Praise for *The Official Ubuntu Server Book*

Murphy's Law is never truer than when it comes to administering a Linux server. You can pretty much count on something happening to your machine at a time when you need it the most. That's when a book with some basic troubleshooting instructions is worth every penny you paid for it. Chapter 11 covers the steps you should take when something goes wrong.

—Paul Ferrill, LinuxPlanet.com reviewer

College-level collections catering to Linux programmers and developers will find *The Official Ubuntu Server Book* a top addition to the collection, covering a complete, free server operating system in a guide to getting going quickly. From making the most of Ubuntu Server's latest technologies to automating installs and protecting the server using Ubuntu's built-in security tools, *The Official Ubuntu Server Book* is packed with keys to success for any Ubuntu user.

—Jim Cox, *Midwest Book Review*

This book will get you started on the path of the server admin, both within the context of Ubuntu server and in the larger realm of managing a server infrastructure. The desktop and server versions of Ubuntu are continuing to mature. Read this book if you want to keep up.

—James Pyles, author

The Official Ubuntu Server Book

Second Edition

The Official Ubuntu Server Book

Second Edition

Kyle Rankin
Benjamin Mako Hill

PRENTICE
HALL

Upper Saddle River, NJ • Boston • Indianapolis • San Francisco
New York • Toronto • Montreal • London • Munich • Paris • Madrid
Capetown • Sydney • Tokyo • Singapore • Mexico City

Many of the designations used by manufacturers and sellers to distinguish their products are claimed as trademarks. Where those designations appear in this book, and the publisher was aware of a trademark claim, the designations have been printed with initial capital letters or in all capitals.

The authors and publisher have taken care in the preparation of this book, but make no expressed or implied warranty of any kind and assume no responsibility for errors or omissions. No liability is assumed for incidental or consequential damages in connection with or arising out of the use of the information or programs contained herein.

The publisher offers excellent discounts on this book when ordered in quantity for bulk purchases or special sales, which may include electronic versions and/or custom covers and content particular to your business, training goals, marketing focus, and branding interests. For more information, please contact:

U.S. Corporate and Government Sales
(800) 382-3419
corpsales@pearsontechgroup.com

For sales outside the United States please contact:

International Sales
international@pearson.com

Visit us on the Web: informit.com/ph

Library of Congress Cataloging-in-Publication Data

Rankin, Kyle.
The official Ubuntu server book / Kyle Rankin, Benjamin Mako Hill. — 2nd ed.
    p.   cm.
  Includes index.
  ISBN 0-13-708133-2 (pbk. : alk. paper)
  1. Ubuntu (Electronic resource) 2. Operating systems (Computers) I. Hill, Benjamin Mako, 1980– II. Title.
QA76.76.O63R3685 2010
005.4'32dc22

                                                    2010021855

ISBN-13: 978-0-13-708133-2
ISBN-10:   0-13-708133-2
Text printed in the United States on recycled paper at RR Donnelley in Crawfordsville, Indiana.
First printing, July 2010

I dedicate this book to my wife, Joy. It is not easy to balance a full-time job and writing a book while still having time for a family. She has endured many a book-writing process at this point and has always been my main source of support and motivation.

—Kyle Rankin

Contents at a Glance

Contents

CHAPTER 10 Fault Tolerance

Preface

WELCOME to *The Official Ubuntu Server Book*!

When most people talk about Ubuntu these days, they tend to talk about the Ubuntu Desktop. After all, it's the easy-to-use "just works" approach to the desktop that has made Ubuntu one of the most popular desktop Linux distributions. What has gotten less attention, although even that is starting to change, is Ubuntu Server. It turns out that desktop Linux users aren't the only ones who want their distribution to "just work"—system administrators appreciate that on their servers as well. In Ubuntu Server you will find all of the powerful server infrastructure from the Debian project plus that extra bit of Ubuntu polish, innovation, and focus on ease of use.

About This Book

This book is the result of the collaborative effort of not just the principal authors, but of the Ubuntu Server team itself. As it is the official, authorized book on Ubuntu Server, the focus has been on a server guide based on our collective experience. Beyond that, the goal is to have something to offer to both the beginner system administrator and the battle-hardened senior sysadmin. On the surface it might seem a tough balance to achieve, but in reality both groups ultimately want the same thing: for their servers to work. Now it's true that some administrators revel in doing things the hard way. Some even treat it as a point of pride. The thing is, all of us who have administered servers for years can do and have done things the hard way as well, but ultimately you realize that there's nothing particularly impressive in doing everything by hand—in the end you just have too much to do and any time-saving steps are welcome.

As you will see, most of this book takes a pragmatic approach to server management. Where Ubuntu offers new programs or features to ease administration and save time, you will find them mentioned here. If you are a beginner administrator, you will find that administering an Ubuntu server isn't nearly as difficult as you might think. Experienced administrators, especially those coming from other platforms, will find numerous time-saving tips and programs, as well as where Ubuntu has updated how a service is organized (Apache being a good example); you can treat this book as a map to point you to all of the right directories.

One great thing about Ubuntu as a server is that there are so many great server packages available for it. Of course, this creates a dilemma for us as writers: It's just not possible to feature every available e-mail and IMAP/POP3 server, for instance. In these cases we've tried to pick out programs that are easy to install, configure, and use under Ubuntu as well as highlight programs that are preferred by the authors and server team. While doing that, there's a good chance that your favorite program for X, Y, and Z was left out. It's certainly no slight against any of those programs—we just had to draw the line somewhere.

How the Book Is Organized

Different people read tech books differently. Some people read them cover to cover, and others skip right ahead to the topic they need immediate help with. You will find that the way this book is organized lends itself well to both approaches. The first few chapters lay the foundation so you can install Ubuntu and navigate the system even if it's your first time. After that the chapters focus on particular server topics, from security to monitoring to system rescue.

- Chapter 1—Installation. In the first chapter you will learn how to use the default Ubuntu Server CD to install Ubuntu on a server. This guide includes a complete walk-through of the installation process from the initial boot screen to partitioning to your first login prompt.

- Chapter 2—Essential System Administration. If you are new to Ubuntu system administration, the amount of learning ahead of you might seem daunting. In this chapter you will find not only a solid foundation of instructions on how to navigate the Linux command line, but also an introduction to the Ubuntu boot process and the standards behind all of the directories on an Ubuntu system. By the end of the chapter you should have a good basis to continue with the rest of the book.

▪ Chapter 3—Package Management. This chapter introduces you to packages and the packaging system—the way that Ubuntu handles the installation, removal, and management of software. We provide a solid foundation in what packages do and how they do it before drilling down into the details of how an administrator can manage software the Ubuntu way. In the final pages, we cover the way that administrators can switch from consumers to producers and begin making their own packages.

▪ Chapter 4—Automated Ubuntu Installs. While you can certainly install Ubuntu step by step from the install CD, that method doesn't work so well when you have tens or hundreds of servers to install. This chapter covers the preseed method for automating Ubuntu installs along with Kickseed—Ubuntu's port of Kickstart. In addition to a description of how to use both of these technologies independently, you will find out it's even better when you use them together.

▪ Chapter 5—Guide to Common Ubuntu Servers. There is an enormous number of services you can run on an Ubuntu server. In this chapter we highlight some of the more popular servers, from Web to e-mail to file services. If you are a new administrator, you will find a simple guide on how to install and configure these services for the first time. If you are an experienced administrator coming from another distribution, you will find this chapter a handy guide to find out how Ubuntu organizes all of the configuration files for your favorite services.

▪ Chapter 6—Security. Security is an important topic for any administrator. Ubuntu Server already is pretty secure by default, and in this chapter we highlight some of these mechanisms along with steps you can take to increase your security even further. Some of the security topics include sudo, firewall configuration, an introduction to forensics, and even Ubuntu's AppArmor software.

▪ Chapter 7—Backups. There are two kinds of administrators: those who back up their servers and those who haven't lost valuable data yet. Backup software abounds for Linux as a whole and for Ubuntu specifically, and in this chapter you will see a few easy-to-set-up approaches to keeping your data secure.

- Chapter 8—Monitoring. Monitoring is one of the most valuable systems an administrator can set up while simultaneously being the most annoying (why do servers always seem to page you in the middle of the night?). In this chapter we cover some different approaches to monitoring systems both for trending purposes and to alert you to any problems. By the end of the chapter you will no longer lose sleep wondering if a server is up—you'll lose sleep only when it goes down.

- Chapter 9—Virtualization. Virtualization is one of the hot topics in system administration today. With more and more powerful hardware out there, virtualization provides you with a way to squeeze the most efficiency out of your servers. In this chapter we will cover two of the most popular server-based virtualization tools out there: KVM and VMware Server. Cloud computing is a new area where virtualization is making a big impact, so this chapter also covers how to set up your own Ubuntu EC2 Cloud environment.

- Chapter 10—Fault Tolerance. If a lot is riding on your servers and your downtime is measured in dollars and not minutes, you realize very quickly that your servers need fault tolerance. The fault tolerance chapter covers Ubuntu software RAID, including steps to migrate from one type of RAID to another. Then we will cover how to set up redundant network connections and finish up with a guide to setting up your own Linux cluster. We also discuss how to get up and running with logical volume management (LVM).

- Chapter 11—Troubleshooting. No matter how great an administrator you are, eventually something on your servers will fail. Over the years you develop a series of troubleshooting steps you go through whenever you find a problem on your systems. In this chapter we condense years of troubleshooting experience into a series of step-by-step guides to walk you through common server and network problems and how to use standard Ubuntu tools and techniques to diagnose them.

- Chapter 12—Rescue and Recovery. We've often said that we've learned more about Linux from fixing a broken system than in any other way. In some environments when a system won't boot, an administrator might just install a new operating system. Under Ubuntu, however, you'll find that most common boot problems also have a common, easy solution. In this chapter we discuss how to use different stages of rescue modes both on Ubuntu and the Ubuntu Server install CD itself to repair your system.

- Chapter 13—Help and Resources. One great thing about Ubuntu is just how many support avenues there are when you need help. Whether it's documentation on the machine itself, guides on the official Ubuntu site, forums, or even professional Canonical support, when you are stuck you aren't alone. In this chapter we cover all of the different ways to get support for your Ubuntu server.

- Chapter 14—Basic Linux Administration. This chapter picks up where Chapter 2, Essential System Administration, left off. Here we discuss some of the core foundation concepts behind Linux administration, including file permissions, different file types, pipes, and other core Linux information. Beginner administrators will find this a very useful guide to flesh out any gaps in their command-line knowledge, and the experienced administrators will find it a good refresher on core concepts.

- Appendix—Cool Tips and Tricks. Over the years you develop all sorts of useful tips, one-liners, and other shell commands that make your life as an administrator easier. Here you will find some of our favorite time-saving tips and hacks in rapid-fire form.

Media with This Book

This book includes two versions of Ubuntu Server: Ubuntu 10.04 for i386 machines and a 64-bit version so you can pick the version that best matches your server hardware. Note that the 10.04 DVD includes the complete Ubuntu Linux operating system for installation on PC platforms, preconfigured with an outstanding desktop environment for both home and business computing. In addition to the Ubuntu Server, it can be used to install other complete variants of Ubuntu, including Kubuntu (with the KDE environment) and Edubuntu (for use in schools).

While we have included both a 32-bit and 64-bit release of Ubuntu 10.04 and have written the book for version 10.04, you might decide to try out a newer Ubuntu release. In that case, just go to http://ubuntu.com and either download the CD image or request a copy to be sent to you. No matter which Ubuntu Server CD you pick, it's relatively easy to use the CDs. Just insert the version you want to install into your computer and boot from the CD-ROM. When the CD boots, you will see a number of options on the screen, but to install Ubuntu Server, just select Install Ubuntu Server. The installer that launches will ask some fairly straightforward questions common to most install discs, and if you get stuck, just turn to Chapter 1 for a more in-depth walk-through of the install process.

Acknowledgments

JORGE, I WOULDN'T HAVE been involved in this book if it weren't for you. I'm one in a long list of people using Ubuntu because of Jorge. His enthusiasm is infectious and I can't count how many times he's introduced me to some cool new program or tool that I write off at first and then somehow find myself using eventually.

Debra and Mako, it has been great working with both of you on this project, and thank you for the opportunity and guidance. Also thanks to Matthew for his help on the support chapter. Robert, thanks so much for your great attention to detail and tracking down all the areas where I had made typos and mistakes. Thanks to Bill "the Cloud" Childers for providing me with equipment for the UEC section.

Extra thanks to Dustin, Nick, Jamie, Kees, Alan, Mathias, Thierry, and the rest of the Ubuntu Server team for all of your excellent feedback and help through this process.

—Kyle Rankin

About the Authors

Kyle Rankin is a systems architect for Quinstreet, Inc., the current president of the North Bay Linux Users' Group, the author of *Knoppix Hacks, Knoppix Pocket Reference, Linux Multimedia Hacks,* and *Ubuntu Hacks,* and he has contributed to a number of other O'Reilly books. Kyle is also a columnist for *Linux Journal* and has had articles featured in *PC Magazine, TechTarget,* and other publications.

Benjamin Mako Hill is a Seattle native working out of Boston, Massachusetts. Mako is a long-time free software developer and advocate. He was part of the founding Ubuntu team, one of the first employees of Canonical, Ltd., and lead author of *The Official Ubuntu Book.* In addition to some technical work, his charge at Canonical was to help grow the Ubuntu development and user community during the project's first year. Mako is currently a fellow at the MIT Center for Future Civic Media and a researcher and Ph.D. candidate at the MIT Sloan School of Management. Mako has continued his involvement with Ubuntu as a member of the Community Council governance board, through development work, and through projects such as this book.

Introduction

THIS INTRODUCTION GIVES AN overview of Ubuntu and Ubuntu Server. After a quick welcome, it includes a brief history of free software, open source, and GNU/Linux and of the Ubuntu project itself with a focus on some of the major players on the Ubuntu scene. This introduction ends where the rest of this book will continue: with a history of the Ubuntu Server project and an overview of that project's goals and accomplishments.

Welcome to Ubuntu Server

In the just over six years of its life, Ubuntu has become one of the most popular GNU/Linux-based operating systems. In the process, however, public perception has been disproportionately focused on Ubuntu's role as a desktop-based operating system. While all popularity is certainly welcome for those of us involved in the project, this success has, at times, overshadowed the rock-solid server operating system that Ubuntu has been constructed to be. For those of us who have helped build out Ubuntu's server-specific features and who use it daily, this is both unfortunate and undeserved. Designed and used as a server since day one, Ubuntu has supported a server team that was one of the first active teams in the Ubuntu community and has been one of the most successful. Although perceptions have changed in large part, many prospective users—and even some current Ubuntu users—often continue to think of Ubuntu as something for desktops.

Perhaps it is just that people are so surprised at the usability of Ubuntu on the desktop—especially in the early days when expectations for desktop GNU/Linux distributions were low—that the public focus naturally has drifted away from Ubuntu's server offering. Lots of other GNU/Linux distributions run great on servers, but a solid desktop experience continues to be surprising to many users. As a result, when people talk about Ubuntu, they often tend to talk about desktops. Perhaps, on the other hand, people just figured that such a well-polished desktop must have come at the cost of the server-oriented features and support. Of course, no such sacrifices were made.

To a large extent, times have changed. The Ubuntu Server team has continued its tireless work both to improve the experience for server users of Ubuntu and to help promote Ubuntu as a server solution. Documentation, testimonials, certification of server-based software, support contracts from a variety of sources, training courses, and more have all contributed to remaking Ubuntu into a powerful player on the server. Although its desktop credentials have not been diminished, Ubuntu's server chops are increasingly difficult to overlook. Over the past two years, Ubuntu has begun to become a major player in the GNU/Linux server market.

More than anything else, testimonials have spread and the small group of early Ubuntu Server users has spread the word. More and more people choose Ubuntu for their servers every day. In fact, this book is simply the latest striking example of just how far Ubuntu on servers has come. Not only do people now know that Ubuntu runs on a server, they know it runs well. This book is publishable only because there is a market for it. That market is made up of people who have heard good things about Ubuntu on the server and who are getting ready to take the plunge themselves. Welcome. We hope we can help make the process easier. We've come a long way, and we're still only just beginning.

Free Software, Open Source, and Linux

A history of Ubuntu Server must, in large part, be a history of Ubuntu itself. A history of Ubuntu must, in large part, be a history of the free software movement and of the Linux kernel. While thousands of individuals have contributed in some form to Ubuntu, the project has succeeded only through the contributions of many thousands more who have indirectly laid the technical, social, and economic groundwork for Ubuntu's success. While introductions to free software, open source, and GNU/Linux can be found in many other places, no introduction to Ubuntu is complete without a brief discussion of these concepts and the people and history behind them. It is around these concepts and within these communities that Ubuntu was motivated and born. Ultimately, it is through these ideas that it is sustained.

Free Software and GNU

In a series of events that have almost become legend through constant repetition, Richard M. Stallman created the concept of free software in 1983. Stallman grew up with computers in the 1960s and 1970s, when computer users purchased very large and extremely expensive mainframe computers, which were then shared among large numbers of programmers. Software was, for the most part, seen as an add-on to the hardware, and every user had the ability and the right to modify or rewrite the software on his or her computer and to freely share this software. As computers became cheaper and more numerous in the late 1970s, producers of software began to see value in the software itself. Producers of computers began to argue that their software was copyrightable and a form of intellectual property much like a music recording, a film, or a book's text. They began to distribute their software under licenses and in forms that restricted its users' abilities to use, redistribute, or modify the code. By the early 1980s, restrictive software licenses had become the norm.

Stallman, then a programmer at MIT's Artificial Intelligence Laboratory, became increasingly concerned with what he saw as a dangerous loss of the freedoms that software users and developers had up until that point enjoyed. He was concerned with computer users' ability to be good neighbors and members of what he thought was an ethical and efficient computer-user community. To fight against this negative tide, Stallman articulated a vision for a community that developed liberated code—in his words, "free software." He defined free software as software that had the following four characteristics—labeled as freedoms 0 through 3 instead of 1 through 4 as a computer programmer's joke:

- The freedom to run the program for any purpose (freedom 0)
- The freedom to study how the program works and adapt it to your needs (freedom 1)

- The freedom to redistribute copies so you can help your neighbor (freedom 2)

- The freedom to improve the program and release your improvements to the public so that the whole community benefits (freedom 3)

Access to source code—the human-readable and modifiable blueprints of any piece of software that can be distinguished from the computer-readable version of the code that most software is distributed as—is a prerequisite to freedoms 1 and 3. In addition to releasing this definition of free software, Stallman began a project with the goal of creating a completely free OS to replace the then-popular UNIX. In 1984, Stallman announced this project and called it GNU—another joke in the form of a recursive acronym for "GNU's Not UNIX."

Linux

By the early 1990s, Stallman and a collection of other programmers working on GNU had developed a near-complete OS that could be freely shared. They were, however, missing a final essential piece in the form of a kernel—a complex system command processor that lies at the center of any OS. In 1991, Linus Torvalds wrote an early version of just such a kernel, released it under a free license, and called it Linux. Linus's kernel was paired with the GNU project's development tools and OS and with the graphical windowing system called X. With this pairing, a completely free OS was born—free both in terms of price and in Stallman's terms of freedom.

All systems referred to as Linux today are, in fact, built on the work of this collaboration. Technically, the term Linux refers only to the kernel. Many programmers and contributors to GNU, including Stallman, argue emphatically that the full OS should be referred to as GNU/Linux in order to give credit not only to Linux but also to the GNU project and to highlight GNU's goals of spreading software freedom—goals not necessarily shared by Linus Torvalds. Many others find this name cumbersome and prefer calling the system simply Linux. Yet others, such as those working on the Ubuntu project, attempt to avoid the controversy altogether by referring to GNU/Linux only by using their own project's name.

Open Source

Disagreements over labeling did not end with discussions about the naming of the combination of GNU and Linux. In fact, as the list of contributors to GNU and Linux grew, a vibrant world of new free software projects sprouted up, facilitated in part by growing access to the Internet. As this community grew and diversified, a number of people began to notice an unintentional side effect of Stallman's free software. Because free software was built in an open way, *anyone* could contribute to software by looking through the code, finding bugs, and fixing them. Because software ended up being examined by larger numbers of programmers, free software was higher in quality, performed better, and offered more features than similar software developed through proprietary development mechanisms. In many situations, the development model behind free software led to software that was *inherently better* than proprietary alternatives.

As the computer and information technology industry began to move into the dot-com boom, one group of free software developers and leaders, spearheaded by two free software developers and advocates—Eric S. Raymond and Bruce Perens—saw the important business proposition offered by a model that could harness volunteer labor or interbusiness collaboration and create intrinsically better software. However, they worried that the term *free software* was problematic for at least two reasons. First, it was highly ambiguous—the English word *free* means both gratis, or at no cost (e.g., as in "free beer") and liberated in the sense of freedom (e.g., as in "free speech"). Second, there was a feeling, articulated most famously by Raymond, that all this talk of freedom was scaring off the very business executives and decision makers whom the free software movement needed to impress in order to succeed.

To tackle both of these problems, this group coined a new phrase—*open source*—and created a new organization called the Open Source Initiative. The group set at its core a definition of open source software that overlapped completely and exclusively both with Stallman's four-part definition of free software and with other community definitions that were also based on Stallman's.

One useful way to understand the split between the free software and open source movements is to think of it as the opposite of a schism. In religious schisms, churches separate and do not work or worship together because of relatively small differences in belief, interpretation, or motivation. For example, most contemporary forms of Protestant Christianity agree on *almost* everything but have separated over some small but irreconcilable difference. However, in the case of the free software and open source movements, the two groups have fundamental disagreements about their motivation and beliefs. One group is focused on freedom, while the other is focused on pragmatics. Free software is most accurately described as a social movement, whereas open source is a development methodology. However, the two groups have no trouble working on projects hand in hand.

In terms of the motivations and goals, open source and free software diverge greatly. Yet in terms of the software, the projects, and the licenses they use, they are completely synonymous. While people who identify with either group see the two movements as being at odds, the Ubuntu project sees no conflict between the two ideologies. People in the Ubuntu project identify with either group and often with both. In this book, we may switch back and forth between the terms as different projects and people in Ubuntu identify more strongly with one term or the other. For the purposes of this book, though, either term should be read as implying the other unless it is stated otherwise.

A Brief History of the Ubuntu Project

A history of Ubuntu, born in April 2004, may seem premature. However, the last six years have been full ones for Ubuntu. With its explosive growth, it is difficult even for those involved most closely with the project to track and record some of the high points. Importantly, there are some key figures whose own history must be given for a full understanding of Ubuntu. This brief summary outlines the high points of Ubuntu's history to date and gives the necessary background knowledge to understand where Ubuntu comes from.

Mark Shuttleworth

No history of Ubuntu can call itself complete without a history of Mark Shuttleworth. Shuttleworth is, undeniably, the most visible and important person in Ubuntu. More important from the point of view of history,

Shuttleworth is also the originator and initiator of the project—he made the snowball that would eventually roll on and grow to become the Ubuntu project.

Shuttleworth was born in 1973 in Welkom, Free State, in South Africa. He attended Diocesan College and obtained a business science degree in finance and information systems at the University of Cape Town. During this period, he was an avid computer hobbyist and became involved with the free and open source software community. He was at least marginally involved in both the Apache project and the Debian project and was the first person to upload the Apache Web server, perhaps the single most important piece of server software on GNU/Linux platforms, into the Debian project's archives.

Seeing an opportunity in the early days of the Web, Shuttleworth founded a certificate authority and Internet security company called Thawte in his garage. Over the course of several years, he built Thawte into the second-largest certificate authority on the Internet, trailing only the security behemoth VeriSign. Throughout this period, Thawte's products and services were built and served almost entirely from free and open source software. In December 1999, Shuttleworth sold Thawte to VeriSign for an undisclosed amount that reached into the hundreds of millions in U.S. dollars.

With his fortune made at a young age, Shuttleworth might have enjoyed a life of leisure—and probably considered it. Instead, he decided to pursue his lifelong dream of space travel. After paying approximately $20 million to the Russian space program and devoting nearly a year to preparation, including learning Russian and spending seven months training in Star City, Russia, Shuttleworth realized his dream as a civilian cosmonaut aboard the Russian Soyuz TM-34 mission. On this mission, Shuttleworth spent two days on the Soyuz rocket and eight days on the International Space Station, where he participated in experiments related to AIDS and genome research. In early May 2002, Shuttleworth returned to Earth.

In addition to space exploration and a less-impressive jaunt to Antarctica, Shuttleworth played an active role as both a philanthropist and a venture capitalist. In 2001, he founded the Shuttleworth Foundation (TSF), a non-profit organization based in South Africa. The foundation was chartered to fund, develop, and drive social innovation in the field of education. Of course, the means by which TSF attempts to achieve these goals frequently involves free software. Through these projects, the organization has been one of the most visible proponents of free and open source software in South Africa and even the world. In the venture capital area, Shuttleworth worked to foster research, development, and entrepreneurship in South Africa with strategic injections of cash into start-ups through a new venture capital firm called HBD, an acronym for "Here Be Dragons." During this period, Shuttleworth was busy brainstorming his next big project—the project that would eventually become Ubuntu.

The Warthogs

There has been no lack of projects attempting to wrap GNU, Linux, and other pieces of free and open source software into a neat, workable, and user-friendly package. Mark Shuttleworth, like many other people, believed that the philosophical and pragmatic benefits offered by free software put it on a course for widespread success. That said, none of the offerings were particularly impressive. Something was missing from all of them. Shuttleworth saw this as an opportunity. If someone could build the great free software distribution that helped push GNU/Linux into the mainstream, he or she would come to occupy a position of strategic importance.

Shuttleworth, like many other technically inclined people, was a huge fan of the Debian project (discussed in depth later). However, many things about Debian did not fit with Shuttleworth's vision of an ideal OS. For a period of time, Shuttleworth considered the possibility of running for Debian project leader as a means of reforming the Debian project from within. With time, though, it became clear that the best way to bring GNU/Linux into the mainstream would not be from within the Debian project—which in many situations had very good reasons for being the way it was. Instead, Shuttleworth would create a new project that worked in symbiosis with Debian to build a new, better GNU/Linux system.

To kick off this project, Shuttleworth invited a dozen or so free and open source software developers he knew and respected to his flat in London in April 2004. It was in this meeting (alluded to in the first paragraphs of this introduction) that the groundwork for the Ubuntu project was laid. By that point, many of those involved were excited about the possibility of the project. During this meeting, the members of the team—which would in time grow into the core Ubuntu team—brainstormed a large list of the things that they would want to see in their ideal OS. The list is now a familiar list of features to most Ubuntu users. Many of these traits are covered in more depth later in this chapter. The group wanted

- Predictable and frequent release cycles
- A strong focus on localization and accessibility
- A strong focus on ease of use and user-friendliness on the desktop
- A strong focus on Python as the single programming language through which the entire system could be built and expanded
- A community-driven approach that worked with existing free software projects and a method by which the groups could give back as they went along—not just at the time of release
- A new set of tools designed around the process of building distributions that allowed developers to work within an ecosystem of different projects and that allowed users to give back in whatever way they could

There was consensus among the group that actions speak louder than words, so there were no public announcements or press releases. Instead, the group set a deadline for itself—six short months in the future. Shuttleworth agreed to finance the work and pay the developers full-time salaries to work on the project. After six months, they would both announce their project and reveal the first product of their work. They made a list of goals they wanted to achieve by the deadline, and the individuals present took on tasks. Collectively, they called themselves the Warthogs.

What Does *Ubuntu* Mean?

At this point, the Warthogs had a great team, a set of goals, and a decent idea of how to achieve most of them. The team did not, on the other hand, have a name for the project. Shuttleworth argued strongly that they should call the project Ubuntu.

Ubuntu is a concept and a term from several South African languages, including Zulu and Xhosa. It refers to a South African ideology or ethic that, while difficult to express in English, might roughly be translated as "humanity toward others," or "I am because we are." Others have described ubuntu as "the belief in a universal bond of sharing that connects all humanity." The famous South African human rights champion Archbishop Desmond Tutu explained ubuntu in this way:

> A person with ubuntu is open and available to others, affirming of others, does not feel threatened that others are able and good, for he or she has a proper self-assurance that comes from knowing that he or she belongs in a greater whole and is diminished when others are humiliated or diminished, when others are tortured or oppressed.

Ubuntu played an important role as a founding principle in postapartheid South Africa and remains a concept familiar to most South Africans today.

Shuttleworth liked the term *Ubuntu* as a name for the new project for several reasons. First, it is a South African concept. While the majority of the people who work on Ubuntu are not from South Africa, the roots of the project are, and Shuttleworth wanted to choose a name that represented this. Second, the project emphasizes the definition of individuality in terms of relationships with others and provides a profound type of community and sharing—exactly the attitudes of sharing, community, and collaboration that are at the core of free software. The term represented the side of free software that the team wanted to share with the world. Third, the idea of personal relationships built on mutual respect and connections describes the fundamental ground rules for the highly functional community that the Ubuntu team wanted to build. *Ubuntu* was a term that encapsulated where the project came from, where the project was going, and how the project planned to get there. The name was perfect. It stuck.

Creating Canonical

In order to pay developers to work on Ubuntu full-time, Shuttleworth needed a company to employ them. He wanted to pick some of the best people for the jobs from within the global free software and open source communities. These communities, inconveniently for Shuttleworth, know no national and geographic boundaries. Rather than move everyone to a single locale and office, Shuttleworth made the decision to employ these developers through a virtual company. While this had obvious drawbacks in the form of high-latency and low-bandwidth connections, different time zones, and much more, it also introduced some major benefits in the particular context of the project. On one hand, the distributed nature of employees meant that the new company could hire individuals without requiring them to pack up their lives and move to a new country. More important, it meant that *everyone* in the company was dependent on IRC, mailing lists, and online communication mechanisms to do their work. This unintentionally and automatically solved the water-cooler problem that plagued many other corporately funded free software projects— namely, that developers would casually speak about their work in person and cut the community and anyone else who didn't work in the office out of the conversation completely. For the first year, the closest thing that Canonical had to an office was Shuttleworth's flat in London. While the company has grown and now has several offices around the world, it remains distributed, and a large number of the engineers work from home. The group remains highly dependent on Internet collaboration.

With time, the company was named Canonical. The name was a nod to the project's optimistic goals of becoming the canonical place for services and support for free and open source software and for Ubuntu in particular. *Canonical*, of course, refers to something that is accepted as authoritative. It is a common word in the computer programmer lexicon. It's important to note that being canonical is like being standard; it is not coercive. Unlike holding a monopoly, becoming the canonical location for something implies a similar sort of success—but *never* one that cannot be undone and never one that is exclusive. Other companies will support Ubuntu and build operating systems based on it, but as long as Canonical is doing a good job, its role will remain central.

The Ubuntu Community

By now you may have noticed a theme that permeates the Ubuntu project on several levels. The history of free software and open source is one of a profoundly effective *community*. Similarly, in building a GNU/Linux distribution, the Ubuntu community has tried to focus on an ecosystem model—an organization of organizations—in other words, a community.

Even the definition of the term *ubuntu* is one that revolves around people interacting in a community.

It comes as no surprise, then, that an "internal" community plays heavily into the way that the Ubuntu distribution is created. While the Ubuntu 4.10 version (Warty Warthog) was primarily built by a small number of people, Ubuntu achieved widespread success only through contributions by a much larger group that included programmers, documentation writers, volunteer support staff, and users. While Canonical employs a core group of several dozen active contributors to Ubuntu, the distribution has, from day one, encouraged and incorporated contributions from *anyone* in the community and rewards and recognizes contributions by all. Rather than taking center stage, paid contributors are *not* employed by the Ubuntu project—instead they are employed by Canonical, Ltd. These employees are treated simply as another set of community members. They must apply for membership in the Ubuntu community and have their contributions recognized in the same way as anyone else. All non-business-related communication about the Ubuntu project occurs in public and in the community. Volunteer community members occupy a majority of the seats on the two most important governing boards of the Ubuntu project: the Technical Board, which oversees all technical matters, and the Community Council, which approves new Ubuntu members and resolves disputes. Seats on both boards are approved by the relevant community groups, developers for the Technical Board and Ubuntu members for the Community Council.

In order to harness and encourage the contributions of its community, Ubuntu has striven to balance the important role that Canonical plays with the value of empowering individuals in the community. The Ubuntu project is based on a fundamental belief that great software is built, supported, and maintained only in a strong relationship with the individuals who use the software. In this way, by fostering and supporting a vibrant community, Ubuntu can achieve much more than it could through paid development alone. The people on the project believe that while the contributions of Canonical and Mark Shuttleworth have provided an important catalyst for the processes that have built Ubuntu, it is the community that has brought the distribution its success to date. The project members believe that it is only through increasing reliance on the community that the project's success will continue to grow. The Ubuntu community won't outspend the proprietary software industry, but it is very much more than Microsoft and its allies can afford.

Finally, it is worth noting that, while this book is official, neither of the authors is a Canonical employee. This book, like much of the rest of Ubuntu, is purely a product of the project's community.

Ubuntu Promises and Goals

So far, this introduction has been about the prehistory, history, and context of the Ubuntu project. After this chapter, the book focuses on the distribution itself. Before proceeding, it's important to understand the goals that motivated the project.

Philosophical Goals

The most important goals of the Ubuntu project are philosophical in nature. The Ubuntu project lays out its philosophy in a series of documents on its Web site. In the most central of these documents, the team summarizes the charter and the major philosophical goals and underpinnings:

> Ubuntu is a community-driven project to create an operating system and a full set of applications using free and Open Source software. At the core of the Ubuntu Philosophy of Software Freedom are these core philosophical ideals:
>
> 1. Every computer user should have the freedom to run, copy, distribute, study, share, change, and improve their software for any purpose without paying licensing fees.
>
> 2. Every computer user should be able to use their software in the language of their choice.
>
> 3. Every computer user should be given every opportunity to use software, even if they work under a disability.

The first item should be familiar by now. It is merely a recapitulation of Stallman's free software definition quoted earlier in the section on free software history. In it, the Ubuntu project makes explicit its goal that every user of software should have the freedoms required by free software. This is important for a number of reasons. First, it offers users all of the practical benefits of software that runs better, faster, and more flexibly. More important, it gives every user the capability to transcend his or her role as a user and a consumer of software. Ubuntu wants software to be empowering and to work in the ways that users want it to work. Ubuntu wants all users to have the ability to make sure it works for them. To do this, software *must* be free, so Ubuntu makes this a requirement and a philosophical promise.

Of course, the core goals of Ubuntu do not end with the free software definition. Instead, the project articulates two new, but equally important, goals. The first of these, that all computer users should be able to use their computers in their chosen languages, is a nod to the fact that the majority of the world's population does not speak English while the vast majority of software interacts only in that language. To be useful, source code comments, programming languages, documentation, and the texts and menus in computer programs must be written in *some* language. Arguably, the world's most international language is a reasonably good choice. However, there is no language that everyone speaks, and English is not useful to the majority of the world's population that does not speak it. A computer can be a great tool for empowerment and education, but only if the user can understand the words in the computer's interface. As a result, Ubuntu believes that it is the project's—and community's—responsibility to ensure that *every* user can easily use Ubuntu to read and write in the language with which he or she is most comfortable.

Finally, just as no person should be blocked from using a computer simply because he or she does not know a particular language, no user should be blocked from using a computer because of a disability. Ubuntu must be accessible to users with motor disabilities, vision disabilities, and hearing disabilities. It should provide input and output in a variety of forms to account for each of these situations and for others. A significant percentage of the world's most intelligent and creative individuals has disabilities. Ubuntu's impact should not be limited to any subset of the world when it can be fully inclusive. More important, Ubuntu should be able to harness the ability of these individuals as community members to build a better and more effective community.

Conduct Goals and Code of Conduct

If Ubuntu's philosophical commitments describe the *why* of the Ubuntu project, the Code of Conduct (CoC) describes Ubuntu's *how*. Ubuntu's CoC is, arguably, the most important document in the day-to-day operation of the Ubuntu community and sets the ground rules for work and cooperation within the project. Explicit agreement to the document is the only criterion for becoming an officially recognized Ubuntu activist—an Ubuntero—and is an essential step toward membership in the project.

The CoC covers "behavior as a member of the Ubuntu Community, in any forum, mailing list, wiki, Web site, IRC channel, install-fest, public meeting, or private correspondence." The CoC goes into some degree of depth on a series of points that fall under the following headings:

- Be considerate.
- Be respectful.
- Be collaborative.
- When you disagree, consult others.
- When you are unsure, ask for help.
- Step down considerately.

Many of these headings seem like common sense or common courtesy to many, and that is by design. Nothing in the CoC is controversial or radical, and it was never designed to be.

More difficult is that nothing is easy to enforce or decide because acting considerately, respectfully, and collaboratively is often very subjective. There is room for honest disagreements and hurt feelings. These are accepted shortcomings. The CoC was not designed to be a law with explicit prohibitions on phrases, language, or actions. Instead, it aims to provide a constitution and a reminder that considerate and respectful discussion is *essential* to the health and vitality of the project. In situations where there is a serious disagreement on whether a community member has violated or is violating the code, the Community Council is available to arbitrate disputes and decide what action, if any, is appropriate.

Nobody involved in the Ubuntu project, including Mark Shuttleworth and the other members of the Community Council, is above the CoC. The CoC is never optional and never waived. In fact, the Ubuntu community recently created a Leadership Code of Conduct (LCoC), which extends and expands on the CoC and describes additional requirements and expectations for those in leadership positions in the community. Of course, in no way was either code designed to eliminate conflict or disagreement. Arguments are at least as common in Ubuntu as they are in other projects and online communities. However, there is a common understanding within the project that arguments should happen in an environment of collaboration and mutual respect. This allows for *better* arguments with *better* results—and with less hurt feelings and fewer bruised egos.

While they are sometimes incorrectly used as such, the CoC and LCoC are not sticks to be wielded against an opponent in an argument. Instead, they are useful points of reference upon which consensus can be assumed within the Ubuntu community. Frequently, if a group in the community feels a member is acting in a way that is out of line with the code, the group will gently remind the community member, often privately, that the CoC is in effect. In almost all situations, this is enough to avoid any further action or conflict. Very few CoC violations are ever brought before the Community Council.

Technical Goals

While a respectful community and adherence to a set of philosophical goals provide an important frame in which the Ubuntu project works, Ubuntu is, at the end of the day, a technical project. As a result, it only makes sense that in addition to philosophical goals and a project constitution, Ubuntu also has a set of technical goals.

The first technical goal of the project, and perhaps the most important one, is the coordination of regular and predictable releases—something particularly important to server users. In April 2004, at the Warthogs meeting, the project set a goal for its initial proof-of-concept release six months out. In part due to the resounding success of that project, and in larger part due to the GNOME release schedule, the team has stuck to a regular and predictable six-month release cycle and has only once chosen to extend the release schedule by six weeks and only after obtaining community consensus on the decision. The team then doubled its efforts and made the next release in a mere four and a half months, putting its release schedule back on track. Frequent releases are important because users can then use the latest and greatest free software available—something that is essential in a development environment as vibrant and rapidly changing and improving as the free software community. Predictable releases are important, especially to businesses, because predictability means that they can organize their business plans around Ubuntu. Through consistent releases, Ubuntu can provide a platform upon which businesses and derivative distributions can rely to grow and build.

While releasing frequently and reliably is important, the released software must then be supported. Ubuntu, like all distributions, must deal with the fact that *all* software has bugs. Most bugs are minor, but fixing them may introduce even worse issues. Therefore, fixing bugs after a release must be done carefully or not at all. The Ubuntu project engages in major changes, including bug fixes, *between* releases only when the changes can be extensively tested. However, some bugs risk the loss of users' information or pose a serious security vulnerability. These bugs are fixed immediately and made available as updates for the released distribution. The Ubuntu community works hard to find and minimize all types of bugs before releases and is largely successful in squashing the worst. However, because there is always the possibility that more of these bugs will be found, Ubuntu commits to supporting *every* release for 18 months after it is released. In the case of Ubuntu 6.06 LTS (Dapper Drake), released in 2006, the project went well beyond even this and committed to support the release for three full years on desktop computers and for five years in a server configuration (LTS stands for LongTerm Support). This proved so popular with businesses, institutions, and the users of Ubuntu servers that Ubuntu 8.04 (Hardy Heron) was named as Ubuntu's second LTS release with similar three- and five-year desktop and server extended support commitments. These five-year support commitments are specifically designed for server users and make Ubuntu a much more attractive option for an important class of server users.

This bipartite approach to servers and desktops implies the third major technical commitment of the Ubuntu project and, in a sense, the most important for this book: support for both servers and desktop computers in separate but equally emphasized modes. While Ubuntu continues to be more well known, and perhaps more popular, in desktop configurations, there exist teams of Ubuntu developers focused on both server and desktop users. The Ubuntu project believes that both desktops and servers are essential and provides installation methods on every CD for both types of systems. Ubuntu provides tested and supported software appropriate to the most common actions in both environments and documentation for each. LTS releases in particular mark an important step toward catering to users on the server.

Finally, the Ubuntu project is committed to making it as easy as possible for users to transcend their roles as consumers and users of software and to take advantage of each of the freedoms central to the Ubuntu philosophy. As a result, Ubuntu has tried to focus its development around the use and promotion of a single programming language, Python. The project has worked to ensure that Python is widely used throughout the system. By ensuring that many applications and many of the "guts" of the system are written in or extensible in Python, Ubuntu is working to ensure that users need to learn only one language in order to take advantage of, automate, and tweak many parts of their systems.

Canonical and the Ubuntu Foundation

While Ubuntu is driven by a community, several groups play an important role in its structure and organization. Foremost among these are Canonical, Ltd., a for-profit company introduced as part of the Ubuntu history description, and the Ubuntu Foundation, which is introduced later in this section.

Canonical, Ltd.

As mentioned earlier, Canonical, Ltd., is a company founded by Mark Shuttleworth with the primary goal of developing and supporting the Ubuntu distribution. Many of the core developers on Ubuntu—although no longer a majority of them—work full-time or part-time under contract for Canonical, Ltd. This funding by Canonical allows Ubuntu to make the type of support commitments that it does. Ubuntu can claim that it will release in six months because releasing, in one form or another, is something that the paid workers at Canonical can ensure. As an all-volunteer organization, Debian suffered from an inability to set and meet deadlines—volunteers become busy or have other deadlines in their paying jobs that take precedence. By offering paying jobs to a subset of developers, Canonical can set support and release deadlines and ensure that they are met.

In this way, Canonical ensures that Ubuntu's bottom-line commitments are kept. Of course, Canonical does not fund all Ubuntu work, nor could it. Canonical can release a distribution every six months, but that distribution will be made *much* better and more usable through contributions from the community of users. Most features, most new pieces of software, almost all translations, almost all documentation, and much more are created outside of Canonical. Instead, Canonical ensures that deadlines are met and that the essential work, regardless of whether it's fun, gets done.

Canonical, Ltd., was incorporated on the Isle of Man—a tiny island nation between Wales and Ireland that is mostly known as a haven for international businesses. Since Canonical's staff is sprinkled across the globe and no proper office is necessary, the Isle of Man seemed as good a place as any for the company to hang its sign.

Canonical's Service and Support

While it is surprising to many users, fewer than half of Canonical's employees work on the Ubuntu project. The rest of the employees fall into several categories: business development, support and administration, and development on the Bazaar and Launchpad projects.

Individuals involved in business development help create strategic deals and certification programs with other companies—primarily around Ubuntu. In large part, these are things that the community is either ill suited for or uninterested in as a whole. One example of business development work is the process of working with companies to ensure that their software (usually proprietary) is built and certified to run on Ubuntu. For example, Canonical worked with IBM to ensure that its popular DB2 database would run on Ubuntu and, when this was achieved, worked to have

Ubuntu certified as a platform that would run DB2. Similarly, Canonical worked with Dell to ensure that Ubuntu could be installed and supported on Dell laptops as an option for its customers. A third example is the production of this book, which, published by Pearson Education's Prentice Hall imprint, was a product of work with Canonical.

Canonical also plays an important support role in the Ubuntu project in three ways. First, Canonical supports the development of the Ubuntu project. For example, Canonical system administrators ensure that the servers that support development and distribution of Ubuntu are running. Second, Canonical helps Ubuntu users and businesses directly by offering phone and e-mail support. Additionally, Canonical has helped build a large commercial Ubuntu support operation by arranging for support contracts with larger companies and organizations. This support is over and above the free (i.e., gratis) support offered by the community—this commercial support is offered at a fee and is either part of a longer-term flat-fee support contract or is pay-per-instance. By offering commercial support for Ubuntu in a variety of ways, Canonical aims to make a business for itself and to help make Ubuntu a more palatable option for the businesses, large and small, that are looking for an enterprise or enterprise-class GNU/Linux product with support contracts like those offered by other commercial GNU/Linux distributions.

Finally, Ubuntu supports other support organizations. Canonical does not seek or try to enforce a monopoly on Ubuntu support; it proudly lists *hundreds* of other organizations offering support for Ubuntu on the Ubuntu Web pages. Instead, Canonical offers what is called second-tier support to these organizations. Because Canonical employs many of the core Ubuntu developers, the company is very well suited to taking action on many of the tougher problems that these support organizations may run into. With its concentrated expertise, Canonical can offer this type of backup, or secondary, support to these organizations.

The Ubuntu Foundation

Finally, in addition to Canonical and the full Ubuntu community, the Ubuntu project is supported by the Ubuntu Foundation, which was announced by Shuttleworth with an initial funding commitment of $10 million. The foundation, like Canonical, is based on the Isle of Man. The organization is advised by the Ubuntu Community Council.

Unlike Canonical, the foundation does not play an active role in the day-to-day life of Ubuntu. At the moment, the foundation is little more than a pile of money that exists to endow and ensure Ubuntu's future. Because Canonical is a young company, many companies and individuals find it difficult to trust that Canonical will be able to provide support for Ubuntu in the time frames (e.g., three to five years) that it claims it will be able to. The Ubuntu Foundation exists to allay those fears.

If something bad were to happen to Shuttleworth or to Canonical that caused either to be unable to support Ubuntu development and maintain the distribution, the Ubuntu Foundation exists to carry on many of Canonical's core activities well into the future. Through the existence of the foundation, the Ubuntu project can make the types of long-term commitments and promises it does.

The one activity in which the foundation can and does engage is receiving donations on behalf of the Ubuntu project. These donations, and only these donations, are then put to use on behalf of Ubuntu in accordance with the wishes of the development team and the Technical Board. For the most part, these contributions are spent on "bounties" given to community members who have achieved important feature goals for the Ubuntu project.

History of Ubuntu Server

The first "production" machines to run Ubuntu were Canonical's own development machines in its data center in London. In this sense, Ubuntu has been used on servers since day one and Ubuntu has *always* been a server operating system. Of course, as we hinted in the welcome at the beginning of this chapter, this has not always been universally recognized. After the first release, public perception was tilted so far toward the idea of Ubuntu as a desktop release that when the developers convened the first of their biannual developer summits after the first full release cycle, one of the most important items on the agenda was thinking about Ubuntu on servers and how to support it.

The Ubuntu Server project, as a result, was at least as much a marketing project as it was a technical project. Sure, there were ways that the team could make Ubuntu better for servers—and they spent plenty of time working and thinking about that—but the biggest problem they faced was simply communicating the message that Ubuntu already was great for servers to all their users and potential users.

Eventually Canonical funded the creation of a graphical installer, but in the first few releases there was just a single, nongraphical installer based on Debian's very descriptively named Debian Installer project. In the initial Ubuntu release, a user installing Ubuntu was given a choice between two modes: "Desktop"—which was self-explanatory enough—and "Custom." Custom, in the minds of the early developers, was what anyone would want for a server. Custom installed just the bare minimum set of packages and then put the users into this base install and prompted them to install the packages that they wanted on their system. It provided users with the bare-bones system and encouraged them to customize it. The first action of the Ubuntu Server project was purely superficial: The "Custom" install was renamed "Server." Although no code had changed, Ubuntu Server almost immediately began getting more recognition. If one had to pick a single point in time that the Ubuntu Server project was born, it would be this moment.

Ubuntu Server isn't actually any different from other flavors of Ubuntu. As the desktop has moved on to a new graphical installer based on a live CD, Ubuntu Server has its own installer that gives users access to features like RAID and LVM that are much more interesting to server users. Certainly, there are some pieces of software that are likely to end up on servers and unlikely to end up on desktops—things like Web servers and mail servers. When we say that the server edition will be supported, we mean these applications plus the core, so it certainly seems most accurate to refer to these as being within the purview of Ubuntu Server.

But at the end of the day, the server and desktop packages come out of a single repository. This fact, plus the integration between the teams of people working on different parts of the project—most core developers work on bits and pieces that get used and reused in server, desktop, and other editions—introduces a fuzziness that makes it hard to pin down just what Ubuntu Server *is*. Of course, it also means that Ubuntu Server gets to benefit from the work, bug reporting, and bug fixing in those core parts of the operating system that every Ubuntu user shares.

Ubuntu Server now can roughly be interpreted to refer to a collection of resources that are particularly aimed at and used by server users. Most obviously, it involves the custom install discs that you'll be using when you install Ubuntu Server on your machine. It also refers to the collections of supported software that are installed primarily on servers—most of the software that the rest of this book will discuss in more detail. It also refers to a mass of documentation, to which this book represents the latest addition, that provides answers to questions. In a broader sense, certifications of software and training programs for administrators occupy another point in the growing Ubuntu Server constellation.

But most of all, and in the Ubuntu tradition, Ubuntu Server refers to a community. It's a community of developers who use Ubuntu on servers, who care deeply about Ubuntu on servers, and who work tirelessly to make sure that Ubuntu performs as well as possible on servers everywhere. Of course, Ubuntu Server also refers to the growing community of people who are primarily not contributing through code but who are at least as important. These people spend time in the support of IRC channels, send e-mail to the mailing lists, and post in the forums. These users help other users, file bugs, may contribute their own fixes to documentation, and contribute in myriad ways and in a variety of venues.

When you "graduate" beyond what this book can teach you, Ubuntu represents those people who will help you take your next steps. They are the people described in more depth in the server resources chapter (Chapter 13) of this book. This is the group you will join when you participate in the Ubuntu project. Let us be the first to welcome to you to the Ubuntu Server community.

Simple, Secure, Supported

Early on, the initial core Ubuntu team—of which one of this book's authors was lucky enough to be a part—resisted the idea of the server version of Ubuntu. Or rather, they resisted the idea of a server distribution in the way that other GNU/Linux distributions had produced them and the way in which they were commonly thought of. The team was more than happy with running Ubuntu on servers, of course, but they resisted the idea of "server distributions" because of the way that Red Hat, SuSE, and the other big distributions built their businesses around "enterprise Linux" distributions that were big, clunky, and expensive. The result was, in the eyes of many of the early Ubuntu core developers and Canonical employees, top-heavy monstrosities. That's not what Ubuntu is about.

The big server-based GNU/Linux distributions seemed to be competing over who included more services, more features, and more bells and whistles. Distribution 1 would have a Web server, an FTP server, a DNS server, several file servers, and a mail server. Distribution 2 would have all of those plus a DHCP server! A brand-new install of one of these "server distributions" would be running dozens of daemons—each taking up many megabytes of memory, loads of disk space, and (most important) lots of administrator time when they failed or interfered with something else. But worst of all, most of these daemons lay completely unused on most installs.

And if that wasn't enough, the server installs would then run firewalls to keep people from accessing all these now-open services and to prevent users from exposing security vulnerabilities from their newly installed machines. Of course, there would be regular upgrades, security releases, and the like, to update all these now-firewalled services that nobody was using. Debian provided one alternative model that focused on custom installations of just what people needed. Among an elite group of sysadmins in the late 1990s and the early 2000s, Debian had become the server OS of choice. Because nearly everyone on the early Ubuntu team was a Debian developer, it was to this model and to Debian technology that the Ubuntu team first turned.

Of course, the commercial GNU/Linux server market was not all horrible. For example, the early Ubuntu developers liked the idea of commercial support for its servers. They liked the idea of regular, predictable releases. As Debian developers, they all knew someone who wanted to install a simple, custom version of Debian on a server but who, because of the lack of commercial support and accountability, had been rejected by a higher-up in the company or organization. They liked the idea of a company using Debian's technology to offer simple, custom server installs but could offer a commercial support contract. The Warthogs, and lots of folks like them, had waited years for this, but nobody had stepped up to the plate.

As we described in the previous section, an Ubuntu server install was simply a bare-bones installation. We were all administrators—at least of our own machines—and when *we* installed servers, we started out with "naked" machines so that we could choose every application, every daemon, every service that would go onto the machine. As administrators, we wanted the *options* of the big enterprise distributions, but we wanted to be able to choose those options ourselves. Like all administrators, we used servers to solve problems and to offer services to our users. These problems and needs are unique and, as a result, the cookie-cutter model of GNU/Linux servers was always a poor match.

And so that is what the Warthogs built and it is what Ubuntu Server remains today. At first, some people were confused. Ubuntu's server offering was panned in several reviews for not including a firewall by default. But Ubuntu installed *no open ports by default*, so there was nothing to firewall! Of course, Ubuntu provided several firewalls for users to install *if they wanted one*, but Ubuntu left the decision to install a firewall, just like the decision to install services that might require one, up to the server's administrator. For all installations but for server installations in particular, Ubuntu's goal is to make the default installation simple and secure and to put the user in the driver's seat. Ubuntu's job, as distribution producer, is to make it as close to drop-dead simple for system administrators to do their jobs. In an Ubuntu Server install, every machine is exactly as complicated as the administrator has requested but never any more than necessary. No extra services or unnecessary features are included—although they are waiting in the wings for when they become necessary and are easily installable in ways that are described in Chapter 3.

One important effect of this simplicity is security. When there is less going on, there is simply less to go wrong. But, of course, the Ubuntu team has taken this many steps further and pursued proactive security in a number of other contexts. Ubuntu's first release was held up for one day because a single open port was found in the default release. The goal of a machine with no open ports by default was more important than an on-time release. Ubuntu's CTO and the chairman of the Ubuntu technical board, Matt Zimmerman, is a longtime security-focused developer who made nearly all of Debian's security updates for more than a year before joining the Warthogs. As Ubuntu struggles over hard decisions about what to include or to pass up for inclusion in the distribution, the most important questions continue to be ones of security and support. "Can we—and we do want to—maintain security support and provide security releases for this software for the next 18 months?" Every piece of software included by default is subjected to this question, and many popular pieces of software are kept out because Ubuntu is reluctant to support them. Inclusion as an officially supported package means that a server admin can trust the software—both because Canonical has indicated that it trusts it and because Canonical has promised to clean up any security messes that occur through fixing important bugs and issuing a fixed package. Canonical's security guarantee goes beyond security bugs to other bugs that might result in data loss. While there are no guarantees beyond this, Canonical makes many dozens of new updates per release that fix other important bugs in the distribution as well. The result is a rock-solid system with a commitment to continue.

With customizability, security, and support, Ubuntu truly is ready for the data room. The rest of this book will show you how.

## CHAPTER 1

Installation

I REMEMBER WHEN IT WAS QUITE the ordeal to install Linux. You had to download a complete set of floppy images and use some strange Linux or Windows tool to dump those images to floppies. After you had your set of floppies and started the installation process, you would quickly realize that the installation program assumed you already knew quite a bit about Linux and about computers in general. I am actively involved in a Linux users' group, and a staple of Linux users' groups is the install-fest—an event to which Linux newbies can bring their computers and have an expert walk them through the installation process.

Well, these days Linux distributions have made great strides to improve the install process. A desktop Ubuntu install asks very few questions that might stump a beginning user, and the server install (unlike some other server installs out there) doesn't assume you are an experienced Linux system administrator either. While the server install is pretty easy to navigate when you just accept the defaults, you'll find that it also allows the advanced administrator a lot of flexibility and control. What's better, you can get this control without toggling an "expert mode" that forces you to answer detailed questions about every aspect of the install. When the default suits you, you can accept it and move on, and when it doesn't, you can easily tweak only those settings you care about.

This chapter walks you through a standard Ubuntu install. Along the way, it covers each of the major parts of the installation process and also highlights areas where the experienced administrator can tweak and tune the settings for a custom server install.

Get Ubuntu

If you have this book, you should already have the Ubuntu install CD for Ubuntu 10.04 LTS, but just in case you don't, or you need an extra copy, it's good to know how to get CDs from scratch. With some distributions you are required to register and log in to a Web site before you have access to CD images, but Ubuntu makes it relatively easy. At www.ubuntu.com/getubuntu/download you can access both desktop and server CDs for each of the platforms Ubuntu supports. Once you have downloaded the ISO image, you can burn it to a CD using your preferred CD-burning tool. Each program is different, so locate your program's option to burn a CD image. If you are already running an Ubuntu desktop, you can just double-click the ISO image after it is downloaded to start the CD/DVD Creator. If you don't have the bandwidth to download the ISO image, you can also purchase CDs or request free CDs from the same page.

Boot Screen

Once you have your CD, insert it into your server's CD-ROM slot and boot the server. Server BIOSs can be quite different from each other. In some cases they are already set up to boot from a CD-ROM if one is present. In other cases you might have to hit a key such as Esc, Del, F12, or others as the server boots so that it presents you with a list of devices from which you can boot. On some systems you might even have to go into the BIOS configuration page to change the boot order.

After you have convinced your BIOS to boot from the CD, you are greeted with the Ubuntu boot splash screen. The very first part of the screen asks you for your language and then presents you with some boot options, as shown in Figure 1-1. If you just hit Enter and select the default option, you will start the Ubuntu install program. You can also perform some diagnostics

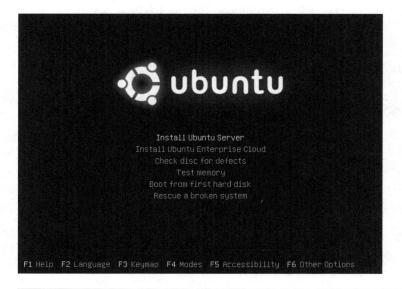

Figure 1-1 Default Ubuntu boot splash screen

from this screen. If you downloaded and burned your own CD from an ISO file, you might want to select the "Check CD for defects" option. You can also test your system memory from this screen—quite useful even later on if your server starts crashing at strange times and you suspect bad RAM might be the cause. This CD also doubles as a basic rescue disk, which is a broad enough topic that it has gotten its own chapter: Chapter 12, Rescue and Recovery. Finally, if you left the CD in the drive by mistake, you can select "Boot from first hard disk" to bypass the CD altogether.

In an ideal world, you could boot the CD, press Enter, and start the installation process with no problems. Unfortunately, for some machines you might have to tweak some of the boot options so the installation works for your system. The Ubuntu developers know this sort of thing happens and have prepared a rich set of options for you. Along the bottom of the boot splash screen are a number of different options you can access with function keys. For instance, if you hit F1 you will see an interactive help screen with documentation for the rest of the options. If you accidentally chose the wrong language at boot time, hit F2 to change it. The boot screen will automatically choose a keyboard mapping based on your language. If you want a different mapping (for instance, you speak English but are doing an install in Germany on a German keyboard), hit F3 to choose from a list of keyboard mappings. The boot screen also has a lot of great accessibility options. The F5 key brings up an accessibility menu that allows you to choose a high-contrast screen, a screen magnifier, a screen reader and Braille terminal, keyboard modifiers, and even an on-screen keyboard.

The F4 and F6 options allow you to actually control aspects of the install. The F4 key displays a list of install modes from which you can choose: you may install an OEM install, a minimal system and a minimal virtualization guest. The OEM install is available for manufacturers. The minimal virtualization guest gives you an easy way to install a virtualized version of Ubuntu. Other Ubuntu CDs allow you to choose text-only install modes, but that isn't necessary here because the Ubuntu server install is already text-only. The real power and control over the boot process are available once you hit the F6 key. Here you can see a menu of common arguments that help the CD to boot on difficult hardware. If you hit the Esc key, you will move from this menu to the boot prompt and can type any extra kernel boot parameters you might need for your hardware. The F1 help screen lists a number of common boot parameters, including some kernel arguments for particular SCSI controllers. If you still can't seem to get the Ubuntu CD to boot after trying these arguments, check out some of the support options in Chapter 13, Help and Resources. Chances are, you aren't the first person to try to boot Ubuntu on that hardware, and someone else might have already discovered the magic list of options you need for it to work.

NOTE   **For Headless Server Installation**
One downside to the pretty boot splash screen Ubuntu uses is that if you install Ubuntu on a headless server (a server without a monitor connected to it that outputs its display over the serial port), you'll notice that you can't see anything over your serial console. There is a work-around. After your system boots past the BIOS, the serial console screen will go completely blank. At that point you will have to type without being able to see the output. First hit Enter to accept the default language. Then hit F6 so you can tweak the boot prompt, and hit Esc to exit out of the F6 menu into the boot prompt. Finally, type `console=ttyS0,9600n8` and hit Enter. If your serial console is on a different port or uses different settings, you will want to change this argument accordingly. Since you can't see what you are typing, you will probably want to pay extra attention to each key. Once you hit Enter, the kernel will boot and within a few seconds you should start to see output over the serial port. At that point you will be able to complete the install over the serial console, and the next time you reboot you'll notice that the GRUB prompt and the kernel arguments are already set up for you.

Disk Partitioning

Any Linux installer is essentially a series of questions, and the Ubuntu server install asks pretty simple questions for the most part. The first phase of the installation prompts you with questions about what language to use for the install, what hostname to use, and, if you don't have DHCP on your network, the network settings for the host. There aren't any real tricky decisions to be made until you get to the partitioning section of the installer.

What Is a Partition?

If you are relatively new to Linux, you might be wondering what a partition is, and why Linux is prompting you to partition in the first place. Think of a hard drive like a house with an open floor plan—no rooms and only outside walls. While many people do live in lofts that are organized like this, most people prefer a house that has rooms. With rooms you can organize your bed and all of your personal things in a bedroom, all of your cooking supplies in your kitchen, and your bathtub, sink, and toilet in a bathroom. Even people in lofts often set up bookcases or other structures to separate, or partition, different sections of the loft into rooms. Disk partitions work in much the same way and for the same reason. Linux uses partitions to separate different parts of its file system that are used for different purposes. One partition might be used for the core of the file system (also known as the root partition) while a separate partition is set up as swap space—a place on the disk that Linux can use as RAM if it doesn't have enough free memory.

Beyond the basic two partitions, system administrators often like to separate out other parts of the file structure into partitions. Chapter 2, Essential System Administration, covers all of the major directories on an Ubuntu system along with their purpose, but for now here are a few directories that administrators often configure as separate partitions:

▪ **/home**
  The /home directory is a popular partitioning candidate among both administrators and desktop users alike because it holds all of the personal files for user accounts on that machine. If you maintain /home as a separate partition, you can install new versions of a distribution or even different distributions altogether without wiping out any user settings.

▪ **/var**
  The /var directory is designed for storing data that varies in size. From mail spools to HTML files to system logs, this directory can often grow pretty quickly. Administrators often separate /var out to its own partition so that if, for instance, a log file grows rapidly and fills up the partition, it is much easier to recover from than if the entire root partition were to be full.

▪ **/opt**
  A lot of third-party software is known to install under /opt. Depending on whether you use any of this software, your /opt directory might be completely empty or might be hundreds of gigabytes in size. On some systems the overall root partition may need to be only a few gigabytes with the bulk of the growth in /opt, so an administrator might put /opt as its own partition.

- **/usr**

  An interesting aspect of the /usr directory is how little it changes after a system is installed. Generally speaking, it is set up so that it changes only when you upgrade programs or install new packages. Because of that, some security-minded administrators put it as its own partition and mount it read-only during normal operation to prevent attackers from replacing programs with Trojan horses or other viruses.

- **/tmp**

  Many programs use /tmp to store temporary files that don't have to persist after a reboot. A common problem, though, is that a program might store far too much data in /tmp, and if it is part of the root partition, the entire root partition can fill up. A common culprit is vi. When you open a file with vi, a temporary copy of the file is placed in /tmp. I can't count the number of times I've been paged because a server's root partition was full, only to find out that a user used vi to open a 500Mb log file and dumped an equivalently sized temporary file under /tmp. I then had to kill the vi session and instruct the user on using a program such as less or more to view large text files.

- **/boot**

  In the past there have been different limitations placed on Linux boot loaders. For some time Linux couldn't boot if the kernel was located past 1024 cylinders on the disk. Even after that issue was resolved, Linux boot loaders sometimes couldn't boot if your root partition used a file system like XFS or if you used LVM or software RAID. A number of these issues have since been resolved, but some (such as booting from a RAID5 root partition) still remain. A common workaround, however, has been to create a small (64–128Mb should be enough) partition at the beginning of the disk for the /boot directory. The kernel, along with its initial root directory, lives in this partition, so if the boot loader can access this partition and load the kernel, the kernel can generally take care of more exotic partitions or RAID/LVM configuration as it boots.

The Ubuntu installer has a few different partitioning options for an administrator. You can choose one of the Guided partitioning methods, which set up a standard partitioning scheme based on sane defaults, or you can choose the Manual option and partition your disk step by step.

NOTE   If your drive already has partitions, you will also get a Guided option to resize the current partitions the installer has found to free up space for your new install. This is mostly a desktop option for people who would like to dual-boot between OSs. Since dual-booting doesn't make sense with most servers, for the most part you will probably want to choose a different option and overwrite the entire drive. This option exists for those of you who know what you are doing and do want to resize existing partitions.

Guided—Use Entire Disk

The first partitioning method is probably the best choice for new administrators who aren't sure what partitions to create and for seasoned administrators who don't need any extra partitions. The installer lets you select among all detected hard drives and partitions your choice with an adequate swap partition and a root partition that fills up the rest of the drive. Before anything gets written to disk you will see a list of both partitions prompted by "Write Changes to Disk." You still have an opportunity to back out of your decisions, or you can choose Yes and Ubuntu will partition the drive and continue with the install.

Guided with LVM

LVM (Logical Volume Management) allows you to group a number of partitions or disks (or even RAID arrays) together and treat them like a single disk that you can grow on the fly later on. An LVM also allows advanced features like snapshots so that you can create a state of your drive that is frozen in time and mount it somewhere temporarily—a feature that is quite useful for backups.

If you would like to use LVM but aren't too experienced with it, the Guided LVM partitioner makes it easy to set up your disk with two LVM volume groups: one for the root partition and one for swap. It will even set up the small /boot partition for you so that GRUB can easily boot from your LVM partition. If you choose the Guided LVM partitioner with encryption, you can even encrypt the entire disk with a key you choose at install time.

Manual

The most flexible option is the manual partitioner. If you would like to deviate at all from the standard two-partition system, if you would like to configure software RAID, if you prefer file systems other than ext3, or if you just like to get your hands dirty and get a clearer view of how your disk will be partitioned, then the manual partitioner is the tool for you.

Initialize a Blank Drive   When you enter the manual partitioner, you will see all visible disks along with any partitions they currently have. For instance, if you have only one disk on the system and it doesn't yet have any partitions, use the arrow keys to highlight the disk and hit Enter. If the disk is completely blank, you will be prompted to initialize the disk and then at that point, as Figure 1-2 shows, you will see free space under that disk that you can use.

Allocate Free Space   Once the drive is initialized or if it already had partitions, you can then highlight any available partition or free space on the screen and hit Enter to edit it. When you select free space, you have the option to create a new partition, automatically partition the free space, or show cylinder, head, and sector information. Generally speaking, you will choose the last option only if you plan to create partitions based on cylinder, head, or sector boundaries. If you aren't sure what I'm talking about, that's OK, as for the most part you don't have to care about these values anymore—the partitioning tool takes care of them for you.

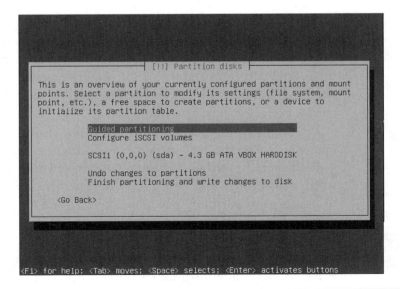

Figure 1-2 Blank drive ready for manual partitioning

If you choose to automatically partition free space, the partitioner will act as though you selected the Guided partitioning option and create a root drive and swap space in the free space for you. Now normally people choose the manual option to avoid the default partitions, so if you want to manually partition, choose the "Create a new partition" option.

For each new partition you choose to create, you are asked a series of questions, including partition size, whether it is a primary or logical partition, and the location of the partition on the free space, and finally you are presented with a list of file system options. For the partition size, you can specify an actual partition size ending in M for megabytes or G for gigabytes, or you can specify a percentage of the free space to use followed by the % sign or just type max to use the entire free space.

Whether a partition should be a primary or a logical partition depends on a few factors based on some limitations to disk partitioning. A disk may have only four primary partitions. If you want more than four partitions on a disk, you have to use a work-around. If you set up one of the primary partitions as an extended partition, then you can create up to 24 partitions within that extended partition (although most people don't need nearly that many). The partitions that you create inside an extended partition are labeled logical partitions. The basic rule of thumb is, if you plan on only two or three partitions on a drive, you can set them all up as primary partitions. If there is a chance that you will have four or more partitions on a drive, you will want to set up an extended partition to span the space of those extra partitions and then set up logical partitions within this. Note that the Ubuntu installer creates the extended partition for you when you choose to create a logical partition.

Figure 1-3 shows the final screen you will see when you create a partition. This screen is devoted to file system settings, and a few of the options are worth extra description. The "Use as" field lets you specify the file system to use for your partition (if you aren't sure what file system to use, the default ext4 or even an ext3 file system is a good choice for all-around use). If you select that option and hit Enter, you will see that along with file system and swap storage choices, this is also where you can set up a partition as a physical volume either for encryption, RAID, or LVM. In Chapter 10, Fault Tolerance, I go into detail about how to set up these RAID partitions

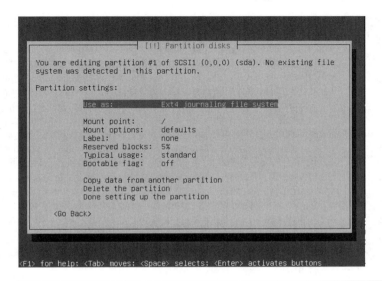

Figure 1-3 File system settings for manual partitioning

from the Ubuntu installer as well as how to use command-line tools to create RAID volumes on an already-running server.

The manual installer doesn't hide too many settings from you even for regular ext4 partitions. Here's a basic rundown of each of the options and why you might want to change them:

- **Mount point**
  If you move beyond the standard root and swap partitions, you need to change this option to point to where you wish to mount this partition when the system boots.

- **Mount options**
  There are a number of advanced options you can pass to file systems as they are mounted. When you select this option, the installer shows you a list of available options to choose from, along with a brief description of what each option does. I recommend sticking with the default relatime option unless you have a good reason to disable it.

NOTE **A Time**
A common complaint with Linux file systems is that by default the disk is written to even when you only read from a file. This is because the file system maintains a set of metadata known as MAC times—an acronym for Modify, Access, and Change. Modified time is the time the inode was last modified (for a file this is when it was last written to). Access time is the time the inode was last accessed (for a file, when it was last read). Change time keeps track of the last time the file's metadata (information like the file's permissions and ownership) was changed. Most administrators tend to not mind the M and C times, but when a file system gets read heavily, you can notice a significant performance boost if you disable A time (the noatime option). The downside, though, is that the A time can be very valuable, especially if you ever need to perform forensics on the file system and want to know the last time a file was accessed. The relatime option is a good compromise between both extremes in that it updates the A time only when a file is accessed and its current A time is older than the M or C time. There is still some overhead to this check, but it is a definite improvement over the default.

▪ **Label**
This option lets you assign a name to your partition. You can then reference this name instead of the device name when you mount the partition.

▪ **Reserved blocks**
A little secret among administrators is that when a user sees a partition at 100%, it may not actually be 100% full. The reserved blocks option lets you reserve a percentage of the file system blocks for the superuser. It can be a very bad situation when a partition fills up (especially the root partition). This option allows the superuser to go into a system where a regular user has filled the disk and still have some room to fix the problem.

▪ **Typical usage**
This option is more for advanced administrators. When a file system is created, it sets the maximum number of total inodes. When you run out of inodes on the system, you can't create any new files even if there is still free space, and you can't increase the number of available inodes without reformatting the file system. If you plan on having only a few large files in the file system, you might choose largefile or largefile4 and create the file system with fewer total inodes to get a performance boost. On the other hand, if you plan on storing millions of small files on the file system, you might choose the news option to make sure you have plenty of inodes.

- **Bootable flag**
  The default for the Ubuntu server is to install the Linux boot code in the MBR (Master Boot Record). If your BIOS will boot only from a partition that has the boot flag set, or if you want to install the boot code at the beginning of a partition instead, then you will need to set the boot flag for your root partition (or /boot if you separated it into its own partition).

Server Roles

The default Ubuntu server install will install only the core system to your drive. Since there are so many types of servers an Ubuntu server can be, Ubuntu just installs the essentials so you have plenty of space for any extra packages or files you need to add. That having been said, unless you have set up an Ubuntu server before, it can take some research to know exactly which packages you need to create, for instance, a DNS or a Samba file server. Ubuntu has streamlined this process for you by choosing a few common server roles, determining what packages they require, and then presenting you with a list of server types during the install process. You can even choose more than one set of software if, for instance, you want to set up a Samba file server that also runs DNS and an SSH server. After you have partitioned and installed the base system, Ubuntu presents you with the following predefined collections of software:

- **Cloud computing**
  The install offers a few different cloud computing options. They are covered in Chapter 9, Virtualization.

- **DNS server**
  This choice is pretty basic and adds the bind9 and bind9-doc packages to your system. These packages provide the Bind 9 DNS server and its documentation, respectively.

- **LAMP server**
  LAMP is an acronym for Linux Apache MySQL PHP (or sometimes Perl or Python). It refers to a recognition that a very common Web server deployment is a combination of Apache using Perl, PHP, or Python for dynamic content with a MySQL database on the back end, all running on Linux. It has become such a common way to set up a

Web site under Linux that even Ubuntu has grouped all of the necessary packages together. If you choose the LAMP server package group, Ubuntu will add the `apache2`, `apache2-mpm-prefork`, `mysql-server-5.0`, `mysql-client-5.0`, and `php5-mysql` packages along with all of their libraries and other dependencies. In addition to the extra packages, when you choose this group, the installer prompts you to choose an optional password for the MySQL root user (a good idea since the default is a blank password).

▪ **Mail server**
This selection installs the Postfix mail server package. When you enable this option, though, the installer starts the initial Postfix configuration script. This is an interactive script that provides you with a few common mail server configuration types, and depending on what you choose, it will ask you a few more questions so that when you are finished, you should at least have a functional mail server. Keep in mind, though, that even though the mail server will function, you must perform extra configuration if you want to add spam checking, greylisting, POP or IMAP servers, or other more advanced options. See Chapter 5, Guide to Common Ubuntu Servers, for a list of mail server configuration types.

▪ **OpenSSH server**
This option installs the `openssh-server` package. Choose this if you would like to remotely manage the server using SSH. Note that even if you don't choose this option, you can still ssh *from* the host; you just won't be able to ssh *into* the host.

▪ **PostgreSQL database**
Choose this option if you would like a PostgreSQL database server. It will install the `postgresql` package along with its documentation and any necessary libraries and dependencies.

▪ **Print server**
This option selects the `cupsys`, `cupsys-bsd` (providing lpr services for cups), `defoma`, `foomatic-db`, `foomatic-filters`, and a number of other printer drives and libraries—everything you need to connect a server to one or more printers (either locally or over the network) and then share them with the rest of your LAN.

- **Samba file server**
  This choice adds the `samba`, `samba-doc`, `smbfs`, and `winbind` packages along with dependencies and libraries. Choose this option if you want to set up a file server to share files with Windows, Linux, and Mac hosts but don't want to use NFS.

- **Tomcat Java server**
  If you plan to install a Tomcat Java server, this selection installs all the Java packages you need.

- **Virtual machine host**
  If you plan to use this machine as a host for other virtual machines, this option installs all of the KVM packages you need. For more information on virtual machines, go to Chapter 9.

If you select any of these options, in some cases the server will be ready to use but in many cases you will still need to do some configuration on your side so that the server is ultimately useful to you. In Chapter 5, I discuss some common Ubuntu servers you might want to configure and provide some example configurations for each type. By the way, if you complete the install and realize that you would like to view this list of packages again, just run `sudo tasksel` from the terminal. Note, however, that the local version of `tasksel` will show you a much larger list of groups, including a number of options that might be more appropriate for a desktop install. You can also run `sudo tasksel -s` so that you get only a list of server tasks.

Installer Console

For the most part you will interface with the default installer screen. Basically all you can do in this screen is answer questions and choose some options. Sometimes, though, an install doesn't go exactly the way you planned, especially if you use exotic hardware or are trying out a new Kickstart script. The Ubuntu installer provides a number of avenues for diagnostics via other consoles you can access. For instance, if you hit Alt-F4, you will see a running log of what the Ubuntu installer has been doing. Or if you don't seem to be getting a DHCP lease on the network, you could hit Alt-F4 to change to this console and see what error you get on the host.

In addition to the F4 installer logs, you can hit Alt-F2 or Alt-F3 to access a limited BusyBox shell. While you won't have access to the same rich list of command-line utilities you might be used to, you can perform some basic diagnostics on the system. You could, for instance, run `fdisk` on a drive to see what partitions are on there or even mount a partition to a temporary location to see what files are there. You could ping a host to test network connectivity or DNS resolution, or you could run `ps` to view the current processes that are running on the installer, and if you have a Kickstart script that is hanging up, you could potentially kill it from this console.

When you are ready to return to the main installer program, just hit Alt-F1. You can always return to any of these windows during the rest of the install process.

Reboot the System

Once you get past the list of package groups, the Ubuntu installer will complete the initial install process and prompt you to reboot. If you booted from a CD-ROM, be sure to eject and remove it unless your BIOS is configured to boot from the hard drive first. Otherwise you could always choose the "Boot from first hard disk" option from the CD boot menu.

## CHAPTER 2

Essential System Administration

AFTER YOU HAVE COMPLETED AN Ubuntu server install, you might think to yourself, "Now what?" If you are new to Linux administration, you might feel a bit overwhelmed at the steep learning curve you see. For one thing, there are a large number of command-line tools to learn. For another, there are all sorts of configuration files scattered in different locations. Even if you are an experienced Linux administrator but new to Ubuntu, you will find that configuration files might not be quite where you expect, and some programs you are used to might not even exist. In many ways trying a new distribution is like driving a new car. Sure, the car has a steering wheel, a gas pedal, and a brake, but it still takes you a minute to adjust the mirrors, find out where all the gauges and controls are, and adjust the seat until you feel comfortable. Think of this chapter as that minute or two behind the wheel of a new car. Here I cover some core commands a new administrator should know, explain the Ubuntu boot process, describe the main directories that make up an Ubuntu system, and talk a bit about networking. By the end of the chapter you should feel pretty much at home while logged in to your Ubuntu server.

Basic Command-Line Administration

Entire books have been written on command-line tools and how to use them effectively, so instead of documenting every major Linux command and process, I'm going to assume you are new to Linux server administration and need at least a basic set of tools just to move around the system, edit files, and check processes. If you are an experienced administrator, feel free to skip ahead to the next section where I document the Ubuntu boot process.

Move Around the System

When you log in to your server, the first thing you see is a blinking cursor. By default, when you log in you will be in your user's home directory. If you want to confirm this, you can use the pwd command:

```
$ pwd
/home/kyle
```

One of the most common commands an administrator runs is the ls command. If you come from a Windows background, this is a lot like the dir command. When you type this command by itself, it will list all of the files in the current directory. If you are in your home directory on a fresh Ubuntu install, you won't see any files because that directory is empty, but if you follow the `ls` command with a directory name, it will list the files in that directory. For instance, / is the name of the root directory (the directory that contains all of the rest of the directories on the system):

```
$ ls /
bin     dev    initrd.img  media  proc   selinux  tmp  vmlinuz
boot    etc    lib         mnt    root   srv      usr
cdrom   home   lost+found  opt    sbin   sys      var
```

If I wanted to see the contents of the etc directory I saw in that output, I could type `ls /etc`. There is a huge number of options for the `ls` command (type man `ls` on the command line to see a list of them), but one of the most common arguments is `-l` (for long). If you type `ls -l`, it will provide much more information about all of the files and directories it sees. For instance, here's what happens when I type `ls -l /`:

```
$ ls -l /
total 85
drwxr-xr-x  2 root root  4096 2010-02-26 15:07 bin
drwxr-xr-x  4 root root  1024 2010-02-26 15:10 boot
drwxr-xr-x  2 root root  4096 2010-02-26 14:58 cdrom
drwxr-xr-x 14 root root  3720 2010-02-26 15:12 dev
drwxr-xr-x 83 root root  4096 2010-02-26 15:24 etc
drwxr-xr-x  3 root root  4096 2010-02-26 15:10 home
lrwxrwxrwx  1 root root    37 2010-02-26 14:59 initrd.img ->
boot/initrd.img-2.6.32-14-generic-pae
drwxr-xr-x 17 root root 12288 2010-02-26 15:22 lib
drwx------  2 root root 16384 2010-02-26 14:56 lost+found
drwxr-xr-x  3 root root  4096 2010-02-26 14:56 media
drwxr-xr-x  2 root root  4096 2009-12-07 16:32 mnt
drwxr-xr-x  2 root root  4096 2010-02-26 14:57 opt
dr-xr-xr-x 80 root root     0 2010-02-26 15:12 proc
drwx------  4 root root  4096 2010-02-26 15:04 root
drwxr-xr-x  2 root root  4096 2010-02-26 15:10 sbin
drwxr-xr-x  2 root root  4096 2009-12-05 13:55 selinux
drwxr-xr-x  2 root root  4096 2010-02-26 14:57 srv
drwxr-xr-x 13 root root     0 2010-02-26 15:12 sys
drwxrwxrwt  4 root root  4096 2010-02-26 15:22 tmp
drwxr-xr-x 10 root root  4096 2010-02-26 14:57 usr
drwxr-xr-x 14 root root  4096 2010-02-26 15:07 var
lrwxrwxrwx  1 root root    34 2010-02-26 14:59 vmlinuz ->
boot/vmlinuz-2.6.32-14-generic-pae
```

All of the output is organized into columns. The first column lists the file's or directory's permissions. If that column starts with a -, then it is a directory; if it starts with a, then it is a regular file; and if it starts with an l, then it is a symbolic link (more on those later). After that you will see a series of rs, ws, or xs grouped into threes. The r, w, and x stand for readable, writable, and executable, respectively. Each group of rwx describes permissions on the file or directory for the owner, group, and everyone else respectively. So if you look at the permissions on the bin directory in the output above you will see drwxr-xr-x. That means it is a directory, that the directory's owner has read, write, and execute permissions, the directory's group has read and execute permissions, and the rest of the users have read and execute permissions.

Further in the ls -l output you will see a column that shows the number of links or directories within a directory, and then after that are columns that list a file or directory's owner and group. In the output above everything is owned by the root user (the superuser on the system who essentially has unlimited access to all files) and the root group. After those columns you will see a number that represents the file or directory's size in bytes. The next column is the date and time the file was last modified, and finally you will see the file or directory's name. Some of the filenames in this output have arrows that point to another filename. This is a special file known as a symbolic link (or symlink). Whenever users read or edit a symlink, they actually open the file to which the symlink points.

To move around in a Linux system, use the cd (change directory) command followed by the directory you want to change to. So, for instance, if I wanted to change to the /etc directory, I would type cd /etc. If I am in a directory and want to change to a directory within my current directory, I don't have to type the full path with all of the / symbols; I can just type the directory name. So if I were in the /etc directory and wanted to go to the /etc/default directory, I could type cd default. Linux also provides aliases to represent the current directory (.) and the directory above your current directory (..), and you can use these with any command that expects a directory as an option. So if I wanted to see the contents of the current directory, I could type ls ., and if I wanted to change to the directory above my current directory, I could type cd .. —this turns out to be much faster than typing the full path to the directory above where you are. You can even nest these aliases, so if you wanted to go two directories up, type cd ../../.

File Ownership

As you administer a system, you will find that you often need to change a file's owner, group, or permissions. The chown and chgrp commands allow you to change the owner and group of a file, respectively, provided that your user has permission to change the ownership to begin with. So if I wanted to change the group of a file to be the staff group, I would type sudo chgrp staff *filename.*

The chmod command allows you to change permissions on a file. There are a number of different ways to describe permissions for a file (type man chmod to see a full list), but one common way is to list u, g, or o for user, group, or everyone else (other) followed by a + or - sign, and then the permission to add or remove. So if I wanted to remove write access for the user who owns a file, I would type chmod u-w *filename.* If I wanted to add read permissions for a file's group, I would type chmod g+r *filename.* To add read permissions on a file for everyone else on the system, type chmod o+r *filename.* There's even a shortcut, a, that applies the change to the user, group, and everyone else, so to add read permissions on a file for user, group, and everyone else, type chmod a+r *filename.*

Check Running Processes

An administrator will often need to check which programs are currently running on the system and what resources they are consuming. You might even need to stop a process on the system. Linux provides a number of tools to manage processes, but top and ps are among the most common. When you type top on the command line and press Enter, you will see a lot of system information all at once (Figure 2-1). This data will continually update so that you see live information on the system, including how long the system has been up, the load average, how many total processes are running on the system, how much memory you have—total, used, and free—and finally a list of processes on the system and how many resources they are using.

You probably won't be able to see every process that is currently running on your system with top because they wouldn't all fit on the screen. By default

```
top - 15:28:40 up 16 min,  2 users,  load average: 0.00, 0.17, 0.22
Tasks:  68 total,   1 running,  67 sleeping,   0 stopped,   0 zombie
Cpu(s):  0.0%us,  1.6%sy,  0.0%ni, 98.4%id,  0.0%wa,  0.0%hi,  0.0%si,  0.0%st
Mem:    508684k total,   304116k used,   204568k free,    10976k buffers
Swap:   397304k total,        0k used,   397304k free,   138948k cached

  PID USER      PR  NI  VIRT  RES  SHR S %CPU %MEM    TIME+  COMMAND
 1331 ubuntu    20   0  2388 1124  896 R  1.6  0.2  0:00.75 top
    1 root      20   0  2616 1576 1192 S  0.0  0.3  0:01.07 init
    2 root      20   0     0    0    0 S  0.0  0.0  0:00.00 kthreadd
    3 root      RT   0     0    0    0 S  0.0  0.0  0:00.00 migration/0
    4 root      20   0     0    0    0 S  0.0  0.0  0:00.00 ksoftirqd/0
    5 root      RT   0     0    0    0 S  0.0  0.0  0:00.00 watchdog/0
    6 root      20   0     0    0    0 S  0.0  0.0  0:00.49 events/0
    7 root      20   0     0    0    0 S  0.0  0.0  0:00.00 cpuset
    8 root      20   0     0    0    0 S  0.0  0.0  0:00.00 khelper
    9 root      20   0     0    0    0 S  0.0  0.0  0:00.00 netns
   10 root      20   0     0    0    0 S  0.0  0.0  0:00.00 async/mgr
   11 root      20   0     0    0    0 S  0.0  0.0  0:00.00 pm
   12 root      20   0     0    0    0 S  0.0  0.0  0:00.02 sync_supers
   13 root      20   0     0    0    0 S  0.0  0.0  0:00.00 bdi-default
   14 root      20   0     0    0    0 S  0.0  0.0  0:00.00 kintegrityd/0
   15 root      20   0     0    0    0 S  0.0  0.0  0:00.04 kblockd/0
   16 root      20   0     0    0    0 S  0.0  0.0  0:00.00 kacpid
   17 root      20   0     0    0    0 S  0.0  0.0  0:00.00 kacpi_notify
   18 root      20   0     0    0    0 S  0.0  0.0  0:00.00 kacpi_hotplug
   19 root      20   0     0    0    0 S  0.0  0.0  0:00.00 ata/0
   20 root      20   0     0    0    0 S  0.0  0.0  0:00.00 ata_aux
   21 root      20   0     0    0    0 S  0.0  0.0  0:00.00 ksuspend_usbd
   22 root      20   0     0    0    0 S  0.0  0.0  0:00.00 khubd
```

Figure 2-1 Output from the top command

top sorts the processes according to how much CPU they use. That way you can see what processes are consuming CPU at a glance. So what if you do notice a process consuming all of your CPU and you want to kill it? The very first column for processes in top is labeled PID and shows a program's process ID—a unique number assigned to every process on a system. To kill a process, press the K key and then type in the PID you wish to kill, then hit Enter when prompted to kill with signal 15. top is a very powerful and informative program and I've only mentioned a small fraction of what it can do. If you want to find out more about top, including detailed information about each field in the output, how to sort by different fields, and much more, type man top in a terminal to bring up the command's manual page.

NOTE You may have noticed that I mentioned the man command a few times already. This command, short for manual, is one of the most useful commands on a Linux system because it provides you with a manual for all of the major Linux commands. No matter how long you have used Linux, you never seem to memorize every argument for every command, but you don't have to. When you are stumped, just type man command to see a list of all of the arguments for a command and overall instructions for how to use the program. While in the man program, hit q to exit. For more information about the man program you can type—you guessed it—man man.

Another useful command-line program for listing processes is the ps command. When you run it with no arguments, it is not very useful—it lists only processes in your current shell. It's the arguments that make ps so powerful. When you type ps -ef, you will see volumes of information about all of the running processes on your system. The very top of the output will show you labels for each of the columns, but in the output you will see the user who owns a process, the PID, the PID of the parent process (the process that started this process), the time the process was started, and even the full command that was run with all of its arguments.

NOTE   When you get columns of output that scroll past your terminal, remember you can type Shift + PgUp to scroll up the terminal. You can also pipe any command to the less program (such as ps -ef | less) so you can page through the output more easily.

The ps command is another useful way to find the PID for a particular process so you can kill it, but unlike top, ps won't kill a process for you. To kill a process on the command line, type kill followed by the PID. So if I wanted to kill a program with a PID of 4023, I would type kill 4023. What you will find is that some programs are stubborn and don't go away even when you kill them. This is because by default the kill command sends a signal to the process that tells it to shut down—a signal that the process could possibly ignore. If you tried to kill a process and it doesn't seem to cooperate, you can force the process to die by passing the -9 option to kill. So, if the 4023 process was being stubborn, I could type kill -9 4023. Just be sure before you use the -9 option that you run the regular kill command first so the process has a chance to clean itself up.

Edit Files

On a Linux server most programs store their configuration in text files. When you want to make changes to a program, the most common way is to locate its configuration file, open it in a text editor, make changes, and then save those changes to the file. Ubuntu has a number of text editors available, and even in the default server install there are two popular editors to choose from, vi and nano. While a number of administrators (myself included) prefer vi, it does have a steep learning curve, so when you are starting out, it's good to have a simpler option with nano.

To edit a file with nano, type nano followed by the file's name. Once the file is open, you can use the arrow keys to move the cursor around in the file. Once you get to a section you want to change, you can use the standard backspace and delete keys to erase text and type text in its place. You will also notice a list of actions you can perform along the bottom of the screen. Each of the actions has a key binding, and each key binding starts with a ^, which represents the Ctrl key. When you are finished editing a file, you can hit Ctrl-X to exit the program. Nano will prompt you to save the file before it closes, so if you don't want to save your changes, you will get a chance to exit without saving.

Become Root

When you administer a system, it quickly becomes pretty apparent how little you can do as a regular user. Basically every configuration file requires extra privileges to edit and every major service does as well. The root user is much like the Administrator user on a Windows system and has access to all of the files and services on the machine. On some Linux systems the root user is like other users and has a password assigned to the account, but on Ubuntu the root password is disabled. Instead, you can log in as a regular user and then use the sudo command to gain root privileges.

There are particular access controls you can put in place to control which users can use the sudo command to become root, and in Chapter 6, Security, I will cover account security and the sudo command in depth, but to get you started you will need to know how to gain root privileges. By default the first user you set up on the system can gain root privileges with sudo. To run any command as root, type sudo followed by the command. So, for instance, if you wanted to reboot the system, you would type sudo reboot. When you are prompted for a password, enter your user password on the system.

Ubuntu Boot Process

As you administer an Ubuntu system, it's important to understand the boot process and how each service starts. Unlike some other Linux distributions, Ubuntu actually uses a totally different start-up process for services called Upstart, although unless you look closely you might not ever notice, since it has added backward compatibility with the classic System V init model. I'll cover both systems below, but first let's walk through some important parts of the initial Ubuntu boot process.

GRUB

When you first start an Ubuntu server, you are greeted with a start-up screen known as the GRUB boot loader. This program sits at least partially within the boot code on the Master Boot Record (the first 512 bytes of your hard drive) and is what controls which Linux kernel the system boots from and which options it uses as it boots.

In the current release of Ubuntu Server (starting with 9.10), the original GRUB boot loader has been updated to GRUB2. This has introduced quite a few changes in how GRUB is configured from what you might be used to if you have used Linux for some time. For instance, the main GRUB configuration file used to be /boot/grub/menu.lst, but now it is /boot/grub/grub.cfg. If you look at that file, however, you will notice a warning that you shouldn't edit it directly. Instead, if you want to change GRUB settings, you should edit /etc/default/grub and then run sudo update-grub to update the main config file. On a standard Ubuntu desktop install, you shouldn't generally have to look at or edit this file. On a server, however, you might run into circumstances that require editing the file. If you want the complete documentation for GRUB, you can start by reading the comments in the configuration files, or you can visit http://www.gnu.org/software/grub/grub.html.

When you look at /boot/grub/grub.cfg or even /etc/default/grub, you will discover references to a program called update-grub. This is a helper program that makes it easier to automate updates to the GRUB configuration file when new kernels are added. This program reads through and executes a number of configuration scripts within /etc/grub.d. Generally speaking, you should stick to /etc/default/grub for any configuration changes you want to make.

One of the great things about GRUB is that you can make temporary changes to its settings at the boot prompt. When GRUB loads, you probably won't be able to see the menu. Hit the Shift key to see all of the available kernel options. Highlight the kernel you want to edit and hit the E key. At that point you can change the particular configuration line you want to edit, make the changes you want, and then press Ctrl x to boot based on those options.

NOTE   If you find it difficult to hit the Shift key in time, you might need to edit the /etc/default/grub file and change the GRUB_HIDDEN_TIMEOUT value to a larger number (say, 10) and then run sudo update-grub. That should give you more time to hit the Shift key.

The Kernel Boot Process

When you select a kernel to boot through the GRUB menu, GRUB then loads the kernel into memory along with its initrd file (initial RAM disk). The initrd file is actually a gzipped cpio archive known as an initramfs file under Ubuntu. If you are curious about which files were included in a particular initramfs file, you can perform the following steps to extract it:

```
$ cp initrd.img-2.6.32-14-generic-pae /tmp/initrd.img-2.6.32-14-
generic-pae.gz
$ cd /tmp
$ gunzip initrd.img-2.6.32-14-generic-pae.gz
$ mkdir initrd
$ cd initrd
$ cpio -idv < /tmp/initrd.img-2.6.32-14-generic-pae
```

Now within your current directory you should see a set of directories that look a lot like a regular root directory. The bin, sbin, etc, lib, and other directories are there but with a limited set of files inside.

When a kernel boots, it needs to be able to at least mount the root file system so that it can access basic configuration files, kernel modules, and system binaries. A number of years ago it was common to have a kernel with file system support and SCSI and IDE device drivers built in. Nowadays there are so many more hardware and file systems to support, along with features like software RAID, LVM, and encryption on the root file system, that it makes much more sense to have this support available in modules that the kernel can load only if it needs them. That keeps the overall kernel size smaller and more flexible across all sorts of different environments.

The problem with a modular kernel is that it needs to get these modules from somewhere. If the modules are on the root file system, you have a chicken-or-egg problem—it has to mount the root file system to access the files it needs to mount the root file system. That's where the initramfs file comes in. The initramfs file provides the kernel with the essential kernel modules and system binaries it must have so that it can mount the root file system and complete the boot process. When the Ubuntu kernel is compiled, part of the build process also builds the initramfs file and identifies and includes all of the core modules and binaries the kernel might need to boot.

When the kernel boots, it then extracts the initramfs into RAM and runs a script called init that sits in the root of the initramfs. If you are more curious about the kernel boot process, extract the initramfs and look at this script. There's honestly not too much magic here—just a standard shell script that creates some system mount points and mounts the actual root partition. By the way, if you were wondering how it knows where the root file system is, GRUB passes that information as an argument to the kernel with the root= boot argument. Finally, after this init script has mounted the real root file system, its last task is to run the /sbin/init program on the root file system, which starts the next phase of the boot process.

/sbin/init

The /sbin/init program is the parent process of every program running on the system. This process always has a PID of 1 and is responsible for starting the rest of the processes that make up a running Linux system. Those of you who have been using Linux for a while know that init on Ubuntu Server is different from what you might be used to. There are a few different standards for how to initialize a UNIX operating system, but most classic Linux distributions have used what is known as the System V init model (described below) while Ubuntu Server has switched to a system known as Upstart. Ubuntu has still retained most of the outward structure of System V init such as runlevels and /etc/rc?.d directories for backward compatibility; however, Upstart now manages everything under the hood.

Classic System V Init   Before I explain Upstart and how it works, it makes sense to first describe how the classic System V init system works and then discuss how Upstart manages everything. System V refers to a particular version of the original UNIX operating system that was developed by

AT&T. In this style of init, the init process reads a configuration file called /etc/inittab to discover its default runlevel. It then enters that runlevel and starts processes that have been configured to run at that runlevel.

RUNLEVELS   The System V init process is defined by different system states known as runlevels. Runlevels are labeled by numbers ranging from 0 to 6, and each number can potentially represent a completely different system state. For instance, runlevel 0 is reserved for a halted system state. When you enter runlevel 0, the system shuts down all running processes, unmounts all file systems, and powers off. Likewise, runlevel 6 is reserved for rebooting the machine. Runlevel 1 is reserved for single-user mode—a state where only a single user can log in to the system. Generally, few processes are started in single-user mode, so it is a very useful runlevel for diagnostics when a system won't fully boot. Even in the default GRUB menu you will notice a recovery mode option that boots you into runlevel 1.

Runlevels 2 through 5 are left for the distribution and finally you to define. The idea behind having so many runlevels is to allow the user to create different modes the server could enter. Traditionally a number of Linux distributions have set one runlevel for a graphical desktop (in Red Hat this was runlevel 5) and another runlevel for a system with no graphics (Red Hat used runlevel 3 for this). The user could define other runlevels to, for instance, start up a system without network access. Then when you boot, you could pass an argument at the boot prompt to override the default runlevel with the runlevel of your choice. Once the system is booted, you can also change the current runlevel with the init command followed by the runlevel. So to change to single-user mode on an Ubuntu server system, you would type sudo init 1.

init Scripts   In addition to /etc/inittab, there are a number of other important files and directories for a System V init system that organize start-up and shutdown scripts, or init scripts, for all of the major services on the system.

▪ **/etc/init.d**
  This directory contains all of the start-up scripts for every service at every runlevel. Typically these are standard shell scripts, and they conform to a basic standard. Each script accepts at least two argu-

ments, start and stop, which respectively start up or stop a service (such as, say, your Web server). In addition, init scripts commonly accept a few extra options such as restart (stops and then starts the service), status (to return the current state of a service), reload (tells the service to reload its settings from its configuration files), and force-reload (forces the service to reload its settings). When you run an init script with no arguments, it should generally return a list of arguments that it accepts.

- **/etc/rc0.d through /etc/rc6.d**
  These directories contain the init scripts for each respective runlevel. In practice these are generally symlinks into the actual files under /etc/init.d. What you will notice, however, is that the init scripts in these directories have special names assigned to them that start with an S (start), K (kill), or D (disable) and then a number. When init enters a runlevel, it runs every script that begins with a K in numerical order and passes the stop argument, but only if the corresponding init script was started in the previous runlevel. Then init runs every script that begins with an S in numerical order and passes the start argument. Any scripts that start with D init ignores—this allows you to temporarily disable a script in a particular runlevel, or you could just remove the symlink altogether. So if you had two scripts, S01foo and S05bar, init would first run S01foo start and then S05bar start when it entered that particular runlevel.

- **/etc/rcS.d**
  In this directory you will find all of the system init scripts that init runs at start-up before it changes to a particular runlevel. Be careful when you tinker with scripts in this directory because if they stall, they could prevent you from even entering single-user mode.

- **/etc/rc.local**
  Not every distribution uses rc.local, but traditionally this is a shell script set aside for the user to edit. It's generally executed at the end of the init process so you can put extra scripts in here that you want to run without having to create your own init script.

So here is an example boot process for a standard System V init system. First init starts and reads /etc/inittab to determine its default runlevel, which in this example is runlevel 2. Then init goes to /etc/rcS.d and runs each script that begins with an S in numerical order with start as an argument. Then init does the same for the /etc/rc2.d directory. Finally init is finished but stays running in the background, waiting for the runlevel to change.

Upstart   System V init is a good system and has worked well on Linux for years; however, it is not without some drawbacks. For one, init scripts don't automatically have a mechanism to respawn if the service dies. So, for instance, if the cron daemon crashes for some reason, you would have to create some other tool to monitor and restart that process.

Another issue with init scripts is that they are generally affected only by changes in runlevel or when the system starts up but otherwise are not executed unless you do so manually. Init scripts that depend on a network connection are a good example. On Ubuntu there is an init script called networking that establishes the network connection. Any init scripts that depend on a network connection are named with a higher number than this init script to ensure they run after the networking script has run. What if you unplug the network cable from a server and then start it up? Well, the networking script would run, but all of the init scripts that need a network connection will time out one by one. Eventually you will get a login prompt and be able to log in. Now after you logged in, if you plugged in the network cable and restarted the networking service, you would be on the network, yet none of the services that need a network connection would automatically restart. You would have to start them manually one by one.

Upstart was designed not only to address some of the shortcomings of the System V init process, but also to provide a more robust system for managing services. One main feature of Upstart is that it is event-driven. Upstart constantly monitors the system for certain events to occur, and when they do, Upstart can be configured to take action based on those events. Some sample events might be system start-up, system shutdown, the Ctrl-Alt-Del sequence being pressed, the runlevel changing, or an Upstart script starting or stopping. To see how an event-driven system can improve on traditional init scripts, let's take the previous example of a system booted with an unplugged network cable. You could create an Upstart script that is triggered when a network cable is plugged in. That script could then restart the networking service for you. You could then configure any services that require a network connection to be triggered whenever the networking service starts successfully. Now when the system boots, you could just plug in the network cable and Upstart scripts would take care of the rest.

Upstart does not yet completely replace System V init, at least when it comes to services on the system. At the moment, Upstart does replace the functionality of init and the /etc/inittab file and manages changes to runlevels, system start-up and shutdown, console ttys, and more and more core functionality is being ported to Upstart scripts, but you will still find some of the standard init scripts in /etc/init.d and all of the standard symlinks in /etc/rc?.d. The difference is that Upstart now starts and stops services when runlevels change.

UPSTART SCRIPTS Upstart scripts reside in /etc/init and have different syntax from init scripts since they aren't actually shell scripts. To help illustrate the syntax, here's an example Upstart script (/etc/init/rc.conf) used to change between runlevels:

```
# rc - System V runlevel compatibility
#
# This task runs the old System V-style rc script when changing
# between runlevels.

description     "System V runlevel compatibility"
author          "Scott James Remnant <scott@netsplit.com>"
start on runlevel [0123456]
stop on runlevel [!$RUNLEVEL]
export RUNLEVEL
export PREVLEVEL
task
exec /etc/init.d/rc $RUNLEVEL
```

Upstart treats lines that begin with # as comments, like most other scripts and configuration files. The first two configuration options are start on and stop on. These lines define what events must occur for the script to start and stop. In this case the script will start when any runlevel 2 is entered and will stop when the runlevel is not set.

The next couple of lines export some environment variables, and then the task option tells init that this script will not be persistent—it will execute and then stop.

The actual programs that are run from an Upstart script are defined with either the script or exec options. In the case of the exec option, Upstart executes the command and all of the arguments that follow the exec option and keeps track of its PID. With the script option, Upstart treats the lines that follow as a shell script until it reaches the end script line.

Even though Upstart is designed to be event-driven, it still provides methods to check the status of Upstart jobs and start and stop them as appropriate. You can check the status, start, and stop Upstart scripts with the appropriately named status, start, and stop commands. One Upstart job on an Ubuntu server is the tty1 job and it starts the getty program on tty1. This gives an administrator a console when he or she types Alt-F1. Let's say, however, that for some reason you believe that the console was hung. Here's how to check the status and then restart the job:

```
$ sudo status tty1
tty1: start/running, process 789
$ sudo stop tty1
tty1 stop/waiting
$ sudo start tty1
tty1 start/running, process 2251
```

You can also query the status of all available Upstart jobs with initctl list:

```
$ sudo initctl list
mountall-net stop/waiting
rc stop/waiting
rsyslog start/running, process 640
tty4 start/running, process 708
udev start/running, process 299
upstart-udev-bridge start/running, process 297
ureadahead-other stop/waiting
apport start/running
hwclock-save stop/waiting
irqbalance stop/waiting
```

```
plymouth-log stop/waiting
tty5 start/running, process 713
atd start/running, process 727
failsafe-x stop/waiting
plymouth stop/waiting
ssh start/running, process 1210
control-alt-delete stop/waiting
hwclock stop/waiting
module-init-tools stop/waiting
cron start/running, process 728
mountall stop/waiting
rcS stop/waiting
ufw start/running
mounted-varrun stop/waiting
rc-sysinit stop/waiting
tty2 start/running, process 717
udevtrigger stop/waiting
mounted-dev stop/waiting
tty3 start/running, process 718
udev-finish stop/waiting
hostname stop/waiting
mountall-reboot stop/waiting
mountall-shell stop/waiting
mounted-tmp stop/waiting
network-interface (lo) start/running
network-interface (eth0) start/running
plymouth-splash stop/waiting
tty1 start/running, process 2251
udevmonitor stop/waiting
dmesg stop/waiting
network-interface-security start/running
networking stop/waiting
procps stop/waiting
tty6 start/running, process 720
ureadahead stop/waiting
```

CHANGE THE DEFAULT RUNLEVEL   In a way, Upstart seeks ultimately to do away with multiple runlevels, since if all of your services were started and stopped via Upstart scripts instead of System V init scripts, you could simply set up particular events that would cause the system to enter one state or the other. That having been said, today the system still does have multiple runlevels, and you might want to set up different runlevels and even change from the default runlevel of 2, so here's how to do that.

The default Upstart runlevel is defined in /etc/init/rc-sysinit.conf:

```
# rc-sysinit - System V initialisation compatibility
#
# This task runs the old System V-style system initialisation
# scripts,and enters the default runlevel when finished.

description      "System V initialisation compatibility"
author           "Scott James Remnant <scott@netsplit.com>"
start on filesystem and net-device-up IFACE=lo
stop on runlevel
# Default runlevel, this may be overridden on the kernel
# command-line or by faking an old /etc/inittab entry
env DEFAULT_RUNLEVEL=2
. . .
```

One way to change the default runlevel is to create your own /etc/inittab file and add an initdefault stanza to it such as with classic System V init. The other, perhaps simpler, way to change it is to edit /etc/init/rc-sysinit.conf and change the value of DEFAULT_RUNLEVEL to the runlevel you want as your default.

Services

The kernel and initial boot process are important parts of an Ubuntu server, but ultimately a server exists (and gets its name) because of services. A service is some function that your computer provides via software on the system. That software, and the computer that runs it, is typically referred to as a server. A computer might run a number of services such as a Web server, a file server, and DNS, all on the same machine.

There are two main ways that services are managed on Ubuntu: through either init scripts or a program called xinetd. While Upstart works behind the scenes to manage runlevels and someday will ultimately also manage the majority of the services on Ubuntu, today many of the services on a system are still started and stopped via init scripts. As I mentioned earlier in the chapter, init scripts reside in /etc/init.d and have symlinks in /etc/rc?.d directories, where ? is a number representing a runlevel. Each of these scripts accepts at least two arguments, start and stop, which start and stop the service, respectively. Most services support extended options, including

- restart: runs the stop portion of the script and then the start
- reload: tells the service to reread its configuration file when it can
- force-reload: forcibly reloads the service's configuration
- status: reports the current status of the service, typically whether it is running or not

Most well-written init scripts will return a list of supported arguments if you run the init script with no arguments:

```
$ /etc/init.d/networking
Usage: /etc/init.d/networking {start|stop|restart|force-reload}
```

If I wanted to restart the networking service, I could type either

```
$ sudo /etc/init.d/networking stop
$ sudo /etc/init.d/networking start
```

or the shorthand form

```
$ sudo /etc/init.d/networking restart
$
```

Now I could also have run the networking script from the /etc/rc?.d directory if I had wanted to, but most administrators I know reference the /etc/init.d directory just because the name of the script is consistent there and you can be assured that all available init scripts are there.

In addition to files in /etc/init.d and /etc/rc?.d, services often have special configuration files in /etc/default. This directory contains configuration files named after the services they manage and generally contain environment variables. When an init script executes, it often checks for a file with its name under /etc/default/, and if one exists, it loads all of its environment variables and other start-up settings from this file. Settings such as extra arguments passed to services are often found here, so if you want to change the default settings of a service on your system, this is a good place to look.

Most init scripts start programs that then run in the background until you explicitly kill them or the system shuts down. A well-written init script also keeps track of the PID of the service it starts so that when it needs to stop the service, it knows the PID to kill. The convention is to keep track of these PIDs in the /var/run/ directory, and if you look there on your Ubuntu system, you will see a number of .pid files (or directories that store .pid files) that contain the PIDs for various system services.

Generally speaking, when you install a new service on your machine, not only should it set up its init script and appropriate symlinks for each runlevel, it should also typically start the service once the package installation is complete. Now those of you who come from a Red Hat background are probably accustomed to using the service and chkconfig command-line tools to manage services. I have good and bad news for Red Hat administrators. The bad news is that currently Ubuntu has not ported chkconfig to Ubuntu. The good news is that it has ported the service command and there is a discouraged but available alternative to chkconfig as well.

The service tool basically provides a shorthand way to start and stop services. Instead of typing `sudo /etc/init.d/networking restart`, you can type `sudo service networking restart`. Red Hat has a very handy tool known as chkconfig that an administrator can use to enable and disable services. On a Red Hat system if you wanted to disable the named service, for instance, you could type `sudo chkconfig named off` and the chkconfig script would remove all of the relevant symlinks within /etc/rc?.d for you. If you wanted to enable the service, you could just type `sudo chkconfig named on`.

Unfortunately, Ubuntu does not yet have a chkconfig-like tool. The closest thing to it is a program known as `update-rc.d`. It's important to know that this script was designed for use by packages, not by users as its syntax shows. The original intention was to make it easy for a package to create all of the symlinks it needed upon installation and remove all of the symlinks upon package removal. That having been said, there are some basic arguments to `update-rc.d` you can use to get similar behavior to chkconfig. To disable an init script from starting up, type `sudo update-rc.d -f` *servicename* `remove`, and to enable a script type `sudo update-rc.d` *servicename* `defaults`.

Write Your Own Init Script   Ultimately when you administer servers, you may need to run your own custom programs at start-up. The simple way to do this is to put the script in /etc/rc.local so it is run at the end of the boot process. However, if you have a more sophisticated script that needs to both start at boot time and stop as part of system shutdown, then you will want to write a custom init script. While you could certainly wing it and write one from scratch, Ubuntu has made the process much easier for you with a cheat sheet init script called skeleton on which you can base your init script. First make a copy of the skeleton init script and name the file after your service:

```
$ sudo cp /etc/init.d/skeleton /etc/init.d/myservice
$
```

Then edit your copy of the skeleton file and replace the generic placeholders you find in the file with custom information for your service:

```
### BEGIN INIT INFO
# Provides:          skeleton
# Required-Start:    $remote_fs
# Required-Stop:     $remote_fs
# Default-Start:     2 3 4 5
# Default-Stop:      0 1 6
# Short-Description: Example initscript
# Description:       This file should be used to construct
#                    scripts to be placed in /etc/init.d.
### END INIT INFO

# Author: Foo Bar <foobar@baz.org>
#
# Please remove the "Author" lines above and replace them
# with your own name if you copy and modify this script.
```

After you change the generic entries in the comments, what you change in the rest of the init script really depends on the complexity of your application. For basic applications you should concern yourself only with the series of environment variables that follow the initial set of comments:

```
PATH=/sbin:/usr/sbin:/bin:/usr/bin
DESC="Description of the service"
NAME=daemonexecutablename
DAEMON=/usr/sbin/$NAME
DAEMON_ARGS="--options args"
PIDFILE=/var/run/$NAME.pid
SCRIPTNAME=/etc/init.d/$NAME
```

The initial set of comments in the skeleton script works for the basic case that your service is an executable program that exists in /usr/sbin. Change the DESC and NAME variables so they are equal to the description and the executable name of your service under /usr/sbin. If your service is installed elsewhere, such as in /usr/local/sbin/ or /opt/, then be sure to change the path in the DAEMON variable to reflect that. If your service needs any special arguments passed to it at runtime, set them in the DAEMON_ARGS variable or otherwise change it to be empty.

Once you are finished with your init script, you will want to create all of the appropriate symlinks for various runlevels. While you could create the symlinks by hand, it's certainly easier to use the update-rc.d script. First look at the current init scripts for your default runlevel such as those in /etc/rc2.d and decide when your init script should start. The lower the number, the sooner it will start in the boot process, but keep in mind that if your service depends on other services running, then you will want to make its sequence number higher. Once you have decided on a number, let's say 90, then run

```
$ sudo update-rc.d myservice defaults 90
$
```

and replace myservice with the filename you gave your service in /etc/init.d.

Xinetd   There are two main ways to start services. While most services on the system are started via init scripts, there are some services that are managed by a program called xinetd. Xinetd is an updated version of the classic inetd service and was created to be more efficient with resources on a server. The problem with init scripts is that when a system boots and a service starts, the service could sit there idly for days or weeks before it gets accessed, wasting valuable server resources. The idea behind xinetd is to listen on all of the ports its child services use. If a connection is made on one of the ports, xinetd will then spawn the service that corresponds to that port, and once the connection is finished, the service exits until it is needed again.

Xinetd is popular for a number of classic UNIX services, including echo (echoes back what you send to it), daytime (returns the system time), and TFTPD (the Trivial File Transfer Protocol Daemon). Xinetd is no longer installed by default, but if you want to use it, just type `sudo apt-get install xinetd`. You can see all of the available xinetd services configured for the system within the /etc/xinetd.d directory. By default all of these services are disabled; however, it's relatively simple to enable a service. For instance, to enable the echo service, open /etc/xinetd.d/echo in a text editor and change `disable = yes` to `disable = no`. Then run `sudo service xinetd reload` to reload the configuration file. Now you can telnet to port 7 on your localhost and anything you type gets parroted back:

```
$ telnet localhost 7
Trying 127.0.0.1...
Connected to localhost.
Escape character is '^]'.
hello
hello
echo
echo
^]

telnet> quit
Connection closed.
```

To quit the telnet session hit Ctrl-] and then press Enter to get to an interactive telnet prompt. Then type `quit` and press Enter to exit telnet.

NOTE I've talked a lot about how Ubuntu starts, but you might also want to know how to stop or reboot it. While you could certainly use a tool like init to change to runlevels 0 or 6, there are two easy-to-remember commands called `halt` and `reboot` that respectively halt and reboot the system. Just run either of the commands with root privileges and your system will immediately start the shutdown process and either reboot or power off after it completes.

File System Hierarchy

On an Ubuntu desktop system these days the overall file system hierarchy (the way directories are organized on the system) shouldn't matter to the average user. On the desktop you generally interact with your personal home directory, your desktop directory, and a few other directories within the home directory. All of the other directories on the system are somewhat obscured and settings are changed via GUI tools. Well, on an Ubuntu server you manage things from the trusty old command line, so you quickly get introduced to a number of directories on the root file system.

The great thing about Linux is that each of these directories has a direct purpose that has evolved over the years based on Linux (and before it, UNIX) having been used as a server. The more you understand what these directories are and why they exist, the faster you can troubleshoot problems, the more secure you can make the system, and the better you can add your own packages and other additions. Below are a number of the important directories on an Ubuntu server. This list is by no means exhaustive or complete. The point is to highlight the core directories with which you will interact as an administrator and explain why they are there. If you do want an exhaustive explanation, however, check out http://tldp.org/LDP/Linux-Filesystem-Hierarchy/html/index.html.

▪ **/bin**
  This directory contains core binaries that might be used by both administrators and regular users on the system. You will find commands like ps, ls, rm, mv, chmod, df, and other core programs in this directory.

▪ **/sbin**
  The /sbin directory has a similar function to /bin. It contains binaries; however, it is for core binaries used only by administrators. This directory should contain only system binaries crucial for mounting the rest of the system and recovering the system if it can't boot. You will find programs such as fsck, ifconfig, mkfs, route, and init here. While a number of the binaries in /sbin can be run by regular users, they are generally intended to be used by the root user.

▪ **/lib**
  Under /lib you will find core system libraries the system needs to complete the boot process and use the binaries under /bin and /sbin. All of the kernel's modules are also found here under /lib/modules/.

- **/usr**

  The /usr directory (short for UNIX System Resources) is intended to store all of the noncritical binaries and libraries for the system. Why the segregation? Well, the idea is that if you keep only the core binaries and libraries in /bin, /sbin, and /lib, you can keep the main root partition relatively small and throughout the life of the system it shouldn't grow too much. The bulk of the disk space can then be devoted to the /usr partition, which could be mounted on a separate, larger disk if you wanted. Another useful fact about /usr is that unless you update packages on the system, /usr stays relatively static. This means that if you separated /usr onto its own partition, you could actually add an extra layer of security and mount it read-only and remount it read-write when performing updates.

- **/usr/bin**

  This directory serves a similar purpose to /bin, only it stores the rest of the binaries on the system that aren't considered critical. You will find commands like man, gzip, nano, and other binaries intended for use both by administrators and regular users here.

- **/usr/sbin**

  This directory is similar to /sbin, only it stores binaries for administrator use that aren't critical to booting. Here you will find tools like traceroute, chroot, and ntpdate along with a majority of the daemons that are started by init scripts like Web servers, ntp daemons, and mail servers.

- **/usr/lib**

  As with /lib, you will find program libraries under this directory, only in this case they are libraries to support the binaries under /usr/bin and /usr/lib.

- **/usr/local**

  The great thing about Ubuntu as a server is that most of the services and other programs you want to run are already packaged and ready to use. In some cases, though, you might want to provide a custom service or binary or even a custom script of your own to the system.

This is where the /usr/local directory comes in. You will notice that it provides bin, sbin, and lib directories just as with /usr, only these directories are intended for any third-party programs you want to make available to the system that aren't provided by Ubuntu itself.

▪ **/opt**

There is an ongoing war between people who favor /usr/local for third-party programs and those who favor /opt. I'll try to not throw fuel on the fire here, but suffice it to say that /opt and /usr/local share the same purpose—the storage of third-party programs. The main difference between the two is organization. Typically programs that install under /opt install under their own directory (such as, say, /opt/someprogram) and then create their own bin, sbin, and lib directories under there. On one hand this means you can remove a program by removing that directory under /opt, but on the other hand it means that your PATH environment variable can grow quite large if you use /opt heavily.

▪ **/boot**

I mentioned the /boot directory already when I discussed the /boot process, but this directory stores kernel images, initramfs files, and also the GRUB configuration files. The /boot directory exists so that you can potentially separate it out into its own small mount point. This can be useful if you want to experiment with LVM or an experimental file system for your root partition. You could format a separate /boot partition as ext2 or ext3 with no software RAID or LVM configured and be sure that your boot loader could read it.

▪ **/etc**

This is a directory of great importance to system administrators. Under /etc you will find all of the configuration files for the system and services on the system. As I mentioned previously, you will also find all of the system start-up scripts under /etc/init and /etc/init.d along with their configuration files under /etc/default. Other core configuration for cron, your mail server, a Web server, your network settings, and all other important configuration files are found here. Some things you won't (or at least shouldn't) find here are binaries and libraries. The great thing about all configuration files being stored in /etc is that configuration files are text and text compresses very well. This makes /etc very easy to back up, and it takes very little space to do so. I highly recommend that if you don't back anything else up on your system you at least back up /etc.

- **/var**

  The /var directory was designed to store files and directories that could be variable in size and change frequently. The idea is to give the administrator the ability to mount /var as its own large partition and potentially as a partition on faster disks than the rest of the system. Under /var you will find system logs, mail spools, Web server documents, and other files that could grow or change frequently. While the /bin, /sbin, and even /usr directories might be pretty consistent across servers, the /var directory could vary widely across different servers depending on what the servers do.

- **/var/log**

  All system logs are stored under /var/log. As any seasoned administrator knows, logs not only vary in size, but they have a tendency to grow out of control when the system is either under load or has a problem. This is yet another reason why you might want to mount /var as a separate partition—if your logs do grow out of control (and trust me, at some point they will), you will fill up /var but won't fill up / and crash the system.

- **/var/spool**

  This directory contains subdirectories that store such information as user crontabs, printer spools, and mail spools. If you run a mail server in particular, this directory will become very important to you, as it can grow quite large if the server spools a lot of mail for delivery.

- **/var/www**

  This directory won't exist on all systems, but if you run a Web server it will be the default place for the Web server's docroot and cgi-bin directories.

- **/home**

  Here you will find the home directories for all of the users you have added to the system. If you plan on having an active set of users log in to the server, you might want to mount this as a separate partition as it could potentially grow quite large. Another advantage to separating out this directory is that if you decide to change distributions, you could install the system on the root partition and overwrite what was there but preserve all user settings here.

▪ **/root**
This is a special home directory just for the root user. It is separated off from /home, among other reasons, so that it can be available for the root user in case the system needs recovery and wasn't able to mount /home.

▪ **/dev**
This is a special directory that contains all of the device files on the system. These files include disk devices, keyboards, mice, and any other devices the system detects. On classic Linux systems these files were pretty static, but on a modern Ubuntu server device files are often created on the fly by the udev program as devices are added or modules are loaded.

▪ **/mnt**
The /mnt directory is intended to be a generic location for an administrator to mount a disk temporarily. You might, for instance, mount an NFS share here temporarily so you can copy information to or from your system. In the past a number of systems have also used /mnt for removable media, but the /media directory has been created recently for that purpose.

▪ **/media**
In the past there have been a lot of differing standards as to where to mount removable media such as floppy disks, CD-ROMs, and USB drives. Some have advocated extra root directories for this purpose, and others prefer /mnt. Ubuntu uses the /media directory for these devices so it can keep /mnt for temporary mount points for nonremovable media.

▪ **/proc**
There are a few virtual file systems under Linux, and /proc is one of the most useful ones. It is not an actual area on disk but instead exists

in RAM. Under this directory you will find live system information. For instance, every process that is created on the system gets a directory under /proc that corresponds to its PID. Within that directory are a number of other files and directories that contain live information about that process. In addition to information about processes, /proc also stores virtual files related to the kernel process itself. You can query such things as the options passed to the kernel at boot (/proc/cmdline) or view settings for different kernel devices or other settings. A number of the kernel /proc files can also be used to not only read settings, but set them by writing to the corresponding file.

- **/sys**
  The /sys directory is a virtual file system much like /proc. The files within /sys provide information about devices and drivers on your system, and the file system was created in part so that these sorts of files would no longer clutter up /proc. As with /proc, not only do many of the files within /sys provide information about parts of the system, but you can also write to various files to change settings on the fly.

- **/tmp**
  The /tmp directory is a special directory set aside to store temporary files. Every user has permission to create files under /tmp, but any files users create are readable and writable only to their user and group (and of course root). A number of programs on the system will use /tmp to store temporary state information. In fact, this use of /tmp provides a common headache for administrators because user programs sometimes store too much information in /tmp and fill up the root partition. It's important to use /tmp only for storage of temporary files, as this directory is wiped out every time the system boots.

Networking

Linux networking is a topic that could fill a number of books, so I won't attempt to document everything an administrator needs to know about networking here. Instead I will provide some basic information you will need to know to change network settings under Ubuntu.

Network Configuration Files

Ubuntu manages network settings like Debian before it. The primary network configuration file is /etc/network/interfaces and contains the configuration for all networking devices on the system. If you come from a Red Hat system, you are probably used to each interface having its own configuration file under /etc/sysconfig/network-scripts, but under Ubuntu all of those settings will be in this one file.

The syntax for /etc/network/interfaces can become complicated, as you will see if you reference its documentation by typing man 5 interfaces, but for most uses, especially for a server, it is very simple. I'm going to assume that since this is a server, we generally have to care about only a few interfaces, loopback, and Ethernet devices. The loopback interface, known as lo, always has the address 127.0.0.1 and is used when programs on the system need to establish network connections with the system itself; that way they don't have to waste time by going out on the network just to be routed back. Generally, you don't have to worry about configuring this interface because Ubuntu should do it for you, but if you did, here is what it would look like:

```
auto lo
iface lo inet loopback
```

The auto line specifies that the lo interface should automatically be brought up at boot. The iface line defines the lo interface and creates its settings (in this case defining lo as a loopback device).

Under Linux, Ethernet devices are generally labeled as eth followed by a number, starting with 0. So if you had two Ethernet ports on your server, they would be referenced as eth0 and eth1. The configuration for Ethernet devices is different depending on whether the device will get its address and settings via DHCP or will have them statically assigned. If your server gets its network settings for eth0 via DHCP, then the following would be a valid configuration:

```
auto eth0
iface eth0 inet dhcp
```

If, on the other hand, your network settings are static, here is a sample configuration:

```
iface eth0 inet static
        address 10.1.1.10
        netmask 255.255.255.0
        gateway 10.1.1.1
```

The fields are pretty self-explanatory. The first defines eth0 as a static interface instead of one that uses DHCP. Then the address of the interface is set (10.1.1.10), then the netmask (255.255.255.0), and finally the gateway (10.1.1.1) address—the IP for the router the machine will use to access other networks.

In addition to /etc/network/interfaces, there are two other core files for network settings. The first is /etc/resolv.conf and the second is /etc/hosts. The /etc/resolv.conf file has long been used by UNIX systems to define name servers to use. Now if your server gets its settings via DHCP, this file will automatically be set, and if you change this file, those settings will be overwritten the next time the machine gets its DHCP lease. Otherwise, if you have a static address and set name servers for this machine during the initial install, they will appear here. If you need to change the settings, the syntax is pretty simple, as this example shows:

```
search example.com site1.example.com
nameserver 10.1.1.2
nameserver 10.1.1.3
```

The first line is optional but configures the DNS search path to use. This way, if I wanted to access web.example.com, I could just reference web and the system would first try to get an address for web.example.com and then web.site1.example.com. The next lines define the IP addresses of name servers to use.

Before DNS existed, all hosts on the Internet were defined in the /etc/hosts file. Of course, there are far too many hosts now to list in /etc/hosts, but you can still use the /etc/hosts file to override or supplement DNS. By default you will find only localhost and loopback addresses configured here, but if you wanted to override a DNS address, or make sure that the system had an IP address for a host even if DNS was down, you could add addresses and names statically to this file.

Core Networking Programs

There are a number of important networking programs an administrator should be aware of on an Ubuntu server. The first of these are `ifup` and `ifdown`. When a system first boots, the /etc/init.d/networking script will read /etc/network/interfaces and automatically bring up any interfaces configured to load at start-up, but sometimes you might want to take down or bring up an interface manually. The `ifup` and `ifdown` scripts will respectively bring up and take down the interface you pass as an argument, so if I wanted to take down eth0, I would type `sudo ifdown eth0`.

NOTE Now be careful when you take down an interface. Not only will you potentially disrupt any services on the system, but if you are connected to the system via SSH and you take down the main interface on the system, you will disconnect yourself.

Another important networking program is `ifconfig`. This command was traditionally the command you used to configure networking interfaces and can actually still be used this way, although `ifup` and `ifdown` were created to make the process simpler. Even though you don't need to run `ifconfig` manually to configure your network anymore, it is still a useful tool to get network information. When run with no arguments, it will return information on all of the interfaces on your system:

```
$ sudo ifconfig
eth0      Link encap:Ethernet  HWaddr 00:30:48:2a:fb:b0
          inet addr:10.1.1.10  Bcast:10.1.1.255  Mask:255.255.255.0
          inet6 addr: fe80::230:48ff:fe2a:fbb0/64 Scope:Link
          UP BROADCAST RUNNING MULTICAST  MTU:1500  Metric:1
          RX packets:803 errors:0 dropped:0 overruns:0 frame:0
          TX packets:741 errors:0 dropped:0 overruns:0 carrier:0
          collisions:0 txqueuelen:100
          RX bytes:70230 (68.5 KB)  TX bytes:68449 (66.8 KB)
          Base address:0x3000 Memory:fc200000-fc220000

lo        Link encap:Local Loopback
          inet addr:127.0.0.1  Mask:255.0.0.0
          inet6 addr: ::1/128 Scope:Host
          UP LOOPBACK RUNNING  MTU:16436  Metric:1
          RX packets:0 errors:0 dropped:0 overruns:0 frame:0
          TX packets:0 errors:0 dropped:0 overruns:0 carrier:0
          collisions:0 txqueuelen:0
          RX bytes:0 (0.0 B)  TX bytes:0 (0.0 B)
```

As you can see, not only will this command tell me the IP address, net-mask, and broadcast settings for interfaces, but I can also see the MAC address for my Ethernet card and also how many packets and bytes have traversed the interface.

NOTE   A common problem beginner administrators run into is that on some systems the PATH environment variable might not contain /sbin or /usr/sbin, so when they run a command like ifconfig they get "ifconfig: command not found." If this happens to you, try specifying the full path to the command, for instance, sudo /sbin/ifconfig.

Another important networking program is the route command. As with ifconfig, this command can be used to both see and set network set-tings—in this case network routes. On many servers you will have only one main route on the system—the default route that points to your default gateway. If you run route without any arguments, it will return the com-plete routing table for your network, including the default route:

```
$ sudo route
Kernel IP routing table
Destination    Gateway    Genmask        Flags  Metric  Ref  Use Iface
10.1.1.0       *          255.255.255.0  U      0       0    0 eth0
default        10.1.1.1   0.0.0.0        UG     100     0    0 eth0
```

A final useful networking program is nslookup. While I also recommend that you ultimately learn the dig program, as it is more full-featured than nslookup, the nslookup tool is a quick way to test what IP address is asso-ciated with a name. Type nslookup followed by a name or IP address to resolve, and nslookup will return the results of the DNS query:

```
$ nslookup ubuntu.com
Server:     192.168.0.1
Address:  192.168.0.1#53

Non-authoritative answer:
Name:       ubuntu.com
Address:  91.189.94.156
```

Most of these networking tools are also very useful for troubleshooting network problems. I cover these and more handy network diagnostic tools in Chapter 11, Troubleshooting.

CHAPTER 3

Package Management

THIS CHAPTER BEGINS WITH a discussion of packages in general while focusing on the core features of packages and package management systems that cross most GNU/Linux distributions. In this discussion, I explain what packages are and what a package management system does. While I turn to examples from Ubuntu throughout, this discussion focuses on building a strong conceptual grounding. After establishing a solid grounding, I introduce Debian packages—the types of packages that Ubuntu uses—and give a brief view of the very different types of packages: source packages and binary packages. Most of the rest of the chapter focuses on package management in Ubuntu using the command-line tools. While many users of Ubuntu on the desktop are familiar with updating their system, this chapter focuses on the way this is done without a desktop system. It covers the basics and works up to some more advanced uses of a packaging system that many server administrators find useful. Finally, I touch on the process through which advanced users and administrators can create, modify, and redistribute their own packages.

Introduction to Package Management

On Ubuntu—and in other GNU/Linux environments—packages are the primary way that software is built, deployed, and installed. Nearly every major GNU/Linux operating system distributes software, both binary software and source code, in packages. These packages are usually either in the Rpm package format (RPM) or in the Debian package format (DEB) for binary software or in corresponding "source" RPM and DEB formats. With its close relationship to the Debian project as a project that continues to be based on Debian's work, Ubuntu naturally uses DEB format packages.

Very simply, packages are an alternative to downloading, building, and installing software from scratch. They offer a host of advantages in terms of installation, removal, monitoring, and handling interactions between pieces of software over the standard "build from source" model. Since packaging is not common outside of the GNU/Linux world—or at least not described in the same terms—it is worth going into some background on packaging before I describe how it is done on Ubuntu systems.

Background on Packages

Nearly every GNU/Linux-based operating system—Fedora, RHEL, open-SUSE, Slackware, Debian, and others—includes an almost entirely overlapping core selection of software. By definition, each of these OSes includes Linus Torvald's Linux kernel and a large chunk of the GNU project's developer- and user-oriented applications that are necessary to build and use it. Most also include server-oriented software like OpenSSH and Apache, either the XFree86 or X.Org implementation of the X Windowing System, and what is often an extremely expansive collection of both command-line and graphically based applications. Although people often throw the term around, it is important to establish that this collection of software is collectively referred to as a distribution. Ubuntu is a distribution. When people refer to "Linux" as an operating system, they are usually referring to a Linux or GNU/Linux distribution.

The primary goal of all distributions is the automatic installation, configuration, removal, maintenance, and update of software—both through the creation of infrastructure for this purpose and in the creation of modified versions of the preexistent software. The latter customization of existing software in this specialized way is the act of "packaging," and it constitutes the vast proportion of work done by Ubuntu developers. It constitutes, to a large degree, what Ubuntu is over and above the software that Ubuntu includes. And while packaging is primarily the work of distribution makers like Ubuntu, it can also be done by both the users of distributions, for the clean integration of "unpackaged" pieces of software into their systems, and by software vendors who wish to allow for easier installation and maintenance of software by their users.

What Are Packages?

The creation of a package—on Ubuntu or elsewhere—begins with the software in need of being packaged. In most, but not all, cases, this involves the procurement of source code. In all situations, it involves code from an original source, usually referred to in the distribution world as an "upstream" source. The packager's first addition to the code here will be the creation of extra metadata, which usually includes

- The name of the software
- The name of the upstream author and the person creating the package
- The license of the software
- The upstream location of the software (or a description of where it was obtained)
- The architecture or architectures on which the software is guaranteed to run
- Information for classifying the software that often has to do with the use of the package, primarily to help people who are browsing for packages
- A description of the software in a computer-parsable format
- Information on the importance or "priority" of the package within the larger Ubuntu system (e.g., essential, optional)

This information will be used by either a packaging system or a series of package selection tools to allow users to search, sort, query, or interact with installed or available software—one of the package system's jobs. However, while this type of metadata is important in that it allows users to find (and find out about) their software, by far the most important group of metadata added to a package relates to the documentation of the relationship of the software in the package to software in other packages within the distribution. While the syntax and semantics of this vary widely between distributions, they include relationships to

- Other software that the software requires to be built
- Other software that the software requires to be installed or configured
- Other software that the software requires to be run
- Other software with which the software cannot be installed or used simultaneously

- Other software for which the software can be used as a drop-in replacement

- Other software that can enhance or improve the software

Modern package systems record even more information. For example, configuration files, unlike normal files, cannot always be simply replaced with a new version when the software is upgraded. As a result, packaging systems have grown to include several pieces of infrastructure for querying users and for maintaining core configuration information over time and across upgrades of the package that requires changes to configuration files. Finally, a more recently realized goal of packages is to provide a structure around which package metadata—such as descriptions—can be translated to provide users with an interface to software localized to their language, script, and culture. Details on accessing and creating all of this metadata in Ubuntu packages are included in the subsequent sections.

Basic Functions of Package Management

A wide range of functionality can be considered core functions of package management systems. The functions are usually implemented by a low-level tool or suite of tools. This script is `dpkg` and associated scripts in the case of Ubuntu and Debian. These tools were, until several years ago, the primary way that most users manipulated packages, but with the creation of higher-level package management tools that provide "front ends" to these tools, most users of package-based systems rarely use them, although they are still highly central for developers or system administrators who build their own packages. Broadly and somewhat imprecisely, many of these tools are referred to as APT on Debian and Ubuntu.

The first goal of packaging is automating the compilation of software. DEB-format packages provide two formats: one for source packages and one for binary packages. These source packages are an excellent system for the distribution and compilation of source code. Packages are, in Ubuntu and elsewhere, designed to be built noninteractively and—in the case of official Ubuntu packages—can be built automatically on a range of different architectures by automatic package-building software called "autobuilders."

Packages provide a simple—usually one command—method for building that is consistent across all packages. Issues of build configurations and choices are addressed ahead of time by the packager. The cost is build-time configurability, but the payoffs, as you will see in the rest of the chapter, are huge. Necessary build-time dependencies are declared in the packages so that these can be satisfied automatically. For example, architecture-dependent source packages (i.e., packages that must be rebuilt for each architecture) are uploaded to Ubuntu as source and are, in most cases, automatically built on all architectures supported by Ubuntu without any changes to the source package.

Any number of binary packages can be created from a single source package. The creation of multiple binary packages from a single source package can be useful for large projects that release large or monolithic source packages containing a wide variety of different pieces of software—or even highly related pieces of software and/or documentation that it may be advantageous to split. An example of the former case is the XFree86 windowing system—now replaced by the already modularized X.Org—which was contained in one source package but would create upward of several dozen binary packages. Packaging, in this case, is what allowed users to distribute, install, and remove the Xserver independently from the terminal emulator, xlib library package, or window manager.

As can be inferred from the preceding discussion, a key benefit of packaging systems is that they help automate the installation of software. When a binary package is installed:

- The "contents" of the software can be verified to assure integrity of the package. The origin of the software can be verified using cryptographic authentication.

- The dependencies of the software can be analyzed and the system can be queried on the installation state of the software on which the software being installed depends. If the dependencies are unsatisfied, the user is prompted as to the lack and the nature of the required software, and the installation is aborted.

- The user installing the package can be queried for configuration options at some point during the installation process. Answers to these queries can be saved on the system and then used in the customization of a configuration file for the software being installed.

- The contents of the package are stored on the system.

- Metadata and accounting information of a variety of forms are placed in a per-system database to include both current information on the packages installed and their state of installation (e.g., installed but unconfigured), the list of files and to which package they belong, and other information.

Perhaps the most central element here is the check against dependencies of the package being installed and the list of packages already installed on the system. With information on dependencies, users can, at a glance, determine which software is required to run the software in the package. As a result, people writing software that will ultimately be packaged can easily write for and deploy software built against shared libraries. The success of package systems is one reason for the wide use of dynamically linked shared libraries in the GNU/Linux environment.

When a user wants to remove a piece of software, the packaging system, with its catalog of the files belonging to the package and the actions done during installation, is well suited to help ensure a clean uninstallation as well.

While similar to installation, the automatic upgrade of software is another area where the package system can be employed with similarly useful results: Users of package systems can safely and easily upgrade from one version of a piece of software to another. The upgrade of the software will work almost identically to the installation of the software. In most cases, software is installed on top of the existing package, and files that are no longer provided by the package are removed. Configuration files that were customized by the installation and have not since been changed by the user can be automatically regenerated by the user, or the user can be prompted to view and merge changes.

Dependency information can play an important role in the upgrade of packages involving shared libraries. In the case of ABI changes, a packaging system will alert users that an upgrade of a package cannot be completed without the installation of a new library, and users can also be alerted to other packages that will break in this upload. As a result, users can structure uploads—or the system can structure it for them—so that API and ABI breakage is not unanticipated, and users can ensure that all packages that depend on a single shared library can be upgraded in tandem.

Finally, at any point, users can use the cryptographic signature on a package and the list of hashes (usually MD5 sums) of the files included in that package to verify the integrity of the files on their system against corruption or compromise by an attacker.

Advanced Functions of Package Management Systems

While these features lead to the powerful potential to manage software on a system, packaging systems with *only* these features—essentially, the state of packaging in the mid-1990s—introduced important limitations. Large-scale API and ABI transitions required downloading many packages and a high degree of coordination by the user. Users were forced to figure out the dependency status of programs during an installation or upgrade and then find, download, and do simultaneous installations of new pieces of software. For complex pieces of software with many dependencies, this process was often exceedingly tedious.

As a result, most system upgrades and ABI/API changes were done with large upgrade scripts between releases of a distribution. Users would be expected to install every package involved in a major transition at once with an upgrade script that would structure the order correctly and handle dependencies appropriately. While these problems are limitations of a limited package management system, they are mostly problems that exist outside of package management systems. Without a package management system, shared libraries that undergo API and ABI changes are either never or rarely approached (with dangerous consistency and security implications to each) or are subject to the same limitations without the warnings that a packaging system provides.

Spurred on by the Debian project's creation of a program called dselect and its frequently lauded Advanced Package Tools (APT, originally named *deity* and implemented primarily in a program called apt-get), the last half-decade has seen a major evolution in the scope and success of package managers. Most of these tools are levels of abstraction upon or "front ends" to the lower-level package management tools previously described. Like most other DEB-based distributions, Ubuntu uses apt-get, Aptitude, dselect, and the graphical front end Synaptic.

As the ability to track and catalog dependencies is perhaps the single most important aspect of any package management system, the primary function of these advanced tools has been to add classes of functionality on top of the extant package tools and to operate on packages in a more-than-one-at-a-time manner. Each of these tools contains additional databases that describe not only the packages installed but also the packages that are *available* as candidates for installation through package archives stored locally, on CD, or (in almost all situations today) over a network.

These systems can automatically sort out dependencies and orders, download packages (including dependencies), install the dependencies first, and then install and configure the package in question using the lower-level tools detailed in the previous section.

Similarly, the same advanced tools can be used to uninstall packages. If, for example, a user wants to uninstall a shared library, he or she is prompted with a screen that describes the consequences as a list of packages that must be uninstalled because their dependencies will no longer exist on the system after the uninstallation. Upgrades that involve changing dependencies (e.g., replaced packages) can also be handled through this system.

The real possibilities of such systems are visible when the dependency aspects of a package change over time or when multiple packages can act as drop-in replacements. A package that requires the ability to send mail can depend only on a virtual package "provided" by other packages. New versions of packages can conflict with and declare that they "replace" other packages or provide the functionality of the original package. If, for example, multiple packages are merged into a single package that obsoletes the three other packages, an advanced package system should be able to track the changing dependency information and make the correct decision during upgrade. Along these lines, most advanced package management tools give users the ability to do strategic "smart upgrades" of every package on the system to the newest version of the packages available using the data declared in the package dependencies.

Even more exciting for some users, it is possible to track an in-development version of a GNU/Linux operating system and upgrade every day to the latest version of everything. The package manager can figure out safe upgrade paths and take it from there. During these upgrades, ABI and API version changes can also be automatically handled because the system will refuse to do a full upgrade of a library until all of the packages installed on the system that depend on the package with the shared library can be upgraded at once. The system will not need to keep or track multiple versions of a shared library over time.

Debian Packages

As was mentioned earlier in this book, the Ubuntu project is based on the Debian GNU/Linux distribution. Among many other technological legacies, Ubuntu has inherited the Debian package system. In fact, many core Ubuntu developers involved early on will credit Debian's packaging system as the reason that Debian proved such an attractive point of departure and represented its major attraction over other GNU/Linux distributions. As a result, almost all aspects of package management—from the formats to the tools—are identical on Ubuntu and Debian. In many situations, unmodified Debian packages can simply be installed on Ubuntu. In nearly all situations, unmodified Debian source packages can be built on Ubuntu. As a result, our first step is to examine an Ubuntu DEB in some depth to understand the anatomy of the package and the way it implements the features described in the preceding sections.

Source Packages

DEB source packages are clearly expressed in what is usually a three- or two-file format but may also include source packages that consist of many more files as well. This means that the package itself contains multiple files and downloading "a source package" may in fact involve downloading a small assortment of different files. Source packages can be broadly classified as either *native* DEB packages or *nonnative* DEB packages. A native DEB is a piece of software where there is no difference between the upstream version and the DEB package. In most cases, native packages are specific to either Ubuntu, Debian, or another Debian-based distribution. In other words, a native package requires no changes in order to create the package. A DEB source package will always consist of a "pristine" source

archive in the form of a gzip-compressed GNU tar file and a DSC file that
will list the contents of the package and can be considered the "core" of a
source package. An example DSC for a program called most that I maintain looks like this:

```
-----BEGIN PGP SIGNED MESSAGE-----
Hash: SHA1

Format: 1.0
Source: most
Binary: most
Architecture: any
Version: 5.0.0a-1
Maintainer: Benjamin Mako Hill <mako@debian.org>
Standards-Version: 3.7.3
Build-Depends: debhelper (>= 4), libslang2-dev
Files:
 30f2131b67f61716f6fe1f65205da48b 155233 most_5.0.0a.orig.tar.gz
 07e3eb05ad5524fe6d885f5cdc2eb902 20160 most_5.0.0a-1.diff.gz

-----BEGIN PGP SIGNATURE-----
Version: GnuPG v1.4.6 (GNU/Linux)

iD8DBQFH4IoAic1LIWB1WeYRAjyOAKCrLCfuZA7b8JcvYTFYeuHrF7r34wCfVTBS
/jGUfIrELNq173sM9CorZA4=
=/Cia
-----END PGP SIGNATURE-----
```

The file is signed with a GnuPG or PGP key to ensure the integrity of the
file and the identity of the author. If you were to check this signature with
GPG, you would see that it was signed by my GPG key. The DSC file also
contains information on the version of the source format (in this case, it's
the "old" format, 1.0), the name of the source package, the version of the
package (split into the version of the upstream source and the version of
the package after the final -), the name and e-mail of the maintainer, the
architecture on which the software will run, the version of policy (marked
as "standards") against which the software was created, the software that
must be present to build the package, and a list of the other files this source
package contains, identified by file size and MD5 hashes.

In a native DEB, there would be only a single compressed tar (tar.gz) file.
In this nonnative package, there would be additional files that represent all
changes to the package. This is so all the changes that the DEB packager

made are clearly visible. This is sometimes done for license reasons but is usually done just so that users can see exactly what the packager has done and what has been changed. This also makes it easy for the package maintainer to understand where a problem lies if there is an error. Changes made to a package are usually expressed in a gzip-compressed diff file that expresses all the differences between the package source and the pristine source. In the case on the previous page, it is listed as most 5.0.0a-1.diff.gz. In newer versions of the DEB source package format, additional tar files containing additions or changes to the pristine source archive are also permitted, as long as they are listed in the DSC file in the list of files.

When unpacked and with all necessary patches applied, every DEB source package will unpack into a single directory of the form packagename-version with a mandatory debian directory as a subdirectory. In the vast majority of packages, almost all changes to the source are made inside this directory. This directory contains a number of files—more than I have space to cover here. Most important among these are the control file and the rules file. The control file includes most of the information about the source package found in the DSC file (which is autogenerated using control file data) and additional information describing each binary package. The control file expresses all interpackage relationships, including Depends, Conflicts, Provides, Replaces, Recommends, Suggests, and Enhances. As the "hard" requirements, the first four are most important. Suggests and Enhances are rarely used by any program. The file also includes both a single-line and a multiline description. A sample control file (the control for most) is shown here:

```
Source: most
Section: text
Priority: optional
Maintainer: Benjamin Mako Hill <mako@debian.org>
Standards-Version: 3.7.3
Build-Depends: debhelper (>=4), libslang2-dev

Package: most
Architecture: any
Depends: ${shlibs:Depends}
Description: Pager program similar to more and less
```

The long-form description was removed from the output but in fact followed the final description line and includes text that is indented by one space and where paragraphs are separated by a single ".". As mentioned previously, the control file consists of a series of stanzas. The first stanza will always begin with Source: and will include information on the source package. Each following stanza will describe a single binary package. In this case, there is only one binary package, which, like the source package, is named most. This situation—a single source package creating a single binary package of the same name—is a very common case.

The rules file is a GNU Make makefile and contains all of the makefile rules to create and build a package. Running debian/rules binary from within the unpacked source package directory results in the creation of a Debian package in one directory above (../) if your system has all the necessary dependencies installed. In most cases, the software will build and "install" into a series of subdirectories within the debian directory; these files in their temporary location will then be included as the package contents.

Additional files in the debian directory include the copyright file, the changelog for the package, optional scripts to be run after and before installation or removal of the package, and extra configuration data plus anything else the packager would like to include.

Binary Packages

Debian binary packages are very simple in format, so it is unnecessary to spend much time on them here. More important, they are almost never manipulated by hand. Binary packages are merely installed and removed. Changes to a binary package are made first in the source package and then new, changed binary packages are rebuilt. In Ubuntu and Debian, binary packages are a single file in an archive in the ar format. In the archive is debian-binary, which contains a series of lines, separated by newlines. At the moment, only the format version number is included. The second member of the archive is named control.tar.gz, and it contains the package control information (as described previously). The third and last member is called data.tar.gz, and it contains the file system archive as a gzipped tar archive.

Package Management in Ubuntu

The administrator of every Ubuntu installation—servers and desktops—must learn the basic mechanics of package management. As administrators need to find new software to solve particular problems, metadata in the packaging system can be a great place to start. When administrators want to install new software, the packaging system provides the best way to do so. The Ubuntu package system will also allow users to install and remove software, check for updates—and for security updates in particular—and install these updates. Finally, when a new release of Ubuntu is made, the packaging system will allow administrators to update their systems.

Ubuntu provides a variety of different tools for package management. On a desktop Ubuntu system, users' interaction with the package management system is primary through a little icon on the desktop that alerts them to new releases of software and through the graphical Add/Remove Programs application and a second graphical package management program called Synaptic that provides functionality to let users browse the package archives. Since these programs are covered in depth in *The Official Ubuntu Book* and because the focus of this book is servers, this section focuses on the command-line tools for package browsing and management.

Most server administrators primarily use tools in the APT family that handle high-level package management. The original tool developed for this purpose was `apt-get`. Aptitude is a frequently used alternative to `apt-get` that provides both an interactive front end and that takes most of the default `apt-get` commands. Many of the commands described in the rest of this chapter that call `aptitude` can also be used with `apt-get` with little or no difference in either output or behavior. The primary differences are in the ways that the systems resolve complicated dependency situations and certainly would not affect the reasonably simple operations described here.

Staying Up-to-Date

Each Ubuntu system stores a list of package repositories in /etc/apt/ sources.list. This describes the list of "places" where your package managers—originally just APT but now several other tools—will look for updated versions of software. These sources may include local repositories on your file system, a CD in your computer, or—as is common in the vast majority of situations—a network location. To update the system's list of packages, you can run `apt-get update` or `aptitude update`.

This command downloads the latest updated package lists for all repositories listed in your /etc/apt/sources.list files and checks any cryptographic signatures on these updates against the keys stored on your machine. On a new system, it checks only the Ubuntu package repositories that include the repositories you installed from and the security repositories.

Installing any new version of packages is as simple as running `aptitude safe-upgrade`, which is a replacement for the `apt-get upgrade` command that may be more familiar to more seasoned users. `safe-upgrade` simply tries to upgrade all installed packages to their most recent versions. Installed packages will not be removed unless they are unused, although additional packages may also be installed in order to resolve added dependencies.

APT can be configured to automatically download and upgrade packages with new versions. This is an attractive proposition to administrators who like the idea of not having to log in to their systems to keep them up-to-date. However, automatic package upgrades are subject to errors because of the particular status of software on the system or even particular configuration changes that have been made, so these automatic package upgrades can leave systems in unstable or unworkable states. As a result, automatic upgrades are neither covered in this book nor recommended by the authors.

Searching and Browsing

Historically, the primary way of searching for new packages was using the program `dselect`. Users of Ubuntu on the desktop will primarily use the Add/Remove Programs application and the graphical program Synaptic. Users on the console have several other options.

First among these is the simple program `apt-cache`, which can provide statistics about and information on packages. If, for example, I decide I want a pager like less, I can search for one in the following way:

```
$ apt-cache search pager less
less - Pager program similar to more
wdiff - Compares two files word by word
console-log - Puts a logfile pager on virtual consoles
gdesklets-data - Applets for gdesklets
jless - A file pager program, similar to more(1) supporting ISO2022
most - Pager program similar to more and less
nagios-plugins-basic - Plugins for the nagios network monitoring
  and management system
```

As you can see from the previous list, the `apt-cache search` command returned eight "hits" for my search on the two keywords *pager* and *less* and returned a list of package names followed by short one-line descriptions. The keyword search looked through the full list of available packages and focused on the package names, short descriptions, and full descriptions that are not shown in the returned list. If I want to know more about a package, `apt-cache` can also show me more about the package with the show subcommand as in the following example:

```
$ apt-cache show most
Package: most
Priority: optional
Section: universe/text
Installed-Size: 172
Maintainer: Ubuntu MOTU Developers <ubuntu-motu@lists.ubuntu.com>
Original-Maintainer: Benjamin Mako Hill <mako@debian.org>
Architecture: i386
Version: 5.0.0a-1
Depends: libc6 (>= 2.7), libslang2 (>= 2.0.7-1)
Filename: pool/universe/m/most/most_5.0.0a-1_i386.deb
Size: 48092
MD5sum: e089c00005b536e1b8848b7087df2bae
SHA1: 4f4ab395f340be4804732452aa112007916f90cb
SHA256:
  ccf50fb49270e7ddf7735da23e699afcd11dcfc8e241973bb17ad03bf49e6f4a
Description: Pager program similar to more and less
 Most is a paging program that displays, one windowful at a time, the
 contents of a file on a terminal. A status line at the bottom of the
 screen displays the file name, the current line number, and the
 percentage of the file so far displayed.
 .
 Unlike other paging programs, most is capable of displaying an
 arbitrary number of windows as long as they all fit on the screen,
 and different windows could be used to view the same file in
 different positions.
 .
 In addition to displaying ordinary text files, most can also display
 binary files as well as files with arbitrary ascii characters.
Bugs: mailto:ubuntu-users@lists.ubuntu.com
Origin: Ubuntu
```

You may recognize that quite a bit of this information looks like the source package information and the corresponding stanza referring to this binary package in the control file described previously. Sure enough, this is exactly where this metadata has been extracted.

Of course, the bulk of the output is made up of the long-form description that was omitted in the previous example. There are some other fields of potential interest, including the "Original-Maintainer" or the person who packaged the system in Debian, the "Maintainer" or the person or group to contact with questions about or issues with the package, and sizes and hashes (e.g., MD5Sum, SHA1, and SHA256), which describe ways to identify that a particular version of the package was downloaded correctly and has not been modified.

Called with no arguments, Aptitude also can provide users with a Curses-based text-based interface that allows for more interactive browsing of all the packages available. For users familiar with Synaptic, this can be thought of as a text-based version of the Synaptic interface. In this mode, many search results can be navigated through with the arrow keys and different applications can be "marked" for installation.

Before concluding this tour of the options for searching and browsing for packages, it is worth pointing to the Web site at http://packages.ubuntu .com. This interface lets users search in ways that are similar to some of the tools I have shown here but with several additional useful options. In particular, the Web site lets users search for particular files in *any* package in Ubuntu. Normally, users are able to find out only which package "owns" a file if they have the package on their system. If, for example, you need a particular header file or shared library and you know only the filename, you can search on the Web site for that filename throughout all packages available in the Ubuntu archive.

Installation and Removal

Installing and removing packages is another simple task that you will do frequently. To install a package, you can invoke apt-get or Aptitude in a similar way, although, unlike searching, a user must be running with root privileges to do so. The recommended way to do this would be to use the sudo command. Since prefixing each command in this section with sudo would be tedious, I have assumed the user is root, although having the user logged in as root would not be considered the best form. If I want to install most, I can simply run the following command as root:

```
# aptitude install most
Reading package lists... Done
Building dependency tree
Reading state information... Done
Reading extended state information
Initializing package states... Done
Writing extended state information... Done
The following NEW packages will be installed:
  libslang2{a} most
0 packages upgraded, 2 newly installed, 0 to remove and 0 not
  upgraded.
Need to get 0B/509kB of archives. After unpacking 1323kB will be
  used.
Do you want to continue? [Y/n/?] y
Writing extended state information... Done
Selecting previously deselected package libslang2.
(Reading database ... 362131 files and directories currently
  installed.)
Unpacking libslang2 (from .../libslang2_2.1.3-3ubuntu1_i386.deb) ...
Setting up libslang2 (2.1.3-3ubuntu1) ...
Selecting previously deselected package most.
(Reading database ... 362143 files and directories currently
  installed.)
Unpacking most (from .../most_5.0.0a-1_i386.deb) ...
Processing triggers for man-db ...
Setting up most (5.0.0a-1) ...

Reading package lists... Done
Building dependency tree
Reading state information... Done
Reading extended state information
Initializing package states... Done
Writing extended state information... Done
```

You can see in the output of the command above that libslang2 was installed alongside most. In this case, Aptitude saw that most required the S-Lang library but that it was not installed. Aptitude prompted me for confirmation about the installation of the additional package (which I approved), downloaded both packages, and then installed and configured them on my system.

Removing a package is similarly simple. If I decide to remove most, I can do so by running

```
# aptitude remove most
```

In this case, libslang2 will *not* be removed (since I have not asked for it to be removed). If I were instead to try to remove libslang2, Aptitude would prompt me and explain that removing libslang2 would also require removing all of the packages that depend on it—on this system, that would just be most, but for other packages or on other systems there could be quite a few packages. This type of dependency management means that, for example, users should not (and cannot easily) remove core or essential packages. Extra "unused" packages can be removed using the command apt-get autoremove.

Finally, while these examples both used Aptitude, the installation and removal of packages can also be done with the lower-level tool dpkg. In fact, in both cases Aptitude is simply calling dpkg on the downloaded package files behind the scenes. Aptitude—or apt-get—will always download packages and work out dependencies before turning to dpkg. If you have already installed existing dependencies, you can install a DEB directly with dpkg by using the -i command and passing the package filename as an argument. For example, if I were given a DEB file for most, I could install it with a command like this:

```
$ dpkg -i most_5.0.0a-1_i386.deb
```

dpkg will check dependencies and produce an error if there are missing dependencies but will not automatically download or install packages since it does not contain the functionality to do this. I could uninstall most with dpkg with the command dpkg -r most.

Manipulating Installed Packages

dpkg provides dozens of methods of querying, searching, and manipulating installed packages. It contains a database of information about packages installed on the system. To get a quick overview of what this might look like, you could run the following command:

```
$ dpkg -l most
Desired=Unknown/Install/Remove/Purge/Hold
| Status=Not/Inst/Cfg-files/Unpacked/Failed-cfg/Half-inst/
  trig-aWait/Trig-pend
|/ Err?=(none)/Hold/Reinst-required/X=both-problems
  (Status,Err: uppercase=bad)
||/ Name           Version        Description
+++-===========-============-=============+=====================
ii  most          5.0.0a-1      Pager program similar to more and less
```

Run without any arguments, dpkg -l will show this basic information on the installation status, name, version, and description of *every* package on your system.

Another simple task is to get a list of files contained within the package. If you have a DEB file that you have not installed, you can get this information by running dpkg --contents as in the example below:

```
$ dpkg --contents /var/cache/apt/archives/most_5.0.0a-1_i386.deb
drwxr-xr-x root/root         0 2008-05-06 12:06 ./
drwxr-xr-x root/root         0 2008-05-06 12:06 ./usr/
drwxr-xr-x root/root         0 2008-05-06 12:06 ./usr/bin/
-rwxr-xr-x root/root     59940 2008-05-06 12:06 ./usr/bin/most
drwxr-xr-x root/root         0 2008-05-06 12:06 ./usr/share/
drwxr-xr-x root/root         0 2008-05-06 12:06 ./usr/share/man/
drwxr-xr-x root/root         0 2008-05-06 12:06 ./usr/share/man/man1/
-rw-r--r-- root/root      5912 2008-05-06 12:06 ./usr/share/man/
  man1/most.1.gz
drwxr-xr-x root/root         0 2008-05-06 12:06 ./usr/share/doc/
drwxr-xr-x root/root         0 2008-05-06 12:06 ./usr/share/doc/most/
-rw-r--r-- root/root      2989 2007-09-09 12:14 ./usr/share/doc/
  most/changelog.gz
-rw-r--r-- root/root      5544 2008-05-06 12:06 ./usr/share/doc/
  most/copyright
-rw-r--r-- root/root      3335 2007-09-06 10:15 ./usr/share/doc/
  most/README
-rw-r--r-- root/root      1386 2006-05-01 13:51 ./usr/share/doc/
  most/lesskeys.rc
-rw-r--r-- root/root       492 2006-05-01 13:51 ./usr/share/doc/
  most/most-fun.txt
-rw-r--r-- root/root      3086 2006-05-01 13:51 ./usr/share/doc/
  most/most.rc
```

```
-rw-r--r-- root/root        2028 2008-05-06 12:06 ./usr/share/doc/most/
  changelog.Debian.gz
drwxr-xr-x root/root           0 2008-05-06 12:06 ./usr/lib/
drwxr-xr-x root/root           0 2008-05-06 12:06 ./usr/lib/mime/
drwxr-xr-x root/root           0 2008-05-06 12:06 ./usr/lib/mime/
  packages/
-rw-r--r-- root/root          94 2008-05-06 12:06 ./usr/lib/mime/
  packages/most
```

Similar information for installed packages can be retrieved with dpkg -L. Working in the other direction, if you have a particular file and you want to know which package "owns" it, you can use dpkg -S to query the database for this information. For example:

```
dpkg -S /usr/bin/most
most: /usr/bin/most
```

The binary file /usr/bin/most belongs to—no surprise here for anyone who's gotten this far—the binary package called most. Since this command is searching through each of the file lists of every package on your system, it may take some time to complete.

Manipulating Repositories

The best way to install new software in the "Ubuntu way" is never to simply download new DEB packages and install them "by hand" with dpkg. But APT is only kept up-to-date with the packages that it already knows about. While dpkg works on packages, APT works on repositories of packages that contain information on different packages, their versions, and their dependencies. As a result, to manage a package through APT, one needs to add to the system not the package, but rather the repository that contains it. This is done by adding or editing the list of "sources." While the Ubuntu desktop distribution includes a graphical tool for manipulating repositories, it can be done easily by hand, which will be the default on most systems.

The sources.list file, already mentioned several times in this chapter, is located at /etc/apt/sources.list on every Ubuntu and Debian system and is made up of a series of lines like this:

```
deb http://us.archive.ubuntu.com/ubuntu/ lucid main universe
deb-src http://us.archive.ubuntu.com/ubuntu/ lucid main universe
```

The first word will be a # symbol marking the line as a comment or else either deb or deb-src. This specifies whether the repository is a source package repository or a binary package repository. The second item is the location in the form of a URI. The third item is the name of the distribution or, as it might more accurately be described, the distribution version. In the previous example, this distribution version is lucid, which refers to the Ubuntu release of the Lucid Lynx. The remaining arguments are the lists of the components. The components provided in the core Ubuntu repositories are detailed in the following section.

An example will help illustrate the process of adding a repository. If I want to install a version of Bazaar that is always the latest released version, I will need to do this from outside the default Ubuntu repositories, which will only be updated based on the Ubuntu release cycle. Luckily, the Bazaar developers provide their own "Personal Package Repository"—a subject I'll come back to at the end of this chapter. On their Web site, they provide the deb and deb-src lines that I can simply drop into my sources.list:

```
deb http://ppa.launchpad.net/bzr/ubuntu lucid main
deb-src http://ppa.launchpad.net/bzr/ubuntu lucid main
```

If I update, I am first greeted by an error that claims that I do not have the correct cryptographic key to verify that the packages in the repository are really coming from the Bazaar developers:

```
W: GPG error: http://ppa.launchpad.net lucid Release: The following
signatures couldn't be verified because the public key is not
available: NO_PUBKEY FE8956A73C5EE1C9
```

I can easily install that by downloading the key from a trusted source like the PPA providers' Web site and saving it into a file (called /tmp/keyfile in the example below), verifying that is correct, and adding to the package manager's key database with a command such as

```
apt-key add - < /tmp/key
OK
```

The apt-key manual page gives more details on how keys for repositories can be managed with this useful command.

Ubuntu Default Repositories

The vast majority of packages that you will need have been packaged for Ubuntu. This is because, leveraging the work of Debian, Ubuntu provides access to a large majority of the most popular pieces of free software as packages in their own repositories.

These tens of thousands of packages are separated into a series of different sections or components. You can toggle these on and off by including them in the list of components in your sources.list. Because these have important consequences for the level of support you will receive for your software, it is worth understanding these different components so that you can decide from which areas you want to pull software. Available components on the Ubuntu server include main, restricted, universe, and multiverse. The following descriptions are adapted from the component descriptions on the Ubuntu Web site.

- **Main**
  The main distribution component contains applications that are free software, can freely be redistributed, and are fully supported by the Ubuntu team. These include the most popular and most reliable open source applications available, much of which is installed by default when you install Ubuntu. Software in main includes a hand-selected list of applications that the Ubuntu developers, community, and users feel are important and that the Ubuntu security and distribution teams are willing to support. When you install software from the main component, you are assured that the software will come with security updates and technical support.

- **Restricted**
  The restricted component is reserved for software that is very commonly used and that is supported by the Ubuntu team even though it is not available under a completely free license. Please note that it may not be possible for Ubuntu to provide complete support for this

software since the Ubuntu team is unable to fix the software but can only forward problem reports to the actual authors.

▪ **Universe**
In universe one can find almost every piece of open source software and software available under a variety of less-open licenses, all built automatically from a variety of public sources. All of this software is compiled against the libraries and using the tools that form part of main, so it should install and work well with the software in main, but *it comes with no guarantee of security fixes and support.*

▪ **Multiverse**
The multiverse component contains software that is not free, which means the licensing requirements of this software do not meet the "main" component license policy. The onus is on you to verify your rights to use this software and comply with the licensing terms of the copyright holder. This software is not supported and usually cannot be fixed or updated. Use it at your own risk.

Using Other Repositories

As you saw when I added the Bazaar repository several sections ago, users will still sometimes want to make use of a variety of outside repositories beyond what is provided in Ubuntu. For example, users might want to install new versions of particular applications or libraries from the development release of Ubuntu but might not want to upgrade all of their packages to the latest version.

The quasi-official "backports" repository in Ubuntu is a useful resource. It contains versions of software from the development version of Ubuntu that have been backported to install cleanly on stable versions of Ubuntu. You can add the backports by installing a DEB package by hand in a one-by-one with dpkg or by adding an extra line to your sources.list. Information on doing both can be found on the Ubuntu Web site at https://help.ubuntu.com/community/UbuntuBackports.

One reason that many users choose to go the à la carte method—that is, the method of downloading packages by hand and installing them with dpkg—as opposed to just adding the repository is because of a limitation in the way that APT works: *APT and other tools will always install the newest version of any package available by default.* This means that if you add the backports repository, or the development repository for that matter, to your sources.list, the latest version of *everything* in that repository will be installed when you try to run an upgrade. For small repositories (like the Bazaar PPA described several sections ago that contained only Bazaar and several closely linked packages) this does not present a problem. However, in situations where you want to add a large repository of many packages like the backports repository or the development release of Ubuntu but only want a few packages, the effects will often not be what you want.

The general solution to this problem is called "pinning" or "apt pinning." Pinning is extraordinarily powerful but, in its advanced forms, can also be very complicated. As a result, a full discussion is outside the scope of this chapter. That said, an example is shown below for the situation where I have Karmic installed but want APT to prefer packages in Lucid. To change this, I would need to create a file in /etc/apt/preferences.d that included something like the following section:

```
Package: *
Pin: release a=karmic
Pin-Priority: 700

Package: *
Pin: release a=lucid
Pin-Priority: 600
```

Each stanza describes one release and, as is represented by the wildcard in the first line, applies to all packages. In the final line of each stanza, the pin-priority describes both relative position (i.e., in the example above, Karmic is preferred to Lucid) and weight that will be given to each. Weights can be tweaked so that packages will be installed, or not, except in special circumstances. Much more information on pinning is available in the apt_preferences manual page and in several excellent pieces of documentation on the Ubuntu and Debian wikis.

Upgrading a Whole System

A final basic task that every system administrator will need to do is to upgrade a full system. On desktop Ubuntu systems, the default way of handling an upgrade is by using the update manager software. However, this software is designed specifically to upgrade graphical systems. Since the process can just as easily be done from the command line, that will probably be more appropriate on most servers.

In the past, upgrading most systems was a two-step process. First, the administrator would update the list of repositories (detailed in the previous section) so that references to the old release were replaced with the new release. For example, if I were upgrading from the Hardy Heron to the Gutsy Gibbon, I would replace every instance of *hardy* with *gutsy* in my source.list file. After doing this, I would run `aptitude update` exactly as I described in the section above on staying up-to-date. This would refresh my local package metadata cache with a list of all the packages in the new distribution.

Finally, I would run `aptitude full-upgrade` which, unlike `safe-upgrade`, described previously, would upgrade all installed packages to their most recent version and would remove or install additional packages as necessary. `full-upgrade` is less conservative than `safe-upgrade` and is much more likely to perform unwanted actions. However, it is capable of upgrading packages that `safe-upgrade` cannot. Because these sorts of situations are much more common between releases, using `full-upgrade` became the recommended course for upgrading between releases. However, neither method is supported anymore.

In current releases of Ubuntu, the correct way to upgrade systems is with the `do-release-upgrade` program. `do-release-upgrade` is a script that automates the process described above in addition to handling a number of corner cases and exceptions intelligently. It is the supported way to upgrade one's Ubuntu server.

Mirroring a System

One common task many system administrators want to accomplish is to mirror the installed software from one machine to another. Because all software on a default Ubuntu system is installed in packages, the packaging system can make this easy. Using `dpkg`, one can get a list of all packages on the machine with the following command:

```
# dpkg --get-selections > package_list
```

This command outputs a simple list of packages and then redirects that output into a file called package_list. I can copy this file to another machine and then use it to set the list of installable packages with the following command:

```
# dpkg --set-selections < package_list
```

Finally, I can install those selections onto the target system using the following command:

```
# apt-get dselect-upgrade
```

dselect-upgrade is a reference to APT's predecessor dselect but will simply work to upgrade packages on the system and install any new packages "marked" for upgrade by dpkg --set-selections in the process.

Making Your Own Packages

The power of a package management system is that you can track dependencies and conflicts, do automatic upgrades, and keep track of every file on the system and which piece of software it belongs to. Installing through packages is much easier than if one simply downloads and builds from scratch, but the package management system truly shines when it comes time to uninstall or upgrade. If you've installed from source, files may be in any number of places on your file system. If you've installed from a package, removing your package will be as simple as apt-get remove.

As a result, many responsible system administrators find it very convenient to ensure that *all* software on their systems is installed from packages. That sounds great, but sometimes a piece of software you want—or a version of a piece of software that you want—isn't packaged or isn't built for the version of Ubuntu that you are running. The result is that you'll need to build, in one way or another, your own packages. The rest of this chapter gives a brief overview of this process and provides a starting spot for the system administrator who wants to move beyond simply consuming packages and become a producer.

Rebuilding Packages

As I hinted earlier in this chapter, many users want to rebuild existing packages as part of backporting a version of a piece of software available in one version of Ubuntu—or Debian—to a current one. Sometimes, if an ABI has changed, a piece of software won't work on a version of Ubuntu simply because it was compiled against a set of libraries that are no longer present. This is the easiest possible case to fix because adjusting for it is simply a matter of downloading the source and rebuilding it against the new version of the libraries. This section will cover doing exactly this.

Doing so will first require a source package. The source package, as you may remember from earlier in this chapter, consists of a DSC file and at least one other file. These can be downloaded as normal files from http:// packages.ubuntu.com and unpacked with dpkg-source -x *filename*.dsc, or they can be installed automatically by using the apt-get source *package* command.

If one wanted to download and compile a package from a particular distribution—as is often the case—one could specify this explicitly with the -t option, which, behind the scenes, sets the default PIN for the distribution at a very high priority (990 in fact) by running (for example)

```
$ apt-get -t jaunty source --compile most
```

This would download and unpack the version of most source packages from Jaunty—assuming, of course, that the necessary deb-src line was included in /etc/apt/sources.list. The unpacked source code will be in a subdirectory of the current directory made up of the package name and version. In this case, the directory would be called most-5.0.0a since 5.0.0.a is the version of most that I've downloaded. By adding a --compile flag to the apt-get invocation above, the binary packages will also be built automatically—even if the program is in an interpreted language and there is no actual compiling taking place. If one does not use the compile flag, it can be invoked afterward in several ways. One of the simplest is by changing into the directory and then running dpkg-buildpackage like this:

```
$ cd most-5.0.0a
$ dpkg-buildpackage -us -uc -rfakeroot
```

This command will create an unsigned package (the -us and the -uc refer to unsigned source and unsigned changelog files) without needing root privileges (fakeroot is a program that allows packages to be built without root). Of course, the package may also require build dependencies that are not installed by running a command in the following form:

```
# apt-get -t jaunty build-dep most
```

The `build-dep` subcommand to `apt-get` automates the process of installing all software necessary to build a given package. Running it is a frequent first step in rebuilding any package for the first time when that package is from an installed repository.

When the software in question is successfully rebuilt, the directory will contain a set of binary packages for this source package that end with .deb in the directory where it is run. In this case, the single binary package created was called most 5.0.0a-1 i386.deb. The -1 following the version number of the software refers to the version of the package and could be incremented each time we made a new version of the package. The i386 in this case simply refers to the architecture for which the binary package was built. In this case, I built it on an Intel machine. For many users, this will say amd64, which is an increasingly popular architecture. For most interpreted programs that will run on any architectures, this will say all.

New Upstream Versions

New upstream versions of packages are slightly more complicated than simply rebuilding an existing package with no modifications. Installing the package `devscripts` provides the user with a program called `uupdate` which helps with this process. To use `uupdate`, a user must first download the source package with a command like `apt-get source most`. Leave off the compile option for the moment, and then download the new upstream version tarball. There is no reason to unpack it at this point and, optionally, rename it into name-version.tar.gz format. Changing into the directory of the *old* package's source and running `uupdate` with the new upstream tarball as the argument will usually do the trick:

```
$ cd most-5.0.0a $ uupdate ../most-5.0.1.tar.gz
```

Usually, `uupdate` then deduces the version number from the upstream tarball and applies all the changes made to the old version to the new upstream source. If uupdate can't decode the version number, the new version number can be specified as a second argument to the command.

The output from uupdate should explain the process that it follows and will end with a description of the location of the new modified source. In this case, changing to ../most-5.0.1 will put me in the new "updated" package directory. It's a good idea to look around first to make sure that things worked well. Especially it is worth checking the debian/ subdirectory and paying attention to both the control file and the changelog file in that directory, the latter of which will have been updated automatically but will probably need a little bit of tweaking. The stanza at the top will include information on the new release and can be updated or tweaked to reflect changes that you made to the file. Once you are satisfied, you can build the package with dpkg-buildpackage in the way described in the previous section.

Building Packages from Scratch

Building packages from scratch is much more complicated and involves getting to know quite a bit about the internals of Debian packages. As a result, it is outside the scope of this chapter. As a hint, new packages can be most easily created using the package dh-make, which installs the program dh_make, which is invoked from inside the unpacked source tarball from the upstream developer. For many simple packages, dh_make does most of the hard work of creating workable packages.

Much more information on creating packages for Ubuntu can be found in the Ubuntu packaging guide, which goes in depth into the process of creating packages from scratch: https://wiki.ubuntu.com/PackagingGuide.

It is worth noting one important caveat to the Ubuntu documentation: The packaging guide is focused on creating packages that are designed to be uploaded to Ubuntu. If you are creating packages that will be installed only on your own machine, the potential for harm is much less, and many of the guidelines in the packaging guide can be treated as just that—especially in the first version of a package. The difference is between workable packages and policy-compliant packages.

If you are going to proceed and create packages to be shared with others or perhaps even uploaded into the Ubuntu repositories eventually, it is a *very* good idea to follow the instructions in the packaging guidelines carefully and to use programs like lintian, which will check your packages for many common errors—useful steps in any situation. If you just want things to work, a brief trip through the guide and use of dh_make will probably put you in good enough shape to get by.

Hosting Your Own Packages

A final step in the creation of your packages will be hosting them in a place where others can get them in the simple "add a line to your source.list file" sort of manner to which I have referred throughout this chapter. There are several different ways to do this. The easiest one and the one most commonly practiced in the Ubuntu world is to use Launchpad—the infrastructure built by Canonical and used extensively in Ubuntu's own development—to host what's called a Personal Package Archives (PPA).

With a PPA, a developer can simply upload a source package to Launchpad and the package will then be built on a variety of architectures and posted into a PPA. PPAs work exactly the same way that developing for Ubuntu does, so using them is a great preview of what you will experience if you decide to eventually upload your software in Ubuntu and get involved on the development side of things. Earlier, when I showed how to add Bazaar packages to the list of packages, I entered the list of the Bazaar PPAs. More information on PPAs is available at the following URLs: https://help .launchpad.net/Packaging/PPA and https://launchpad.net/ubuntu/+ppas.

Alternatively, you can host your own repository on your own server with any of several different tools. Although the classic tool for running these is a package called apt-ftparchive, the newer project reprepro is probably a better fit. Installing the package with that name and looking in the documentation is a good way to get started.

## CHAPTER 4

Automated Ubuntu Installs

AFTER YOU HAVE GONE THROUGH the Ubuntu Server install a few times, you start to realize that you generally pick the same options for a majority of the install no matter what type of server it is. It might be OK to manually enter install options when you have a single server to set up, but what if you have ten or a hundred? At some point you start to wish you could hire an intern or build a robot to press Next for you. While this might work, Ubuntu has provided a cheaper (free) option with two automated installation methods: preseeding and Kickstart. Preseeding is derived from the Debian Linux distribution, and Kickstart has been ported from Red Hat and is often referred to as Kickseed under Ubuntu. Both have their advantages and shortcomings, and in fact the recommended method of automating Ubuntu server installs is a combination of both.

In this chapter I cover both automation methods and how to use them to supplement a CD-ROM install. Finally, I show how to use Kickstart and preseeding together for a fully automated installer over the network. By the end you will be able to set up one or a hundred Ubuntu servers with about the same amount of effort. Then your robot can focus on more important tasks like bringing you coffee.

There are two different ways you can read this chapter. I discuss preseeding first because it is the classic way to automate Debian and Ubuntu installs, and even if you Kickstart servers, you often need to supplement it with preseed values. So if you are interested in how the entire process works and fits together, you should read the chapter straight through. You'll gain a good foundation on preseeding so that when you learn about Kickstart, you can truly see how it eases the process. On the other hand, if you just want to get started with an automated installer, I recommend skipping ahead to the Kickstart section in the chapter. There is a lot of useful information in the preseed section, but preseeding is a pretty vast and complex topic, especially if you are new to it. If you just want to get things working on a basic automated install, you will want to use Kickstart. The Kickstart section will get you up and running, and then if you need to do anything that isn't yet possible in Kickstart, you can return to the preseeding section.

Preseeding

The concept behind preseeding is pretty simple. Every possible option in the Ubuntu install is represented by a variable. Once you discover what those variables are, you can set them ahead of time in a file and instruct the Ubuntu installer to load and apply them for you. The key to preseeding, of course, is to know what those values are. There are a number of good online guides for preseeding, but I've noticed that most of them, even those for Ubuntu, still seem to provide Debian-based examples.

The main way to discover all of the available preseeding options is to use `debconf-get-selections` (included in the debconf-utils package). For instance, to find out all of the current preseed settings from your current install, you would run

```
$ debconf-get-selections --installer > alloptions.cfg
```

This would dump all of the installation-focused preseeding options into alloptions.cfg. The great thing about preseeding, though, is that it isn't limited to installer options—every package you install that asks you questions can have its answers preseeded. To dump the entire debconf database containing these values into the same alloptions.cfg file, run

```
debconf-get-selections >> alloptions.cfg
```

Now you might be tempted to simply use this alloptions.cfg file as your preseed.cfg file. The problem is that this file contains all of the configuration options, including many that should not be preseeded. Use this file only as a guide when you want to discover a particular preseeding option that you want to set; instead I recommend that you start with the base preseed.cfg I will provide below and tweak that.

Basic Preseed Configuration for CD-ROM

There are a few different ways to introduce preseeding options to the installer, but probably the simplest way is to use the default Ubuntu install CD while specifying options directly at the boot prompt and putting a preseed.cfg file full of options on a local Web server. It turns out that if you are going to use preseeding by itself, there are certain options that you can't set strictly in a preseed file—either they must go on the boot prompt, or you will have to answer the questions manually.

The first step is to set up a default preseed.cfg file. Below is a basic preseed file that describes a default Ubuntu server install for a system in the United States. Copy these settings into a file named preseed.cfg:

```
## Options to set on the command line
d-i debian-installer/locale string en_US
d-i console-setup/ask_detect boolean false
d-i console-setup/layoutcode string us
d-i netcfg/get_hostname string unassigned-hostname
d-i netcfg/get_domain string unassigned-domain

d-i netcfg/choose_interface select auto
d-i netcfg/wireless_wep string

d-i base-installer/kernel/override-image    string linux-server
d-i clock-setup/utc-auto    boolean true
d-i clock-setup/utc boolean true
d-i time/zone string US/Pacific
d-i clock-setup/ntp boolean true

d-i mirror/country string US
d-i mirror/http/proxy string
d-i pkgsel/install-language-support boolean false
d-i pkgsel/update-policy select none
tasksel tasksel/first multiselect standard, ubuntu-server

d-i partman-auto/method string regular
d-i partman-auto/purge_lvm_from_device boolean true
d-i partman-lvm/confirm boolean true
d-i partman-auto/choose_recipe select atomic
d-i partman/confirm_write_new_label boolean true
d-i partman/choose_partition select finish
d-i partman/confirm boolean true
d-i passwd/user-fullname string Ubuntu User
d-i passwd/username string ubuntu
d-i passwd/user-password password insecure
d-i passwd/user-password-again password insecure
user-setup-udeb user-setup/encrypt-home boolean false

d-i grub-installer/only_debian boolean true
d-i grub-installer/with_other_os boolean true
d-i finish-install/reboot_in_progress note
```

Keep in mind that with these default settings the installer will find the first disk it can, format over it, and install the base system on top of it, so make sure before you try this on a server that you are willing to lose all of the data on its disks. Otherwise, if you do want to preserve data on a server, be sure to first check out the Partitioning section in this chapter to find out how to tweak the default settings.

Once you have set up the preseed.cfg file, put it on a local Web server that your test server can access. For this example let's assume the server is at www.example.net and you put the file in the main document root so it can be found at www.example.net/preseed.cfg. Now boot the server on which you wish to install Ubuntu off of the Ubuntu Server install CD. Once you answer the language prompt, hit F6 and then Esc so you can edit the default boot arguments, as shown in Figure 4-1. Use the arrow keys to move to the left past the `initrd=` argument and backspace over the `file=/cdrom/preseed/ubuntu-server.seed` section of the prompt. That is actually Ubuntu's own preseed file that it uses for the install, but we will replace it with our own. To do that we use the `url` option to point to our Web server, so type

```
url=http://www.example.net/preseed.cfg
```

Of course, change that to point to the path to your actual Web server and preseed file. Unfortunately we will need to specify a few extra options on the command line so the installer can get past the initial phase of the

Figure 4-1 Ubuntu install boot screen with boot arguments

install, get on the network, and retrieve the rest of its settings. If you look at the top of my example preseed.cfg file, you will see that I set apart a few options to go on the boot prompt:

```
d-i debian-installer/locale string en_US
d-i console-setup/ask_detect boolean false
d-i console-setup/layoutcode string us
d-i netcfg/get_hostname string unassigned-hostname
d-i netcfg/get_domain string unassigned-domain
```

To add these to the boot prompt, just type the full path to a particular option (such as debian-installer/locale), an = sign, and then the option to set it to. After you are finished, your complete boot prompt, including all the options that were there before that you need to keep, will look like this:

```
url=http://www.example.net/preseed.cfg
  debian-installer/locale=en_US console-setup/ask_detect=false
  console-setup/layoutcode=us
  netcfg/get_hostname=unassigned-hostname
  netcfg/get_domain=unassigned-domain
  initrd=/install/initrd.gz quiet --
```

Now that's quite a bit of typing, but Ubuntu has provided some short-hand for some of the options. For instance, debian-installer/locale can be replaced with just locale, netcfg/get_hostname can be replaced with hostname, and netcfg/get_domain can be replaced with domain. With all of the shortcuts in place the command line looks a bit more manageable:

```
url=http://www.example.net/preseed.cfg locale=en_US
  console-setup/ask_detect=false console-setup/layoutcode=us
  hostname=unassigned-hostname domain=unassigned-domain
  initrd=/install/initrd.gz quiet --
```

Once you have typed all of these values into the boot prompt, press Enter and go get a cup of coffee. The installer should get its own IP address over DHCP, retrieve the preseed.cfg file from your Web server, complete the install, and then reboot. When you get back, you should be welcomed with a default Ubuntu login prompt. Of course, if everything didn't go smoothly, you might see, for instance, an error retrieving the preseed.cfg file. If that is the case, try retrieving the same file from a Web browser on the same network and make sure your path is correct and your Web server is configured correctly.

Other things that might halt the installation process could be the installer not being able to get a DHCP lease or, as is most often the case, a mistake in the preseed.cfg file. As you will discover, a good preseed file is something you get after a lot of trial and error. When you set an option incorrectly, the installer will simply stop at that point in the install and prompt you for that particular option. As you create more sophisticated preseed.cfg files, you might run through the same install multiple times before you get it exactly right.

The default preseed.cfg will get you started, but where do you go from there? This chapter digs into each of the main configuration categories and explains how to customize the default preseed.cfg file for your needs.

Networking Options

In my sample preseed.cfg I introduced the following networking options:

```
d-i netcfg/get_hostname string unassigned-hostname
d-i netcfg/get_domain string unassigned-domain
d-i netcfg/choose_interface select auto
d-i netcfg/wireless_wep string
```

The first two options I used on the boot prompt with their aliases hostname and domain to set the hostname and domain, respectively, for this machine. The choose_interface option allows you to choose which network interface to use on the machine for the install. In my case I chose auto, which will pick the first interface that has link, if possible. Instead of choosing auto, you could also set this option to a specific interface, such as eth1. Now if eth1 were a wireless card and your wireless network uses WEP, you could use the wireless_wep option to set the WEP key. Even though I didn't use a wireless connection in my example, I still set this to a dummy value so I wouldn't get prompted for a WEP key during the install.

With these default settings the installer will attempt to get all of its network settings via DHCP, which is probably what most administrators want, especially if they intend to install a machine over PXE. However, you might want to statically assign an IP for a machine, and in that case there are a number of preseed options you will need to use. The following is an example set of preseed options that will set up a network manually:

```
d-i netcfg/disable_dhcp boolean true
d-i netcfg/get_nameservers string 192.168.1.1
d-i netcfg/get_ipaddress string 192.168.1.50
d-i netcfg/get_netmask string 255.255.255.0
d-i netcfg/get_gateway string 192.168.1.1
d-i netcfg/confirm_static boolean true
```

Most of these options are pretty self-explanatory, so you can just replace the IPs listed here with the IPs you want to use for your name server, the IP of the host itself, gateway, and netmask. The `disable_dhcp` option is what tells the installer to skip DHCP and use the static settings, and `confirm_static` simply confirms all of the static options you set; otherwise the installer would prompt you to confirm all of the settings in the middle of the install.

NOTE One downside to installation with DHCP is that on many installs the machine could potentially attempt to get a lease multiple times. When this happens, you will often notice that the actual physical port will also reset. Now, depending on how your networking equipment is configured, it could take longer than 30 seconds (the default DHCP time-out) for the port to come back up because the switch needs to perform spanning tree calculations. I've had installs that seemed to get a lease only one out of ten or more times because of a race for the port to come back up before DHCP timed out. A Red Hat install I had got a new lease three or four times, and it was basically impossible to win the race that many times in a row. If you notice this is the case, you have a few options. For one, you (or your network administrator) can enable PortFast on that particular switch port so that it speeds up the spanning tree calculations, or you can set the `netcfg/dhcp_timeout` preseed option to a longer value, such as

```
d-i netcfg/dhcp_timeout string 60,
```

to set the DHCP time-out to 60 seconds.

There might be some circumstances when you have a preseed file you want to use both on a network with DHCP and on a network without it. There is a way to configure that with preseeding. Combine all of the `netcfg` options you would use for a DHCP install with the static settings, except comment out or remove the disable_dhcp option. Finally, add the following options to the preseed:

```
d-i netcfg/dhcp_failed note
d-i netcfg/dhcp_options select Configure network manually
```

With these options in place, on networks where DHCP works, the install will use those settings. In case DHCP fails, the installer will then fall back to your static settings.

Partitioning

As you saw in the installation chapter (Chapter 1), there are many different ways to partition an Ubuntu server, and so it should be no surprise that there are also many preseeding options for partitioning. First, let's break down the options I used in my default preseed.cfg:

```
d-i partman-auto/method string regular
d-i partman-auto/purge_lvm_from_device boolean true
d-i partman-lvm/confirm boolean true
d-i partman-auto/choose_recipe select atomic
d-i partman/confirm_write_new_label boolean true
d-i partman/choose_partition select finish
d-i partman/confirm boolean true
```

With these options, the installer will simply select the first available disk it can find and then overwrite it with one big / partition and a swap partition. For something so basic it certainly took quite a few options, so let's go through these options one by one and discuss what part they play.

- **partman-auto/method**
  This option defines what partitioning method to use for the automatic partitioning and can accept the options regular, lvm, or crypto. As the options suggest, the latter two set up partitions as LVM or encrypted volumes.

- **partman-auto/purge_lvm_from_device and partman-lvm/confirm**
  These options just save you from having to acknowledge warning prompts in the installer. The former option will purge any old LVM

configuration from the disk if it exists, and the latter confirms writing any LVM partitions you may have set up.

▪ **partman-auto/choose_recipe**
The Ubuntu partition program allows a few different predefined partitioning recipes from which the user can choose. The `atomic` recipe sets up everything on a single partition. If you set the option to `home`, it will separate out a /home partition as well, and if you set it to `multi`, you will get separate /home, /usr, /var, and /tmp partitions.

▪ **partman/confirm_write_new_label, partman/choose_partition, and partman/confirm**
These are more options that tell the installer to proceed with partitioning without extra user confirmation. If you did, however, want to require a user to confirm settings (possibly while debugging your preseed file), you could comment out one of these options.

Expert Partition Recipes   The predefined partition recipes that Ubuntu provides are probably adequate for basic servers, but most administrators I know have strong feelings about how their systems are partitioned. In these cases you will likely want to create your own custom partitioning scheme for your servers. In the preseeding world this is known as an `expert_recipe`. Custom partitioning recipes can get rather complex as there are a lot of options available. The complete documentation is available at http://d-i.alioth.debian.org/svn/debian-installer/installer/doc/devel/partman-auto-recipe.txt, but even that can be difficult to follow without some examples.

First let's examine a basic partitioning recipe that is provided in a lot of the example preseed files in official documentation. The following recipe will set up a small /boot partition and a swap partition and use up the rest of the disk for /:

```
d-i partman-auto/expert_recipe string            \
boot-root ::                                      \
    40 50 100 ext3                                \
        $primary{ } $bootable{ }                  \
        method{ format } format{ }                \
        use_filesystem{ } filesystem{ ext3 }   \
        mountpoint{ /boot }                       \
        .                                         \
```

```
500 10000 1000000000 ext3                       \
    method{ format } format{ }                  \
    use_filesystem{ } filesystem{ ext3 }  \
    mountpoint{ / }                             \
    .                                           \
64 512 300% linux-swap                          \
    method{ swap } format{ }                    \
    .
```

Note that this entire configuration is intended to appear on a single line, so to make it more readable you are allowed to use the \ symbol at the end of the line to extend your options to multiple lines, as with shell scripts.

The first line labels this recipe as boot-root, and all of the rest of the lines are considered part of the boot-root recipe. The way that the lines are formatted separates each of the three partitions from the others. First let's take a closer look at the /boot partition:

```
40 50 100 ext3                              \
    $primary{ } $bootable{ }                \
    method{ format } format{ }              \
    use_filesystem{ } filesystem{ ext3 }    \
    mountpoint{ /boot }                     \
    .
```

The first line has four different fields corresponding to the minimal size of the partition, the priority, the maximal size, and the parted-style file system. All disk sizes in this file are in megabytes, so here we would have a disk that is at least 40Mb but if available could grow up to 100Mb, and it is a standard Linux partition with an ext3 file system. If you compare this line with the corresponding line for the swap partition, you will notice that for its maximal field it uses 300%. When a percentage is used, the size is determined based on the amount of RAM on the system. What 300% means in this case is that the swap partition's maximal size will be 300% of the amount of RAM on the machine.

The priority field deserves a little extra description. It also represents a partition size in megabytes and usually is set to some value between the minimal and maximal values. The installer uses the priority setting of each partition when it decides how much of the available space to give each partition. The higher the priority compared to that of other partitions, the more likely it is that a particular partition is going to get the space. In fact, for some small partitions you might even want to set the priority higher than the maximal value if you want to make sure it gets enough space (or you could just increase the minimum value). Ultimately this is another exercise in trial and error to make sure all of your partitions get enough space.

The next line, `$primary{ } $bootable{ }`, sets two different options for the partition. The first makes the partition the primary partition (if that is possible; it's worth noting that the partitions will be created in the order in which they are listed in this file). The second option sets the bootable flag on this partition.

The third line tells the partition to be formatted. The `method{ }` setting takes three different arguments: `format` (formats the partition), `swap` (formats the partition as swap space), or `keep` (keep the current partition as it is and do not format it). The `format{ }` argument is also needed to ensure that this partition is formatted. If the file system you have chosen for a partition supports labels, you can also add the `label{ }` option here to assign it a label. So to label a partition `boot` you could add `label{ boot }`.

Whereas the third line defines that the partition *should* be formatted, the fourth line defines *how* it should be formatted. The `use_filesystem{ }` option tells the installer that this partition will have a partition on it, and the `filesystem{ }` option defines which file system to format it with.

The fifth line contains the `mountpoint{ }` option, which tells the partitioner where to mount this partition on the final installed system. The installer will take care of the /etc/fstab settings for you, but you can also add special mounting options for a partition if you wish. For instance, to mount a partition read-only, you would typically add `ro` to the list of mount options in /etc/fstab. In this case you would add a line containing `options/ro{ ro }`. If you wanted to add the `noatime` option as well (stops the logging of A time on a file system, which can boost its performance), you would add `options/noatime{ noatime }`.

Note that each partition uses a single period at the end of the last line to signify the end of its options and separate it from any other partitions you might define.

LVM You can also configure LVM partitions in your preseed file with only a few changes. First, change the `partman-auto/method` option from `regular` to `lvm` and then add `lvmok{ }` to each partition you want to use LVM. However, you will get a warning in your install if you haven't configured a non-LVM /boot partition. A simple way to solve this is to be sure that your expert recipe has a /boot partition configured without `lvmok{ }` in it. A simple example uses the expert recipe I listed above and adds an extra option `lvmok{ }` to the root and swap partitions. The final expert recipe will look like the following:

```
d-i partman-auto/expert_recipe string              \
    boot-root-lvm ::                               \
      40 50 100 ext3                               \
           $primary{ } $bootable{ }                \
           method{ format } format{ }              \
           use_filesystem{ } filesystem{ ext3 }    \
           mountpoint{ /boot }                      \
      .                                             \
      500 10000 1000000000 ext3                    \
           method{ format } format{ }              \
           use_filesystem{ } filesystem{ ext3 }    \
           mountpoint{ / }                          \
           lvmok{ }                                 \
      .                                             \
      64 512 300% linux-swap                       \
           method{ swap } format{ }                \
           lvmok{ }                                 \
      .
```

Finally, you can create your own custom LVM physical volume in your partition recipe. Here is an example physical volume that will consume the entire /dev/sda drive and set up a volume group named vg00. Note that the `method{ }` option is set to `lvm` in this case.

```
100 1000 1000000000 ext3         \
      $defaultignore{ }           \
      $primary{ }                 \
      method{ lvm }               \
      device{ /dev/sda }          \
      vg_name{ vg00 } .
```

When you set up your own volume groups, you might also want to control which volume groups particular partitions are a part of. Use the `in_vg{ }`

option to specify which volume group a particular partition is a member of and `lv_name{ }` to name the logical volume. For instance, if I wanted the swap partition I created above to be a part of vg00 explicitly and labeled testswap, I could change it to the following:

```
64 512 300% linux-swap                            \
    method{ swap } format{ }                      \
    lvmok{ }                                      \
    invg{ vg00 }                                  \
    lv_name{ testswap }                           \
    .
```

NOTE   Since each line in these partition declarations is a continuation of the previous line, you can separate each option on its own line or put multiple options on the same line—it's up to you. Just make sure to use the \ symbol at the end of each line and use a . at the end of each partition.

Packages and Mirrors

What differentiates one type of server from another is what services it runs, and on Ubuntu that ultimately comes down to which packages you decide to install on the system. While you could certainly use the installer just to set up a base install image and then go in and add packages yourself later, if your goal is complete automation you should look into the package settings built into the preseed process.

The basic package options in the preseed file are pretty straightforward and self-explanatory. Let's start with the options I used in my default preseed file:

```
d-i mirror/country string US
d-i mirror/http/proxy string
d-i pkgsel/install-language-support boolean false
d-i pkgsel/update-policy select none
tasksel tasksel/first multiselect standard, ubuntu-server
```

The first option defines what Ubuntu mirror to use to retrieve packages and updates (the default mirror for the United States). I don't use a proxy, but I also didn't want to get prompted for it, so I left this option blank. I didn't want to install additional language packages, so I set `pkgsel/`

install-language-support to false. The pkgsel/update-policy option lets you define whether the system will apply updates automatically. We set this to none so any updates must be applied manually. Finally, you can see that you can also preseed values for tasksel; in my case I told it to select the standard packages along with the ubuntu-server task. I could have also added other tasks that are available via the manual tasksel process such as lamp-server if I had wanted. Sometimes the extra packages you want to install aren't part of specific tasks. In that case you can use the pkgsel/include option to add a list of specific packages the installer will add for you. This example adds the openssh-server and build-essential packages:

```
d-i pkgsel/include string openssh-server build-essential
```

Custom Package Repositories In addition to the standard settings you need to define, there are a number of tweaks you can make to the APT configuration within your preseed file. For instance, you can choose which repositories to include within APT. The values below include the restricted, universe, and backports repositories:

```
d-i apt-setup/restricted boolean true
d-i apt-setup/universe boolean true
d-i apt-setup/backports boolean true
```

You might also decide you want to specify from which Ubuntu mirror to retrieve packages, because either you have your own repository or you know of a repository that is faster for you. In either case, all you need to do is set the mirror/country option to manual and then specify which mirror to use. I left the mirror/http/proxy value blank, but if you use an HTTP proxy you would put its value there.

```
d-i mirror/country string manual
d-i mirror/http/hostname string us.archive.ubuntu.com
d-i mirror/http/directory string /ubuntu
d-i mirror/http/proxy string

d-i apt-setup/local0/repository string \
      http://apt.example.net/ubuntu &releasename; main
d-i apt-setup/local0/comment string local server
d-i apt-setup/local0/source boolean true
d-i apt-setup/local0/key string http://apt.example.net/key
```

This example adds the local repository stored at apt.example.net and labels it `local server`. The `apt-setup/local0/source` line will also add the source code repository, and the `apt-setup/local0/key` points to the GPG key that your APT repository must have set up to sign packages. If you don't have this key set up and available, the install will complain.

User Settings

One thing you will find in just about every Linux install program is a section to configure user accounts. As with every other part of the installer, this section can be preseeded. Here's what I used in my default preseed.cfg file:

```
d-i passwd/user-fullname string Ubuntu User
d-i passwd/username string ubuntu
d-i passwd/user-password password insecure
d-i passwd/user-password-again password insecure
user-setup-udeb user-setup/encrypt-home boolean false
```

Each field is pretty self-explanatory, but note that I had to specify the password twice. The last option lets you define whether the home directory is encrypted. Since this is a server and we want the install to be automated, it's simplest if we just set that option to `false`. Now if you don't want to list the password in plain text, substitute the following in the `user-password` lines:

```
d-i passwd/user-password-crypted password [MD5 hash]
```

If you are sure how to figure out an MD5 hash for a particular password, change the password for a user on another system to the password you want to use and then see what MD5 hash is set for it in the /etc/shadow file.

Ubuntu will set up the default user with a default UID and group membership. You can also use preseeded values to override that:

```
d-i passwd/user-uid string 1010
d-i passwd/user-default-groups string audio cdrom video
```

One thing Ubuntu does to increase security is to disable the root account by default. Instead of a root account, users use the `sudo` program to gain superuser privileges. You can override this with preseeded values, of course. The following set of options will set up the root user along with the default user:

```
d-i passwd/root-login boolean true
d-i passwd/root-password password insecure
d-i passwd/root-password-again password insecure
# or encrypted using an MD5 hash.
#d-i passwd/root-password-crypted password [MD5 hash]
```

Finally, if you want, you can disable the default user account altogether and stick with only root, although I would discourage this:

```
d-i passwd/make-user boolean false
```

GRUB

For the most part you will probably want to stick with the default GRUB setup for your server, in which case the entries in my sample preseed.cfg would be all that you need:

```
d-i grub-installer/only_debian boolean true
d-i grub-installer/with_other_os boolean true
d-i finish-install/reboot_in_progress note
```

The first option will install GRUB to the MBR if no other operating system is found. The `grub-installer/with_other_os` option will additionally set up any other operating systems it finds on the host. You typically don't have a dual-boot setup with a server, but this is probably safe to keep as is. The final option will preseed away the prompt to reboot the machine so that it automatically reboots to the newly installed OS.

In some situations you might not want GRUB to be installed on the MBR but instead at the beginning of a particular partition or to multiple disks (handy for software RAID). In these cases you can specify the boot device for GRUB to use:

```
d-i grub-installer/only_debian boolean false
d-i grub-installer/with_other_os boolean false
d-i grub-installer/bootdev  string (hd0,0)
```

The first two lines disable the default behavior of installing to the MBR, and the final line specifies which boot device GRUB should use. Note that it uses GRUB's syntax for boot devices and not /dev entries. Also, if you want to install GRUB across multiple devices, just list them one after another, separated by spaces on the `grub-installer/bootdev` line.

If you want extra security for your server to protect against users tweaking GRUB to boot into single-user mode, for instance, you have the option of password-protecting GRUB. This option can also be automated with preseed:

```
d-i grub-installer/password password insecure
d-i grub-installer/password-again password insecure
```

As with the user password settings, you can either use a plain-text password as shown above, or use an MD5 hash as shown below.

```
d-i grub-installer/password-crypted password [MD5 hash]
```

Miscellaneous

Finally, there are a few extra options that aren't critical but could prove useful, depending on your environment. For instance, by default Ubuntu will eject the CD after the install has finished. Well, if you are installing Ubuntu remotely and are thousands of miles away, that means you have just one shot at getting the install right before you have to get someone to reinsert the CD. Instead, you can set a preseed option to disable that:

```
d-i cdrom-detect/eject boolean false
```

Alternatively, you may not want to immediately reboot into the new system but instead halt it. This could be useful, for instance, if you wanted to build out a cluster of machines ahead of time but won't be using them immediately.

```
d-i debian-installer/exit/halt boolean true
```

Dynamic Preseeding

There is incredible flexibility in preseeding your install process, but as you develop your preseed infrastructure, ultimately you will find that one preseed configuration file won't work for all of the different servers you want to install. At that point you will probably develop a second, third, or fourth preseed.cfg file for those circumstances and then manually point to those files on the command line. That works, but it can be a pain to maintain over time. A better approach is to take advantage of the installer's ability to dynamically load preseed settings at different points of the install. That way you can maintain a base preseed.cfg file that contains options that work for all of the installs, and then create custom preseed files that contain only what needs to be changed from the base config. Then you can load those files, and their changes will ultimately overwrite the settings in your main preseed.cfg.

Chain Loading Preseed Files One way to manage all of your preseed settings is to separate the differences into multiple files. You could, for instance, put all of the partitioning information into a partition.cfg file, or if you have different network settings for each network, you might have the same base preseed.cfg file but different network.cfg files. Each of these networks might have its own preseed server that shares the preseed.cfg but has a custom network.cfg. Within the preseed.cfg file you would then add a line like the following:

```
d-i preseed/include string network.cfg
```

The installer would then retrieve the network.cfg file from the same location where it found the original preseed file. You can specify multiple files on this line; just separate them with spaces. You can also use relative directory paths if you wish. The installer will start from the directory where the main preseed file was retrieved and move from there. So if my preseed.cfg file was at http://example.com/preseed.cfg but my network file was at http://example.com/network/network.cfg, my include string would read

```
d-i preseed/include string network/network.cfg
```

Using static include files such as this can help with organization, but often what you'll find is that you want to include only certain preseed files for certain situations. In this case there is an include_command preseed option that allows you to write a short shell script that will output the filename to include. This allows you to choose custom preseed files based on the environment. This simplistic example just echoes a particle filename:

```
d-i preseed/include_command \
    string echo partition.cfg
```

This feature actually can open up a lot of options for an administrator. For instance, let's say that you manage three data centers in New York, London, and Tokyo. As a good administrator, you have set up a unique subdomain for each of these data centers, so the New York, London, and Tokyo servers use ny.example.net, london.example.net, and tokyo.example.net respectively as their domains. More likely than not you would have custom preseed options you would want to set for each of the different data centers, so you could then put these custom options in ny.example.net.cfg, london.example.net.cfg, and tokyo.example.net.cfg on the same server as your generic preseed.cfg file. Then in your preseed.cfg file you could add

```
d-i preseed/include_command \
    string echo `hostname -d`.cfg
```

The `hostname -d` command will output a host's domain name, so if a host in New York's fully qualified domain name is web1.ny.example.net, then `hostname -d` would output ny.example.net. Our preseed command would then echo ny.example.net.cfg.

Run Custom Commands During the Install   If you find yourself writing longer and longer one-liners into the `include_command` option, you will definitely want to look into some of the other preseed options that allow you to run entire scripts. There are three different preseed options that allow you to execute commands within the installer environment.

The first option I will mention is in a way an extension of the `include` options. Where those options allowed you to list an additional preseed file to download and read in, the `preseed/run` option will instead download and execute a script of your choice:

```
d-i preseed/run string command.sh
```

This `command.sh` script could perform all of the shell logic you might have used before in `include_command`, only now it's much easier to organize. You can even read and set preseed values within your script. Just use the `debconf-get` and `debconf-set` commands to get and set different preseed settings for your install. For instance, if I wanted to retrieve the preseeded hostname, I could run

```
debconf-get netcfg/get_hostname
```

If I wanted to set that option to web1 from within my script, I would run

```
debconf-set netcfg/get_hostname web1
```

The next preseed option that allows you to run commands within your install is preseed/early_command. This option allows you to specify a command that will be run as early as possible in the install—basically as soon as the preseed file is read. This is similar to the preseed/run command, except that you don't have to retrieve a script to execute—you can run shell commands directly from the install environment. If you want, though, you can make preseed/early_command behave just like preseed/run with the use of the preseed_fetch command that will retrieve a file from your preseed server for you. Its first argument is the file to retrieve, and the second argument tells the command where to place the file it has downloaded. In this example I have re-created the functionality of my preseed/run example from above.

```
d-i preseed/early_command string preseed_fetch command.sh \
/tmp/command.sh; sh /tmp/command.sh
```

Whereas the preseed/early_command is executed as soon as possible in the install process, the preseed/late_command is executed as late as possible. The early_command is useful to set dynamic values for the installer before it has started the bulk of the installation process, but the late_command is handy for running your own custom programs after you know the base image has been installed. At this phase in the installer, the server's root partition is still mounted under the /target directory, so you could potentially chroot into that directory and run commands as though you were running them directly from the installed server.

As with the early_command, you can use preseed_fetch to retrieve scripts to run. Some of the most common things you might want to do have been automated for you with the in-target and apt-install commands. The in-target command automates the chroot process for you so that any command you list after in-target will be executed within the installed environment. The apt-install command will use APT to install any extra packages you might want to add. The following example will install the Mutt e-mail client on your server and then dump the current set of environment variables into a file in your /root directory:

```
d-i preseed/late_command string apt-install mutt; \
in-target set > /root/environment
```

While you can certainly list extra packages to install in other parts of your preseed.cfg file, the real power here is that with `late_command` you could download a script that dynamically pulls information from the environment and then decides which packages it wants to install based on that. Later in the chapter, when I discuss how to deploy servers with PXE booting using both Kickstart and preseeding, I will go into more detail on how to leverage dynamic scripting in your automated installs.

Kickstart

The second main method you can use to automate Ubuntu server installs is with Kickstart. Kickstart is a technology used originally by Red Hat that has been ported for use by Ubuntu. Like preseeding, Kickstart works via a configuration file with answers to the installer's questions that you can grab over HTTP or FTP or from a local file. Kickstart is arguably easier to use, and since many administrators already have a Kickstart environment in place for their Red Hat machines, it makes sense to stick with Kickstart as your main automation tool for Ubuntu as well. Most of the Kickstart features, but not all, have been ported, but because of the ease of configuration and the benefit of a graphical configuration management tool, I advocate starting with Kickstart and supplementing it with a preseed file where necessary.

Basic Kickstart Configuration for CD-ROM

As in the preseeding section of this chapter, I will start with the simplest Kickstart scenario: a default Ubuntu server installed from the CD-ROM. Even though the Kickstart file's options are pretty self-explanatory, the great news is that there is a graphical program available for Ubuntu that will help you generate a Kickstart file. Not only does this save you from looking up the syntax for every Kickstart option, it saves you time—something a sysadmin never has enough of. As someone who has created plenty of Kickstart configuration files by hand, I recommend using the GUI as much as you can to set up your base template and then tweaking the resulting configuration file by hand only if you need to.

The Kickstart GUI tool is not installed by default on a typical Ubuntu desktop system, so use your preferred package management tool to install the `system-config-kickstart` package. Once it is installed, you can find the program in Applications->System Tools->Kickstart. As you launch the program, you will see that it is broken up into a basic two-pane window, as shown in Figure 4-2. On the left side is the set of configuration categories you can change, and as you select one of them, the right pane changes to list the options you can configure. Go through each of the categories and make sure the default settings match what you want on your server. Also be sure to go to the Partition Information category and set up your partitions. Unlike with preseeding, you do have to give the Kickstart file some sort of guide on how to partition the system. Once you finish your settings in the GUI, click File->Save and save the file to ks.cfg.

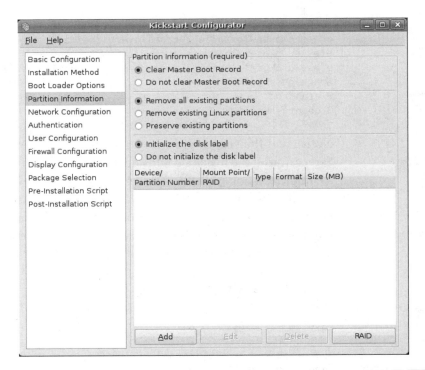

Figure 4-2 Kickstart Configurator program

NOTE   A great thing about the GUI program is that it already knows the correct syntax to use for each option, so it makes a great reference for Ubuntu Kickstart options. Just start the program and set the options you want to look up, and then click File->Preview. The tool will then output a sample ks.cfg to the screen so you can see the syntax.

As I mentioned, I will need to tweak this file so that it will create a default Ubuntu server. Essentially it needs a few server-specific preseed options that the Ubuntu Server CD-ROM typically provides, along with the list of default tasks to install. To add those preseed options to the Kickstart file, I would just add lines to the main configuration section, starting the lines with the word preseed followed by the particular preseed option I want to set. All of the extra tasks and packages you need to install on a server are defined in a %packages section (the different sections of a Kickstart file are named with a % at the beginning). The two tasks we need for this server are standard and ubuntu-server. The following is the combined preseed options and %packages section I appended to the end of the ks.cfg file the GUI tool created:

```
preseed base-installer/kernel/override-image string linux-server
preseed pkgsel/language-pack-patterns string
preseed pkgsel/install-language-support boolean false
%packages
@ standard
@ ubuntu-server
```

Notice that the tasks begin with an @ sign, so if I wanted to select LAMP Server during the install I could add @ lamp-server to this list. If you want a complete list of available tasks, run tasksel --list-tasks. You can also add individual packages to this list; just put each package name on its own line without the @ in front of it. Since I just wanted a default Ubuntu install that mirrored my previous preseed.cfg file, I didn't add any extra packages. Here is the resulting ks.cfg file:

```
#Generated by Kickstart Configurator
#platform=x86

#System language
lang en_US
#Language modules to install
langsupport en_US
#System keyboard
```

```
keyboard us
#System mouse
mouse
#System timezone
timezone America/Los_Angeles
#Root password
rootpw --disabled
#Initial user
user ubuntu --fullname "ubuntu" --password insecure
#Reboot after installation
reboot
#Use text mode install
text
#Install OS instead of upgrade
install
#Use CDROM installation media
cdrom
#System bootloader configuration
bootloader --location=mbr
#Clear the Master Boot Record
zerombr yes
#Partition clearing information
clearpart --all --initlabel
#Disk partitioning information
part / --fstype ext3 --size 1 --grow --asprimary
part swap --recommended
#System authorization information
auth  --useshadow  --enablemd5
#Firewall configuration
firewall --disabled
#Do not configure the X Window System
skipx
# This section was added by hand
preseed base-installer/kernel/override-image string linux-server
preseed pkgsel/language-pack-patterns string
preseed pkgsel/install-language-support boolean false
%packages
@ standard
@ ubuntu-server
```

As I did with the preseed file, I set up a single / partition with the --grow option so that it filled the entire drive (actually I just toggled that setting within the GUI). Then I copied this ks.cfg file to the same Web server I used before. One other great thing about using this Kickstart file is that I don't have to manually enter a lot of settings at boot. In fact, all I need to do is replace the file preseed option that is already there with an option that points to my Kickstart file. Boot the CD-ROM and then press F6 to see the full list of boot options as before. This time, though, after you back-space over the `file=` option, use the `ks=` option to point to your Kickstart file. Your final boot prompt will look like this:

```
ks=http://example.net/ks.cfg initrd=/install/initrd.gz quiet --
```

Of course, replace `http://example.net/ks.cfg` with the URL for your Kickstart file. As with preseeding, the install should complete without any interaction from you unless any typos or other mistakes were introduced to the Kickstart file.

Changes and Limitations in Ubuntu Kickstart

As I mentioned before, Kickstart in Ubuntu is a port of the original Red Hat system. Since Red Hat and Ubuntu are quite different from each other, not every feature of Red Hat's Kickstart currently works the same way with Ubuntu. Also, some additional options needed to be added for Ubuntu. Next I will discuss some of the major differences you will find between the two Kickstart systems.

New Options

▪ **Preseed**

I already mentioned the new preseed option in my example ks.cfg file. The basic syntax is

```
preseed [--owner pkgowner] package/question type value
```

Honestly, the main difference you will see here as opposed to the syntax in a standard preseed file is that each line starts with `preseed` instead of the typical `d-i`. I said "typical" because while most of the preseed options you set are installer options, some preseed options actually don't start with `d-i` in a preseed file because they are owned by a different package. If you run into a setting like that, use the `--owner` option set to the argument that would have gone at the beginning of a preseed file. For instance, tasks that you select in a pre-seed file look like the following:

```
tasksel tasksel/first multiselect standard, ubuntu-server
```

These settings already are managed in a Kickstart file in the `%packages` section, but if they weren't you could set this setting with

```
preseed --owner tasksel tasksel/first multiselect \
standard, ubuntu-server
```

■ **Account options**

Two other major additions in the Kickstart syntax provide extra options for account management. Because Ubuntu disables the root user by default, the `rootpw` Kickstart command now can take the `--disabled` option. This disables the root password and gives the first user root privileges from `sudo`.

The Ubuntu Kickstart file has also added a `user` command to add settings for the initial user. The syntax for this command is

```
user --disabled | username [--fullname "Firstname Lastname"] \
--password insecure [--iscrypted]
```

This command either takes the `--disabled` option to disable an initial user altogether or takes as options the username, optionally the user's full name, and finally the password. By default the password is in plain text, but you can optionally list the MD5 hash for the password; just be sure to add the `--iscrypted` option so that Kickstart knows.

Limitations   Currently the Ubuntu Kickstart does not implement the full range of features of Red Hat's Kickstart. These limitations are one reason for advocating a combination of Kickstart and preseeding. The Kickstart file can take care of the base configuration, and where features aren't available, they can be supplemented by preseed options. Here is a list of major features not yet implemented in Ubuntu's Kickstart:

■ There is no LDAP, Kerberos 5, Hesios, or Samba authentication.

■ There are no `bootloader --linear`, `--nolinear`, or `--lba32` options for lilo.

■ There is no `lilocheck` command.

■ Ubuntu handles system upgrades outside of the Kickstart file.

▪ Partitioning in Ubuntu's Kickstart is not yet as full-featured. As a result, if you have more sophisticated partitioning in mind, I recommend supplementing this with preseed options. Here are the current partitioning limitations:

  ▪ Can partition only the main disk

  ▪ No LVM configuration

  ▪ No bad sector checks

  ▪ No RAID partitions

▪ You cannot restrict a partition to a particular disk or specify the starting or ending cylinder.

▪ There is no support for a supplemental driver disk during install.

▪ The device command is not supported.

▪ Firewall configuration is not supported.

▪ There is no automated discovery of Kickstart source via DHCP; you must specify Kickstart source explicitly.

▪ NFS and local disk are not supported as installation sources.

▪ The xconfig --monitor option is not supported (selects a specific monitor name).

▪ Package groups in Ubuntu and Red Hat have different names and under Ubuntu, package groups reference Ubuntu tasks instead.

▪ You cannot exclude packages in the %packages section.

▪ You can use shell scripts only in pre- and post-installation sections.

Run Custom Commands during the Install

Like preseeding, Kickstart supports running custom commands during the install. Also like preseeding, this is done via a pre-install and a post-install script. In a Kickstart file these are defined in %pre and %post sections. Any shell commands you place in those sections will be executed immediately before or after the install process, respectively. A nice feature of these scripts in Kickstart is that they can span multiple lines as long as they stay within the %pre or %post section.

NOTE   Even though it's easy to put a large shell script in the %pre and %post sections, once your scripts get to a certain complexity, you should probably consider putting them into a script on your Kickstart server that you then retrieve via wget and execute. An extra benefit of this approach is that you could perform logic within the %pre and %post sections to pull custom shell scripts based on the type of server you are installing.

Probably the simplest way to start your pre- or post-installation script is with the Kickstart Configurator tool. Each installation script is set up as a category in the left pane with a section in the right pane where you can write your script. You can even specify a custom interpreter for your shell script via the GUI. Even the GUI provides a warning in these sections that a mistake in these shell scripts can cause the Kickstart as a whole to fail.

An important distinction to make between the pre- and post-installation scripts is that the pre-installation script is run within the installer environment whereas the post-install script by default is run within a chroot environment inside the installed system. That means that you can install additional packages or perform other custom tweaks within the installed system in the post-install section, while in the pre-install section you would mostly want to tweak preseed settings.

PXE Boot Server Deployment

While the examples I gave earlier are a good place to start, when you want to automate server installs, you ultimately need to set up a PXE boot server to manage the process. After all, do you really want to manually go to each new server and insert a CD-ROM? What if your server is on another continent or you have 200 servers to install? With PXE boot deployment, your new server boots from the network, pulls down its install image from the PXE server, and then starts the installation process—all over the network.

There are a number of different services you need for PXE boot deployment to work:

- A DHCP server configured for PXE booting to give each install an IP address and point it to the TFTP server and boot program to load
- A TFTP server to serve the PXE boot loader program over the network
- A Web server to host any Kickstart and preseed files and any custom scripts

While each of these services could reside on totally different hosts, for my example I will step you through how to set up each of them, starting with the same default Ubuntu image with the same default settings I have been using so far in this chapter. In this example I will set up a PXE server with an IP address of 10.1.1.5. On this network my gateway router is at 10.1.1.1 and my DNS servers are at 10.1.1.2 and 10.1.1.3.

DHCP

The first step is to set up a DHCP server that can hand out IP addresses to each installation candidate. First install the dhcp3-server package:

```
$ sudo apt-get install dhcp3-server
```

By default your DHCP server won't be configured. All you really need to get everything started is a short subnet section in the /etc/dhcp3/dhcpd .conf file. When you open the file with your preferred text editor, you will notice there is a basic skeleton of a configuration there along with many commented-out examples. Just go to the bottom of the file and add the following subnet section:

```
subnet 10.1.1.1 netmask 255.255.255.0 {
    option domain-name-servers 10.1.1.2, 10.1.1.3;
    option routers 10.1.1.1;
    range dynamic-bootp 10.1.1.50 10.1.1.99;
    next-server 10.1.1.5;
    filename "pxelinux.0";
}
```

I will go more into overall DHCP configuration in Chapter 5, but here I have told DHCP to answer queries on the 10.1.1.0/255.255.255.0 subnet. I have listed the two DNS servers on that network along with the router to use. The dynamic-bootp line defines the range of IP addresses this DHCP server will hand out. In this case I will hand out addresses between 10.1.1.50 and 10.1.1.99. The next-server line configures the IP address for TFTPD server to use so that any hosts that PXE boots can retrieve their boot loader (in this case this server) via TFTPD. The filename line tells it the name of the file to retrieve. More on that in the next section.

Obviously, tweak this sample configuration so that it matches the settings on your particular network, and then start the DHCP server by typing `sudo service dhcp3-server start`. You should see

```
$ sudo service dhcp3-server start
* Starting DHCP server dhcpd3              [OK]
```

If the service fails to start because of an error in the configuration file, you should see a reference to the error in the output on the screen. Track down that line in the dhcpd.conf file and look for missing semicolons at the end of lines or any other syntax errors you might have made.

TFTPD

Once the DHCP server is set up, the next step is to install a TFTPD service on your PXE boot server. Type

```
$ sudo apt-get install tftpd-hpa
```

and APT will pull down the TFTPD server and the `openbsd-inetd` package it depends on. As this service is managed by inetd, it will be started only when a user accesses UDP port 69 on this machine. The firewall is disabled by default in my Kickstart and preseed examples, but if you have enabled it, be sure to open a port for UDP port 69.

Configure Pxelinux

Now that TFTPD is installed, you are ready to install and configure pxelinux. Pxelinux is a component of the syslinux package that provides a boot loader for CD-ROMs (including Ubuntu) called isolinux, a standard boot loader known as syslinux, and a PXE boot loader called pxelinux. While you could install the syslinux package and copy the files yourself, Ubuntu has already provided a netboot configuration ready for you to use on its mirrors. All you have to do is go to the TFTPD root directory and then download and extract the netboot tarball for your Ubuntu version. For instance, here are the steps to grab a netboot tarball for Lucid Lynx:

```
$ sudo cd /var/lib/tftpboot
$ sudo wget http://us.archive.ubuntu.com/ubuntu/dists/lucid/main/
  installer-i386/current/images/netboot/netboot.tar.gz
$ sudo tar -xzvf netboot.tar.gz
```

This tarball already contains the pxelinux.0 binary, an excellent sample pxelinux configuration file in pxelinux.cfg/default, and a series of boot menus and help documents under the ubuntu-installer directory.

When pxelinux loads, it will search the pxelinux.cfg directory on the TFTP server for a number of different configuration files. You can take advantage of this search order to pass custom settings to particular hosts. Pxelinux will search for files in the following order:

▪ Files named 01-MACADDRESS with hyphens between each hex pair. So for a server with a MAC address of 88:99:AA:BB:CC:DD, a configuration file that would target just that machine would be named 01-88-99-aa-bb-cc-dd (and I've noticed that it does matter that it is lowercase).

▪ Files named after the host's IP address in hex. Here pxelinux will drop a digit from the end of the hex IP and try again as each file search fails. This is often used when an administrator buys a lot of the same brand of machine, which will often have very similar MAC addresses. The administrator can then configure DHCP to assign a certain IP range to those MAC addresses. Then a boot option can be applied to all of that group.

▪ Finally, if no specific files can be found, pxelinux will look for a file named default and use it.

For this example we will stick with the pxelinux.cfg/default configuration file provided by netboot.tar.gz. You can always create a custom configuration file later on for specific servers, and there are a number of different ways to organize and define separate install options, as I will discuss next.

The great thing about using Ubuntu's netboot tarball is that it sets up a nice PXE boot environment out of the box with menus, help, and most of the hard work already done for you. All you need to do is tweak the default so that it points to your Kickstart file. Open /var/lib/tftpboot/ubuntu-installer/i386/boot-screens/text.cfg in your favorite text editor and you will see the following lines:

```
default install

label install
    menu label ^Install
    menu default
```

```
      kernel ubuntu-installer/i386/linux
      append vga=normal initrd=ubuntu-installer/i386/initrd.gz --
  quiet
label cli
      menu label ^Command-line install
      kernel ubuntu-installer/i386/linux
      append tasks=standard pkgsel/language-pack-patterns=
pkgsel/install-language-support=false vga=normal initrd=ubuntu-
installer/i386/initrd.gz -- quiet
```

The `default` line tells pxelinux that the section labeled `install` is the one to load by default if a user just presses Enter at the boot prompt. The `label` `install` section defines a particular configuration a user can select. Every section that begins with `label` defines another configuration. As you look through this configuration file, you will see a number of different labels already set up for you. You can choose between different sections by typing the specific label at the boot prompt and pressing Enter. So while I could just hit Enter to select the section above labeled `install`, since it is set as the default, I could also type `install` at the boot prompt and press Enter. All we need to do to this file is change the default boot options so that they also point to our Kickstart file. To do this I just add my options to the append line. The beginning section of the file changed from this:

```
default install
label install
      menu label ^Install
      menu default
      kernel ubuntu-installer/i386/linux
      append vga=normal initrd=ubuntu-installer/i386/initrd.gz --
quiet
```

to this:

```
default install
label install
      menu label ^Install
      menu default
      kernel ubuntu-installer/i386/linux
      append vga=normal initrd=ubuntu-installer/i386/initrd.gz
  ks=http://10.1.1.5/ks.cfg -- quiet
```

Save your changes and exit your text editor. Pxelinux is now configured and you are ready to move on to the final step.

Web

The last step in the process is to set up a Web server to host your Kickstart and preseed files and any custom scripts you might have. First install the apache2 package, which will provide your Web server software and all its necessary dependencies:

```
$ sudo apt-get install apache2
```

The apache2 package will automatically set up and start a functioning Web server for you with a default docroot of /var/www. I won't cover any more advanced configuration of Apache here because all we want is a Web server to host a few text files. At this point all you need to do is move your ks.cfg file to /var/www on this server. You will need to make only one change to your ks.cfg file for PXE booting. Since we won't be pulling down files from the CD-ROM, we need to tell our Kickstart file to grab files from an Ubuntu mirror, so find and change the line that reads

```
cdrom
```

to

```
url --url http://us.archive.ubuntu.com/ubuntu
```

NOTE   Since this server will be pulling all of its packages directly from an Ubuntu mirror, the installation will undoubtedly take longer than it would from the CD-ROM. If you plan to do a lot of automated Ubuntu installs, you will probably want to consider setting up your own mirror of the Ubuntu archive.

Before you go any further, try to access your ks.cfg file either from a Web browser or using a tool like wget and make sure that Apache is serving that file. If you can't access the file, check the Apache error logs in /var/log/apache2/error.log for clues as to what may be wrong, and check the permissions on ks.cfg to make sure that it is world-readable. If not, type chmod a+r ks.cfg to make it so.

Test Your PXE Server

At this point you should be ready to test your PXE server with a new install. There's no single instruction on how to set a server to PXE boot.

On some servers it's just a matter of hitting a function key to get a list of boot options and then selecting network boot. On other servers you need to go into the BIOS and change the boot order. Still other servers provide a function key that automatically netboots. You will need to research how to tell your particular server to netboot and also make sure that it is connected to the same subnet as your PXE boot server.

Once you PXE-boot your server, you will be greeted with an Ubuntu menu as shown in Figure 4-3. Since we set up the default label to boot with our Kickstart options, all we need to do here is press Enter.

NOTE   Even this automated install requires some user interaction since you need to at least hit Enter at every boot prompt to start the installation process. This is a safety mechanism in a sense, since what happens if six months from now one of your servers reboots and then netboots? If everything were completely automated, that server would start the installation process again and potentially overwrite all of its current files—which could be a very bad thing. Now for some organizations this is desirable behavior (particularly for large clusters of identical machines). They have put in appropriate safeguards so that no machine boots on the network unless they want it to, and if it does, they definitely want it to perform a reinstall. If you want a 100% automated install that requires no user interaction apart from turning on the server, then just locate the TIMEOUT value in the pxelinux.cfg/default file. By default it is set to 0, which means that it will never time out. Just change that to a 1 and any server that boots and grabs that configuration file will automatically load the default label after a one-second time-out.

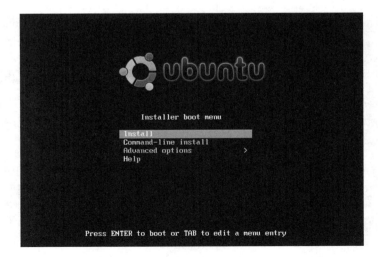

Figure 4-3 Ubuntu PXE boot menu

Customize Automated Installs

You will quickly realize that one size does not fit all when it comes to automated server deployments. As you start to expand your base Kickstart file into multiple offshoots, you will find that there are about as many ways to organize such a process as there are sysadmins. Instead of covering all of them, I will discuss some of the more popular ways to organize your Kickstart server for multiple install types.

Two popular ways to customize your automated installs involve changing settings to the pxelinux menu, and using DHCP to bypass the menu altogether and automatically install Ubuntu on any server that boots on the network. Each approach has its advantages and disadvantages. With the pxelinux menu approach, the administrator can provide one final confirmation before a machine starts the installation process. That way you prevent a machine that accidentally boots over the network from overwriting its settings. Another advantage is that you don't have to look up a machine's MAC address ahead of time and set up a special configuration option for each server. You get to specify at the boot prompt what sort of server you wish to install and it goes from there.

The main advantage to the DHCP approach is that it provides you with a completely unattended install. All you have to do is set up DHCP ahead of time, and then any time in the future once the server is powered on and netboots for the first time, it will automatically install itself. Some administrators even get the list of MAC addresses from their vendor ahead of time so their DHCP server is ready before the machines even arrive. Once they arrive and are physically installed, anyone could then power on the machines when it's time for them to go live.

Multiple Kickstart Files

Since the default pxelinux configuration file that Ubuntu includes already sets up a menuing system for you, why not use it to your advantage? You can set up any number of different boot options and assign them different labels. Let's say, for instance, that you wanted to be able to choose among three different Kickstart files: the default, one specifically for a Web server, and one for a MySQL server. We already have the default Kickstart configured:

```
default install
label install
      menu label ^Install
      menu default
      kernel ubuntu-installer/i386/linux
      append vga=normal initrd=ubuntu-installer/i386/initrd.gz
  ks=http://10.1.1.5/ks.cfg -- quiet
```

So all we need to do is clone the `label install` section twice and tweak each section to point to our other Kickstart files:

```
default install
label install
      menu label ^Install
      menu default
      kernel ubuntu-installer/i386/linux
      append vga=normal initrd=ubuntu-installer/i386/initrd.gz
  ks=http://10.1.1.5/ks.cfg -- quiet
label web
      menu label ^Install
      menu default
      kernel ubuntu-installer/i386/linux
      append vga=normal initrd=ubuntu-installer/i386/initrd.gz
ks=http://10.1.1.5/ks-web.cfg -- quiet
label mysql
      menu label ^Install
      menu default
      kernel ubuntu-installer/i386/linux
      append vga=normal initrd=ubuntu-installer/i386/initrd.gz
  ks=http://10.1.1.5/ks-mysql.cfg -- quiet
```

As you can see, the only real change I made in each section was to point to a different Kickstart file I had created. Now once I boot, I can type `web` or `mysql` and then hit Enter to select those particular options.

Boot Cheat Codes

Another useful way to differentiate between different install types is to use cheat codes (a name I'm borrowing from Knoppix). A cheat code is an option you type on the command line that gets passed down to the system. The interesting thing about the boot prompt is that everything that is on the boot prompt is accessible during the install via the /proc/cmdline file. If you want to create custom cheat codes, all you need to do is provide a pre- or post-install script that parses /proc/cmdline and stores those settings into environment variables. Then you can refer to those environment variables in your script and make custom changes to the pre- or post-install process based on them.

For instance, let's say we want to define two cheat codes at the boot prompt: mytype, to label what type of server it is (Web, MySQL, DNS), and myraid, which tells whether it should use RAID or not. Instead of setting up three different Kickstart files, I could use a single Kickstart file that then has logic in its pre-installation script to parse these options and change settings based on them. Here's a sample pre-install script that would parse the /proc/cmdline file, set the environment variables, and then perform special actions based on them:

```
%pre
for i in `cat /proc/cmdline` ; do
        echo $i | grep -iq MYTYPE=
        if [ $? -eq 0 ] ; then
            export MYTYPE=`echo $i | awk -F"=" '{ print $2; }'`
        fi
        echo $i | grep -iq MYRAID=
        if [ $? -eq 0 ] ; then
            export MYRAID=`echo $i | awk -F"=" '{ print $2; }'`
        fi
done

if [ $MYTYPE == "web" ]; then
# Change preseed settings for web servers
elif [ $MYTYPE == "mysql" ]; then
# Change preseed settings for mysql servers
elif [ $MYTYPE == "dns" ]; then
# Change preseed settings for dns servers
fi

if [ $MYRAID ]; then
# Change preseed settings for RAID
fi
```

Now at the boot prompt if I wanted to set up a MySQL server with RAID, I could type install mytype=mysql myraid=1. Again, the advantage to this approach is that it allows you to maintain a single Kickstart file that has the logic within it to change settings for specific server types. The downside to this approach is that the resulting Kickstart file can get rather large and complex over time.

DHCP Selection

This approach works particularly well if your organization uses static DHCP assignment for your servers. With static DHCP leases, a DHCP server assigns each host that requests an IP address the same IP address every time based on that host's MAC address. Typically in this setup your server will automatically install a new image whenever it boots off of the network. You will find this approach popular for large clusters or in environments where servers are physically installed sometime before they may ever get an operating system. Once you change the pxelinux configuration to automatically install the default image, your DHCP configuration file controls what each server will ultimately become. All an administrator needs to do to install Ubuntu on a server is connect it to the network and turn on the power.

In this scenario you create multiple directories under /var/lib/tftpboot, each of which contains an extracted copy of the netboot.tar.gz. For instance, if I wanted to set up three separate configurations for Web, MySQL, and DNS servers, I could do the following:

```
$ sudo cd /var/lib/tftpboot
$ sudo wget
http://archive.ubuntu.com/ubuntu/dists/hardy/main/installer-i386/
  current/images/netboot/netboot.tar.gz
$ sudo mkdir web mysql dns
$ cd web
$ sudo tar -xzvf netboot.tar.gz
$ cd ../mysql
$ sudo tar -xzvf netboot.tar.gz
$ cd ../dns
$ sudo tar -xzvf netboot.tar.gz
```

Now I would change the pxelinux.cfg/default files in each of those subdirectories to reflect any special settings I wanted to change. In addition, if I wanted this installation to require no user interaction at all, I would edit the pxelinux.cfg/default configuration files and set the TIMEOUT value to 1 so that after one second it will automatically start the installation process.

Again, if you use this method, put appropriate safeguards in place so that a machine doesn't accidentally netboot and overwrite its settings.

Once my TFTP server is set up, the bulk of the configuration occurs on the DHCP server. I need to modify my /etc/dhcp3/dhcpd.conf file so that, depending on which MAC address requests a lease, it gets pointed to a particular pxelinux.0 file under one of those subdirectories. For each MAC address I would add an individual section. Below I have added three specific servers, each pointing to a Web, MySQL, or DNS configuration:

```
host web1 {
    hardware ethernet 00:0c:c0:ff:ee:00;
    option host-name "web1";
    fixed-address 10.1.1.101;
    filename "/web/pxelinux.0";
}
host mysql1 {
    hardware ethernet 00:0c:c0:ff:ee:01;
    option host-name "mysql1";
    fixed-address 10.1.1.101;
    filename "/mysql/pxelinux.0";
}
host dns1 {
    hardware ethernet 00:0c:c0:ff:ee:02;
    option host-name "dns1";
    fixed-address 10.1.1.101;
    filename "/dns/pxelinux.0";
}
```

The main downside to this approach is that it means you have to maintain multiple pxelinux configuration files on your TFTP server. Another downside is that you have to look up the MAC address for each server before you can install anything on it. Of course, if you use static DHCP, that is a step you already have to perform anyway.

One benefit to this method, especially if you set the time-out so that a machine that PXE boots automatically starts installation, is that once you set up your environment, when a new host appears you just grab its MAC address and set up the dhcpd.conf file. Anyone at that point can set up Ubuntu on the server just by connecting to the network and powering on the server (provided it is set up to boot from the network by default).

DHCP Selection by Subnet

One variation on this method takes advantage of the fact that many networks segregate different server types into their own subnets. If your network is like this, then all you need to do is set up different subnet sections in your dhcpd.conf file for each type of server. For instance, let's say that all of my Web servers are on the 10.1.1.0 subnet and all of my MySQL servers are on the 10.1.2.0 subnet. Instead of setting up a specific section for each and every server, I could just point each subnet to a particular file:

```
subnet 10.1.1.0 netmask 255.255.255.0 {
    option domain-name-servers 10.1.1.2, 10.1.1.3;
    option routers 10.1.1.1;
    range dynamic-bootp 10.1.1.50 10.1.1.99;
    next-server 10.1.1.5;
    filename "/web/pxelinux.0";
}
subnet 10.1.2.0 netmask 255.255.255.0 {
    option domain-name-servers 10.1.1.2, 10.1.1.3;
    option routers 10.1.2.1;
    range dynamic-bootp 10.1.2.50 10.1.2.99;
    next-server 10.1.1.5;
    filename "/mysql/pxelinux.0";
}
```

Notice that the next-server section stayed the same in both subnets since I'm still using the same TFTP server. I'm also assuming that this single DHCP server serves leases for both subnets. With this type of install environment, I can control what gets installed on a server simply by controlling which subnet it is a member of. Depending on your environment, this might be as simple as changing a setting on a switch.

## CHAPTER 5

Guide to Common Ubuntu Servers

WHILE LINUX HAS BEEN USED AS a desktop operating system for a long time, it has arguably been used longer and by many more people as a server. Over the years Linux has accumulated hundreds of different services either ported from another operating system or developed primarily on Linux. This means that when you want to use Ubuntu as a server, there are literally hundreds of different servers Ubuntu could be, many of which can be installed by a simple call to a package manager.

It would be extremely difficult, if not impossible, to document all of Ubuntu's possible services in a book, much less a chapter. What I realize, though, is that among the hundreds of services you could install, there are a handful of common services that most administrators deal with on a daily basis. This chapter covers some of the most common Ubuntu server types that an administrator will run into. If you are a beginning administrator, I will provide you with a step-by-step guide to set up what might be your first DNS server with some common configuration schemes and best practices. If you are an advanced administrator, think of this chapter as a guide to the Ubuntu approach to servers. I show you how Ubuntu organizes configuration files along with any particular tools or shortcuts it provides for a service. I also cover major file locations so you'll know exactly where to look for the core configuration files, which init scripts are important, and where logs are stored.

Entire books have been written about how to administer basically every service discussed here. I don't attempt to document all of the major Apache modules, for instance, nor do I discuss every configuration option for BIND or Postfix. What I give you is a good departure point with working example configuration files. A sysadmin is always busy, so where Ubuntu has provided time-saving shortcuts, I point them out. After all, you only have to do something the hard, "old-school," time-consuming way so many times before it loses its mystique.

DNS Server

The first service I discuss also happens to be one of the oldest. DNS, or Domain Name System, is one of the fundamental services that keep the Internet running. In a nutshell, DNS is the service that among other things translates a hostname, such as www.ubuntu.com, into an IP address, like

91.189.94.8. DNS servers maintain a local directory of names and IP addresses for which they are authoritative, so that if you ask a DNS server for the IP address for a name for which it is authoritative, it should generally respond with the answer. Many DNS servers can serve recursive requests as well. With a recursive query, a DNS server might not itself contain the record you are looking for, but it can go out on the Internet and find the answer for you.

There are many different programs that provide DNS services on Ubuntu, but the most common has also been around the longest—BIND. BIND, short for Berkeley Internet Name Domain, has many advanced features, but with many features often comes a more complicated configuration file. Honestly, what trips up most administrators is simply building a BIND server from scratch, but as you will see, under Ubuntu the heavy lifting has already been done for you.

Install BIND

There are a few ways to install BIND under Ubuntu. During the initial Ubuntu install you can select DNS Server from the list of server types. If you have already installed Ubuntu, you can type sudo tasksel to get to the same menu. Once you select DNS Server and then OK, the bind9 and bind9-doc packages will automatically be downloaded and installed for you. Alternatively you can just run

```
$ sudo apt-get install bind9 bind9-doc
```

What you will discover (and what I will cover in more detail next) is that once the Ubuntu BIND package has been installed, you will actually have a fully configured and functioning name server ready, at least, to act as a caching name server for recursive queries. Sample configuration files, root zone files, local zones, and even rndc keys have already been configured for you.

Ubuntu Conventions

There are a few key file conventions that Ubuntu's BIND uses that might be different from what you are accustomed to, depending on what other

Linux distributions you have used. Here are some of the key Ubuntu file locations:

- **/etc/bind/**
  This directory contains the main BIND configuration file, named.conf, as well as any individual zone files. Any new master zone files should also be stored in this directory or, if you have many zone files you wish to organize, in a subdirectory below /etc/bind.

- **/etc/bind/named.conf**
  This is BIND's main configuration file and is where you change BIND's options and behavior. All of BIND's individual zone files (files containing name and IP information) are also referenced here. The main options that are enabled in BIND are included from a separate file named /etc/bind/named.conf.options.

- **/etc/bind/db.***
  As a convention, all zone files start with db. and then some name or number to identify the particular zone. Names are typically used when the zone contains traditional forward DNS records (names mapped to IPs), and numbers are typically used for reverse DNS records (IPs mapped back to a name). For instance, by default Ubuntu's BIND will include a few zone files such as db.root (information about the root name servers on the Internet), db.local (localhost zone information), and db.127 (reverse DNS records for localhost).

- **/var/cache/bind**
  This is BIND's working directory and where it will store slave zone files. If your server will act as a slave for a particular zone, configure it to store its files here.

- **/etc/init.d/bind9**
  This is BIND's init script. Once you install the bind9 package, it will automatically be set up to start on system boot, but you can run the init script manually with /etc/init.d/bind9, or run sudo service bind9.

▪ **/var/log/syslog**
  This is the default log file for BIND. A number of different services
  log to this file, but log entries for BIND will be prefixed by the keyword named, so if you wanted to see only the BIND log entries you
  could run sudo grep named /var/log/syslog.

Caching Name Server

The default Ubuntu BIND configuration is ready out of the box to be a
caching name server. Essentially a caching name server acts as a middle-
man for DNS queries. Once you configure some hosts to point to a
caching name server, when one host requests a particular record, the
caching name server goes out to the Internet, retrieves a record, and stores
that record locally. If a second host requests the same record, and that
record hasn't expired from the cache, a caching name server will simply
return the cached result. This can dramatically improve the response times
for a network of hosts, especially for Web browsing, since often the same
records (like, say, www.google.com) are requested by multiple hosts.

DNS Master

Caching name servers are very useful, but when most people install BIND,
they intend to host some zone files of their own. When a name server hosts
zone files locally and doesn't need to retrieve them from any other source,
it is known as a master. When you want to add zones to a DNS server, there
are basically three steps: Create a zone file, add a reference to that zone file
in named.conf, and tell BIND to reload its configuration.

For my example let's assume that I have a name server inside my network
at 192.168.0.5 and I registered example.net. I want this name server to
have the following entries:

▪ ns1.example.net points to 192.168.0.5 (the name server itself).

▪ example.net also points to 192.168.0.7.

▪ www.example.net points to 192.168.0.7.

▪ gateway.example.net points to 192.168.0.1.

The simplest way to create a new zone file is to copy one you already have and change it. In this case the best candidate is the /etc/bind/ db.local file, so I copy it to db.example.net:

```
$ sudo cp /etc/bind/db.local /etc/bind/db.example.net
```

When I open db.example.net in a text editor, I will see the following configuration:

```
;
; BIND data file for local loopback interface
;
$TTL    604800
@   IN   SOA    localhost. root.localhost. (
                      2          ; Serial
                  604800         ; Refresh
                   86400         ; Retry
                 2419200         ; Expire
                  604800 )       ; Negative Cache TTL
;
@    IN    NS   localhost.
@    IN    A    127.0.0.1
@    IN    AAAA ::1
```

Because this isn't intended to be a complete guide to BIND I won't go into every option in this file, but by default it is configured for a TTL (Time to Live, the amount of time before a name server that has requested a record considers it stale) of 604,800 seconds, or seven days. Next it lists localhost as the SOA (Start of Authority, the server that should be considered the best source of information), and root@localhost is the contact e-mail address to use for this host (referenced by root.localhost). Further down, the file lists localhost as a name server for this zone with an NS record, then sets localhost's IP address to be 127.0.0.1 and even adds an IPv6 address for localhost with the AAAA record.

I then changed this record to suit the requirements I set out previously, and this is the resulting zone file:

```
;
; BIND data file for example.net
;
$TTL    1d
```

```
@   IN   SOA   ns1.example.net. root.example.net. (
                    2          ; Serial
               604800          ; Refresh
                86400          ; Retry
              2419200          ; Expire
               604800 )        ; Negative Cache TTL
;
@   IN   NS   ns1.example.net.
@   IN   A    192.168.0.6
ns1 IN   A    192.168.0.5
www IN   A    192.168.0.7
gateway   IN   A   192.168.0.1
```

There are a number of things to note in this zone file. For one, I changed the TTL from seven days to one day. While I could have specified it in seconds, BIND supports shorthand, so I can use 1d to mean one day, or 4h to mean four hours. I set ns1.example.net as the SOA and root@example.net as the contact e-mail address. I also set ns1.example.net as the name server to use for this zone, but notice that the NS record references the name of the host. Since this name server is in the same domain, example.net, I needed to make sure I added a record for it here that listed its IP address. Also note that I didn't need to add .example.net to any of the A records.

NOTE Be sure once you save your zone file that it has the same permissions and ownership as the other zone files in the directory—that's the best way to avoid any permission headaches later on once you reload BIND.

Now that I have created the zone file, I need to add a reference to it in named.conf. When I open it with my text editor, I can see a number of similar zone examples such as the one for the db.local file:

```
zone "localhost" {
        type master;
      file "/etc/bind/db.local";
};
```

So I just add a similar entry to the very bottom of the file:

```
zone "example.net" {
        type master;
      file "/etc/bind/db.example.net";
};
```

Once I save my changes, I just need to tell BIND to reload its configuration, and then I should be able to query the name server for one of the new records:

```
$ sudo service bind9 reload
 * Reloading domain name server... bind          [OK]
$ nslookup www.example.net localhost
Server:         localhost
Address:        127.0.0.1#53

Name:    www.example.net
Address: 192.168.0.7
```

If the BIND reload fails, it will say so on the command line. If that command-line output doesn't tell you why BIND refuses to reload, you can view /var/log/syslog for clues.

DNS Slave

A DNS slave is a DNS server that retrieves its zone information from a different DNS server known as its master. In fact, a BIND server can act as a master for one zone and a slave for a different zone. Having a master and one or more slave servers greatly simplifies your DNS administration because you have to update zone information only on the master and it automatically propagates to the slaves. When you update a zone on the master server and increment the serial number inside that zone, once BIND reloads, all of the slaves get notified that the zone has changed and will automatically pull down the updates.

Since a slave DNS server retrieves its zone information from the master, its configuration is much simpler. Provided the master is configured to allow zone transfers from the slave, on the slave you simply have to add an entry to /etc/bind/named.conf. For our example, let's assume I wanted to add a second name server, ns2.example.net at 192.168.0.10.

Configure the Master Server   On my master server, 192.168.0.5, I would need to edit my db.example.net file and add the references to ns2.example .net:

```
;
; BIND data file for example.net
```

```
;
$TTL  1d
@    IN   SOA   ns1.example.net. root.example.net. (
                          3          ; Serial
                     604800          ; Refresh
                      86400          ; Retry
                    2419200          ; Expire
                     604800 )        ; Negative Cache TTL
;
@    IN   NS    ns1.example.net.
@    IN   NS    ns2.example.net.
@    IN   A     192.168.0.6
ns1  IN   A     192.168.0.5
ns2  IN   A     192.168.0.10
www  IN   A     192.168.0.7
gateway   IN    A    192.168.0.1
```

Now I need to add a line to the example.net configuration in named.conf so that it allows zone transfers from 192.168.0.10, so example.net's entry in named.conf becomes

```
zone "example.net" {
    type master;
    file "/etc/bind/db.example.net";
    allow-transfer { 192.168.0.10; };
};
```

Configure the Slave Server   On the slave server I install the bind9 package either through `tasksel` or `apt-get`, and then all I need to do is add a slave entry for example.net at the bottom of /etc/bind/named.conf:

```
zone "example.net" {
    type slave;
    file "/var/cache/bind/db.example.net";
    masters { 192.168.0.5; };
};
```

Reload BIND with `sudo service bind9 reload`. Once BIND reloads, it will immediately attempt a zone transfer for example.net from 192.168.0.5. When it completes the zone transfer, if I check the /var/cache/bind/ directory I will see that the db.example.net zone file was created there. Now the next time I want to make a change to db.example.net, I just have to change the file on the master, update the serial number, and then reload BIND on the master. The slave will automatically get the updates.

Manage BIND with rndc

So far I have reloaded BIND with the bind9 init script. Ubuntu includes another tool named `rndc` that helps you with BIND administration. For instance, to reload the BIND configuration using `rndc`, I would type

```
$ sudo rndc reload
```

You can pass a number of other arguments to `rndc` to get more information about the BIND service or submit commands to it. One useful aspect of the `rndc` command is that if you want an administrator to be able to update DNS but not have full root privileges, you can give that person `sudo` access to the `rndc` command. If you type `rndc` with no arguments, you will get a help page that lists the available commands. Here are some of the more interesting ones:

- `reload`—reloads all configuration files and zones. If you specify a specific zone after the `reload` command, it will reload only that zone.

- `retransfer zone`—retransfers the zone whether the serial number has been incremented or not.

- `reconfig`—like the `reload` command, except it only reloads named.conf and any new zones.

- `flush`—flushes all of a server's caches. This is handy on a caching name server if it is holding on to a stale IP address that is no longer valid.

- `status`—outputs some statistics about the current status of the BIND process, including how many zones it is managing and some statistics on its current workload.

There are numerous resources available if you want more information about BIND configuration file syntax or DNS administration in general. The bind9-doc package includes a series of documentation files under /usr/share/doc/bind9-doc/ that are a great place to start. For instance, to view the first chapter of the BIND version 9 HTML manual, type `w3m /usr/share/doc/bind9-doc/arm/Bv9ARM.ch01.html`.

Web Server

LAMP is an acronym for Linux Apache MySQL PHP (or sometimes Perl or Python). It refers to the recognition that a very common Web server deployment is a combination of the Apache Web server program using Perl, PHP, or Python for dynamic content and a MySQL database on the back end, all running on Linux. It has become such a common way to set up a Web site under Linux that even Ubuntu has grouped all of the necessary packages together.

The fact is, there are many different approaches to LAMP environments. With high-traffic Web sites often the Web servers run on different hardware from the MySQL database servers. Even if you select the LAMP server option at install, there might be extra Apache modules or other software you also need to install. I will cover MySQL servers in the Database Server section of this chapter, so if you plan to run a full LAMP environment on a single server, be sure to check out that section as well.

Install a Web Server

There are a few different ways to set up a Web server on a default Ubuntu server install. Probably the easiest method is to select LAMP Server during the initial install or afterward with the tasksel tool. This will add the apache2, apache2-mpm-prefork, mysql-server-5.1, mysql-client-5.1, and php5-mysql packages along with all of their libraries and other dependencies. Alternatively you could install each of these packages from the command line with

```
$ sudo apt-get install apache2 apache2-mpm-prefork \
mysql-server-5.1 mysql-client-5.1 php5-mysql
```

In either case the package manager will prompt you during the install to enter a root password for MySQL. This is an optional step, but I highly recommend you set the password at this point. For one thing, without a password, anyone on the system can access your databases and change and delete data. Another less technical reason is that it's simply easier to specify it at this stage than to run extra MySQL commands at the command line. Both the apache2 and mysql init scripts will be configured to start automatically at boot.

Now if your Web site does not use a MySQL back end, or you plan to run MySQL on a separate server, you can skip the `mysql-server-5.1` package:

```
$ sudo apt-get install apache2 apache2-mpm-prefork \
mysql-client-5.1 php5-mysql
```

Ubuntu Apache Conventions

Like most other distributions, Ubuntu has certain conventions when it comes to Apache administration. Configuration files are organized in a particular way, as are administrative tools and logs. If you aren't used to the way that Debian and Ubuntu organize Apache, it is quite different from what you may have seen on other distributions. Here are the major file conventions for Apache:

- **/etc/apache2**
  All Apache configuration files can be found under this directory. Traditionally Apache was configured via one large httpd.conf file containing scores of options, settings, and different virtual hosts. Of course, if you were to simply start with the httpd.conf file here, you would discover that it is empty. Ubuntu has moved away from the monolithic httpd.conf model and has split up its configuration across a number of files and subdirectories.

- **/etc/apache2/apache2.conf**
  This is the main Apache configuration file used by Ubuntu's `apache2` binary. The default apache2.conf is heavily commented, so it works well as a guide in and of itself to each configuration option and what it does.

- **/etc/apache2/envvars**
  There are a number of environment variables used by different scripts when Apache starts that define settings like the location of PID files. Those environment variables are defined here.

- **/etc/apache2/ports.conf**
  This file is used to define which ports Apache listens on when it starts. The default settings have it listen on the standard port 80 and additionally port 443 if the SSL module is enabled.

- **/etc/apache2/conf.d/**
  This directory is listed as an included directory in the main apache2.conf file, which means that when Apache starts it will also include any configuration files found in this directory and add them to the overall configuration. Some administrators (such as yours truly) have in the past used this directory to store all of their virtual hosts, each separated in its own file, but Ubuntu now has a better solution, which is mentioned later in the chapter. Instead of containing virtual host entries, this directory is used for additional Apache options an administrator (or a package) might want to add separately from the core apache2.conf.

- **/etc/apache2/mods-available/**
  It always used to be such a pain to add modules to Apache. Once the module itself was installed, you had to dig through a huge httpd.conf file and locate a possibly commented-out reference to include the module and most of the time also had to paste in some sort of IfModule logic as well just to make it load. Ubuntu offers a simpler, more modular approach. All of the modules that are available on the system are represented within this directory by .load and .conf files. The .load files contain all of the configuration necessary to load the modules into Apache, and the optional .conf files contain any extra configuration Apache may need to use the file after it is loaded. If you are wondering what modules you have available for your Apache install, you just need to glance in this directory.

- **/etc/apache2/mods-enabled/**
  This directory operates much like the different runlevel directories in System V init, so if mods-available is like your init.d directory, this directory is like rcS.d (if you aren't sure what I mean by that, check out my description of System V init in Chapter 2). Basically this directory contains symlinks to .load and .conf files in the mods-available directory. When Apache starts, it will scan this directory and load all of the modules referenced within. So if I wanted to enable the CGI module, for instance, I could type

```
$ sudo ln -s /etc/apache2/mod-available/cgi.load \
/etc/apache2/mods-enabled/cgi.load
```

Of course, Ubuntu even provides tools to simplify that. To enable a module, just run `a2enmod` followed by the module you want to enable. To enable the CGI module as I did above, I just run

```
$ sudo a2enmod cgi
```

Likewise, there is an `a2dismod` program that will disable a module for you. It takes the same syntax as `a2enmod`, so to disable CGI type

```
$ sudo a2dismod cgi
```

▪ **/etc/apache2/sites-available/**
Ubuntu organizes Apache virtual hosts similarly to modules. Before Apache was created, the available Web server software on the market could host only a single site per physical server. Apache introduced the concept of virtual hosts, which allowed it to host multiple sites on the same physical server. Each virtual host could have a completely different domain name with a completely different document root. Under Ubuntu, each virtual host, or site, that is available to be served by Apache on this machine has its configuration in a separate file under sites-available. By default the only file in there is the aptly named default file that defines the default virtual host that will show up if no others are configured, or if no other site's configuration matches the hostname that is requested.

▪ **/etc/apache2/sites-enabled/**
Like mods-enabled, this directory contains symlinks to configuration files in sites-available. So when you want to add a new virtual host to Apache, just create a new configuration file for that host that contains a complete `<VirtualHost>` block under sites-available and symlink it here:

```
$ sudo ln -s /etc/apache2/sites-available/mysite \
/etc/apache2/sites-enabled/mysite
```

Or you can use the `a2ensite` script that works just like `a2enmod`. Just run a2enmod with the site you wish to enable as an argument. To enable `mysite` I would type

```
$ sudo a2ensite mysite
```

and to disable it I can use `a2dissite`:

```
$ sudo a2dissite mysite
```

The default site is a special case in that it prepends `000` to its symlink under sites-enabled to make sure that it loads first and works properly as the default virtual host.

- **/var/www/**
  This is the default document root for Apache. Any HTML file that is readable by Apache and placed in this directory will be available once you point a Web browser at the server. There is already a default index.html in that directory.

- **/usr/lib/cgi-bin/**
  This is the default location for CGI scripts. Any scripts referenced on the Web server by /cgi-bin will point here.

- **/var/log/apache2/**
  This is the standard directory where Apache logs are stored. The access.log file contains information about what files have been accessed on the Web server, and the error.log file lists any Apache errors. If, for instance, you have trouble starting Apache, look in error.log for clues.

apache2ctl

The `/usr/sbin/apache2ctl` program is the primary command-line program you will use to manage Apache under Ubuntu. The syntax for the command is fairly straightforward. Run `apache2ctl` from the command line and pass a single command to it as an argument. The simple commands `start`, `stop`, and `restart` will, as you might imagine, start, stop, and restart the Apache process respectively. You could also achieve the same functionality with the `apache2` init script, so three commands that do the same thing are

```
$ sudo apache2ctl restart
$ sudo /etc/init.d/apache2 restart
$ sudo service apache2 restart
```

Stop Apache Gracefully   There is a potential risk associated with the restart and stop commands. When you restart or stop Apache with these commands, all currently running Apache processes are killed, even if they are in the middle of serving files to a user. If you issue a restart when a user is in the middle of loading a page, it will only load as much information as it currently has and then stall—forcing the user to reload the page. To avoid this, apache2ctl has provided the graceful and graceful-stop commands. These commands respectively restart and stop Apache, but when they do, they wait for each process to finish any outstanding requests first. On an active site a graceful restart shouldn't even be noticed by anyone using the service. In general, unless you know that a site is not actively serving traffic (or unless you don't care whether all active connections are closed), you should use graceful and graceful-stop. The only exception is when you add new SSL certificates to a site or make other changes that do require a full Apache restart to take effect.

Diagnostic apache2ctl Commands   The other main commands for apache2ctl provide more diagnostic features. The first, configtest, will test your current Apache configuration files for errors. This can be very useful if you decide to automate the deployment of your Apache scripts. One challenge when you set up a script to deploy configuration files and restart Apache is that if you have made a mistake in your configuration files, Apache might not start back up. If you deploy the same file to your entire Web farm, you could potentially bring the entire farm down with a single syntax error and a script that blindly deploys and restarts Apache. With configtest, you can set up logic in your deployment scripts that restarts Apache only once a server has passed the configtest.

As an Apache server gets traffic, you typically want to get diagnostic information from it, such as how many Apache processes are active and what those processes are doing, and how many open slots you still have available. The status and fullstatus apache2ctl commands provide you with a lot of great diagnostic data. The status command outputs a general-purpose overall status of your Apache server, including how long the server has been up, how many requests are active, and how many processes are idle, and in addition outputs an ASCII art map of all available processes with different letters representing different process states, as shown in Figure 5-1. The fullstatus command outputs similar information, just more of it and in more detail.

```
tu@kickseed:~$ apache2ctl status
_W__he Server Status for localhost
....
....er Version: Apache/2.2.8 (Ubuntu) PHP/5.2.4-2ubuntu5.4 with Suhosin-Patch
....er Built: Jun 25 2008 13:54:13
Scor_____
" "
"W" ent Time: Tuesday, 06-Jan-2009 20:04:20 PST
"C" art Time: Tuesday, 06-Jan-2009 19:01:33 PST
"I" nt Server Generation: 0
    er uptime: 1 hour 2 minutes 47 seconds
PID quests currently being processed, 4 idle workers

    4_..........................................................................
    4............................................................................
    ............................................................................
    ............................................................................
To o
Exteeboard Key:
____Waiting for Connection, "S" Starting up, "R" Reading Request,
    Sending Reply, "K" Keepalive (read), "D" DNS Lookup,
ApacClosing connection, "L" Logging, "G" Gracefully finishing,
localdle cleanup of worker, "." Open slot with no current process
ubuntu@kickseed:~$ _
```

Figure 5-1 `apache2ctl` status output

Apache Documentation

While this guide is good enough to get you started, as you develop complicated Web sites of your own, you will need more complete Apache documentation. Entire books have been written about Apache configuration,
but you can also get great documentation directly from your Ubuntu
server. Just install the `apache2-doc` package:

```
$ sudo apt-get install apache2-doc
```

This package installs the Apache documentation under /usr/share/doc/
apache2-doc/manual in HTML files. You could use `w3m` on these files
directly, but why not use your desktop's Web browser instead? The default
Apache virtual host is configured to point to this directory for you. Just
browse to the /manual/ folder on your Web server. For example, if my Web
server were at 192.168.0.5, I could go to http://192.168.0.5/manual/ in a
Web browser and view the complete documentation.

WordPress, a Sample LAMP Environment

There are any number of different Web sites you can set up on an Ubuntu
LAMP stack, but to illustrate how easy it is to set up a new site under

Ubuntu, I walk you step by step through a common LAMP deployment—a WordPress install. WordPress is popular blogging software that is packaged by Ubuntu and provides a nice, feature-rich platform for one or multiple blogs.

Install WordPress   In this example I run both the Web server and the MySQL database on the same host, named blog.example.net, so I chose the LAMP Server task during the install. I've also already made sure that blog.example.net is set up in my DNS server to point to this particular Web server. Next I use a package manager to install the WordPress package, which will pull down the WordPress software along with any extra libraries it needs:

```
$ sudo apt-get install wordpress
```

Configure Apache   There are a few different ways you can configure Apache for use with WordPress, and the included example Apache file at /usr/share/doc/wordpress/example/apache.conf provides the main options you are looking for. The first example in the file provides the best all-around case because it makes it easy to host multiple WordPress blogs on the same site. Save the following configuration under /etc/apache2/sites-available/wordpress:

```
NameVirtualHost *:80

<VirtualHost *:80>
UseCanonicalName    Off
VirtualDocumentRoot /var/www/%0
Options All
</VirtualHost>
```

With the configuration file in place I use a2ensite to enable the site and a2dissite to disable any default sites that might be there:

```
$ sudo a2ensite wordpress
$ sudo a2dissite default
```

Since the configuration uses the VirtualDocumentRoot option, I need to make sure that the vhost_alias module is enabled, so I use the a2enmod command:

```
$ sudo a2enmod vhost_alias
```

NOTE   How did I know that `VirtualDocumentRoot` needed the `vhost_alias` module? Well, for
one thing, if you try to reload Apache without the module, Apache will complain about the
unknown configuration option. At that point a quick Web search on `VirtualDocument-
Root` will point you to the `vhost_alias` module as the one that provides that feature.

Now I need to create a symlink for my Web site under /var/www and point
it to the root WordPress directory that contains all of the PHP files. If I
wanted to host multiple WordPress sites, I could potentially create multiple symlinks here.

```
$ sudo ln -s /usr/share/wordpress /var/www/blog.example.net
```

Now I can reload Apache:

```
$ sudo apache2ctl graceful
```

Configure MySQL   WordPress provides a simple script under /usr/share/
doc/wordpress/examples/setup-mysql that will set up a WordPress MySQL
configuration for the specified MySQL user and domain name for the Web
site:

```
$ sudo bash /usr/share/doc/wordpress/examples/setup-mysql \
-n wordpress blog.example.net
```

That's it. The blog is ready to be used. All I need to do at this point is open
http://blog.example.net in a Web browser and I will be greeted with the
WordPress install Web page as shown in Figure 5-2. The final step is to
enter your site name and e-mail address in the fields provided and click
the large button that says Install WordPress. The database will then be set
up for your site and a new page will load that lists your admin username
and temporary password as well as a link to log in to your blog. At this
point the rest of the configuration is up to you. You can change themes,
create a Hello World post, install plug-ins, or, even better, change your
password to something you can remember.

Figure 5-2 WordPress Web install page

Mail Server

Along with the Web, e-mail is probably the service most people think of when they think of the Internet. Like Web servers, mail servers have traditionally been pretty tricky to set up, and there are many guides and books on the subject. You will find, though, that mail servers are pretty easy to set up and use under Ubuntu. Now there are a number of different mail servers one can choose from, but for this section I am going to discuss Postfix. For one reason, it is the default mail server Ubuntu uses when you select "Mail server" in tasksel. Second, it is a good, secure, easy-to-administer mail server.

Install Postfix

Postfix can be installed with the same methods used by many of the other services I mention in this chapter. You can choose Mail Server either during the initial install or when you run the tasksel program, or alternatively you can type

```
$ sudo apt-get install postfix
```

When you install Postfix, the installer will start the initial Postfix configuration script. This is an interactive script that provides you with a few common mail server configuration types, and depending on what you choose, it will ask you a few more questions so that when you are finished, you should at least have a functional mail server. Keep in mind, though, that even though the mail server will function, you will have to perform extra configuration if you want to add spam checking, greylisting, POP or IMAP servers, or other more advanced options.

Postfix Configuration Types

If this is your first exposure to a Postfix mail server configuration, you might not be sure exactly which mail server configuration type to choose. Here are the different configuration types along with why you might want to choose them:

- **No configuration**
  This option does no Postfix configuration at all. Choose this option if you already have a Postfix configuration file you want to add, or if you want to build the configuration file from scratch.

- **Internet site**
  This option creates a basic mail server that can receive incoming mail directly from the Internet and also can send e-mail directly to other mail servers on the Internet. Choose this option if you need a basic mail server, and this server will not be prohibited (by firewall or other network configuration) from sending and receiving e-mail over the Internet.

- **Internet with smarthost**
  This option is a lot like the Internet site except that all outgoing e-mail is sent via a smarthost. A smarthost is another e-mail server that acts as a sort of proxy for e-mail. Organizations often use a smarthost so that they have a single e-mail server that has outbound e-mail access. This way they can centralize outbound spam and virus scans and can firewall off the rest of the e-mail servers from directly sending e-mail over the Internet. Don't forget to confirm that the smarthost is configured to accept e-mail from this new server.

▪ **Satellite system**

This configuration option forwards both outgoing *and* incoming mail through a smarthost. You might select this option if you want to provide mail server redundancy. Your smarthost could be the ultimate destination for e-mail and could act to send out all outbound mail, but your satellite system could be your primary, secondary, or tertiary mail server that can help offset the load from your smarthost.

▪ **Local only**

If you choose this option, this server will deliver only local mail such as e-mail sent to root from cron processes or other e-mail sent to a local user from another local user. The server will not accept any mail from the network. Choose this option if you want to use Postfix as your local mail server but don't intend to send or accept any e-mail from the rest of the network.

Depending on which configuration you choose for Postfix, you will be prompted to select a hostname the mail server will use for outgoing mail. This may or may not be the same as your server's hostname. This is the hostname that Postfix will use to label outgoing e-mail. So, for instance, if you named your server zeus internally, but on the Internet the host will be referred to as mail2.example.com, then you would put mail2.example.com in this field.

Ubuntu Postfix Conventions

There aren't too many surprises with Ubuntu's Postfix conventions, but the following are the major directories and files used by Postfix under Ubuntu:

▪ **/etc/postfix/**

This directory contains all of the major Postfix configurations. Of course, programs that work with Postfix, like spam filters and greylisting software, will typically store their configuration elsewhere.

▪ **/etc/postfix/main.cf**

This is the main Postfix configuration file. The upstream main.cf is heavily commented and lists all of the major options, their defaults, and nice descriptions. It's great when you want to learn about Postfix, but it can be cumbersome to actually use as a configuration file. Because of this, the Ubuntu install script for the Postfix package generates its own smaller main.cf file, although you can still reference the fully commented version at /usr/share/postfix/main.cf.dist.

- **/etc/aliases**
  This file contains a mapping of user aliases Postfix will reference for mail delivery. The basic syntax is essentially username1: username2, which tells Postfix to redirect mail addressed to username1 to username2. You can also redirect mail to piped commands to do more sophisticated redirection.

- **/var/spool/mail/**
  This directory by default contains the mailboxes for each user on the system. By default Postfix will use the mbox format, so every e-mail for a user will be in a single file under this directory named after the user. This, of course, could change if you install POP or IMAP servers or store mail in Maildirs instead, but more on that in the POP/IMAP section of the chapter.

- **/var/spool/postfix/**
  Postfix stores many different subdirectories within this directory and uses them to organize mail that is being spooled by the system either for delivery on the server or delivery to a different mail server. Generally speaking, you won't want to meddle in this directory. Postfix provides tools you can use to get information on the current mail spool.

- **/var/log/mail.***
  Postfix logs are organized into a few different log files under Ubuntu so you can more easily find the information you need. The mail.log file stores all mail logs, so if you aren't sure what other logs to check (or are going to just use grep to find the information you need anyway), use this log file. Similarly, the mail.info log contains all of the informational logs such as new mail that has been queued, log entries for each transaction with a remote server, and other common log entries. The mail.err and mail.warn files segregate out errors or

warnings from the rest of the Postfix logs, respectively, so look here if you want a quick view of errors or warnings.

▪ **/etc/init.d/postfix**
This is Postfix's init script and should automatically be set up to start at system start-up.

Administering Postfix

The main tool you will use to administer Postfix is aptly named `postfix`. It works much like `apache2ctl` in that it accepts a few different commands as arguments and can also be used as a substitute for the init script to start and stop the service. For instance, to stop Postfix and then start it back up, you would type

```
$ sudo postfix stop
$ sudo postfix start
```

The other commands generally work the same way. Here are the major commands you can pass to Postfix along with their functions:

▪ **reload**
Use this command whenever you have made changes to the Postfix configuration and want to load it. This operates much like the `apache2ctl graceful` function in that it allows each process to terminate and reload when it can, so it is much safer and provides a much smoother process than if you were to stop and then start Postfix.

▪ **flush**
This command tells Postfix to flush its mail queue. Typically Postfix spaces out its mail delivery so as not to throttle the network, and when a message gets deferred for some reason, it will be delayed in the queue for some time before Postfix attempts redelivery. Sometimes you will have some issue, such as a network outage, that causes a large number of e-mails to spool on the server, and once the problem is remedied you would like to deliver them. When you use the `flush` command, Postfix forces delivery of all of the deferred messages immediately. Generally speaking, you should let Postfix spool and

deliver messages on its own schedule, so use this command only if you really need it.

▪ **status**
Returns the current Postfix status. If Postfix is running, this command also returns the PID of the master process.

▪ **abort**
This is a more forceful version of the `stop` command and immediately kills all running Postfix processes whether they are finished or not.

▪ **check**
This command is much like `apache2ctl check`. It scans the Postfix directory structure for bad file or directory permissions and warns you about and corrects any problems it finds.

In addition to the Postfix command-line tool, Postfix provides a few other tools to help administration of the service. The `postqueue` command can be used by regular users to get information about the current mail queue. This is useful so that you can keep track of deferred messages and answer the "I sent this e-mail two hours ago and the recipient said they didn't get it. What happened?" questions. For instance, to get a full listing of all messages currently in the queue, type

```
$ postqueue -p
```

Sometimes you want to take action on messages in the queue besides simply flushing them. Occasionally you might want to delete a message (or maybe even all messages) in the queue. The `postsuper` command allows a superuser to perform privileged operations on the queue. For instance, to delete a message in the queue with a queue ID of 522, you would type

```
$ sudo postsuper -d 522
```

If you actually did want to delete all messages in the queue, you can use the word ALL in uppercase instead of a particular queue ID. You might also want to put a message on hold so that Postfix keeps it in the queue but doesn't attempt to deliver it. Use the -h option followed by the queue ID to put a message on hold and then use the -H option with the same queue ID to put the message back in the queue.

Previously I discussed the /etc/alias file and how it is used to map one username to another for mail delivery. The /etc/alias file is actually just for humans to edit. Postfix doesn't directly read it. Instead, it creates a database out of that file that it can reference much more quickly. Whenever you edit that file, type sudo newaliases to update the /etc/alias.db file. In addition, for some more advanced Postfix configuration such as canonical maps, virtual accounts, or other features, you will have a separate file within /etc/postfix that also needs a database. You can identify these files in the main.cf file as their paths are preceded by hash:. If you do create or edit one of these lookup tables, run sudo postmap /path/to/file. If I set up virtual users in /etc/postfix/virtual, I would update the database with

```
$ sudo postmap /etc/postfix/virtual
```

Finally, there are occasions when you are tweaking your main.cf file and want to see what the current and active setting is on the running instance of Postfix. The postconf command outputs every (and I mean every) Postfix setting to the screen along with its value. So if I wanted to see the current value of myhostname in the running config, I could type

```
$ sudo postconf | grep ^myhostname
myhostname = mail1.example.net
```

Default Postfix Example

One of the great things about the Postfix install script is that once you have completed it, you should have a functioning mail server. Of course, depending on how you plan to use the server, there might still be more configuration to do. While there is almost infinite tuning and tweaking you can perform with Postfix, there are a number of common configuration options you will want to look into. I cover some of the major options and then provide a few examples of different mail server configurations.

For all of these examples, I start with a basic main.cf file for an Internet site set up by the Postfix install script. This configuration accepts mail from the local network as well as mail sent to example.org and mail1.example.org. Here is the full main.cf file:

```
# See /usr/share/postfix/main.cf.dist for a commented, more
complete version


# Debian specific:  Specifying a filename will cause the first
# line of that file to be used as the name.  The Debian default
# is /etc/mailname.
#myorigin = /etc/mailname

smtpd_banner = $myhostname ESMTP $mail_name (Ubuntu)
biff = no

# appending .domain is the MUA's job.
append_dot_mydomain = no

# Uncomment the next line to generate "delayed mail" warnings
#delay_warning_time = 4h

readme_directory = no

# TLS parameters
smtpd_tls_cert_file=/etc/ssl/certs/ssl-cert-snakeoil.pem
smtpd_tls_key_file=/etc/ssl/private/ssl-cert-snakeoil.key
smtpd_use_tls=yes
smtpd_tls_session_cache_database =
btree:${data_directory}/smtpd_scache
smtp_tls_session_cache_database =
btree:${data_directory}/smtp_scache

# See /usr/share/doc/postfix/TLS_README.gz in the postfix-doc
# package for information on enabling SSL in the smtp client.

myhostname = mail1.example.org
alias_maps = hash:/etc/aliases
alias_database = hash:/etc/aliases
myorigin = /etc/mailname
mydestination = mail1.example.org, example.org,
localhost.example.org, localhost
relayhost =
mynetworks = 127.0.0.0/8 [::ffff:127.0.0.0]/104 [::1]/128
mailbox_size_limit = 0
recipient_delimiter = +
inet_interfaces = all
```

The beginning of the file mostly sets Ubuntu defaults that differ from standard Postfix defaults. The core configuration for you to tweak starts at myhostname. To get full documentation on each of these options, type man 5 postconf. That manual contains all of the Postfix configuration options along with a description of their use. Here are a few of the options in the sample configuration file that you will use frequently:

▪ **myhostname**
This is the Internet hostname of the mail server. If you haven't set it explicitly in this file, it will use gethostname() and use that value. A number of other options, such as myorigin, will use or reference the myhostname value if it isn't explicitly set.

▪ **myorigin**
The domain name listed here is the domain that mail sent from this machine appears to come from. If, for instance, your server is named mail1.example.org but you want e-mail sent from it to appear to come from example.org, you would set this value to example.org.

▪ **mydestination**
This is a list of domain names for which this mail server will accept mail and consider itself the final destination. If mail arrives on this server addressed to one of these domains, Postfix will deliver it locally.

▪ **relayhost**
In this example this value is blank, but if you did want to route all of your outbound mail through a different mail server, you would set this value to the hostname of that server. You might use this value on all of your servers in a data center so they all point to a single outbound mail host. You could then more tightly control firewall access and have a single choke point from which to view all outbound messages.

▪ **mynetworks**
This value is a comma-separated list of networks (IP addresses and subnet masks) for which this server will relay mail. Be very careful with this value! If you were to set this to too broad a value and allow

random hosts on the Internet to relay through your server, you will have just set up what's known as an open relay. Open relays are often used by spammers to relay their spam, and if you mistakenly make your server an open relay it won't take long for someone to discover it and for your server to be put on a spam blackhole list. Generally speaking, this will be set to `localhost` and possibly your internal network interface if you want to allow other hosts on your network to relay mail through you.

- **mailbox_size_limit**
  This option sets the maximum value of any local user's mailbox. The default in this example sets it to `unlimited`.

Secondary Mail Server

The default example I gave will work fine as a default Internet mail server for a small domain, such as your own personal mail server. Once you set up a mail server that accepts messages for a domain and you start to rely on it, you should consider setting up a secondary mail server to act as a backup. If you have only one mail server and it goes down for some reason, any host that wants to deliver mail to it will ideally queue the messages for a few days. If the server does not come back up in a set amount of time, though, the messages will bounce back to the sender as undeliverable. Each administrator might set up his or her mail server to bounce after a different period of time. Postfix by default will set this to five days via the `bounce_queue_lifetime` option.

To avoid bounced messages, you will want to set up at least one additional mail server that can accept and spool mail for your domain. This server will then deliver the messages to the primary mail server once it is back up.

It's actually pretty easy to set up a secondary mail server with Ubuntu and Postfix. First we will start with the Internet site install-time option which will give you a main.cf much like the one I listed above. At this point the only other option you really need to add to the main.cf is the `relay_domains` option. This option defines the domains for which this machine will accept and relay mail. So, for instance, if you wanted to set up a secondary mail server for example.org and example.net, you would set this value to

```
relay_domains = example.org, example.net
```

Once you reload this configuration with `postfix reload`, all you need to do to start using the secondary mail server is to add an MX record to your domain's DNS zone and be sure that its priority number is larger than the primary mail server's. If my primary mail server is mail1.example.org and the secondary is mail2.example.org, the zone entries might look like the following:

```
example.org.   IN    MX    100     mail1.example.org.
example.org.   IN    MX    200     mail2.example.org.
```

Once the DNS changes have propagated, your mail server will start to be used. One final setting you may want to consider for your secondary mail server is an increase in the number of days it will queue mail before it bounces. If you know that a primary mail server will be down for more than five days, you might want to increase the limit so that the secondary mail server will still hold mail for you until the primary mail server comes back online. To increase the queue limit to two weeks, for instance, add the following settings to your /etc/postfix/main.cf:

```
bounce_queue_lifetime = 14d
maximal_queue_lifetime = 14d
```

Once the primary server does come back online, run `postfix flush` on the secondary server so that it immediately starts delivering all of the deferred messages.

Greylisting Mail Server

Spam is a definite problem for just about every mail server administrator. There are many solutions out there to help cut down on the amount of spam a server receives, and one such concept is known as *greylisting*.

Greylisting is based on the notion that since spammers send out millions of e-mails, they generally don't set up a deferred queue if an e-mail is not immediately delivered. There is a special response in the SMTP protocol called 450 that basically says, "Please come back later." Most legitimate mail servers on the Internet will honor that request and come back later. Most spammers won't. With greylisting, your mail server will respond to all new mail servers with a 450 command. Once a server does come back, the greylisting program makes a note of it in a local database of servers, To:, and From: addresses. That means (depending on how many successes you configured before a server is whitelisted) that after a server waits once, it won't have to wait anymore in the future.

There are a number of different programs that implement greylisting for Ubuntu, but one of the simplest to set up with Postfix is called Postgrey. It implements greylisting as I mentioned above and also includes whitelists for major mail servers that are known to not work well with greylisting; it also allows you to whitelist servers so that they never see the initial delay.

Install and Configure Postgrey   To install Postgrey, use your package manager to install the package of the same name:

```
$ sudo apt-get install postgrey
```

The Postgrey program is started via an init script at start-up and listens on the local 10023 port for queries from Postfix. Once it is installed and running, all you need to do is modify the `smtpd_recipient_restrictions` option in Postfix's main.cf to add the localhost:10023 service. If you haven't tweaked your `smtpd_recipient_restrictions` setting at all, here's a sample that should work for you:

```
smtpd_recipient_restrictions = permit_mynetworks, \
        permit_sasl_authenticated, \
        reject_unauth_destination, \
        check_policy_service inet:127.0.0.1:10023
```

Once you add that option, reload Postfix and it will start implementing greylisting immediately. If you aren't too familiar with greylisting, then this should work well for you to start. If you do wish to tweak the whitelists, for instance, the default Postgrey configuration is stored under /etc/postgrey. The `whitelist_clients` and `whitelist_recipients` are provided by the Postgrey package and have some good defaults set. If you would like to add additional entries, create a whitelist_clients.local or whitelist_ recipients .local file so you can keep your settings separated. Then type sudo service postgrey reload so Postgrey will reload its settings. If you would like more specific information on configuration file syntax or other Postgrey options, check out the documentation under /usr/share/doc/postgrey/.

POP/IMAP Server

Most people who set up mail servers no longer actually log in to the mail server to retrieve the mail. They generally use some sort of mail client that then connects to some destination mail server and retrieves mail via POP or IMAP. With POP, the messages are downloaded and removed from the server as you access them, whereas with IMAP the messages continue to be stored on the server. Ultimately it's good to provide both as options, but these days most people prefer IMAP so they can connect to the mail server from multiple clients and still see all of their mail.

There are a number of different packages that provide POP and IMAP support, and choosing one is at least partially a matter of preference. For this example I cover the Dovecot POP and IMAP servers, as they integrate well with Postfix, support Maildirs, and have a number of additional packages available that provide more advanced features such as LDAP, MySQL, and Postgres support. The steps are pretty simple. They start with enabling Maildirs on Postfix, then installing Dovecot.

Enable Maildirs on Postfix

There are a number of different ways that mail servers can store e-mails. For a long time the primary format for mail storage was the mbox format. With the mbox format, all of a user's mail is stored in a single large text file. This method works; however, it's not without its shortcomings. For one, with an mbox all of your eggs are in one basket. If that file is corrupted, so are all of your e-mails.

Nowadays in addition to the mbox format mail is often stored in databases (Exchange) or in a Maildir. A Maildir basically breaks up each e-mail folder into its own directory on a host. Within that directory are subdirectories to store new and read e-mail. Within those subdirectories each e-mail is stored as its own text file. The nice thing about Maildirs is that there is already a large number of tools on any Linux system to parse through and manage files, making it simple to find an individual e-mail on the system and back it up, delete it, or copy it.

To enable Maildirs under Postfix, you just need to set the `home_mailbox` option to specify the directory name you will use for your Maildirs. Open /etc/postfix/main.cf and add the following option:

```
home_mailbox = Maildir/
```

Be sure to remember the trailing / after the directory name, as it is needed when you use Maildirs. In this example Postfix will use the Maildir directory in each person's home directory to store e-mail. Once you have made the change, type `sudo postfix reload` to reload the configuration. At this point all new e-mail will be delivered to the Maildir directory in the local user's home directory. If the directory doesn't exist, Postfix will create it.

Install Dovecot

All of the Dovecot packages you need are available by default in Ubuntu. If you installed Postfix during the install or afterwards with tasksel, the Dovecot packages are included. Otherwise, you can just use your package manager to install them. The packages I will install will enable POP, POP with SSL, IMAP, and IMAP with SSL:

```
$ sudo apt-get install dovecot-imapd dovecot-pop3d
```

By default Dovecot will be set up for POP, POP with SSL, IMAP, and IMAP with SSL. If for some reason you want to disable any of these options, open Dovecot's default configuration file, /etc/dovecot/dovecot.conf, and locate the line that says

```
protocols = imap imaps pop3 pop3s
```

Just remove any of the protocols you don't want enabled and run `sudo /etc/init.d/dovecot reload` to enable the changes. The next step is to tell Dovecot to use Maildirs and also let it know where it can find them on the system. To do this, see if there is already an uncommented line that starts with `mail_location` (in the default install it's commented out). If it doesn't

exist, then add the following line; if it does exist, then modify the `mail_`
`location` line so that it looks like the following:

```
mail_location = maildir:~/Maildir
```

Then reload Dovecot with `sudo /etc/init.d/dovecot reload`. Now you
should be able to configure your mail clients to point to the server and
access their local mail.

NOTE   By default Dovecot is configured to use the system's local accounts. Note, however, that it
will allow you to use plain-text authentication only if you do so over a secure protocol like
IMAPS or POP3S. If you want to use IMAP or POP3 with plain-text passwords and don't
have a problem with user passwords being transmitted over the wire unencrypted, then set
the configuration option `disable_plaintext_auth` in dovecot.conf to no:

```
disable_plaintext_auth = no
```

then reload Dovecot so it takes the new changes.

Ubuntu Dovecot Conventions

▪ **/etc/dovecot/**
    This is the default configuration directory for Dovecot and contains
    all of the configuration files, including dovecot.conf, the main file you
    will use to configure the service.

▪ **/etc/init.d/dovecot**
    This is Dovecot's init script. The script is set up at install time to auto-
    matically start at system start-up.

▪ **/var/log/syslog and /var/log/mail.log**
    Dovecot sends copies of its logs to both of these files so you can use
    either to look for errors or monitor logins.

OpenSSH Server

While I can understand why this service is not installed by default, most
system administrators these days use SSH to remotely manage their
servers. SSH provides you with a secure encrypted channel so that you can
log in and execute commands on a remote machine. In addition to the

standard remote console uses, SSH also allows a number of interesting hacks so that you can set up tunnels, run remote X applications, and do all sorts of other interesting tricks. It seems an article on a new SSH trick shows up online every few days.

To install OpenSSH, you can either select OpenSSH Server during the task selection process in the installer, run `sudo tasksel` after the install and select it there, or run

```
$ sudo apt-get install openssh-server
```

Once the package is installed, the `sshd` process will start. To log in to the server from a remote host, type

```
$ ssh username@hostname
```

Replace `username` and `hostname` with your username on the machine and the hostname or IP address of the machine, respectively. Once you log in over SSH, you can run commands on the remote server as though you were on the machine with a keyboard and mouse. To log out of a current SSH session, just type `exit` in the terminal.

Ubuntu OpenSSH Conventions

- **/etc/ssh/**
  This directory contains all of the major configuration files for both the OpenSSH server and the client.

- **/etc/ssh/ssh_config**
  This file defines the default client settings for SSH clients on this machine. Local users can override these options with their own options in ~/.ssh/config.

- **/etc/ssh/sshd_config**
  In this file you will find the default settings for the SSH server. It's worth noting that by default root logins over SSH are enabled, even though Ubuntu doesn't set up root logins on the system itself by default. If you want to disable root logins, edit the file and set the `PermitRootLogin` value to `no`.

- **/etc/ssh/ssh_host_dsa_key and /etc/ssh/ssh_host_dsa_key.pub**
  These files provide the private and public DSA keys for the system, respectively. These keys are used to authenticate the system so that you can better detect man-in-the-middle attacks.

- **/etc/ssh/ssh_host_rsa and /etc/ssh/ssh_host_rsa.pub**
  These files are like the DSA keys I mentioned above, only they are created using the RSA algorithm instead.

- **/etc/init.d/ssh**
  This is the init script for the OpenSSH server and provides the standard `start`, `stop`, and `restart` commands as well as `reload` and `force-reload` commands for when you change its configuration files.

- **/var/log/auth.log**
  The OpenSSH server will log its information to this log file, including informational messages, errors, and user logins.

DHCP Server

It's easy to take DHCP for granted these days. After all, even the most basic home wireless routers seem to provide a DHCP server as part of the firmware, and most corporate networks seem to use DHCP, at least for desktops. If you've ever had to administer a large network of desktop machines without DHCP, though, you probably recall the pain of manually entering static IP information into Windows desktop after Windows desktop.

DHCP stands for Dynamic Host Control Protocol, and with this protocol a new host on the network can issue a request for IP information. The DHCP server will then provide the host with all of the necessary information it needs to communicate on the network, such as its IP address and netmask and the gateway and DNS servers to use.

Install DHCP

To install a DHCP server under Ubuntu, type

```
$ sudo apt-get install dhcp3-server
```

Ubuntu DHCP Conventions

- **/etc/dhcp3/dhcpd.conf**
  This is the configuration file for the DHCP server. By default it is a heavily commented file that should provide plenty of examples for you to work from.

- **/var/lib/dhcp3/dhcpd.leases**
  This file contains the current list of DHCP leases your server has handed out. If you are wondering what MAC address got a particular IP, or when a particular lease will expire, look in this file.

- **/var/log/syslog**
  DHCP uses the standard syslog file for all of its logs. Here you will be able to find any requests from the network for a DHCP request along with the DHCP server's reply.

Configure DHCP

Ubuntu provides a heavily commented DHCP configuration file that explains all of the major options and gives a number of different configuration examples. For basic DHCP services you generally want to set up one or possibly two scenarios: dynamic DHCP and static DHCP. In a dynamic DHCP configuration new hosts get assigned an IP out of a possible range of IPs. There's no guarantee a host will get assigned the same IP every time. With static DHCP you can bind a particular IP address to a host's MAC address and ensure that every time it shows up on the network it will get the same IP. Dynamic DHCP is good for a simple, easy-to-maintain DHCP server, and static DHCP gives you a lot of the benefits of static IPs without nearly as many headaches. Plus with static IPs, if you do want to change the IP address of a host, you can do so in the dhcpd.conf file and reload DHCP instead of having to track down and change the host.

For both of my examples I set up DHCP for a local office network, example.net, on 10.1.1.0, subnet 255.255.255.0. The gateway is at 10.1.1.1 and the name servers are at 10.1.1.2 and 10.1.1.3.

Dynamic DHCP Configuration   To set up dynamic DHCP, open the /etc/dhcp3/dhcpd.conf file and move to the bottom of the file to pass all of the example options. All you need to add is a single subnet declaration that provides all of the information about your subnet that DHCP needs to hand out, along with the range of IP addresses DHCP can use. In my example I hand out 10.1.1.50 through 10.1.1.99, so I add the following settings to the bottom of the file:

```
subnet 10.1.1.0 netmask 255.255.255.0 {
    range 10.1.1.50 10.1.1.99;
    option routers 10.1.1.1;
    option domain-name-servers 10.1.1.2, 10.1.1.3;
}
```

Now to reload DHCP and enable my settings, I would run `sudo service dhcp3-server restart`. If I didn't make any syntax errors, the DHCP server will stop and then start back up. If there is an error in the file, it should output to the screen along with its location. A common error is a missing semicolon at the end of a particular line.

Static DHCP   You can use static DHCP assignments along with a dynamic DHCP subnet declaration if you want. If a server matches a static assignment, it will get that address; otherwise it will default with an address in the dynamic range. Each host that gets a static assignment needs its own host declaration. For instance, here is a host declaration for a host with a MAC address of 00:0c:c0:ff:ee:00 that will be assigned 10.1.1.10:

```
host examplehost {
    hardware ethernet 00:0c:c0:ff:ee:00;
    option host-name "examplehost";
    fixed-address 10.1.1.10;
}
```

You can add as many host declarations as you want; just keep in mind that each one needs to have a unique MAC address and a unique IP address in this file. Once you have added all of your host declarations, save your changes and restart the `dhcp3-server` init script.

NOTE   If you aren't sure how to tell what MAC address a particular host has, log in to the host and then run `sudo ifconfig`:

```
$ sudo ifconfig
eth0      Link encap:Ethernet  HWaddr 00:0c:c0:ff:ee:00
          inet addr:10.1.1.10  Bcast:10.1.1.255  Mask:255.255.255.0
```

```
             UP BROADCAST MULTICAST  MTU:1500  Metric:1
             RX packets:0 errors:0 dropped:0 overruns:0 frame:0
             TX packets:0 errors:0 dropped:0 overruns:0 carrier:0
             collisions:0 txqueuelen:1000
             RX bytes:0 (0.0 B)  TX bytes:0 (0.0 B)
             Interrupt:10

lo           Link encap:Local Loopback
             inet addr:127.0.0.1  Mask:255.0.0.0
             inet6 addr: ::1/128 Scope:Host
             UP LOOPBACK RUNNING  MTU:16436  Metric:1
             RX packets:2741 errors:0 dropped:0 overruns:0 frame:0
             TX packets:2741 errors:0 dropped:0 overruns:0 carrier:0
             collisions:0 txqueuelen:0
             RX bytes:148411 (148.4 KB)  TX bytes:148411 (148.4 KB)
```

Look for the `HWaddr` section in the output. That section will show that network device's MAC address, in my case `00:0c:c0:ff:ee:00`.

Database Server

Flat files and spreadsheets can work for data storage for some time, but at some point you will recognize the need for a real database. Most complex Web sites these days (including the WordPress example in this chapter) expect a database at the back end to store account information, blog posts, forum settings, and any other information about the site. There are a number of different databases available for Ubuntu, including Oracle, but here I discuss how to set up the two most common databases: MySQL and Postgres.

MySQL

MySQL has long been a favorite database server, particularly as a back-end database for Web sites because of its simple setup and fast performance. It's so popular for this purpose that an acronym, LAMP (Linux Apache MySQL Perl/PHP/Python), was created to describe it.

Install MySQL There are a few different ways to install the MySQL server. If you choose LAMP Server during the Ubuntu install or afterward with `tasksel`, MySQL will get installed along with Apache and PHP. Alternatively, you can install the MySQL server package directly:

```
$ sudo apt-get install mysql-server
```

During the package installation you will be prompted to set a password for the root MySQL account. You can choose to leave it blank; however, I recommend that you take this opportunity to set the password. It's certainly simpler to set it here than to look up the MySQL commands to set it later. Once the package installs, the MySQL daemon will start and it will be ready for you to use.

NOTE   If you do change the password of the root MySQL user (and you should), you will need to set up a small configuration file for cron to use so that it can run its MySQL /etc/cron.daily/ script successfully. To do this, create a /root/.my.cnf file containing the following information:

```
[mysqladmin]
user      = root
password  = yourpassword
```

Since this file contains a password in plain text, you will want to secure the permissions to make sure that no one other than root can read it:

```
$ sudo chown root:root /root/.my.cnf
$ sudo chmod 0600 /root/.my.cnf
```

Ubuntu MySQL Conventions

▪ **/etc/mysql/**
This directory contains the main configuration files for MySQL.

▪ **/etc/mysql/my.cnf**
This is the core MySQL configuration file. Individual users can create their own custom configurations as well and store them in ~/.my.cnf (as we did for the root user).

▪ **/etc/mysql/debian-start and /etc/mysql/debian.cnf**
These files are a script and configuration file, respectively, that manage processes that Ubuntu runs whenever the MySQL init script is started or restarted. This script checks for crashed tables and corrupt data, and overall checks to make sure that the database came up cleanly. You can think of this script almost like the file system check the system performs at start-up.

- **/etc/mysql/conf.d/**
  This directory is included by the main my.cnf and allows a better way
  to organize configuration files for particular databases or sites. Any
  configuration file created here will be included along with the main
  settings for MySQL when it starts.

- **/etc/init.d/mysql**
  The main MySQL init script is set to automatically start at boot time
  and stop when the system is rebooted or halted. Like many service init
  scripts, it supports extra options such as reload and force-reload to
  reload configuration files, as well as status to report the current status of the service. As you will see below, Ubuntu also includes a better
  command-line tool for managing MySQL.

- **/var/log/syslog**
  Ubuntu sets MySQL to log to the standard system log file, instead of
  /var/log/mysql.log or files under /var/log/mysql/. So to view only
  MySQL-related log entries from your syslog, you can use a simple
  grep command:

  ```
  $ sudo grep mysqld /var/log/syslog
  ```

- **/var/lib/mysql/**
  Under this directory you will find all of the database files used by the
  active database.

mysqladmin   Ubuntu includes the mysqladmin tool to help with MySQL
administration. You can think of it as being like the apache2ctl program in
that it accepts certain commands on the command line and then interacts
with the mysqld process for you. For instance, to get the current status of
your MySQL process, you can run

```
$ sudo mysqladmin -p status
```

The program will return information such as the current uptime, how
many threads are active, how many slow queries are running, and the average queries it processes per second. Note that I used the -p argument in
this command, which will tell mysqladmin to prompt me for the password

on the command line. If you set a password for the root user, you will need to use -p with your commands, or if you plan to run a batch of commands and don't want to enter the password every time, you can add the password to the -p option. So, for instance, if my MySQL password was *insecure*, I would type the following:

```
$ sudo mysqladmin -pinsecure status
```

The mysqladmin manual page (type man mysqladmin on a console) lists the full set of commands, but a few of the common ones are highlighted here:

- **create and drop**
  The create and drop commands take a database name as an argument and respectively create or remove a database from your MySQL instance.

- **flush-***
  There are a number of commands that flush caches or other settings within MySQL. The flush-hosts, flush-threads, and flush-logs commands flush the host cache, thread cache, and all logs, respectively. The flush-privileges, flush-status, and flush-tables commands reload the grant tables, clear status variables, and flush all tables, respectively.

- **password**
  If you never set the root password to begin with, or you want to change it, use this command with the new password as the next argument. If the password contains any special characters or spaces, be sure to put them in double quotes.

- **status, extended-status, processlist**
  All of these commands provide you with information about the current MySQL instance. I've already discussed the status command. The extended-status command provides a more complete set of status information, and the processlist command lists all of the active server threads along with their IDs. You can use that ID as a reference if you need to kill a particular process.

■ **kill**

The `mysqladmin processlist` command lists all of the processes along with their IDs, and the `kill` command kills all of the process IDs you pass as arguments. If you specify multiple processes, separate them with commas.

MySQL Web Administration While hard-core database administrators might scoff at using a Web interface to administer MySQL, it is a popular way to create and modify databases, particularly among Web designers. The phpMyAdmin program is a popular Web interface to MySQL, and it is easy to set up under Ubuntu.

INSTALL PHPMYADMIN To install phpMyAdmin, use your package manager to install the `phpmyadmin` package:

```
$ sudo apt-get install phpmyadmin
```

This will grab not only the `phpmyadmin` package but also its dependencies, including `apache2`, if you don't already have a Web server installed. During the package installation you will be presented with some questions to configure phpMyAdmin. The first question is which Web server to use. Unless you specifically set up another Web server for this task, select `apache2` here.

Once the package installation completes, phpMyAdmin should be ready to use. Just open a Web browser and point to the IP address or hostname of the phpMyAdmin server and append `/phpmyadmin` to it. So if my server was at 192.168.1.7, I would browse to http://192.168.1.7/phpmyadmin. The first screen you will see is a login screen, as shown in Figure 5-3. It's important to remember that phpMyAdmin does not maintain any user accounts on its own—it simply passes your login and password directly to MySQL—so type in `root` and your MySQL password (or if you have set up other users on MySQL, type that information in here). Once you log in, you will see the main configuration screen as shown in Figure 5-4, and from there you can tweak your MySQL settings, create and modify databases and tables, and access the phpMyAdmin documentation itself.

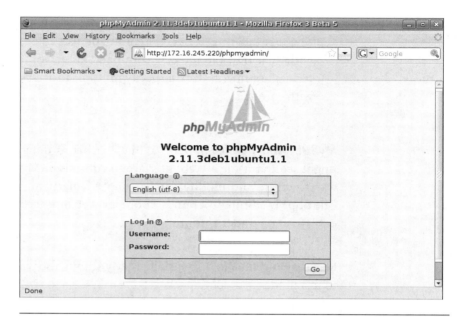

Figure 5-3 phpMyAdmin login screen

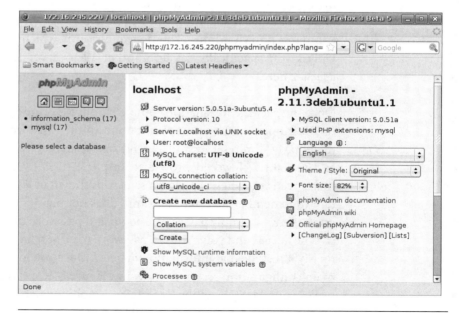

Figure 5-4 Main phpMyAdmin configuration screen

PostgreSQL

PostgreSQL and MySQL are the yin and yang of the open source database world. Whereas MySQL focused on speed and ease of use early on and then started to add more advanced database features, PostgreSQL focused on advanced database features first and then worked on optimization and ease of use. Both databases have their following, and all of the major open source database-backed Web software supports both databases. PostgreSQL moves far beyond Web site databases, though, with an advanced feature set including full ACID compliance, foreign keys, joins, views, triggers, and stored procedures.

Install PostgreSQL   Even though MySQL has the reputation of ease of use, PostgreSQL under Ubuntu is also simple to install and use. To install PostgreSQL, you can either select PostgreSQL Server as you install Ubuntu or afterward with `tasksel`, or you can use a package manager to install the `postgresql` package:

```
$ sudo apt-get install postgresql
```

Once the `postgresql` package has been installed, the database service will start in the background and you can then set up your superuser account and create a database. The initial administration will be performed by the postgres user, so first use sudo to become that user:

```
$ sudo -u postgres -s
```

Now from this shell you can create a new user account. You can choose to maintain the postgres user as the main superuser and then control who can become that user with sudo, or alternatively you can set up a new database user with superuser privileges. If I wanted to create a new superuser on my PostgreSQL database with the username kyle, I just need to pass the right flags to the `createuser` program:

```
$ createuser -P -s -e kyle
Enter password for new role:
Enter it again:
CREATE ROLE kyle PASSWORD 'md56966c432c869202883876a8b4f925ccc'
SUPERUSER CREATEDB CREATEROLE INHERIT LOGIN;
```

Alternatively, if I just wanted to create a regular unprivileged user:

```
$ createuser -P -DRS kyle
Enter password for new role:
Enter it again:
```

If you make a mistake and want to try again, or if you want to delete a user in general, just use the dropuser command with the username as an argument. Now that I have created a user, I can set up a database owned by that user. The createdb does all of the heavy lifting; I just need to specify the owner and the name of the database, in this case kyledatabase. So while I'm still the postgres user:

```
$ createdb -O kyle kyledatabase
```

Now I can type exit to exit out of the postgres shell and back to my normal user. To access the database I can use the psql command as my regular user:

```
$ psql --password kyledatabase
```

Now if my PostgreSQL username is different from the name of my shell account, this will error out as by default it tries the username of the local account. In that case I can add the PostgreSQL username at the end of the command:

```
$ psql --password kyledatabase kyle
```

Ubuntu PostgreSQL Conventions

■ **/etc/postgresql/**
Here you will find the main configuration files for all PostgreSQL instances on the system. Because the configuration files between different PostgreSQL versions can be incompatible, Ubuntu gives each PostgreSQL version its own subdirectory here. That way you can easily maintain multiple PostgreSQL versions on the same machine. For instance, the default postgresql package under Lucid will install PostgreSQL version 8.4, so all of its configuration will fall under /etc/postgresql/8.4/.

▪ **/etc/postgresql/8.4/main/postgresql.conf**
The /etc/postgresql/8.4/main/ directory contains the main configuration files for PostgreSQL 8.4, with postgresql.conf being the primary configuration file. This file is heavily commented, so you can use the file as a reference when you change options.

▪ **/etc/postgresql/8.4/main/pg_hba.conf**
This is the configuration file that stores all host authentication information. Here you can control which hosts on the network can access the PostgreSQL database.

▪ **/etc/postgresql/8.4/main/pg_ident.conf**
The pg_ident.conf file allows you to map a local username on the server to a different PostgreSQL username. So if your local username and PostgreSQL username don't match, you can add a mapping here and avoid having to add the PostgreSQL username to the command line each time you run psql.

▪ **/etc/init.d/postgresql-8.4**
This is the init script for PostgreSQL 8.4. As you can see, Ubuntu labels the init script based on the database version, so you can install and use multiple PostgreSQL versions on the same host.

▪ **/var/log/postgresql/**
Unlike MySQL, which logs to syslog, PostgreSQL separates all of its logging under /var/log/postgresql. From there each log is labeled according to its version, so the default PostgreSQL 8.4 database under Lucid logs to /var/log/postgresql/postgresql-8.4-main.log.

Web-Based PostgreSQL Administration   If you think hard-core MySQL administrators balk at Web-based administration, you should see how hard-core PostgreSQL administrators react. Even so, if you just want to create a Web site that is backed on a solid PostgreSQL database, you might appreciate the simplicity of managing the database from the Web. As with MySQL, there is a PHP-based administration tool called phpPgAdmin. To install phpPgAdmin, you simply need to install the phppgadmin package:

```
$ sudo apt-get install phppgadmin
```

The package will download all of its dependencies, including a Web server if one is not already installed. Once the package installs, create a symlink to its Apache configuration file under /etc/apache2/sites-available and then use a2ensite to enable the site:

```
$ sudo ln -s /etc/phppgadmin/apache.conf /etc/apache2/
  sites-available/phppgadmin
$ sudo a2ensite phppgadmin
$ sudo apache2ctl graceful
```

By default phpPgAdmin is configured to allow only localhost to access the site, so to allow access from your local network, open /etc/phppgadmin/apache.conf and locate the line that says

```
allow from 127.0.0.0/255.0.0.0
```

To allow the 192.168.1.0 network to access the tool as well, add

```
allow from 192.168.1.0/255.255.255.0
```

below the other allow from line and then run sudo apache2ctl graceful to reload your changes. Now you can open a Web browser on your network and browse to the /phppgadmin directory on the phpPgAdmin host. So if its IP address was 192.168.1.7, you would browse to http://192.168.1.7/phppgadmin/ and see the default Web page shown in Figure 5-5.

The main page lists all of the available PostgreSQL servers in the left side-bar. By default you will have just one configured, so click it and then use your PostgreSQL credentials to log in and manage the server. As Figure 5-6 shows, the interface is different from phpMyAdmin's, but as with php-MyAdmin you can modify databases, change tables, and perform all of the other major database administration you might want.

File Server

I suppose you could think of a Web server as a file server in a way—it does share files—but generally speaking, when people think of file servers they think of a machine on the local network with a lot of storage and the ability for multiple hosts on the network to access and modify files on that

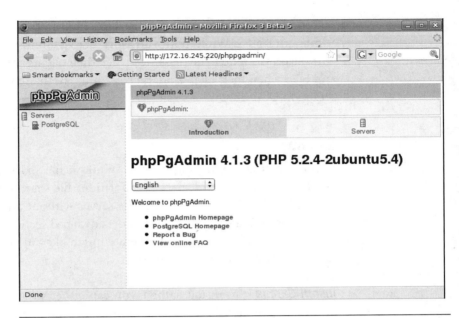

Figure 5-5 phpPgAdmin default page

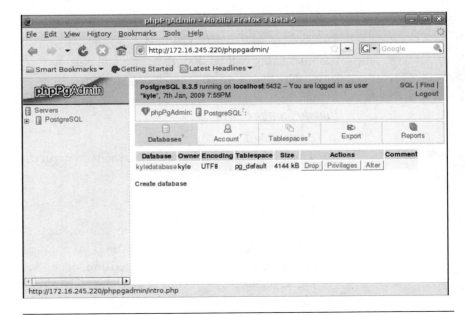

Figure 5-6 phpPgAdmin database administration

server. There are two main file servers for Ubuntu that most people favor: Samba and NFS. While both can work across multiple platforms, most administrators tend to favor Samba when their clients are mostly Windows, and NFS when their clients are mostly Linux. Both are relatively simple to set up on Ubuntu.

Samba

Samba is a program that implements Windows file-sharing protocols, SMB and CIFS. As such it's ideal as a platform for file sharing under Windows, since all of the clients can access the server without additional software. Over time Samba has grown to support advanced sections of Windows file sharing to the point that it can operate much like any other Windows file server or Primary Domain Controller.

Install Samba   To install Samba, you can either select the Samba Server option during the Ubuntu install or after the install with the `tasksel` program, or you can install the `samba`, `samba-doc`, `smbfs`, and `winbind` packages separately with the package manager:

```
$ sudo apt-get install samba samba-doc smbfs winbind
```

The Samba service will start automatically; of course, by default nothing too interesting will be shared, so you will need to tweak Samba's configuration files before any directories are shared.

Ubuntu Samba Conventions

- **/etc/samba/**
  This directory contains all of the main configuration files used by Samba, including local password files.

- **/etc/samba/smb.conf**
  The smb.conf file is the core configuration file for Samba and is used to define file shares and global settings for Samba itself. The default smb.conf file is heavily commented and sets up sane defaults for the file server such as a default workgroup of Workgroup. The file also contains a number of different examples of how to set up shares,

including a useful example configuration that shares out all of the users' home directories, but by default all of these sample shares are commented out.

- **/etc/init.d/smbd, /etc/init/smbd.conf**
  Samba's init script has been converted to an Upstart script, although there is still an old init script available as a placeholder. This means that you will use the standard Upstart programs like start, stop, and status to manage the service. Samba automatically starts at system boot by default.

- **/etc/init.d/nmbd, /etc/init/nmbd.conf**
  Like the smbd init script, the nmbd init script is also managed by Upstart now.

- **/usr/bin/smbpasswd**
  This tool is used to create user accounts for Samba. If you want to set up Samba shares that require authentication, you use this tool to create a Samba user database. Samba usernames that you add need to already exist on the system as well. For example, to add an ubuntu user to Samba, I would type

```
$ sudo smbpasswd -a ubuntu
```

  I can also use this command when I want to change the password for a particular user. To delete a user from Samba, replace the -a option with -x. You can also temporarily disable Samba users without deleting their accounts. To do this, use the -d and -e options to disable and enable the user, respectively.

- **/usr/share/doc/samba-doc/**
  If you installed the samba-doc program, you will find Samba documentation and example configuration files under this directory.

- **/var/lib/samba**
  This directory contains all of the different databases used by Samba, including the user and password database used by smbpasswd.

▪ **/var/log/samba/**

Samba logs in to its own directory and creates separate log files for the smbd and nmbd processes (log.nmbd and log.smbd respectively) as well as a separate log for each host that accesses Samba. This organization can make it easier to narrow down to the logging information you need.

Sample Samba Configuration   A good way to set up a new Samba share is to read the comments in the /etc/samba/smb.conf file. There are many different examples that show you how to share the user home directories or the CD-ROM drive, for instance. In this example I will show how to share a directory located at /mnt/share so that everyone on the network can access and write to it as a general storage location. Open /etc/samba/smb.conf in your preferred text editor and move to the bottom of the file. Then add the following:

```
[general]
    path = /mnt/share
    comment = General Storage
    writeable = Yes
    browseable = Yes
    guest ok = Yes
    force user = ubuntu
```

In this example I have set up the /mnt/share directory so that anyone on the network can write to it (writeable = Yes, guest ok = Yes) and use the force user = ubuntu option so that when a user creates a file on the share, it will be owned by the local user named ubuntu. Of course you would want to change this user from ubuntu to a user that exists on your system. Now I can create the shared directory and make sure that its permissions are set so that the local ubuntu user can write to it:

```
$ sudo mkdir /mnt/share
$ sudo chown ubuntu:ubuntu /mnt/share
```

One nice feature of Samba is that I can add or tweak a share like the one above without having to restart Samba. This is handy because when you restart Samba, any user accessing a file on the share will temporarily be disconnected from the file. Certain programs react very poorly to having their files pulled out from under them, even temporarily, and I've seen some simply crash when this happens.

Now that Samba is configured, go to another host on the network and attempt to connect to your Samba server. On an Ubuntu desktop you would click Places > Connect to Server..., then select "Windows share" from the "Service type" drop-down menu. Finally you would enter the IP address or hostname for your Samba server and then enter general for the name of the share (or otherwise whatever name you put between the brackets in your smb.conf). Click Connect and Ubuntu will mount and display the mounted share on your desktop.

NFS

NFS is a file-sharing service that originated on UNIX instead of Windows. These days both Linux and Windows can mount NFS shares, but you still tend to see NFS used with a network of Linux or UNIX clients. As you will see, there isn't too much involved if you want to share a directory over NFS.

Install NFS   To install NFS, select the nfs-kernal-server in your package manager. This will download and install the service along with any extra dependencies you need.

```
$ sudo apt-get install nfs-kernal-server
```

After the package installs, NFS is ready to be configured. By default no NFS exports will be configured, so nothing will be shared until you explicitly configure it.

Ubuntu NFS Conventions

- **/etc/exports**
  This is the core configuration file for NFS and contains a list of all file systems that NFS will export to users.

- **/etc/init.d/nfs-kernel-server**
  This init script controls the NFS server and accepts the standard list of init script options, including reload, so that you can reload the configuration without restarting the service.

- **/var/log/syslog**

    NFS logs to the standard syslog file as the NFSD process. This is the place to look if a remote host can't access a share and you want to track down exactly what is failing. To view only NFS logs from this file, run `sudo grep NFSD /var/log/syslog`.

Sample NFS Configuration   It is relatively simple to add NFS shares, and all of your work will be done in the /etc/exports file. The syntax of the file is covered in detail in the exports man page, which you can access by typing `man 5 exports`. Generally, the file will contain one export per line, and each line has two columns separated by one or more spaces. The first column is the path to the directory to share, and the second column is the host or network allowed to access the share along with a set of options within a pair of parentheses.

I create a sample share much like the example I gave in the Samba section. I export the /mnt/share directory owned by the ubuntu user to everyone on the 192.168.1.x network. To do this, I just need to add the following line to /etc/exports:

```
/mnt/share 192.168.1.0/255.255.255.0(rw)
```

Now I set up the /mnt/share directory if it isn't already there:

```
$ sudo mkdir /mnt/share
$ sudo chown ubuntu:ubuntu /mnt/share
```

Finally, I can reload NFS to enable this share:

```
$ sudo service nfs-kernel-server reload
```

Once NFS has reloaded, I can go to any host on the 192.168.1.0 network and mount the share. If the NFS server were at 192.168.1.7 and I wanted to mount it at /mnt/local, I would type

```
$ sudo mount -t nfs 192.168.1.7:/mnt/share /mnt/local
```

If your Ubuntu host gets an error about wrong file system type, you likely haven't installed NFS client support on your system. Just run

```
$ sudo apt-get install nfs-common
```

and try the mount command again.

NFS User Permissions   One interesting and controversial feature of NFS is how it handles user permissions. When you mount an NFS share, the file ownership will be based on the user IDs of the users on the NFS server. For users on a remote system to be able to read and write to the share, their user IDs need to match up with the NFS server. If you use LDAP or some other system to keep user IDs consistent across servers, this shouldn't present much of a problem, but if, for instance, the ubuntu user on my NFS server had a user ID of 1000 but the ubuntu user on my client had a user ID of 1001, the client wouldn't be able to write to the mount point.

Another matter of interest with NFS permissions is how it handles root. On Ubuntu by default the root account will be squashed, because NFS blocks any attempts by a remote root user to access shares with its root privileges. Otherwise any host on the network with an Ubuntu live CD could boot it, mount the NFS share, and read and write to any files on that share, regardless of the permissions. With this security issue in mind, you still might want to disable root squashing. To do so, add the no_root_squash option to your list of export options in /etc/exports. Each option is separated by commas, so if I wanted to disable root squashing on the share I created earlier, the file would look like the following:

```
/mnt/share 192.168.1.0/255.255.255.0(rw,no_root_squash)
```

Edubuntu and LTSP

The community-driven Edubuntu project aims to create an add-on for Ubuntu specially tailored for use in primary and secondary education. Edubuntu exists as a platform for tools for teachers and administrators. But the real thrust, of course, and the real purpose, is to put free and open source software into the hands of children. In doing so, Edubuntu provides children with a flexible and powerful technological environment for learning and experimenting. Based on free software, it offers educational technologies that are hackable and that can ultimately be used by students and teachers on *their own terms*. Distributed freely, its gratis nature serves an important need for schools where technology programs are always understaffed and underfunded. Fluent in Ubuntu and in free software, the children who, right now, are growing up using Edubuntu are offering the Ubuntu community a glimpse of where it might go and the generation of Ubunteros who may take us there.

While the Ubuntu, Kubuntu, and Xubuntu desktops highlight the products of the GNOME, KDE, and Xfce communities respectively, the Edubuntu project provides the best of everything in Ubuntu—properly tailored for use in schools and as easy to use as possible. One thing that made Edubuntu popular was its amazing ability to integrate thin clients, allowing the use of one powerful machine (the server) to provide many very low-powered, often diskless machines (the clients) with their entire OS. (See the next section for more information.) This model, while uninteresting for most workstation and laptop use by home or business users, is a major feature in classroom settings where it can mitigate configuration and maintenance headaches and substantially reduce the cost of classroom deployments.

What Is LTSP?

LTSP stands for Linux Terminal Server Project. It provides the same functionality to current client/server models that was present in the mainframe/dumb terminal setups prevalent many years ago.

The LTSP model centers on one powerful machine that acts as a server and several often much lower-powered machines that act as clients. The machines are all connected on a local area network.

This network allows all data required for booting the client's computer, which is normally held on the client's hard drive, to be served to the client over the network. If all the data required for booting the computer is provided over the network, the client machine requires no storage media at all, which leads to the term *diskless clients*.

TIP   Clients require a network card, which can boot either via PXE or via Etherboot to allow initial booting for local media before piggyback booting from the network. More information can be found at http://rom-o-matic.net, where you can create bootable images for your network hardware. Etherboot is essentially a convenient way to emulate the PXE system on older hardware. Most newer motherboards and network cards come with PXE software on the chip.

Technical Details of the LTSP Boot Process

A client machine is switched on. After the hardware is initialized, the network card looks for an IP address via the DHCP protocol. The LTSP server in most cases acts as the DHCP server to the local network and sends the client machine its IP address. Figure 5-7 shows a diagram of the LTSP booting process.

Once the network card has bound the IP address to itself, it makes a connection to the LTSP server and asks for the PXE configuration file. The LTSP server sends this file back to the client machine, which then makes a request for the kernel image. This is the base of the OS, which provides the client with all the hardware drivers required to communicate with the server.

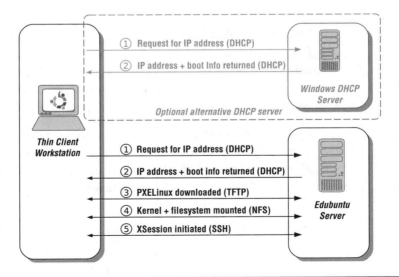

Figure 5-7 LTSP booting process

Next, an NFS connection is set up with the server. This is almost like a standard network share. The NFS share holds a very cut-down installation of Ubuntu, which consists almost entirely of an X server and an SSH-based login manager to connect to the server. Once the client machine has finished booting this small version of Ubuntu, the login screen is displayed to the user.

When a user logs in, an SSH tunnel is opened to the server, and an X session is initiated through this tunnel. All programs are run on the server, and only the graphical interface is piped back to the client machine. This allows the user to interact with the session and use a computer as normal.

The whole process is totally transparent to the user, but it is important to have a basic understanding of the underlying technologies present in LTSP to assist in the troubleshooting process and to be able to evaluate LTSP for a given task.

The Benefits of LTSP

Booting computers in this way does have some distinct advantages over the current preferred model of many powerful desktops, particularly where only a low budget is available.

- **Singular point of administration:** Working with this model means that only one computer needs to have new software installed on it. By using the Add/Remove tools, as demonstrated later in this chapter, you can make applications automatically available to all clients because they are essentially all using the same machine.

- **Low-cost hardware:** Thin client machines are not required to be incredibly powerful because all processing is done by the server. This allows people to use much older hardware for their client machines, often reusing machines that were taken out of service for being sluggish several years ago.

- **Diskless clients:** Anyone who has spent time administrating a network knows that often a computer used regularly suffers from corrupt files on the hard disk and needs reinstalling. If a client has no disk, there is no chance of a user corrupting data on the client's hard drive.

- **Easy replacement:** If one of your thin client machines breaks down, you still have all your data stored on the server. Just replace the client hardware and carry on working. It really is as easy as changing a light bulb.

TIP   Thin clients can run on incredibly low-specification machines. People are running thin clients on recycled computers that are as low-powered as 133MHz Pentiums with 64MB of RAM. While performance becomes an issue on hardware this slow, simple tweaks to avoid encryption over SSH can mitigate these. Generally, a machine running at least a 400MHz processor with 128MB of RAM will make an excellent thin client.

Other Uses

The LTSP system has its uses in many other applications too. Imagine you are running an Internet cafe, where many people use the computers in exactly the same way. Each workstation would need the same set of applications installed. The tasks they are performing are not hugely CPU intensive, so a thin client system is perfectly suited to this type of application. You will also find LTSP solutions very commonly used in information systems (e.g., in airports) and in point-of-sale systems.

LTSP Availability in Ubuntu

The ability to install and configure the LTSP system automatically is available to the user with the Ubuntu alternate CD. Since Edubuntu is no longer available as a live or alternate CD, the LTSP server installation has been moved to the Ubuntu alternate CD. If installation of LTSP is required to an already installed Ubuntu, Kubuntu, or Xubuntu desktop or Ubuntu server, you should follow the instructions provided in the next section.

Installing an LTSP Server

Starting with Ubuntu 9.04, the LTSP installation process requires one minor step before proceeding. The first thing you need to do is acquire the Ubuntu alternate CD. LTSP server installation is no longer provided via an Edubuntu CD because the status of Edubuntu has changed from a distribution to an add-on. If you would like to add LTSP to an Ubuntu server you have already installed, skip ahead to the section titled "Installing the LTSP Environment in Ubuntu or on a Desktop Installation."

LTSP Server Configurations

The LTSP server install allows a great deal of flexibility and is designed to allow it to fit into any current network configuration. Essentially these fall into two categories: those that use the LTSP server as a primary gateway for all their LTSP clients and those that do not. Let's take a few minutes to discuss the relative merits of each system.

Using the recommended configuration requires the LTSP server machine to have two network interface cards (NICs). One of these cards is connected to the rest of the network, that is, to the Internet or to other servers on the internal network. The other card is usually connected to a private subnet of the network where only Edubuntu LTSP clients reside. Figure 5-8 shows this two-NIC setup. No network data is routed from the second network card to the first, so client machines must be authenticated on the LTSP server before having access to the Internet or the rest of the network. This makes for a secure network setup.

The benefit to this setup is that client computers cannot connect to the network unless the LTSP server permits them to. This also reduces net-

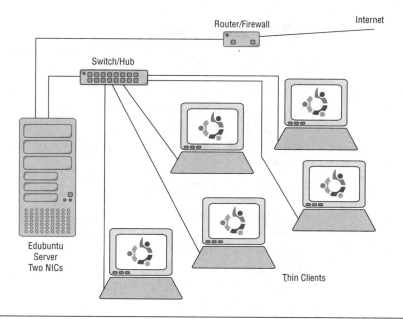

Figure 5-8 Two-NIC setup

work traffic on the rest of the network because while the LTSP clients are booting from the LTSP server, data is being transferred only on the private subnet and not on the rest of the network. Also, the clients receive their network addresses from the LTSP server, which frees up addresses on the rest of the network.

Using LTSP as simply another server on a network allows for a more flexible atmosphere. For a start, you require only one network interface card in the server to run using this configuration. The LTSP clients are connected to the normal network and could, assuming they had the capabilities to boot, access the network without the help of the LTSP server. Figure 5-9 shows this one-NIC setup.

The benefits of this setup are that thin clients can be used with more than one OS. One establishment, for example, runs dual-booting Microsoft Windows and Edubuntu clients. This setup also allows users to have their LTSP thin clients receiving their DHCP network addresses from a single network server.

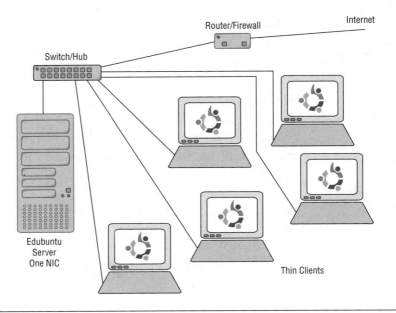

Figure 5-9 One-NIC setup

Essentially the choice of network design layout will impact the number of network cards installed in your server. It is primarily this that affects the difference between the standard Ubuntu install and the LTSP install.

The Installation Procedure

The installation procedure from the Ubuntu alternate CD looks very different from that of the desktop CD, but the questions asked are largely the same. The alternate CD is all text based, which can be a little daunting at first, but you will find installing Ubuntu in this way quicker because it doesn't require the entire desktop session to be loaded.

TIP   Remember that the server CD sets up LTSP for you. If you are planning to run an LTSP server, the easiest installation method is to use the Ubuntu alternate CD.

After the CD has booted, press F4 and select "Install an LTSP server," and then select the "Install to the Hard Disk" option. Confirm by pressing Enter to begin the installation. Notice also the workstation and command-line options at this point.

The first question you are asked simply sets up the language used for the install procedure as well as the language for the final system. You are then asked to choose your location.

Now you must choose your keyboard layout. The text-based installer has an auto-detection routine that asks you to press a series of keys on the keyboard. From these keys, the installer can work out which keyboard layout will best suit you. If there are any keyboard variations, these are now presented for you to choose from.

The installer now loads various components. If you have more than one NIC in your computer, you are asked to choose the primary card for the installation (Figure 5-10). By this, the installer wishes to know which network card is connected to the outside network or the Internet.

If your network has DHCP enabled, this card will be set up with an IP address from the network. You are then prompted to choose a hostname

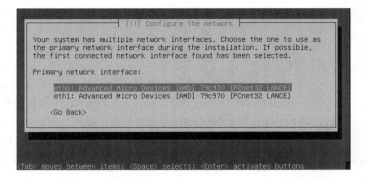

Figure 5-10 Selecting the primary network interface

for the LTSP server. If your network doesn't have DHCP enabled, you must set up the IP address manually.

The next step is to set up the hard disk for installation. By far the easiest method here is to select the default option of Guided Partitioning. If you require more in-depth partitioning or already have data on the hard drive that you do not want to lose, you must plan how you are going to proceed. If you are installing onto a computer that has partitions Ubuntu can resize, it will offer you that option. This option allows you to have two OSes installed on one computer and to switch between them at bootup. Whichever method you select, you are asked to confirm your partitioning choices.

TIP While the resizing utilities in Ubuntu are excellent, you should always back up your data before performing an operation such as this.

After this, you must choose whether or not your clock is set to Coordinated Universal Time (UTC). Your system clock should be set to UTC. Your OS is then responsible for converting the system time into local time. Unless you have another OS that expects the system time to be the local time, you should answer yes here.

Now it's time to set up the first user on the system. Remember that this user will have full administrative rights. First, enter the user's full name, then the desired username, followed by the password twice. After this, the base system is installed.

After plowing through several steps, you are presented with a question about screen resolutions. For the type of system you are installing, a very high screen resolution could result in a slow connection between the server and the client. The default options are fine.

When this is completed, the installer begins building the LTSP client root filesystem (Figure 5-11). This is the very small version of Ubuntu mentioned earlier in this chapter. Essentially it consists of just a kernel and an X server.

TIP   This step appears to take a long time, and the progress bar isn't updated often. Be patient, have a snack—it will finish eventually.

Once the installation is complete, a prompt asks you to remove the CD and press Enter to reboot the system into your new Edubuntu server.

Initial LTSP Server Setup

The DHCP server installed on your Ubuntu machine should start up automatically, so all that is left to do is to make your thin clients bootable from the network. If you are using the single–network card setup described earlier and your network already has a DHCP server running, *do not* start the Ubuntu DHCP server, because doing so will likely cause both DHCP services to be unavailable.

Figure 5-11 Building the LTSP filesystem

TIP   If you are still running the Dapper 6.06 LTS version of Edubuntu, there is a little bit more work to do. The latest versions of Ubuntu have an automatic DHCP configuration generator. This means that they do not require manual configuration in usual LTSP environments. The 6.06 LTS release needs manual configuration of the DHCP server; please visit https://www.edubuntu.org/GettingStarted for further instructions.

Initial LTSP Client Setup

Modifying a client computer to boot from the network is usually done by altering a setting in the machine's BIOS. It's a good idea to look at the manual for the computer's motherboard to find out how to alter these settings. For most machines it is simply a case of entering the BIOS by pressing the Delete key at bootup and changing the boot device priority.

Once you've set up your client machines to boot from the network card, you should see a screen similar to the one Figure 5-12 shows on each of the clients. This means that the client machine has been issued with a DHCP address and that the PXELinux file has been loaded from the network.

```
PXELINUX 3.11 Debian-2006-03-16  Copyright (C) 1994-2005 H. Peter Anvin
UNDI data segment at:    0009C7F0
UNDI data segment size: 24D0
UNDI code segment at:    0009ECC0
UNDI code segment size: 0A0D
PXE entry point found (we hope) at 9ECC:0106
My IP address seems to be C0A800FA 192.168.0.250
ip=192.168.0.250:192.168.0.254:192.168.0.1:255.255.255.0
TFTP prefix: /ltsp/i386/
Trying to load: pxelinux.cfg/01-00-0c-29-a3-9c-0a
Trying to load: pxelinux.cfg/C0A800FA
Trying to load: pxelinux.cfg/C0A800F
Trying to load: pxelinux.cfg/C0A800
Trying to load: pxelinux.cfg/C0A80
Trying to load: pxelinux.cfg/C0A8
Trying to load: pxelinux.cfg/C0A
Trying to load: pxelinux.cfg/C0
Trying to load: pxelinux.cfg/C
Trying to load: pxelinux.cfg/default
Loading vmlinuz........................
Loading initrd.img.....................
.....
Ready.
_
```

Figure 5-12 DHCP boot

If your client boots up to the graphical login and the screen looks similar to the one shown in Figure 5-13, congratulations—you have successfully set up your LTSP thin client system.

Installing the LTSP Environment in Ubuntu or on a Desktop Installation

Perhaps you already have an Ubuntu machine and wish to make it available in an LTSP setup. To do this is a simple procedure and requires very little configuration. To begin, you must decide whether you require a DHCP server. If so, install the ltsp-server-standalone package. If you already have a DHCP server and are going to configure it to point to the LTSP server, by modifying the `filename`, `next-server`, and `root-path` options, you should install the ltsp-server package. Along with this, you will need the openssh-server package.

The easiest way to do this is to log in to your server and type the following commands to install the LTSP server and the SSH server. In our example, a DHCP server was not required.

```
sudo apt-get install ltsp-server openssh-server
```

Figure 5-13 LDM login screen

TIP   If you require a DHCP server, modify the line above from `ltsp-server` to `ltsp-server-standalone`. You will also need to configure a second network device to an IP address of 192.168.0.1 before running the procedures described in this subsection.

All that is left to do now is to install the client chroot by running the following command:

```
sudo ltsp-build-client
```

After this, you should be able to boot your first thin client.

Special LTSP Cases

Setting Up LTSP to Coexist with an Existing DHCP Server

Sometimes you might not want your machines to be on a totally separate subnetwork. However, the problem then becomes that the current DHCP server will not be set up to serve the correct options to enable the clients to boot from the network. Modifying a Linux-based DHCP server is well documented; however, some establishments will require the modification of a Microsoft Windows DHCP server to allow network clients to boot from the network.

The following setup assumes that there are currently no thin client systems running on the Windows network. Opening up the Windows DHCP administration tool will allow you to create *reservations* for your machines. A reservation is an IP address tied to a specific MAC address. In this way, each time a machine requests an IP address from the DHCP server, it is always given the same IP address. This has its benefits because you can then set advanced options for the client as well.

For each client, you must create a reservation and then add the following options to each one (Figure 5-14).

- 017 Root Path: /opt/ltsp/i386
- 066 Boot Server Host Name: *<server ip>*
- 067 Bootfile Name: /ltsp/i386/pxelinux.0

Figure 5-14 Windows DHCP Reservations

It is recommended that you restart the DHCP server. After this, the clients should be able to correctly pick up their IP address from the server and then boot from the LTSP server via NFS.

TIP You can also set these options as global parameters to be rolled out over the entire network. However, it is often advisable, at least in the beginning, to keep track of which machines are booting from the LTSP server.

Dual-Booting with Another Operating System on the Hard Disk   Perhaps
you have a suite of computers that are already happily running another OS, and you would prefer to keep both systems running for a while. Hopefully, after using Edubuntu for any length of time, you will eventually make the switch permanent. In these situations, it is easy to set up the server to allow the client to boot from either the network or the first hard disk in the computer.

The bulk of the editing takes place in the pxelinux.cfg/default configuration file in the directory /var/lib/tftpboot/ltsp/<arch>/. The format of this file is very similar to the old LILO configuration syntax (for those of you familiar with that bootloader). The following sample configuration will present a message to the client, which is explained later. The user can then choose to either allow the system to boot its default configuration, which in this example would be the local hard disk, or to type in the word linux and press Enter, which would load the LTSP thin client.

```
DEFAULT localboot
TIMEOUT 50
PROMPT 1
DISPLAY display.msg

LABEL linux
   KERNEL vmlinuz
   APPEND ro initrd=initrd.img quiet splash

LABEL localboot
   LOCALBOOT 0
```

Let's take a look at the configuration file and break it down so that you can create your own to suit your environment. (If this sample file fits the bill for you, you can skip down to the part about creating the display.msg file.)

The DEFAULT keyword specifies which boot option will be chosen once the timeout expires. The TIMEOUT option specifies how long to wait before booting the default option. This timeout is measured in one-tenth of a second; thus a value of 50 sets it for 5 seconds. The PROMPT option specifies whether the PXE software displays the boot: prompt to enable users to choose an operating system. The DISPLAY option displays a text file on the screen as an introduction. In this case, the file is called display.msg and must be placed in the root LTSP directory alongside the pxelinux.0 file. An example of this file is proposed a little later.

The three lines starting with *LABEL linux* define the *linux* option for booting. This is configured by the KERNEL and APPEND options, which you will notice are extracted from the original default file, as shown here:

```
DEFAULT vmlinuz ro initrd=initrd.img quiet splash
```

All that is needed now is the option for booting from the local hard drive, shown by the two lines starting LABEL localboot. These lines define the *localboot* option as used with the DEFAULT keyword earlier in the file. The only definition included in this option is the LOCALBOOT option, with a parameter of 0. This provides normal hard disk booting. Other parameters are available, as you can see by visiting the Syslinux home page, http://syslinux.zytor.com.

The display.msg file should contain some information that tells the user what to do to choose an operating system. Following is an example file that is suitable for the configuration above. When creating this file, it is helpful to use a number of blank lines before the text actually begins. This has the effect of clearing the screen so that users don't get confused by the PXELinux start-up text.

```
===================================================================

                   Welcome to the Multiboot System

                  The system will start in 5 seconds...

         for Linux users type :  linux
         at the boot: prompt and press <enter>

===================================================================
```

After rebooting the client, you should see the text from the display message file. It should look similar to that shown in Figure 5-15.

Changing Your IP Address

At some point it may become necessary to change the IP address of the server. Changing the IP address of a normal machine would not usually have much consequence on the client machine. However, in an LTSP environment, changing the IP address will result in clients being unable to log in. This is because when the LTSP root is built, it is populated with SSH authorization keys, which allow authentication between the client and the server without a password.

The procedure for solving this issue is fairly simple. First, log in to your server and then run the LTSP SSH key update script by typing the following command into the terminal and pressing Enter. You will be prompted for your password.

```
sudo ltsp-update-sshkeys
```

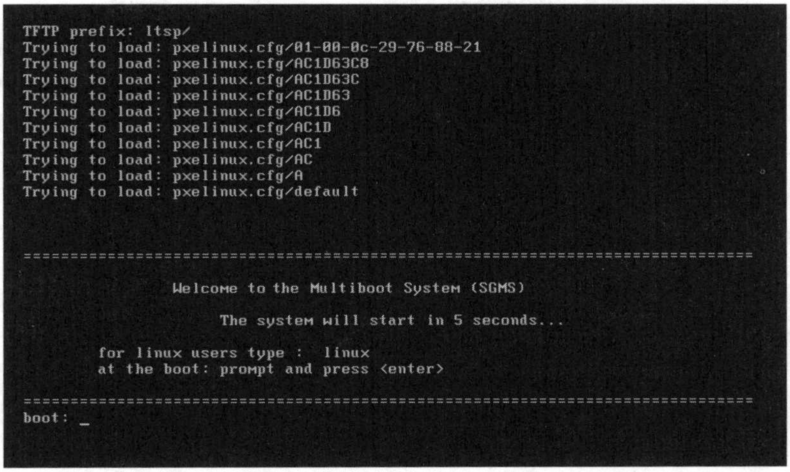

```
TFTP prefix: ltsp/
Trying to load: pxelinux.cfg/01-00-0c-29-76-88-21
Trying to load: pxelinux.cfg/AC1D63C0
Trying to load: pxelinux.cfg/AC1D63C
Trying to load: pxelinux.cfg/AC1D63
Trying to load: pxelinux.cfg/AC1D6
Trying to load: pxelinux.cfg/AC1D
Trying to load: pxelinux.cfg/AC1
Trying to load: pxelinux.cfg/AC
Trying to load: pxelinux.cfg/A
Trying to load: pxelinux.cfg/default



=============================================================================
               Welcome to the Multiboot System (SGMS)

                  The system will start in 5 seconds...

         for linux users type :   linux
         at the boot: prompt and press <enter>
=============================================================================
boot: _
```

Figure 5-15 Multiboot system in action

TIP When entering your password, nothing is displayed on the screen, although your password is still being read by the computer. The password is not displayed for security reasons, but it is also not obfuscated. This prevents people who may be looking over your shoulder from seeing how many characters your password has.

TIP It is possible here to update the SSH keys by simply restarting the network interface, using a command similar to the following one. You will need to replace *<iface>* with the interface identifier, usually something like eth0 or eth1.

sudo ifdown *<iface>* && sudo ifup *<iface>*

Once completed, your SSH keys will be updated, and after the clients reboot, they should be able to log in again.

Local Devices over LTSP

Since Ubuntu Edgy 6.10, Edubuntu has included the update to LTSP to allow what are called local devices. Plugging a USB storage device into a thin client machine, for example, will trigger the local devices mechanism, and the device will be correctly mounted and shown on the desktop of the client machine.

When using USB sticks with Ubuntu, you would normally have to unmount the device before removing it physically. This is so that Ubuntu has time to write all the data it needs to the USB stick and can safely unmount it. In the LTSP environment, using a USB stick is a little different. There is no unmount option because the data is written to the USB stick on a very regular basis. Hence you do not need to unmount it and can just remove it once the computer has finished writing information to it.

Local device support is set up by default in Edubuntu; however, to use it you must add to the fuse group the users who require access to such support. You can do this from the user manager. Start by going to System > Administration > Users and Groups option. From here, select the user to whom you wish to give local device access and click on the User Properties button. Click on the User Privileges tab, and from here tick the checkbox for allowing use of fuse filesystems, as shown in Figure 5-16.

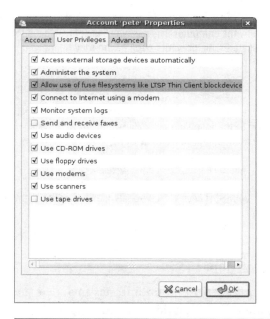

Figure 5-16 Setting fuse preferences

Sound over LTSP

Since Ubuntu Dapper 6.06, Edubuntu has the ability to play sound through the speakers of the client machine. For versions of Edubuntu prior to 6.10 and LTSP setups installed on top of Ubuntu, you must add an entry to the /opt/ltsp/i386/etc/lts.conf file to enable sound for client machines.

The easiest way to edit this file is to hold down Alt-F2, which will bring up the run command dialog box. Type in the following command:

```
gksudo "gedit /opt/ltsp/i386/etc/lts.conf"
```

Clicking OK will bring up an editing window. Make sure to have at least a [default] section in the lts.conf file where you will add the following line:

```
SOUND=True
```

NOTE   Dapper 6.06 LTS is very particular about the SOUND=True statement. You must type it exactly as shown, taking extreme care with capital letters and so on.

For all versions after 6.10 of Edubuntu, this is already done for you, and sound should work on client machines out of the box.

CHAPTER 6

Security

SECURITY IS DEFINITELY A HOT TOPIC both inside and outside the computer world. It can be difficult to distinguish legitimate threats from basic paranoia, but as anyone who has connected to a high-speed connection and monitored the logs knows, these days there are armies of servers out there trying to attack you.

Even though other operating systems and products seem to get the majority of the press for their security breaches, Ubuntu users aren't completely in the clear. Even though Ubuntu has good security out of the box, the moment you set up new services you risk opening holes to attack. This chapter discusses some common security practices and simple steps you can take to keep your Ubuntu server secure. Just in case you still get attacked, I also include a section at the end on how to respond to a security breach.

General Security Principles

There is a saying in security circles: "Security is a process, not a product." What that means is that despite what your vendor might tell you, you can't solve all your security problems with some appliance or software. Instead, you find real security when you follow sound security principles and develop sound security procedures. While I cover some specific tools and options you can use to increase your system's security later in the chapter, there's no way I can discuss how to lock down every major service under Ubuntu. These principles, though, are something that you can apply no matter what software you might run:

- **Keep it simple.**
  Another saying you will hear in security circles is "Complexity is the enemy of security." The more complex a system, the more difficult it is to understand every part of it and the greater the likelihood that the security of some aspect of the system was overlooked. Whenever you design a system, try to keep the number of interoperating pieces as small as you can. Not only will it help with security, it will help with troubleshooting and overall administration as well.

- **Follow the principle of least privilege.**
  The principle of least privilege is the idea that programs and people should operate with the lowest possible level of power. This is the

concept behind the separation of root and the regular users. Since most daily tasks don't require full system privileges, give users fewer privileges. Programs like Apache and Postfix follow this principle; they use the root privileges only when they are absolutely necessary, and then the bulk of the work is done via child processes owned by a different user. When these practices are in place, and you do get attacked, the amount of damage an attacker can do is limited.

■ **Provide layers of protection.**
Some refer to this as "defense in depth." The best security occurs in layers. Slapping a firewall in front of your servers won't automatically make them secure, but it will help increase their security. Instead, you want multiple layers of defense, such as a firewall between you and the outside world, a local software firewall, strong passwords, and sudo roles.

■ **Avoid security by obscurity.**
On the surface it might seem as if moving the SSH server from port 22 to port 257 would add extra security. After all, no one will think to look for it there. Unfortunately, steps like this slow down, but don't stop, an attacker. The real danger of these sorts of security methods is that they create a false sense of security. This isn't to say that moving ports around and using other means of obscurity are completely bad, just that they should be recognized for what they are—things that only slow down attackers and that must be combined with other security procedures.

■ **Keep on top of security patches.**
You can have all sorts of security procedures in place and still be attacked if a vulnerability is found in a service and you fail to patch it. It's important to monitor security updates and use Ubuntu's package management to keep your systems up to date.

Sudo

Out of the box Ubuntu implements a number of practices to make the default install more secure. One of these is the disabling of the root account and the use of sudo for superuser privileges. The sudo program provides a much more robust set of features to increase user privileges compared to the traditional su program. Here is a list of some of the more interesting features of sudo:

▪ **Uses the user's password for authentication**
When the sudo command is run and the user is prompted for a password, each user enters his or her own password instead of the password for the user he or she wants to become. This helps with security because it means that you can give people superuser privileges without having to tell them the root password (if it is enabled) or the password for any other users on the system. It also means that a user can't directly log in to the system as the root user since there is no password—since all Linux machines have a root user, it's the most common account someone will try to brute force.

▪ **Limitation on superuser access**
With sudo a user doesn't have to have complete root access. Instead, you can define a list of programs a user can execute with superuser privileges. With this feature you can better follow the principle of least privilege. If a user really needs root privileges only to run apache2ctl, why give the user root access over the entire system? With sudo you can easily limit the user's access strictly to apache2ctl.

▪ **Support for group-based and host-based access**
The sudo configuration file allows you to put users into groups and then assign access to that group. If you find that you have a number of different sudo rules for the same set of users, this makes it much easier to organize the file and add or remove users from the group. You can also define rules based on the host. With this feature you can maintain a single sudoers file (sudo configuration file) that can be copied to all hosts on your network (or even shared via LDAP).

▪ **Auto-expiration of sudo access**
Once you pass the password check once, you can continue to run sudo commands and sudo won't prompt you for a password for a configurable amount of time. This certainly saves time when you need to run multiple sudo commands in a row and provides extra protection in case you forget to lock your terminal and leave your desk.

- **Logging of all sudo access**

  Every time users run sudo they generate a new log entry in
  /var/log/auth.log that lists the time, the users who ran sudo, and what
  commands they ran. This gives an administrator a nice forensics trail.
  Also, sudo can send the administrator an e-mail whenever a user fails
  the password check.

- **Can configure passwordless access to rules**

  While you wouldn't necessarily want to enable this for every sudo
  rule, there is sometimes a need for a script (particularly cron scripts)
  to gain root access to run a particular command. Since it's a cron
  script, it's much easier if it can run without your having to code support for the interactive password prompt. It might be tempting to
  give complete passwordless sudo access to a user, but I recommend
  you limit rules like this to individual commands.

Configure sudo

sudo's configuration file can be found at /etc/sudoers. Ubuntu provides a
basic file by default that allows the root user to do anything as any other
user and allows members of the admin group to become root (the user
you create at install time is automatically added to this group). Your natu-
ral inclination might be to open the file with your favorite text editor;
however, this is not recommended. The sudo package provides a tool called
visudo that you should use whenever you want to make changes to the file,
so to view and edit the /etc/sudoers file, type

```
$ sudo visudo
```

The reason you want to use visudo is that it automatically checks your
sudoers file for mistakes. Since a mistake in the sudoers file could potentially lock you out of root access, this syntax check is pretty important. If
you do make a mistake, visudo will tell you about it after you save and exit.
You will have the option to go back and fix your mistake, exit without saving, or ignore its warnings and save anyway (which is not recommended).

While the basics of sudoers syntax are pretty straightforward, the full set
of features and syntax for things like user or command groups can get

complicated rather quickly, especially without an example to work from. Luckily you can access the sudoers manual by typing man sudoers. This manual defines this file's syntax and gives a number of examples you can use for your own sudoers file. Instead of documenting that manual again here, to start let's look at two lines from the default /etc/sudoers file and break down each of the fields:

```
root   ALL=(ALL) ALL
%admin ALL=(ALL) ALL
```

The first column defines which user or group this rule applies to. To refer to a user, you can just list the user, or you can list multiple users separated by commas. To reference a group add the % sign in front of the group's name. The second column before the = sign defines which hosts this rule applies to. In this case it is set to ALL, which means it applies to all hosts. The value within the parentheses sets which user this sudo rule will be run as. In this case it is also set to ALL so it can be run as any user. The final column defines which commands the user can run. In this example it is set to ALL so any command can be run.

It's easier to see how all of these options fit in when you see an example that isn't set to ALL. Let's assume I have a Web server named web1. I have an administrator with a username of jorge who manages only this Web server. I don't want to give him full root access to the machine because he has a history of accidents with the rm -rf command. All I really want to give him is the ability to use apache2ctl so he can reload and restart Apache on this one server. I copy my sudoers file to all of the servers on my network, so I need to restrict the rule to web1 only. The resulting rule would look like this:

```
jorge web1 = (root) /usr/sbin/apache2ctl
```

Notice that I specified the full path to apache2ctl. If I had just listed apache2ctl without the path, I would have opened up a way to full root access on the system. The user could have created a bash script in his home directory named apache2ctl and run whatever he wanted as root.

Now let's say that the jorge user never really used apache2ctl except to reload changes he made to configuration files. He wanted to automate this process and wrote a script to deploy his configuration files, but he still has to manually log in to run apache2ctl because it asks for a password. To remove the password requirement for this rule, add the NOPASSWD: statement before the command:

```
jorge web1 = (root) NOPASSWD: /usr/sbin/apache2ctl
```

Keep in mind that you want to restrict how often you use NOPASSWD since it bypasses one of sudo's main security measures. You also want to avoid using it if the command is set to ALL if you can help it. Even in this case I may not want the full apache2ctl command available without a password. If I wanted to restrict this further, I could create my own shell script that ran /usr/sbin/apache2ctl graceful and then give the jorge user NOPASSWD access to that script instead.

sudo Aliases

As your sudoers file gets larger and more complicated, or as you deploy it to a larger number of servers, you will see that it easily becomes disorganized and difficult to manage. A new developer gets hired and needs sudo access to a machine, and you find yourself poring over line after line in the sudoers file looking for all of the different rules that might apply. Aliases save you from that trouble and allow you to define groups for each of the columns in an entry. The basic syntax for each of these aliases is as follows:

```
User_Alias ALIASNAME = user1,user2,user3
Host_Alias ALIASNAME = host1,host2,host3
Runas_Alias ALIASNAME = user4,user5,user6
Cmnd_Alias ALIASNAME = /bin/command1,/sbin/command2
```

There are some restrictions given to the alias name. You can use only uppercase letters, 0–9, and the _ symbol for them. That not only helps you distinguish them from regular users, it helps sudo distinguish them as well.

So let's extend our previous scenario to incorporate groups. Instead of just the jorge user, I have a number of users, jorge, allan, and ben, who work on our Web cluster, web1, web2, and web3. I want to grant them access both to apache2ctl and also some of the other useful Apache commands Ubuntu includes, such as a2enmod, a2dismod, a2ensite, and a2dissite, so they can enable and disable modules and sites. Finally, I want them to be able to run any command as the webadmin and apache users—two special users we set up just for Web administrators. Here are the resulting rules I would add to /etc/sudoers:

```
User_Alias WEB_ADMIN = jorge,allan,ben
Host_Alias WEB_CLUSTER1 = web1,web2,web3
Cmnd_Alias WEB_COMMANDS = /usr/sbin/apache2ctl, \
                          /usr/sbin/a2enmod, \
                          /usr/sbin/a2dismod, \
                          /usr/sbin/a2ensite, \
                          /usr/sbin/a2edissite
RunAs_Alias WEB_ACCOUNTS = webadmin,apache

WEB_ADMIN WEB_CLUSTER1 = (root) WEB_COMMANDS
WEB_ADMIN WEB_CLUSTER1 = (WEB_ACCOUNTS) ALL
```

Notice with the WEB_COMMANDS alias I can span multiple lines as long as I use a \ at the end of the line. With these aliases in place, if we hire new users, all I have to do is add them to the WEB_ADMIN alias. If we add a fourth Web server to the cluster, I need to update only the WEB_CLUSTER1 alias.

AppArmor

The UNIX permissions model has long been used to lock down access to users and programs. Even though it works well, there are still areas where extra access control can come in handy. For instance, many services still run as the root user, and therefore if they are exploited, the attacker potentially can run commands throughout the rest of the system as the root user. There are a number of ways to combat this problem, including sandboxes, chroot jails, and so on, but Ubuntu has included a system called AppArmor, installed by default, that adds access control to specific system services.

AppArmor is based on the security principle of least privilege; that is, it attempts to restrict programs to the minimal set of permissions they need to function. It works through a series of rules assigned to particular programs. These rules define, for instance, which files or directories a program is allowed to read and write to or only read from. When an application that is being managed by AppArmor violates these access controls, AppArmor steps in and prevents it and logs the event. A number of services include AppArmor profiles that are enforced by default, and more are being added in each Ubuntu release. In addition to the default profiles, the universe repository has an `apparmor-profiles` package you can install to add more profiles for other services. Once you learn the syntax for AppArmor rules, you can even add your own profiles.

Probably the simplest way to see how AppArmor works is to use an example program. The BIND DNS server is one program that is automatically managed by AppArmor under Ubuntu, so first I install the BIND package with `sudo apt-get install bind9`. Once the package is installed, I can use the `aa-status` program to see that AppArmor is already managing it:

```
$ sudo aa-status
apparmor module is loaded.
5 profiles are loaded.
5 profiles are in enforce mode.
   /sbin/dhclient3
   /usr/lib/NetworkManager/nm-dhcp-client.action
   /usr/lib/connman/scripts/dhclient-script
   /usr/sbin/named
   /usr/sbin/tcpdump
0 profiles are in complain mode.
2 processes have profiles defined.
1 processes are in enforce mode :
   /usr/sbin/named (5020)
0 processes are in complain mode.
1 processes are unconfined but have a profile defined.
   /sbin/dhclient3 (607)
```

Here you can see that the /usr/sbin/named profile is loaded and in enforce mode, and that my currently running /usr/sbin/named process (PID 5020) is being managed by AppArmor.

AppArmor Profiles

The AppArmor profiles are stored within /etc/apparmor.d/ and are named after the binary they manage. For instance, the profile for /usr/sbin/named is located at /etc/apparmor.d/usr.sbin.named. If you look at the contents of the file, you can get an idea of how AppArmor profiles work and what sort of protection they provide:

```
# vim:syntax=apparmor
# Last Modified: Fri Jun  1 16:43:22 2007
#include <tunables/global>
```

```
/usr/sbin/named {
  #include <abstractions/base>
  #include <abstractions/nameservice>

  capability net_bind_service,
  capability setgid,
  capability setuid,
  capability sys_chroot,

  # /etc/bind should be read-only for bind
  # /var/lib/bind is for dynamically updated zone (and journal) files.
  # /var/cache/bind is for slave/stub data, since we're not the origin
  #of it.
  # See /usr/share/doc/bind9/README.Debian.gz
  /etc/bind/** r,
  /var/lib/bind/** rw,
  /var/lib/bind/ rw,
  /var/cache/bind/** rw,
  /var/cache/bind/ rw,

  # some people like to put logs in /var/log/named/
  /var/log/named/** rw,

  # dnscvsutil package
  /var/lib/dnscvsutil/compiled/** rw,

  /proc/net/if_inet6 r,
  /usr/sbin/named mr,
  /var/run/bind/run/named.pid w,
  # support for resolvconf
  /var/run/bind/named.options r,
}
```

For instance, take a look at the following excerpt from that file:

```
/etc/bind/** r,
/var/lib/bind/** rw,
/var/lib/bind/ rw,
/var/cache/bind/** rw,
/var/cache/bind/ rw,
```

The syntax is pretty straightforward for these files. First there is a file or directory path, followed by the permissions that are allowed. Globs are also allowed, so, for instance, /etc/bind/** applies to all of the files below the /etc/bind directory recursively. A single * would apply only to files within the current directory. In the case of that rule you can see that /usr/sbin/

named is allowed only to read files in that directory and not write there. This makes sense, since that directory contains only BIND configuration files—the named program shouldn't ever need to write there. The second line in the excerpt allows named to read and write to files or directories under /var/lib/bind/. This also makes sense because BIND might (among other things) store slave zone files here, and since those files are written to every time the zone changes, named needs permission to write there.

Enforce and Complain Modes

You might have noticed that the aa-status output mentions two modes: enforce and complain modes. In enforce mode, AppArmor actively blocks any attempts by a program to violate its profile. In complain mode, AppArmor simply logs the attempt but allows it to happen. The aa-enforce and aa-complain programs allow you to change a profile to be in enforce or complain mode, respectively. So if my /usr/sbin/named program did need to write to a file in /etc/bind or some other directory that wasn't allowed, I could either modify the AppArmor profile to allow it or I could set it to complain mode:

```
$ sudo aa-complain /usr/sbin/named
Setting /usr/sbin/named to complain mode
```

If later on I decided that I wanted the rule to be enforced again, I would use the aa-enforce command in the same way:

```
$ sudo aa-enforce /usr/sbin/named
Setting /usr/sbin/named to enforce mode
```

If I had decided to modify the default rule set at /etc/apparmor.d/usr .sbin.named, I would need to be sure to reload AppArmor so it would see the changes. You can run AppArmor's init script and pass it the reload option to accomplish this:

```
$ sudo /etc/init.d/apparmor reload
```

Be careful when you modify AppArmor rules. When you first start to modify rules, you might want to set that particular rule into complain mode and then monitor /var/log/syslog for any violations. For instance, if

/usr/sbin/named were in enforce mode and I had commented out the line in the /usr/sbin/named profile that granted read access to /etc/bind/**, then reloaded AppArmor and restarted BIND, not only would BIND not start (since it couldn't read its config files), I would get a nice log entry in /var/log/syslog from the kernel to report the denied attempt:

```
Jan  7 19:03:02 kickseed kernel: [ 2311.120236]
  audit(1231383782.081:3): type=1503 operation="inode_permission"
  requested_mask="::r" denied_mask="::r" name="/etc/bind/named.conf"
  pid=5225 profile="/usr/sbin/named" namespace="default"
```

Ubuntu AppArmor Conventions

▪ **/etc/apparmor/**
   This directory contains the main configuration files for the AppArmor program, but note that it does *not* contain AppArmor rules.

▪ **/etc/apparmor.d/**
   You will find all of the AppArmor rules under this directory along with subdirectories that contain different sets of include files to which certain rule sets refer.

▪ **/etc/init.d/apparmor**
   This is the AppArmor init script. By default AppArmor is enabled.

▪ **/var/log/apparmor/**
   AppArmor stores its logs under this directory.

▪ **/var/log/syslog**
   When an AppArmor rule is violated in either enforce or complain mode, the kernel generates a log entry under the standard system log.

SSH Security

If you are going to run services on your servers, these days it's a safe bet that one of them will be SSH. SSH provides a secure, encrypted channel between your desktop and a server so that you can run commands and manage the machine without having to physically be there with a keyboard and mouse. Even though SSH was designed with security at the forefront, poor management of the service can open you up to attack. In fact, one of the most common ways that Linux servers are attacked at the moment is via SSH brute-force attacks. I cover how to manage those attacks, but first I discuss a few other methods to enhance the security of SSH.

sshd_config

The /etc/ssh/sshd_config file is where you will find all of the settings for the SSH server. The default Ubuntu sshd_config file is pretty secure out of the box, as it allows only SSH protocol 2, uses privilege separation, and allows authentication keys to be used. The only questionable setting is `PermitRootLogin yes`. This option allows the root user to log in via SSH. In a way this setting is useless on a default Ubuntu install, since the root account is disabled, but if you decide to enable the root account, you might want to set this option to `no` and run `sudo service ssh reload` to save the settings. This way you force users to log in with their regular accounts and `sudo` up to root, and you also prevent a user from being able to guess the root password and gain access.

Key-Based Authentication

If there is a weak link in SSH security, password authentication would probably be it. I know plenty of people who have been hacked simply because of a weak user password. There are many brute-force SSH scripts active in the wild that constantly scan for new machines and run through a dictionary full of passwords until one works. I know of a honeypot server intentionally set with weak passwords that was hacked and used as part of a botnet within hours of showing up online.

The good news is that you don't need password authentication to log in to an SSH server. SSH supports key-based authentication. In this approach the user generates a public and private key. The public key is then placed in a special file on the remote server. When the user logs in, these keys are used to authenticate the user instead of a password. It's certainly more convenient to be able to log in to a machine without typing a password every time, although if you want an extra layer of security, you can set a passphrase on your keys as well.

It is relatively simple to set up key-based authentication. In this example we have a user named ubuntu on desktop1 who wants to set up key authentication on server1. The first step is to use the ssh-keygen program to create an RSA public and private key on desktop1. At each prompt you can press Enter to accept the defaults.

```
ubuntu@desktop1:~$ ssh-keygen -t rsa
Generating public/private rsa key pair.
Enter file in which to save the key (/home/ubuntu/.ssh/id_rsa):
Created directory '/home/ubuntu/.ssh'.
Enter passphrase (empty for no passphrase):
Enter same passphrase again:
Your identification has been saved in /home/ubuntu/.ssh/id_rsa.
Your public key has been saved in /home/ubuntu/.ssh/id_rsa.pub.
The key fingerprint is:
91:ae:0c:ff:16:a2:67:98:19:34:71:5b:71:e3:d2:2c ubuntu@ubuntu
```

The script creates the keys in the .ssh directory under your home directory, in this case /home/ubuntu/.ssh. The private key and public key are named id_rsa and id_rsa.pub respectively. It's very important (especially if you chose an empty passphrase) to keep the private key (id_rsa) safe! If anyone else gets access to this file, he or she can copy it and will be able to log in to any machines you have set up with this key.

Once you have created the keys, the next step is to copy the id_rsa.pub key to the server and then append it to the ~/.ssh/authorized_keys file. There are a number of ways you can do this. You could SSH into the remote machine, open ~/.ssh/authorized_keys with a text editor, and paste in the contents of id_rsa.pub, for instance. Here are two other ways to do this. The first way is simple to understand but takes multiple steps. The second method does the entire operation in one command. In method one I use the scp command to copy the id_rsa.pub file to the home directory on the remote server, then I append it to the ~/.ssh/authorized_keys file:

```
ubuntu@desktop1:~$ scp ~/.ssh/id_rsa.pub
ubuntu@server1:/home/ubuntu/id_rsa-desktop1.pub
ubuntu@desktop1:~$ ssh ubuntu@server1
ubuntu@server1:~$ mkdir ~/.ssh
ubuntu@server1:~$ chmod 700 ~/.ssh
ubuntu@server1:~$ cat ~/id_rsa-desktop1.pub >>
  ~/.ssh/authorized_keys
```

If you already have the ~/.ssh directory on the remote host, you can skip most of those steps. Also, if you already have a ~/.ssh directory, you can add your public key in a single one-liner that takes advantage of file redirection:

```
ubuntu@desktop1:~$ ssh ubuntu@server1 "cat >>
  ~/.ssh/authorized_keys" < ~/.ssh/id_rsa.pub
```

Once you have keys set up on a machine, you should be able to log in without a password prompt, unless you set a passphrase for your key, in which case you will need to type it. After your keys work, you might want to disable SSH password authentication altogether. Just make sure that your SSH keys work first or you could lock yourself out! To disable password authentication, edit /etc/ssh/sshd_config and locate the line that says

```
#PasswordAuthentication yes
```

Uncomment that line and set it to no:

```
PasswordAuthentication no
```

Finally, run sudo service sshd reload to load the new change.

SSH Brute-Force Attacks

As mentioned earlier in this chapter, SSH brute-force attacks have become a very common threat to Linux servers. Even if your password is hard to guess, unless you impose strong password restrictions on the server, there's no way of knowing that every other user has a strong password. The best way to combat SSH brute-force attacks is to simply disable password authentication and use SSH keys. Unfortunately, that isn't an option for every administrator. If you must use password authentication, there is another way to protect against these attacks: a package named denyhosts.

The way that denyhosts works is to monitor for failed SSH logins. When a host attempts to log in either as a user that doesn't exist or too many times, that host is added to /etc/hosts.deny and blocked from future SSH access.

Also, if a host tries to log in as a valid user but fails too many times, the host is blocked.

A number of administrators use this tool or tools like it to protect against brute-force attacks and like the results, but I find it hard to recommend. I mention it so that you know it is available, since you might disagree with my opinion. In case you do decide to deploy it, here are some things to watch out for:

- Any program that automatically modifies firewall (or TCP wrappers) rules is dangerous. If an attacker can detect that such a tool exists, he or she can remotely modify your firewall rules. What happens if the attacker can appear to come from a different host, such as your desktop, and lock you out?

- Set your thresholds carefully. Even with reasonably large thresholds, such as ten failed attempts for a valid user, you might still lock out valid users who forgot their password. I've even seen this happen with a user who set up keys and had a cron script log in and perform various tasks. When the server got overloaded and the SSH connections timed out, the failed SSH connections crossed the threshold and locked out the script.

- Set whitelists for trusted hosts. Be sure to add any hosts or networks that you can't risk being blocked into /etc/hosts.allow. Be sure to keep your whitelists up-to-date with new hosts or networks. Just keep in mind that if attackers do manage to hack into another machine on any of these networks, they will be able to attack these machines.

- Botnets know about denyhosts and can work around it. It's true that denyhosts makes a brute-force attack more difficult, but a large-enough botnet can work around this problem by having a particular host attack only a few times, or shift to a different host once the first is locked out.

Firewalls

One of the most common ways to protect machines on a network is with a firewall. Essentially a firewall gives you the ability to restrict access to services over the network. With a firewall you could limit access to SSH, for instance, to hosts only within your internal network, while allowing HTTP access to everyone. There are two major types of firewalls used in an organization: so-called hardware and software firewalls. A hardware firewall is generally a stand-alone machine that sits between your hosts and another network (often the Internet). This machine is then configured with a set of rules to control what access is allowed. A software firewall is a program that is run on a host itself and has a similar ability to restrict access, except in this case it applies only to that specific host.

Many organizations deploy both hardware and software firewalls, which is in line with the "Provide layers of protection" security principle. The hardware firewalls often double as the gateways for a particular network and help restrict access in and out of the network, while software firewalls on each host help reinforce the rules from the hardware firewall and can provide additional protection from hosts inside their own network—something a separate hardware firewall can't do. Honestly, many "hardware firewalls" out there are simply stand-alone machines that run Linux and use the same software firewall tools. In this chapter I discuss how to use Ubuntu's tools to set up a secure software firewall on your server.

Traditionally, firewall rules under Linux required that one delve deeply into the dark arts of the `iptables` program. `iptables` (and before that, `ipchains`) is a program included with Linux distributions that works with the Linux kernel to evaluate and potentially block packets based on rules that you define. In addition to standard port and host blocking, `iptables` supports stateful packet matching, which means it monitors and can identify traffic as belonging to a particular pair of hosts and can keep track of the state of that connection. You can then define rules that activate based on these states.

You can (and I have done so) create very complicated `iptables` rule sets, but honestly, the way that the `iptables` syntax is constructed, even the most basic rules can seem complex at times. This complexity fights against the "Keep it simple" security principle so that the beginner administrator either ends up disabling the firewall altogether or relies on some long set of `iptables` rules found on the Internet—rules the admin doesn't understand and therefore can't easily debug. The advanced administrator soldiers on and either develops a minimal set of rules or learns the dark art of stateful packet matching and develops a long rule set that is bound to have mistakes.

At some point the initial pride of writing heavy-duty, complicated iptables rules wears off and you just wish it were simpler. Eventually your common iptables administrator discovers the OpenBSD pf firewall tool and fills with envy. In pf you have simple, easy-to-understand syntax that is still secure. Luckily for Ubuntu administrators, there is now a similar tool, ufw, that aims to simplify firewall administration by providing a front end to iptables commands.

The ufw program will be installed by default on your server but will be disabled. Since a default Ubuntu install has no external network services enabled, there really isn't anything for a firewall to protect. As you start to add services, however, you will want to enable the firewall and add rules.

ufw Commands

The basic set of ufw commands is pretty straightforward. If you run ufw -h, you will get a help page that describes the main ufw commands, but if you want full syntax information, you should type man ufw to read the full manual page. First I identify the main commands and then provide some examples.

- **enable and disable**
  These commands enable and disable ufw, respectively. By default ufw is disabled, so if you wanted to enable it, you would type sudo ufw enable.

- **status**
  If you aren't sure whether or not your firewall is enabled, type sudo ufw status to check. If ufw is enabled and you have any rules defined with ufw, the status command will also output all of your rules.

- **default**
  A very important command to consider is the default command. This command defines the default policy of your firewall, as in whether by default all packets are allowed or denied. The general

consensus is that a firewall is more secure if you deny all packets by default, and then enable services as you need to. That way, if you start a new service (or worse, a user starts a service) and you forget to set firewall rules for it, by default it will be blocked. So to deny by default, you would type `sudo ufw default deny`. To allow by default, type `sudo ufw default allow`. Note that `ufw` will deny by default unless you change it.

- **logging**
  This command toggles whether or not you want your firewall to dump logs of anything it blocks along with anything against your default policy. To enable logging, type `sudo ufw logging on`. To disable it, type `sudo ufw logging off`.

- **allow and deny**
  These are the commands that you will run more often than not, as they define your firewall rules. The arguments they accept are more involved because they can define complex firewall rules, so I discuss their syntax below.

- **delete allow and delete deny**
  These commands will undo a particular firewall rule you have created. Whenever you want to remove a rule, you copy the same command you used to create the rule and then add `delete` to the very beginning.

NOTE For all of my examples, I'm going to assume your firewall denies by default. When you deny by default (`sudo ufw default deny`), you construct your rules so that they are focused on what access to allow. If instead you decide to allow by default, your set of rules has to be focused on what access to deny. Generally speaking, you will find that denying by default results in a shorter list of rules for a secure firewall.

ufw Rule Syntax

A basic `ufw` rule takes a port or service as an argument. To open port 53 (used for DNS servers), you would type

```
$ sudo ufw allow 53
```

ufw also accepts service names that are defined in the /etc/services file instead of specific ports. If you look in the /etc/services file, you can see that port 53 TCP and UDP is set to the domain service. So another way to state this rule is

```
$ sudo ufw allow domain
```

This name-based access makes it really simple to define rules because you don't need to concern yourself as much with ports as with service names. For instance, to open up access to a mail server, you could type

```
$ sudo ufw allow smtp
```

The SMTP service operates only over TCP, not UDP, and ufw will see this in the /etc/services file and allow only port 25 TCP traffic through. You can specify TCP or UDP on the command line as well, so the equivalent to the command above would be

```
$ sudo ufw allow 25/tcp
```

Once you have created some rules, you can view them with the status command:

```
$ sudo ufw status
Status: active

To              Action  From
--              ------  ----
53              ALLOW   Anywhere
25/tcp          ALLOW   Anywhere
```

Extended ufw Rules

When you view the ufw status after you have set some basic rules, you will notice that by default these ports are open to any IP address. This may be exactly what you want. You may, however, want to lock down specific services further so that only certain hosts can access them. To do this, you need to extend the basic ufw rules.

A good example of why you might want to limit based on IP address is an intranet site, like an internal wiki. If you use a wiki for your internal documentation, you probably don't want the entire world to read it. You might even host a wiki just for a particular group of users and want to restrict access so that only their network can see it. When you define more advanced ufw rules, you must use the extended ufw syntax. This syntax requires you to specify the protocol and port number explicitly, so you can't use the same shortcuts as in the simpler commands. Here's an example command to limit Web access (port 80) to just the 10.1.1.0 network:

```
$ sudo ufw allow proto tcp from 10.1.1.0/24 to any port 80
```

Let's break this command down. The proto tcp section defines whether this rule applies to TCP or UDP. I limit what networks this rule applies to with from 10.1.1.0/24. The to any port 80 section of the command says that this rule applies to port 80 on any destination address on the machine.

Even if you deny by default, there might be circumstances when you also add a deny rule. For instance, let's say that you are running an external SMTP (mail) server and you notice that a host inside your network at 10.1.1.75 appears to be infected with a virus and is flooding your mail server with invalid messages. To block just that IP address, you would type

```
$ sudo ufw deny proto tcp from 10.1.1.75 to any port 25
```

If you wanted to block all packets from that host, not just SMTP, you wouldn't need to define the proto or to arguments:

```
$ sudo ufw deny from 10.1.1.75
```

Later on, once the virus has been removed and the host is back to normal, you can remove the rule with

```
$ sudo ufw delete deny proto tcp from 10.1.1.75 to any port 25
```

or, if you dropped all packets from the host, this command would remove it:

```
$ sudo ufw delete deny from 10.1.1.75
```

NOTE   Notice that when I wanted to undo a rule, I used the `delete` command. At first you might logically conclude that you just need to write an `allow` command so the host can connect again. This works, but when you do this, `ufw` just changes your existing rule, so you will have an unnecessary rule in your list. When you want to undo a rule, just delete it.

ufw Examples

The following is a list of start-to-finish `ufw` commands to set up a firewall for a particular service. I assume you are starting from the default state, that is, `ufw` is disabled. Also, I assume you will probably want to manage your server remotely with SSH even if it's a Web, mail, or DNS server, so I add rules to enable SSH in each example.

NOTE   **About Remote Firewall Management**
If this is the first time you have enabled `ufw`, and you plan to set this up remotely over the network, you should be careful about your steps. It's very easy to make a mistake and lock yourself out. Specifically, when `ufw` is enabled, it flushes all connection data, so if you manage the server over SSH, your connection will be closed, and if you deny by default and haven't set up an SSH rule yet, when `ufw` is enabled, you will be locked out. One simple safeguard you can put in place is a cron job that disables `ufw` every 15 minutes or so. That way, if you make a mistake and lock yourself out, you just have to wait at most 15 minutes for the firewall to be reset. To do this, add the following line to your /etc/crontab file:

```
*/15 *  * * * root    ufw disable
```

Of course, the downside to this is that every 15 minutes while you are tweaking your firewall, `ufw` will be disabled and you will have to remember to enable it. Still, it's better than being locked out of the system completely. Just remember to delete the `crontab` rule once you are finished tweaking. On Ubuntu 8.10 and later, `ufw` actually warns you if you enable `ufw` while using SSH and prompts you before it enables.

SSH   I'm assuming you will probably want to have SSH enabled on just about any server you manage. Note the order in which I run the commands here, as I enable `ufw` at the very end. That way I don't risk locking myself out because the SSH rule is defined before `ufw` is enabled:

```
$ sudo ufw allow ssh
$ sudo ufw default deny
$ sudo ufw enable
$ sudo ufw status
Status: active
```

```
To              Action  From

--              ------  ----
22              ALLOW   Anywhere
```

DNS

```
$ sudo ufw allow ssh
$ sudo ufw allow domain
$ sudo ufw default deny
$ sudo ufw enable
$ sudo ufw status
Status: active
```

```
To              Action  From

--              ------  ----
22              ALLOW   Anywhere
53              ALLOW   Anywhere
```

Web   Here I open up ports for both HTTP (80) and HTTPS (443), but if you don't use HTTPS, you can remove that particular rule from the list:

```
$ sudo ufw allow ssh
$ sudo ufw allow www
$ sudo ufw allow https
$ sudo ufw default deny
$ sudo ufw enable
$ sudo ufw status
Status: active
```

```
To              Action  From

--              ------  ----
22              ALLOW   Anywhere
80              ALLOW   Anywhere
443             ALLOW   Anywhere
```

SMTP

```
$ sudo ufw allow ssh
$ sudo ufw allow smtp
$ sudo ufw default deny
$ sudo ufw enable
$ sudo ufw status
Status: active
```

```
To              Action  From

--              ------  ----
22              ALLOW   Anywhere
25/tcp          ALLOW   Anywhere
```

POP/IMAP   To simplify things, I list rules to enable POP2, POP3, and POP3 with SSL, IMAP2, IMAP3, and IMAP with SSL, since many administrators end up supporting all of them on the same server.

```
$ sudo ufw allow ssh
$ sudo ufw allow pop2
$ sudo ufw allow pop3
$ sudo ufw allow pop3s
$ sudo ufw allow imap2
$ sudo ufw allow imap3
$ sudo ufw allow imaps
$ sudo ufw default deny
$ sudo ufw enable
$ sudo ufw status
Status: active

To            Action  From
--            ------  ----
22            ALLOW   Anywhere
109           ALLOW   Anywhere
110           ALLOW   Anywhere
995           ALLOW   Anywhere
143           ALLOW   Anywhere
220           ALLOW   Anywhere
993           ALLOW   Anywhere
```

MySQL   This example uses the default MySQL ports. Of course, if you have moved MySQL to listen on a different port, you will have to manually specify the port to open.

```
$ sudo ufw allow ssh
$ sudo ufw allow mysql
$ sudo ufw default deny
$ sudo ufw enable
$ sudo ufw status
Status: active

To            Action  From
--            ------  ----
22            ALLOW   Anywhere
3306          ALLOW   Anywhere
```

PostgreSQL   This example uses the default PostgreSQL ports. Of course, if you have moved PostgreSQL to listen on a different port, you will have to manually specify the port to open.

```
$ sudo ufw allow ssh
$ sudo ufw allow postgresql
$ sudo ufw default deny
$ sudo ufw enable
$ sudo ufw status
Status: active

To              Action  From
--              ------  ----
22              ALLOW   Anywhere
5432            ALLOW   Anywhere
```

Samba   Samba is a little trickier to open because it listens on a set of ports and none of them are labeled in /etc/services with "Samba."

```
$ sudo ufw allow ssh
$ sudo ufw allow netbios-ns
$ sudo ufw allow netbios-dgm
$ sudo ufw allow netbios-ssn
$ sudo ufw default deny
$ sudo ufw enable
$ sudo ufw status
Status: active

To              Action  From
--              ------  ----
22              ALLOW   Anywhere
137             ALLOW   Anywhere
138             ALLOW   Anywhere
139             ALLOW   Anywhere
```

NFS   NFS is a little trickier to firewall off than most other services because the connections don't necessarily use a defined set of ports. As a result, it can be difficult to open up a range of ports for NFS that will work long-term. The simplest solution, if you want to enable a firewall on an NFS server, is to deny by default and then allow access to all ports from specific NFS clients. If you don't want to add a firewall rule for each individual host because there are many, you might consider putting all NFS clients on their own subnet and then allowing that subnet. I show two examples. The first allows all access from the 10.1.1.7, 10.1.1.8, and 10.1.1.9 hosts. The second example opens up access for the entire 10.1.2.0/24 subnet:

```
$ sudo ufw allow ssh
$ sudo ufw allow from 10.1.1.7
$ sudo ufw allow from 10.1.1.8
```

```
$ sudo ufw allow from 10.1.1.9
$ sudo ufw default deny
$ sudo ufw enable
$ sudo ufw status
Status: active

To              Action  From
--              ------  ----
22              ALLOW   Anywhere
Anywhere        ALLOW   10.1.1.7
Anywhere        ALLOW   10.1.1.8
Anywhere        ALLOW   10.1.1.9
```

Here are the steps to allow all of 10.1.2.0/24 access to NFS:

```
$ sudo ufw allow ssh
$ sudo ufw allow from 10.1.2.0/24
$ sudo ufw default deny
$ sudo ufw enable
$ sudo ufw status
Status: active

To              Action  From
--              ------  ----
22              ALLOW   Anywhere
Anywhere        ALLOW   10.1.2.0/24
```

Ubuntu ufw Conventions

For the most part you should be able to set up a firewall using ufw without worrying about configuration files. The ufw program will update its configuration files for you, so that if you set it to be enabled from the command line, you won't have to tweak anything else. That being said, you might be interested in how ufw works behind the scenes, so I list ufw's file conventions here:

▪ **/etc/ufw/**
This directory contains all of the configuration files for ufw, including /etc/ufw/ufw.conf, the main configuration file. The only default setting in that file, though, defines whether the firewall is enabled at boot—something you can set with ufw itself.

▪ **/etc/ufw/before.rules and /etc/ufw/before6.rules**
These files contain a set of IPv4 and IPv6 iptables rules, respectively, that ufw will set before any ufw rules are enabled. Advanced iptables

users can refer to these files if they are curious about ufw's behavior. If you really know what you are doing and want to modify this behavior with your own iptables rules, you can add them to the ufw-before-input, ufw-before-output, or ufw-before-forward chains, depending on which chain they belong to. If you don't know what I'm talking about, then don't worry; the average user shouldn't need to edit these files.

▪ **/etc/ufw/after.rules and /etc/ufw/after6.rules**
These files are like the before.rules and before6.rules files, except they are loaded after ufw rules are enabled. Again, if you really know iptables, you might want to set up specific iptables rules in this file to be started after ufw.

▪ **/etc/init.d/ufw**
This is the init script for ufw. Generally speaking, you shouldn't need to touch this script because you can add and delete rules and enable and disable ufw from the command line.

▪ **/etc/defaults/ufw**
Like other init scripts, ufw has a file under /etc/defaults that defines the environment variables it uses when it starts. There are some settings in this file that are of interest to more advanced administrators; for example, you would come here to enable IPv6 support or add or delete extra connection tracking modules for iptables.

▪ **/lib/ufw/user.rules and /lib/ufw/user6.rules**
When you define your own ufw rules, they end up in the user.rules file, or user6.rules file for IPv6 rules. If you want to know exactly what iptables command a particular ufw rule creates, you can look here. Generally speaking, you do not want to edit these files directly.

▪ **/var/log/syslog**
If you have enabled logging, ufw will dump its logs to the standard /var/log/syslog file. If logging is enabled, each connection attempt that is against your ufw policy will be logged here, so you can see the source host and port, the protocol, and the destination host and port for each connection attempt.

Intrusion Detection

Once you have set up a firewall and locked down your system, how can you tell whether the system has been compromised? One way is to set up an intrusion detection system (IDS). If you think of your computer system like a house, your firewall and file permissions could be thought of as locks on the windows and doors. Think of an intrusion detection system as a burglar alarm—its job is not to prevent someone from breaking in, but instead to alert you when it happens.

There are a number of different intrusion detection systems out there, and most of the time you hear about network intrusion detection systems that sniff network traffic and look for suspicious activity. In this case I'm not talking about that sort of IDS, but instead a system to detect that an attacker has intruded into a particular server. One of the oldest and most common of these types of systems is Tripwire. Tripwire maintains a database of information about core files on the system. Once the database has been created, Tripwire scans the system once per day and e-mails you a report. If any of the files in the database has been altered, Tripwire alerts you in its report. Most of the files in Tripwire's database are files that are common to replace with Trojan horse programs. Others, such as the /etc/passwd file, are files that only root can change. This means that if any of the files change, and you know you and your staff didn't change it, you can be pretty confident of some sort of system breach.

Because Tripwire detects a breach based on files being different from the version in its database, Tripwire can't detect if your system was attacked *before* Tripwire was installed. In addition, the effectiveness of Tripwire is based on the integrity of its database. If attackers can write to that database, they can update it with signatures for hacked versions of system files and continue undetected. Because of all of this, it's important to install Tripwire as soon as possible on the system, preferably at install time. Also, if possible, you might consider switching to single-user mode beforehand (type sudo init 1 in a console). Note that single-user mode works only if you are physically logged in to the machine (no SSH). In single-user mode you can be sure that no other users can interfere with the initial Tripwire install.

Tripwire is packaged by Ubuntu; however, it is not ready to use out of the box. You must tweak its policy database and think about how you will store the signature database securely before the install is complete. First, install the Tripwire package:

```
$ sudo apt-get install tripwire
```

If you don't have an MTA (Mail Transport Agent) installed, the Tripwire package will add one as a dependency. As the Tripwire package installs, you will be asked a number of questions about keys. Tripwire uses two different keys to sign files and ensure that they have not been altered. The first key is a site-wide key that you might use for all of the servers on a particular network. The second key is a local key that is unique for this particular machine. If you do not yet have a site key or you aren't sure what this means, answer Yes to create a site key. Next you get a similar prompt about a local key. Unless you already have a local Tripwire key, answer Yes here as well so the installer can create one. At the next prompt, answer Yes to rebuild the Tripwire configuration file, and Yes one final time to re-create the policy file. Finally, enter passphrases to use for the site and local keys. Be sure to note what passphrases you selected, because there's no method to retrieve or reset them if you forget.

Update Tripwire Policy

The Tripwire policy file is located at /etc/tripwire/twpol.txt and defines all of the files and directories Tripwire will monitor along with what information to monitor and how to respond to changes in each file. The default twpol.txt file is a good starting place, but it contains a few files and directories that you will want to remove to avoid a lot of false positives every time you run a Tripwire check. Open the file in a text editor and remove the lines as indicated for each file below:

- **/etc/rc.boot**
  Ubuntu doesn't have this file, so remove the line that says

  ```
  /etc/rc.boot     -> $(SEC_BIN) ;
  ```

- **/proc**
  Files in the /proc directory change constantly, so you will get tons of false alarms if this is scanned. Delete the following line from the file:

  ```
  /proc     -> $(Device) ;
  ```

▪ **/root**

There is a large section of the twpol.txt file that lists files under the /root directory. The problem is that by default these files don't exist, so they will generate false positives. Locate the section of the file that looks like this:

```
# These files change the behavior of the root account
(
  rulename = "Root config files",
  severity = 100
)
{
    /root      -> $(SEC_CRIT) ; # Catch all additions to /root
```

Delete the references to all of the files under the /root directory except for /root/.bashrc. The resulting segment of the twpol.txt file looks like this:

```
# These files change the behavior of the root account
(
  rulename = "Root config files",
  severity = 100
)
{
    /root      -> $(SEC_CRIT) ; # Catch all additions to /root
    /root/.bashrc    -> $(SEC_CONFIG) ;
}
```

Save all of your changes, and then use the twadmin tool to update the policy file:

```
$ sudo twadmin -m P /etc/tripwire/twpol.txt
```

Initialize the Tripwire Database

Once the policy file has been changed, you are ready to initialize the database. Note that the system's state at this point in time is what Tripwire considers the gold standard, so you want to initialize the database as soon after the system has been created as possible. Here is the command to initialize Tripwire's database:

```
$ sudo tripwire -m i
```

Don't worry about any errors you see about the /var/lib/tripwire/foo.twd file not existing—this is the database you are creating now. Once the database has been initialized, you should store it somewhere safe, because if attackers get root privileges they could update the database and hide their tracks. There are a few ways to secure the database. One, you could store the database on a floppy disk with the physical write-protect bit set and change the /etc/tripwire/twcfg.txt file to point to that new location. Alternatively, you could set up an NFS server that you consider secure to host all of the Tripwire database files and set all of the databases as read-only.

Since floppies are getting hard to come by, I describe how to set this up with NFS. Let's assume that your Tripwire database is at /var/lib/tripwire/ host1.twd. You have an NFS server at 10.1.1.7 and have copied the host1 .twd file at /mnt/tripwire/host1/. Then you would use `sudo chmod 400 /mnt/tripwire/host1/host1.twd` to ensure that the file could not be changed. Since Tripwire checks are run as the root user, you will probably have to disable root squashing on the NFS server, at least whenever you need to update the database. If you wanted additional security, you could also modify the /etc/exports file so that this share could be mounted only as read-only. NFS server administration is out of the scope of this chapter, but for more information on NFS server configuration, check the NFS section of Chapter 5. With NFS configured, create a directory called /mnt/ tripwire on your local machine and mount the NFS share:

```
$ sudo mkdir /mnt/tripwire
$ sudo mount -o ro 10.1.1.7:/mnt/tripwire/host1/ /mnt/tripwire
```

If you get an error that this is an unknown file system type, be sure that you have the `nfs-common` package installed. Once the share mounts successfully, add a new line to /etc/fstab to make sure that it mounts automatically each time the system boots:

```
10.1.1.7:/mnt/tripwire/host1 /mnt/tripwire nfs defaults,ro 0 0
```

Now if you run `sudo ls -l /mnt/tripwire/`, you should be able to see the /mnt/tripwire/host1.twd file (the filename will be named after your host's name, of course). Edit the /etc/tripwire/twcfg.txt file as root and change the part of the file that reads

```
DBFILE      =/var/lib/tripwire/$(HOSTNAME).twd
```

to

```
DBFILE      =/mnt/tripwire/$(HOSTNAME).twd
```

Finally, you need to re-create the encrypted Tripwire configuration file:

```
$ sudo twadmin -m F -S /etc/tripwire/site.key /etc/tripwire/
  twcfg.txt
```

Once the Tripwire database is in a safe location, your base Tripwire configuration is complete. Now any time you want to check the system, you can run

```
$ sudo tripwire --check
```

and Tripwire will output a report that lists any files that have changed. In addition to the output on the screen, Tripwire stores all of its reports in date-stamped files under /var/lib/tripwire/reports/. By default, Tripwire runs a system check every night and e-mails you a report.

Update the Tripwire Database

The very first time that you run a sudo tripwire --check you will probably notice that it complains because you modified /etc/tripwire/ twcfg.txt and a few other Tripwire files. Now and then, such as when you update major packages on the system, you will end up legitimately updating files that Tripwire scans, and unless you update the Tripwire database to note these changes, you will get false positives at every nightly scan. In fact, you might want to run a Tripwire check after you do major package updates to make sure that you catch any changes and update them immediately.

To update the Tripwire database, first you must set it so that you can write to the .twd file. If you set this up on an NFS share as in the example, you will need to go to the NFS server and run sudo chmod a+w /mnt/tripwire/ host1/host1.twd (replace that path with the path to the file you are exporting). In addition, you need to disable root squashing and set the share to rw during the short time the database is updated. You will also need to remount the NFS share as rw. Once the NFS server is ready, go to the host itself and locate the report that contains the errors you want to override. This will probably be the newest file in /var/lib/tripwire/report. Then run the following Tripwire command to update the database:

```
$ sudo tripwire -m u -r /var/lib/tripwire/report/
  hostname-20090107-190736.twr
```

Replace the filename under here with the name of your report. The update tool outputs the report to the screen in the root user's default text editor (probably vi, unless you set the EDITOR environment variable to something else). If this is the default vi editor, you should be able to use the arrow keys (or the standard H, J, K, and L keys) to move throughout the report. Each item slated to be updated in the database will be on a line with [x] at the beginning. As long as that x is inside the box, that file will be updated. If you do not want to update a particular file, move the cursor over that x and type r and then the spacebar to remove it. When you are finished editing the file, hit :wq. You will be prompted for the local key, and then the database will be updated.

Once this command is finished and the database is updated, you must go back to the NFS server and reinstate all of the permissions and other protections you put in place to make this file read-only.

Ubuntu Tripwire Conventions

- **/etc/tripwire/**
  This directory contains all of the main configuration files used by Tripwire.

- **/etc/tripwire/*-local.key and /etc/tripwire/site.key**
  These files are your local and site keys, respectively. The local key will be named after the localhost.

- **/etc/tripwire/tw.cfg and /etc/tripwire/twcfg.txt**
  The tw.cfg is the encrypted database of Tripwire settings, and the twcfg.txt is the plain-text version. Whenever you want to change

Tripwire settings, such as the location of the database file, you will make the changes in twcfg.txt and then use twadmin to update the encrypted database.

▪ **/etc/tripwire/tw.pol and /etc/tripwire/twpol.txt**
These files define the policy that Tripwire uses when it scans the file system. This policy includes which files to scan, what attributes of those files to pay attention to, and with what severity to rate any changes to those files. The tw.pol file is the encrypted database, and the twpol.txt file is the plain-text file you edit to make changes. Once you have made changes to twpol.txt, you must run twadmin to update the tw.pol file.

▪ **/var/lib/tripwire/**
This directory is the default location for the Tripwire database. Generally, you will end up moving the database file to another, more secure, read-only location.

▪ **/var/lib/tripwire/reports**
When you run sudo tripwire --check (or when it runs automatically every night), a new report file is generated and stored in this directory. This provides a good history of how core files have changed on the system.

▪ **/var/log/syslog**
Tripwire logs to the standard system log. To see only Tripwire logs, you could run sudo grep tripwire /var/log/syslog.

Incident Response

Most of this chapter focuses on how to protect your systems so that they can't be breached by an attacker, but what do you do when an attacker succeeds? Here I provide an overview of how to prepare for and respond to a successful attack.

Preparation before an attack occurs is just as important as the actions you take when it occurs. Even if you are naturally cool and calm during a crisis, there's a good chance other members of your team won't be, so a plan you have thought through when you are calm will be better than a plan you have thought up at the last minute with upper management breathing down your neck.

Do You Prosecute?

Before you develop any other responses, the first thing you should decide is under what circumstances you will wish to prosecute an attacker. If you are running a home office, that answer might be never. If you are part of a large organization, your company's legal department might have to answer the question for you. In either case it's important to have an idea of what circumstances will prompt prosecution, because it will define the rest of the steps you can take. Generally, investigators want to collect untainted evidence, and if you and your team have been touching a bunch of files on the system, their job will be that much harder. How you respond (and how you set up a system) so you can prosecute effectively will vary depending on your location, so if at all possible, consult an attorney.

Pull the Plug

Another question you should answer before an attack occurs is what you do the moment you have confirmed that a host has been attacked. There are different schools of thought on this, but I believe that the moment you detect an attack, you should immediately pull the power from the server. If the host is a virtual machine that supports snapshots, take a snapshot, then power off the VM. The reason I advocate this approach is that while there can be valuable data in RAM on the system, every command you run and every file you touch on the system potentially erases forensic clues you could use later. Plus, if the attacker has installed a root kit, you can't even trust any output from the running machine—you could have Trojan versions of ps, bash, and lsmod, for instance, that mask the attacker's existence.

Image the Server

Once the power has been pulled, do whatever you can to ensure that the machine doesn't boot back up until you have been able to image all of the

partitions on the system from a rescue disc. That way you can then perform forensic analysis on the image without overwriting the original evidence. Plus, once you have an image to work from, you can consider
redeploying the server. If the host is a VM and you were able to take a
snapshot, you have even more data to work from. Create a copy of the
entire VM, snapshot and all. Then you can potentially replay the time you
discovered the attack over and over and run tools on the running snapshot
image without fear of corrupting data. If you have the space, consider creating two images. One is a gold image that you put away and don't touch,
and the other is an image that you use for any forensic analysis you might
perform. When you have multiple images, if you make a mistake and accidentally write to one during your analysis, you will at least have the gold
image to copy from.

Server Redeployment

Another thing to consider before a crisis occurs is whether and when you
should rebuild a server. The best practice is to rebuild a server whenever
there has been a breach. It can be easy, at least if the attacker was sloppy, to
prove he or she *did* install a root kit if you see the software out in the open,
but unless you are skilled at forensic analysis it can be difficult to prove an
attacker *didn't* install a root kit or some sort of Trojan horse on the system.
A root kit can hide all sorts of things from the administrator, so unless you
are absolutely sure there is no root kit, rebuild the machine.

How you go about rebuilding the server might be decided on a case-by-case
basis. Some servers (particularly those in a cluster) often can be rebuilt
from scratch without a thought. Other servers, such as large database or
e-mail servers that aren't in a cluster, can be more difficult because they
hold data you need to transfer to the new host. These types of machines
might have to go into quarantine until you can make sure that the data can
be trusted. To be safe, you might even have to try to track down when the
attack occurred and roll back the files on the system from a previous
backup. Also, you might need to keep the machine in quarantine until you
can track down how the attacker got in and patch the hole before risking
another intrusion.

Forensics

Once you have a valid image of the system's partitions, you might want to perform some sort of forensic analysis on it. Computer forensics is a vast topic and it can take years of work for you to become proficient. That having been said, even if you aren't a skilled forensics expert, you might want to try your hand at identifying how the attacker got in.

One basic method of forensic analysis is simply to take the image of your attacked server to another host, mount it loopback and read-only, and then look around the mounted system for clues. For instance, if I had an image of a partition on an external USB drive mounted at /media/disk1/ and the image itself was at /media/disk1/web1-sda1.img, I could use the following command to mount the disk at /mnt/temp:

```
$ sudo mkdir /mnt/temp
$ sudo mount -o loop,ro /media/disk1/web1-sda1.img /mnt/temp
```

If you are ready for more advanced forensic analysis, I recommend you check out Sleuth Kit (http://sleuthkit.org). Sleuth Kit is a complete set of forensics tools including a Web-based front end called Autopsy. These tools are packaged in Ubuntu as sleuthkit and autopsy, so you can install them on an Ubuntu desktop with your preferred package manager. Once both tools are installed, type autopsy in a terminal to start the program and then follow the instructions on the screen to see where Autopsy stores its files (/var/lib/autopsy by default) and what URL to open on a Web browser to use Autopsy (http://localhost:9999/autopsy by default). That URL will display the default Autopsy page as shown in Figure 6-1, and from there you can navigate through the tool, start a new investigation, and add images to scan. For more information on how to use Autopsy, read the official Autopsy user's guide at http://wiki.sleuthkit.org/index.php?title=Autopsy_User's_Guide.

Another useful forensics tool is chkrootkit. This program can check a file system for common root kits and then output a report. This tool is also packaged for Ubuntu with the package name chkrootkit. Note that you generally don't want to run this on a live system because you will potentially overwrite evidence. Instead, mount an image somewhere on your

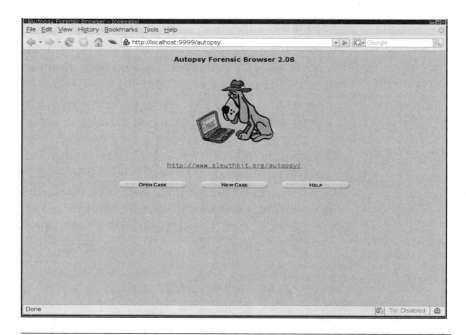

Figure 6-1 Default Autopsy page

system (for instance, in this example I mount the root file system image under /mnt/temp), and then point chkrootkit to it:

```
$ sudo chkrootkit -r /mnt/temp
```

Ultimately, complete forensics on a host could take days, weeks, or even months to complete, depending on your experience, the nature of the attack, and how thorough you want to be. Even if you decide to just rebuild the host and already know how the attacker got in, it's worth experimenting with these forensics tools as they will provide you with greater insight into how your system works long term.

## CHAPTER 7

Backups

THERE ARE SO MANY ENEMIES of your data. When it comes to disks, it's not a question of whether your hard drives will fail, it's a question of when. Beyond hard drive failure you find rm, dd, and a number of other Linux commands that are incredibly efficient at destroying your data. Just ask a good friend of mine who was trying to clean up his MP3 directory. A number of us were helping him perfect a find script that would delete all of the files in his MP3 directory that did not end in .mp3. Despite our warnings to test the script with echo first, he ran the full command: find . -type f ! -name '*.mp3' -exec rm -f {} \;. At first it appeared to be working, until he discovered he hadn't run the command in his MP3 directory—he ran it in ~, his home directory. True, he had cleaned up his MP3 directory, along with the rest of his files. The bottom line is that the only real way to ensure that your data is safe is to back it up.

There are any number of ways to back up data under Ubuntu, and in this chapter I cover a graphical tool called BackupPC. I also discuss some commonsense backup tips and describe how to create a full image of a drive or partition. I include some special considerations for when you're backing up a database. By the end of the chapter, if you haven't set up a backup system yet, I hope you will be encouraged by how easy it is under Ubuntu.

Backup Principles

There are a number of principles that should guide you when you set up your backup strategy. Most of these are common sense but bear repeating:

- **Back up data to a separate system.**
  That separate system might be a separate drive, a tape, or ideally a completely separate host. The point is not to back up data on a drive to the same drive. You really want your backups to be as far removed from the system as possible—even for my personal data at home I have a backup system in place to copy my most important files to a server out of state. That way, if my house burned down or serious file system corruption hit my server, my important data would still exist.

▪ **Test your backups.**
If you haven't successfully restored from backup, you haven't truly
backed anything up. After you set up a backup system, you must make
sure that you can restore from it. It's a good practice to follow up with
tests of your restore process periodically afterward. The worst time to
find out a backup didn't work is when you really need a file.

▪ **RAID is not a substitute for backups.**
A common mistake among beginner administrators is to mistake
RAID for backups. RAID provides you with redundancy for hard
disks so that if a particular disk fails, your data still remains safe on
the other disks. RAID does *not* protect you from a user deleting a file
or, worse, complete file system corruption. In the case of a RAID mirror, if you write bad data to one drive, that bad data will simply be
replicated to the second. On top of this, it's not unheard of for a RAID
controller to die and write bad data to the disks as it goes down. In
any of these cases if you did not keep a backup that is separate from
your RAID, your data would be gone.

▪ **Create full and incremental backup schedules.**
The majority of files on a server tend to stay the same, particularly
when you are talking about the core OS files. For this reason most
administrators opt for a combination of full backups (a complete
copy of every file) over a longer period of time, such as every week,
and incremental backups (only files that have changed since the last
backup) over a shorter period of time, usually daily. Since incremental backups generally involved fewer files, they take up less space and
are faster to complete. Just keep in mind that if you restore multiple
files, there's a chance that some of the files aren't included in the latest
incremental backup. The safe approach is to restore from the full
backup and then all subsequent incrementals if you aren't sure every
file made it into the last backup.

▪ **Decide how often to back up.**
A common question one might ask is "How often should I back up?"
The basic answer is "How much work can you afford to lose?" Many
organizations can stand losing up to a day's work, so they back up

nightly. If you can afford to lose only a few hours of work, then you need to back your data up every few hours.

▪ **Archive your backups.**
While it would be nice to save backups forever, the reality is that back-ups can consume an incredible amount of space. You may be able to keep only a month's worth of backups on your system before you run out of space. Even if that is the case, consider archiving old backups to separate storage like a tape, a USB drive, or even DVDs that you label and store in a vault. Many organizations maintain a month's worth of backups, and then archive off a full backup every month, every quarter, or every year. That way they have a snapshot of their data at that point so even if the backup server itself were to catch fire, there's still a version of the data available.

Drive Imaging

An image is a complete bit-for-bit copy of a drive. Once you image a drive, its image should be indistinguishable from the original drive. One of the most guaranteed, if wasteful, methods for backing up a system is to take an image of its drives. Even if you don't use drive imaging as your backup strategy, you will find a number of other circumstances where drive images come in handy, from cloning a system to file system recovery to forensics.

NOTE When imaging a drive, it's important that the drive not be in use. If the drive changes while you image it, you will not be able to guarantee that the image is consistent, so be sure that any file systems on a drive are unmounted. The requirement that a drive you image not be in use is yet another reason why most people don't use imaging as their primary backup strategy.

The classic UNIX imaging tool is dd, and you will find it on just about any Linux system and definitely on any Ubuntu server. This straightforward and blunt tool in its most basic form reads an input file bit by bit and copies it to an output file bit by bit. If you had two drives of identical size, /dev/sda and /dev/sdb, here is the command to image sda to sdb:

```
$ sudo dd if=/dev/sda of=/dev/sdb
```

Of course, dd can use any file as its input and output file, so instead of imaging to another drive, you could image to a file. This is particularly handy for forensics, when you might have a number of file system images stored on a single large USB drive. Assuming you have mounted your USB drive at /media/disk1, here is how you could image /dev/sda to a file on that drive:

```
$ sudo dd if=/dev/sda of=/media/disk1/sda-image.img
```

To restore from this image, you would just reverse the two arguments. Here are the commands to restore the two previous examples:

```
$ sudo dd if=/dev/sdb of=/dev/sda
$ sudo dd if=/media/disk1/sda-image.img of=/dev/sda
```

You can also image individual partitions. This can be useful since you can easily mount the images loopback and read through them. First let's image a partition on /dev/sda:

```
$ sudo dd if=/dev/sda1 of=/media/disk1/sda1-image.img
```

Now you can create a directory, /mnt/temp, and use the loop mount option to mount this image:

```
$ sudo mkdir /mnt/temp
$ sudo mount -o loop /media/disk1/sda1-image.img /mnt/temp
```

This is handy when you need to recover only a few files from an image. You can browse /mnt/temp like any other file system and copy individual files or entire directories from it. To copy this image back to the original drive, reverse the arguments once again:

```
$ sudo dd if=/media/disk1/sda1-image.img of=/dev/sda1
```

Another useful trick is imaging over the network. The fact is that with some servers you might not have a separate disk attached that can hold an image. One method might be to set up a remote NFS server with plenty of storage. Then you could mount the NFS share on the local system and create an image file that way. Of course, that requires that you have an NFS server set up. Another method is to pipe dd's output to SSH. Since most servers will probably have SSH, you won't have to set up anything special to create this image, and all of the data will be transferred over an encrypted channel.

To transfer /dev/sda from the local machine over the network to 10.1.1.5 and dump the image at /media/disk1/sda-image.img, you would type

```
$ sudo dd if=/dev/sda | ssh username@10.1.1.5 \
"cat > /media/disk1/sda-image.img"
```

To restore this image:

```
$ ssh username@10.1.1.5 "cat /media/disk1/sda-image.img" |
sudo dd of=/dev/sda
```

Database Backups

For the most part, backing up a system is as easy as making a copy of its files. On a database system, however, things aren't quite so simple. A database often won't commit changes to disk immediately, so if you simply make a copy of the database files, the database itself might be in an inconsistent state. When you restore it, you can't necessarily guarantee that it is an uncorrupted copy.

The solution to this problem is to use tools included with the database to provide a consistent dump of the complete database to a file that you *can* back up. Below I describe how to use the tools provided for MySQL and PostgreSQL databases under Ubuntu.

MySQL

The tool MySQL uses to create a backup of its database is called `mysqldump`. This tool dumps an entire database or databases to the screen. Most people then redirect the output to a file or pipe it to a tool like `gzip` to compress it first. For instance, if your user had a database called wordpress, here is how you would back it up:

```
$ mysqldump wordpress > wordpress_backup.sql
```

If you wanted to compress the database as it was dumped, you would put a pipe to `gzip` in the middle:

```
$ mysqldump wordpress | gzip > wordpress_backup.sql.gz
```

Now if you wanted to back up more than one database, there are two main ways to do it. The first way is to use the `--databases` argument followed by a space-separated list of databases to back up. The other method is to use the `--all-databases` argument, which backs up everything:

```
$ mysqldump --all-databases > all_databases_backup.sql
```

Of course, I assume you have set passwords for your database users so these commands won't work for any of those users. This especially won't work if you want to back up all databases, because at least some are owned by the root user. The solution is to use the `-u` and `-p` options to specify the user and password to use:

```
$ mysqldump --all-databases -u root -pinsecure >
all_databases_backup.sql
```

The command above would back up all of the databases as the root user using the password *insecure*. I list this example only to say that while this option works, it is insecure. The reason is that the full list of arguments, including the password, will be visible to all users on the system who run the `ps` command. A better method is to use `-p` without specifying a password:

```
$ mysqldump --all-databases -u root -p >
all_databases_backup.sql
```

When you specify `-p` without a password, `mysqldump` behaves like the `mysql` command and will prompt you to enter one. This provides good security, but of course it also means that you have to enter the password manually. Most people who back up their MySQL databases set up a cron job to do it at night. The way that MySQL recommends you solve this problem is to add the password to the client section in the ~/.my.cnf file for the user performing the backups. If you don't already have a ~/.my.cnf file, create a new one and add the following text:

```
[client]
password=moresecure
```

Replace moresecure with the password your user will use to log in. Once you set up this file, you don't need to specify the -p option anymore because mysqldump will pick up the password from this file. Of course, the downside here is that this password is in a plain-text file on the system, so you will want to set its permissions so that only your user can see it:

```
$ chmod 400 ~/.my.cnf
```

Restore MySQL Backups   A backup isn't much use if you can't restore from it. To restore a backup on MySQL, use the mysql command-line tool and point it at your backup. For instance, to back up the test database to test_backup.sql, you would type

```
$ mysql test < test_backup.sql
```

If instead you were backing up a number of databases, just type

```
$ mysql < multiple_database_backup.sql
```

To restore all databases, you need to log in as the root user. Of course, you are a secure MySQL administrator and have set a root password, so you must use the -p option (unless you set up a .my.cnf file, in which case you can leave out -p):

```
$ mysql -u root -p < all_databases.sql
```

MySQL Backup Cron Job   Since most people generally want to provide a MySQL backup at least once a day, here's a quick and simple way to set up the cron job. First choose the location where you will store your backups. In this example I still store the backups in /root because I know only root can read that directory, but you will probably want to store them somewhere else with more space.

The main thing to consider is how many backups you want to keep. If you have some sort of other backup system in place to back up all of your files, you may need to keep only one database backup file on the system, since older versions will be stored on your remote backup server. If you want to store, say, a week's worth of backups, you can use a simple shell trick. The date command with no arguments can be used to output the current date, but you can add some arguments to it so that it outputs, for instance, only the current day of the week:

```
$ date +%A
Friday
```

When you run mysqldump, you can enclose that entire command in backticks, and the shell will replace that section of your script with the output of the command. So if you were to write

```
$ mysqldump -u root --all-databases >
/root/all_databases_backup-`date +%A`.sql
```

the shell would actually save the database to /root/all_databases_backup-Friday.sql. That means the next day it runs the command it will name it Saturday, and so on. After a week, the new backup will automatically overwrite the one from the previous week without your having to write in any extra shell logic. To make this command run every night, you just have to create a file as root called /etc/cron.daily/mysqlbackup containing the following script:

```
#!/bin/sh

mysqldump -u root --all-databases >
/root/all_databases_backup-`date +%A`.sql
```

Then you would type chmod a+x /etc/cron.daily/mysqlbackup so that the script is executable.

Finally, if you set up a root password for MySQL, you must create a /root/.my.cnf file with the password in it, as discussed earlier. Now every night when the cron.daily scripts run, this script will run as well. If you want to change how many backups you keep, it's as easy as changing the date command within the backticks. If you want only one backup, you can just save to an ordinary file. If you want to keep a month's worth of back-ups, for instance, just replace %A with %d, which lists the day of the month starting with 01.

PostgreSQL

PostgreSQL uses a backup mechanism similar to MySQL's in that it provides a command-line dump tool called pg_dump that dumps one or more databases to the command line. In its simplest form it behaves a lot like the mysqldump command. To back up a database named test, created by your user, you could type

```
$ pg_dump test > test_backup.sql
```

The main database user for PostgreSQL is the postgres user, so you are more likely to do backups as that user:

```
$ sudo -u postgres pg_dump test > test_backup.sql
```

To back up all PostgreSQL databases, use the pg_dumpall command instead:

```
$ sudo -u postgres pg_dumpall > all_databases_backup.sql
```

Restoring PostgreSQL databases works much like MySQL except you use the psql tool. Here is how you would restore each of the backups I did previously:

```
$ psql test < test.sql
$ sudo -u postgres psql test < test.sql
$ sudo -u postgres psql < all_databases_backup.sql
```

PostgreSQL Backup Cron Job   The cron job to back up PostgreSQL is very similar to the one for MySQL, except in this case there's no need to set up any /root/my.cnf files. You just need to create a new file called /etc/cron .daily/postgresqlbackup containing the following:

```
#!/bin/sh

/usr/bin/sudo -u postgres /usr/bin/pg_dumpall >
/root/all_databases_backup-`date +%A`.sql
```

Then you would make the script executable with `chmod a+x /etc/cron.daily/postgresqlbackup`. Now every night when the cron.daily scripts run, this script will run as well. Changing how many backups you keep is as easy as changing the `date` command within the backticks. If you wanted only one backup, you can just remove the backticks and everything between them. If you wanted to keep a month's worth of backups, for instance, just replace `%A` with `%d`, which will output the day of the month starting with 01.

BackupPC

One of the simpler but still powerful backup programs for Ubuntu is called BackupPC. BackupPC is written in Perl and can make use of `tar` and `rsync` to back up Linux and UNIX hosts, and it can mount and back up SMB shares. Unlike many other backup programs, BackupPC does not necessarily back up a particular machine at the same time every day. This software was designed with networks of desktops that power off at the end of the day in mind, so as you add hosts, it probes them to see if they are up. If BackupPC is able to back them up during the evening backup window it will, but if it can't, it will attempt to back up the host during the day.

A nice feature of BackupPC is that it not only compresses files it has backed up, it also scans through all of the files daily and, where it sees duplicates, creates a hard link. Since a lot of servers tend to have the same system files, this method means that you can squeeze a lot more data on a lot less disk. BackupPC is packaged for Ubuntu, so you can use your package manager to install it:

```
$ sudo apt-get install backuppc
```

BackupPC includes a Web-based interface you can use to manage backup jobs, view logs, and restore files, so it will include the Apache packages it needs if they aren't already installed. During the install process you will be prompted to select a Web server for BackupPC. Unless you set up your own Web server ahead of time and know what you are doing, select `apache2` here. BackupPC uses Apache htpasswd accounts to password-protect the page, and the installer creates a backuppc user and outputs a random password to the screen, so be sure to jot it down. If you forget to do that or forget the password later on, you can use the `htpasswd` command against the /etc/backuppc/htpasswd file.

After the installer completes, open a Web browser and point it to the /backuppc directory on that host, so if your host was 10.1.1.7, you would point it to http://10.1.1.7/backuppc/. You will be prompted for login credentials, so use the login and password you were given during the install. Once you are logged in, you will see the default BackupPC admin page as shown in Figure 7-1.

BackupPC Storage

As with any other backup server, BackupPC needs a lot of storage. All of the backups are ultimately stored under /var/lib/backuppc, so if you have a separate disk (or set of disks in a RAID) for BackupPC, this is a good place to mount it. Let's assume you have a second SCSI partition at /dev/sdb1 that you want to use for BackupPC. First move the old directory out of the way, mount the new drive, and copy over the current /var/lib/backuppc

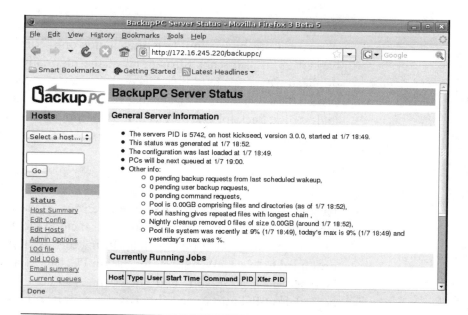

Figure 7-1 Default BackupPC Web interface

files. BackupPC must be stopped while you do this so that it doesn't write to that directory while you're changing it:

```
$ sudo service backuppc stop
$ sudo mv /var/lib/backuppc /var/lib/backuppc.orig
$ sudo mkdir /var/lib/backuppc
$ sudo chown backuppc:backuppc /var/lib/backuppc
$ sudo mount /dev/sdb1 /var/lib/backuppc
$ sudo rsync -av /var/lib/backuppc.orig/ /var/lib/backuppc/
$ sudo service backuppc start
```

Finally don't forget to add the new /dev/sdb1 mount point into /etc/fstab so it will mount automatically the next time the system boots.

Default BackupPC Configuration

Of course, the default Web interface isn't very useful until you add a host. BackupPC's default behavior is defined in /etc/backuppc/config.pl, its core configuration file. If you are unfamiliar with Perl, this file may seem a bit daunting at first as all of the options are configured in Perl data structures. I walk you through adding an Ubuntu host that you will back up with rsync, and as you will see, once you get the core configuration file set, it is relatively simple to add hosts.

The config.pl file defines the default settings for all hosts BackupPC backs up, such as how often to back up, what directories to back up, whether to use smb, rsync, or tar to back up, and even what arguments to pass to those commands. What you want to do is generate a config.pl that works for the majority of your hosts and then create host-specific configuration files when a host needs special options. Any host-specific configuration goes into a .pl file under /etc/backuppc/ named after the host. So if you had a host named web1 and wanted to change some settings just for it, you would copy those specific options from /etc/backuppc/config.pl to /etc/backuppc/web1.pl. Any options you set in web1.pl will override anything in config.pl when web1 is being backed up.

In this example I assume a network mostly made up of other Ubuntu servers and use rsync for the backup. This is all-important because by default BackupPC logs in over SSH as root. On a network of Ubuntu servers this wouldn't work, because root is disabled by default, so we need to change some settings.

There are two different ways to edit the BackupPC configuration. The first (and easier) is through the Web interface; with the second you just open /etc/backuppc/config.pl with a text editor and locate and tweak settings directly.

Web-Based Configuration   You can actually change all of the options you need directly from the Web interface. From the BackupPC home page click the Edit Config link in the left pane and then click the Xfer link along the top of the right pane. You will then see a configuration screen like the one in Figure 7-2. On the XferMethod drop-down menu change from smb to rsync. Then scroll down until you see the RsyncClientCmd and RsyncClientRestoreCmd options. Change both of them from

```
$sshPath -q -x -l root $host $rsyncPath $argList+
```

to

```
$sshPath -q -x -l backuppc $host sudo $rsyncPath $argList+
```

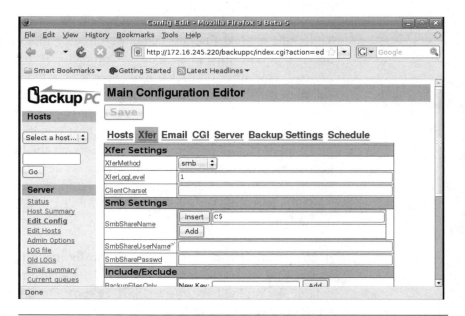

Figure 7-2 BackupPC Xfer configuration options

Then scroll back up to the top of the page and click the Save button. Once you are done with all of your changes, click the Admin Options link in the left sidebar and then click Reload so BackupPC can read your new settings.

Command-Line Configuration   While the Web interface provides an easy way to configure BackupPC, some people prefer doing it all through the command line. If you are one of those people, open the /etc/backuppc/config.pl file in your preferred text editor and then search for the line that matches this one:

```
$Conf{XferMethod} = 'smb';
```

This option defines the default method BackupPC uses to transfer files. SMB might work well for a network of Windows machines, but since we have Ubuntu hosts, we change this to rsync:

```
$Conf{XferMethod} = 'rsync';
```

Next, we need to set BackupPC so that it logs in to each machine as a regular user and then uses sudo to become root. We create a backuppc user on each host along with a secure sudo role so that BackupPC can log in and back up the machine. First locate the following line:

```
$Conf{RsyncClientCmd} = '$sshPath -q -x -l root $host $rsyncPath
  $argList+';
```

This defines what command BackupPC uses when it backs up with rsync. Change it to

```
$Conf{RsyncClientCmd} = '$sshPath -q -x -l backuppc $host sudo
  $rsyncPath $argList+';
```

We need to do the same thing for the command BackupPC uses when it restores to a host, so find the line that matches

```
$Conf{RsyncClientRestoreCmd} = '$sshPath -q -x -l root $host
  $rsyncPath $argList+';
```

and change that along the same lines as the previous option:

```
$Conf{RsyncClientRestoreCmd} = '$sshPath -q -x -l backuppc $host
  sudo $rsyncPath $argList+';
```

By default, BackupPC backs up the entire root file system along with all mounted file systems. I'm leaving this setting alone for now because I do want to back up all of the files on the host, but I discuss how to change it later in the chapter.

Configure the Client Machine

Now that you have changed the config.pl option, you are ready to set up BackupPC so that it can log in and back up your client. In this example we call our client web1, so where you see web1 listed in the example, replace it with your client's hostname.

Configure SSH Keys   Since BackupPC needs to be able to log in to hosts without interaction, you must set up passwordless SSH keys for the backuppc user. On the BackupPC server type

```
$ sudo -u backuppc ssh-keygen -t rsa
```

Hit Enter at each of the prompts to accept the defaults. The public and private keys will be stored at /var/lib/backuppc/.ssh/.

Set Up the Client   Now log in to your client and create a backuppc user (hit Enter when prompted for the name and room number and other information about the user) and create a .ssh directory for the same user:

```
$ sudo adduser backuppc --disabled-password
$ sudo mkdir /home/backuppc/.ssh
$ sudo chown backuppc /home/backuppc/.ssh
```

NOTE   If your client does not yet have an SSH server running, then run sudo apt-get install openssh-server.

Now you need to copy the contents of the /var/lib/backuppc/.ssh/id_rsa.pub file from your BackupPC server to the /home/backuppc/.ssh/

authorized_keys file. One way to do this is to log in to both machines on separate terminals, open both files, and then use your mouse to copy and paste between them. Another method is to use scp on the server to copy the file to the /tmp directory on the client and then log in to the client and copy it from there.

On the server:

```
$ sudo scp /var/lib/backuppc/.ssh/id_rsa.pub user@web1:/tmp/
```

Replace user@web1 with the username and hostname on the client. Then on the client:

```
$ sudo sh -c "cat /tmp/id_rsa.pub >>
/home/backuppc/.ssh/authorized_keys"
```

Now you should be able to go to the BackupPC server and log in to the client as the backuppc user without a password:

```
$ sudo -u backuppc ssh web1
```

Configure sudo   Now we need to configure sudo on the client machine so that the backuppc user can run rsync as root without a password. To do this, run sudo visudo on the client and add the following line to the /etc/sudoers file:

```
backuppc ALL=(root) NOPASSWD:/usr/bin/rsync
```

Add the Client to BackupPC

Now that BackupPC can log in to the client and run rsync as root, we are ready to add it to the list of hosts BackupPC backs up. All of the hosts are defined in /etc/backuppc/hosts, and you can add hosts either by editing the file directly or via the Web interface.

Web Interface   To add a host in the Web interface, click Edit Config in the left sidebar and then click the Hosts link on the top of the right pane. Click the Add button to add a new host, and once you are finished, click the Save button. Finally, click Admin Options in the left sidebar and then the Reload button so BackupPC will reload the changes.

Command Line   To add a host via the command line, open /etc/backuppc/ hosts in a text editor and add the following line at the bottom:

```
web1 0 backuppc
```

Change web1 to the hostname of the server you want to back up. The 0 tells BackupPC that this host has a static IP address, and the backuppc at the end sets what user can manage this host on the Web interface. I just used a single space in this example, but you can separate the columns with multiple spaces so everything lines up and looks nicer. If you wanted other users to also be able to back up and restore this host from the Web interface, you could add a fourth column to this line and list those users separated by commas. So if I had two users, allan and jorge, that I wanted to be able to manage web1, the line would read

```
web1 0 backuppc allan,jorge
```

Once you save the changes to /etc/backuppc/hosts, tell BackupPC to reload its configuration with sudo service backuppc reload or sudo /etc/ init.d/backuppc reload.

Start the First Backup Job

Once the BackupPC program reloads its configuration, go back to the Back-upPC Web interface and reload the page. You should be able to see your host in the "Select a host..." drop-down menu on the left side of the page. Select that option and you will see the default host page as shown in Figure 7-3. To test that everything is set up correctly, click Start Full Backup to initiate the first backup for the host. Then you can click Status in the left sidebar to go to the main status page and see that your backup job has started. It should look something like Figure 7-4. To stop a job for a particular host, go to that host's page and then click the Stop/Dequeue Backup button.

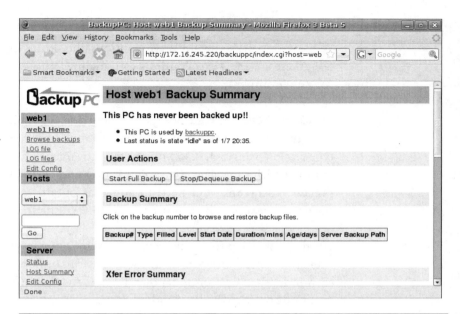

Figure 7-3 BackupPC host management Web page

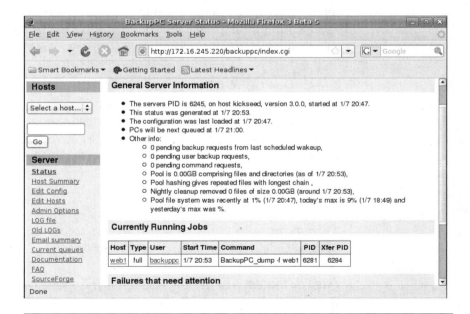

Figure 7-4 BackupPC full backup running

rsync Tweaks

While most of the default rsync options should be fine for the average user, there are a few extra options you might want to enable depending on your environment.

Checksum Seed   If your host is relatively new, it should have a version of rsync greater than or equal to 2.6.3 (if you aren't sure what version you have, type rsync --version). If so, you can take advantage of the --checksum-seed option, which can cache rsync's checksums and overall speed up the rsync process. To do this you need to add that option to the RsyncArgs and RsyncRestoreArgs option in your BackupPC configuration.

To add this setting from the Web, click Web Config in the sidebar, then the Xfer link. Then scroll down to the RsyncArgs option where you can see each individual option on its own line. At the end of these options is an Add button. Click that and add --checksum-seed=32761. Then scroll down and add the same option to the RsyncRestoreArgs section.

To make the same change on the command line, open /etc/backuppc/config .pl in a text editor and find the line that starts with $Conf{RsyncArgs}. Each rsync option is on its own line, but if you are still using the config.pl that came with the package, you will see this option commented out:

```
#'--checksum-seed=32761',
```

Just remove the # from the beginning of that option. If you don't see the commented-out option, just add a line below the last RsyncArgs option that reads

```
'--checksum-seed=32761',
```

Then move down to the RsyncRestoreArgs section (generally it's the next option) and do the same thing for this option.

One File System   By default, BackupPC traverses all of the file systems on the host and backs up absolutely everything. There are circumstances when you might not want that to be the default behavior, especially in a cluster when you can easily replace the main system files by rebuilding the host. In these circumstances what you want to do instead is tell `rsync` to stick to one file system at a time, and then specify which mount points BackupPC should back up.

The first step is relatively simple because this option goes in the same place as the `--checksum-seed` option. Follow the steps I described above to add the `--checksum-seed` option to `RsyncArgs` and `RsyncRestoreArgs`, in either the Web interface or the command line. This time, though, the option you add is

```
--one-file-system
```

Once you set that option, you must define each file system that BackupPC will back up. In this example, let's assume that you have /home and /var on separate partitions and want to back up only them. The option you will change is called `RsyncShareName`. In the Web interface return to the Xfer configuration screen you used to add `--one-file-system` to `RsyncArgs`. Above that section you will see the section named `RsyncShareName`. Each share is on its own line, as with `RsyncArgs`. First you change the first option from / to /home. Then you click the Add button and add a new share named /var.

To change the same option on the command line, open config.pl, find the line that looks like

```
$Conf{RsyncShareName} = '/';
```

and change that to

```
$Conf{RsyncShareName} = ['/home', '/var'];
```

Exclude Directories   You might find that you typically want to back up all of the files on the host apart from a few different directories. For instance, in the example above, you might want to back up /home and /var, but perhaps you want to skip /var/spool/mail and /var/tmp. To do this you go back to the Xfer configuration screen on the Web interface and scroll down to the `BackupFilesExclude` option. Then you type in /var/tmp under the New Key field and click Add. Once the screen refreshes, you can scroll down and add /var/spool/mail the same way.

If you want to change this on the command line instead, you search through the file until you see a line that looks like this:

```
$Conf{BackupFilesExclude} = undef;
```

By default no files are excluded. To add the two directories you change that option to

```
$Conf{BackupFilesExclude} = ['/var/tmp', '/var/spool/mail'];
```

As with any configuration changes, once you have changed everything, don't forget to save and then reload BackupPC so the changes take effect.

Host-Specific Tweaks   While you can set up a default BackupPC config that works for most of your hosts, you will likely run into a few machines that need something slightly different from the default. With BackupPC it's particularly easy to branch off from the default config and customize options. For instance, you might want to apply the `--one-file-system` option or exclude directories only on one host.

Basically, to add custom options for a particular host, copy those options from the /etc/backuppc/config.pl file into /etc/backuppc/hostname.pl, where hostname is the name of the host you want to change. So if, for instance, you wanted to back up only /home and /var on your BackupPC host and not traverse file systems on the host called web1, you would copy the entire `RsyncArgs` and `RsyncRestoreArgs` in a file named /etc/backuppc/web1.pl along with the `RsyncShareName` option. The result would look something like this:

```
$Conf{RsyncShareName} = ['/home', '/var'];
$Conf{RsyncArgs} = [
    #
    # Do not edit these!
    #
    '--numeric-ids',
    '--perms',
    '--owner',
    '--group',
    '-D',
    '--links',
    '--hard-links',
```

```
        '--times',
        '--block-size=2048',
        '--recursive',

            # my custom options
        '--one-file-system',
];
$Conf{RsyncRestoreArgs} = [
        #
        # Do not edit these!
        #
        '--numeric-ids',
        '--perms',
        '--owner',
        '--group',
        '-D',
        '--links',
        '--hard-links',
        '--times',
        '--block-size=2048',
        '--recursive',

            # my custom options
        '--one-file-system',
];
```

Change the Backup Schedule   By default, BackupPC takes one full backup
per week and in between takes an incremental backup of every host.
BackupPC keeps one full backup and six incremental backups before it
deletes anything. Finally, BackupPC will *not* start up new jobs for hosts that
are always on the network between 7:00 a.m. and 7:30 p.m. during the
week. These defaults are not suitable for everyone. For instance, you might
be required to keep a month's worth of full backups, or everyone might be
out of the office by 6:00 p.m. so you can start backups then. All of these
options are easy to change in the BackupPC Web interface.

To start, click the Edit Config link in the left sidebar and then click the
Schedule link on the top right-hand side of the screen. You will see a
schedule-editing screen as shown in Figure 7-5. The first set of options lets
you schedule your full backups. Each of the options is hyperlinked to a
manual page so you can read about what they change.

The FullPeriod option defines how much time should pass (in days)
before a new full backup should be scheduled. This option is always set

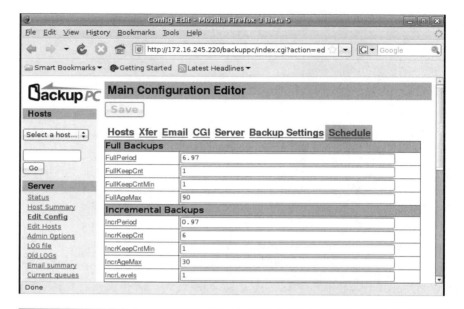

Figure 7-5 BackupPC schedule configuration screen

slightly below a full number. In the case of the default, 6.97, a full backup will be scheduled every seven days. The FullKeepCnt and FullKeepCntMin options configure how many full backups to keep and the minimum number to keep, respectively, and FullAgeMax defines the maximum number of days before an old full backup is deleted. Incremental backups can save backup resources as they back up only what has changed since the last full backup. They take most of the same options as the full backups, and by default they are run every day and the last six are saved.

The Blackouts section of this page lets you define BackupPC's blackout period. The blackout period is the range of time during which BackupPC will *not* attempt to back up hosts that are always on the network. This way, if you have desktops that might be powered off in the evening, BackupPC will back them up during the day, but for servers that are always on, BackupPC knows it can wait until the evening when they are presumably under less load. When you add a new host to BackupPC, it will try to ping it periodically to determine whether it is always on the network. If it is, BackupPC will back it up only during the blackout period. The hourBegin option defines what hour or fraction of an hour the blackout period begins, and the hourEnd option sets when it ends. The weekDays option sets which days of the week the blackout period is in effect. By default the blackout period is between 7:00 a.m. and 7:30 p.m. Monday through Friday.

To demonstrate how you would change these options, I define a different backup policy that might be used in an organization. In this organization we want weekly full backups and daily incremental backups, but we want to save the full backups up to a month before discarding them. We also want to keep the last two weeks of incremental backups. Finally, everyone in the office leaves by 6:00 p.m., so we want to start backups then. To make these changes I need to change only the following values:

```
FullKeepCnt = 4
IncrKeepCnt = 12
hourEnd = 18
```

Restore Files

Backing up files is all well and good, but it isn't too useful unless you can restore them. One of the best features of BackupPC in my opinion is its easy-to-use Web-based restore. If you set up additional Web accounts for backuppc (use `htpasswd -c /etc/backuppc/htpasswd username`), you can add those accounts to specific hosts in the /etc/backuppc/hosts.conf (or on the Web interface) and those users can log in to BackupPC and restore their own files.

To restore a file or directories for a host, first go to the host's home page on BackupPC (select the host in the drop-down menu in the left sidebar). On the host's main page you will see a list of completed backups in a table that lists whether the backup was full or incremental, when the backup started, how long it took, and where those files are stored on the file system. Click the hyperlinked backup number at the beginning of a particular row to restore from that backup. You will then see the entire directory structure of your host on the page with checkboxes next to files and directories (Figure 7-6). The interface is like that of most file managers, and you can click on an individual directory to expand it. Once you have selected all of the files you wish to restore, click the "Restore selected files" button at the top or bottom of the page.

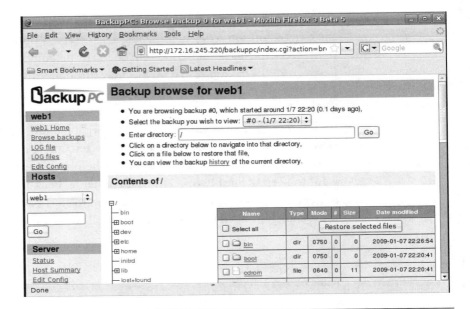

Figure 7-6 BackupPC restore file browser

BackupPC provides you with three different restore options:

▪ **Direct restore**

In a direct restore, BackupPC restores the files or directories directly to a host. You can actually choose which host to restore to, as BackupPC lets you choose any host it has configured. By default BackupPC restores to the share and directory below the share that the files originally came from, so if you want to overwrite or replace what is currently there, you can just click the Start Restore button. You can even completely overwrite the entire / directory on the remote host with the full backup if you need to. Instead of restoring the files to their original directory, you could also restore to a different directory if you wanted to compare the two files.

▪ **Download zip archive**

This option is very useful when you back up Windows desktops and allow your users to restore their own files. Instead of restoring a file directly to a host, you can instead generate a .zip file that contains all of your restored files and directories and download it to your current computer.

- **Download tar archive**
  This and the zip archive option are essentially the same, except in this case you get a tar archive instead, which is more useful for Linux desktops.

Ubuntu BackupPC Conventions

- **/etc/backuppc**
  This directory contains all of the configuration files for BackupPC, including its Apache config and any host-specific configuration files.

- **/etc/backuppc/config.pl**
  All of the default BackupPC options are set in the config.pl file. The version of config.pl that comes with the package by default is full of documentation that explains each option and gives examples. Any host-specific configuration goes into a separate file named after the host and ending in .pl.

- **/etc/backuppc/hosts**
  All of the hosts that BackupPC will back up are defined here.

- **/etc/backuppc/htpasswd**
  Web users along with their passwords are set in this file by default. This is a standard Apache password file, so you can use the htpasswd command to make changes (type man htpasswd for details on how to use the program).

- **/etc/backuppc/apache.conf**
  This file defines all of the virtual host settings for the BackupPC Web administration page. BackupPC creates a symlink from /etc/apache2/conf.d/backuppc.conf to this file, although these days it would fit better under /etc/apache2/sites-available.

- **/etc/init.d/backuppc**
  Here is BackupPC's init script. BackupPC starts the service by default once it is installed and automatically starts at boot time.

- **/var/lib/backuppc**

  This directory contains all of the files that BackupPC backs up, so you should consider putting this directory on a separate large mount point or at least make sure it has plenty of free space.

- **/var/lib/backuppc/log**

  All of the logs for each backup can be found under this directory. You can also access the logs from the Web interface.

- **/var/lib/backuppc/pc**

  Each host has its own directory here that contains its latest set of files. BackupPC pools together identical files from multiple hosts with hard links, but if you have removed a host from BackupPC and want to delete its files as well, delete the host's directory under here first.

CHAPTER 8

Monitoring

A SERVER IS NOT VERY USEFUL if it's down. If you have skipped ahead and read Chapter 10, Fault Tolerance, you are well aware of the lengths to which some administrators go to ensure that a service stays up. No matter how much work you put into your environment, though, eventually a service or server will go down. When that happens, you want to make sure you are alerted. If it's your job to maintain a server, it's embarrassing if someone else has to come to you with the news that it's down—that's something you should be the first to know. Getting alerts is only one aspect of monitoring, though. In addition to getting alerts whenever a service goes down, you should also monitor the overall health of your environment. With the proper monitoring in place you can often see a problem before it causes an outage. Good monitoring also provides you with the health statistics you need after an outage so you can piece together what happened.

In this chapter I discuss how to set up monitoring for your network so that you will be alerted to any problems. In addition I discuss a few different monitoring tools you can use to keep track of a system's health that even provide manager-friendly graphs of system statistics. While there are many different monitoring tools available for Ubuntu, I have picked a few that are easy to set up and use that should provide you with a good foundation for any additional monitoring you want to add.

Local Monitoring Tools

A good place to start your monitoring is on the machine itself. Network-based monitoring is great, but it's even better to have some monitoring on each host that will give you statistics even when the network goes down. I describe a few monitoring tools you can easily add to a server.

Smartmontools

I have mentioned Smartmontools elsewhere in this book because it provides an excellent way to diagnose hard drive problems. This tool works via the SMART features most modern hard drives include. The SMART features give you information on a drive's overall health, including its firmware revisions and drive temperature, as well as any hardware errors or pending drive failures. One of the more useful features of Smartmontools, however, is its ability to scan your hard drives for failures and warn you before a failure actually happens.

The first step is to install the smartmontools package:

```
$ sudo apt-get install smartmontools
```

The package includes a daemon called smartd that can launch at system start-up and start monitoring your drives. By default smartd will not start, so you need to edit /etc/default/smartmontools and uncomment the line that reads

```
# start_smartd=yes
```

Now smartd will start at boot, but you will also want to start it up manually so it's available right now:

```
$ sudo /etc/init.d/smartmontools start
```

By default smartd scans through all of your drives for any that are SMART-enabled and monitors them, so you don't need to perform any special configuration at this point. When smartd detects an error, it runs any scripts it finds under /etc/smartmontools/run.d/. By default there is only one script under that directory, named 10mail, that e-mails the root user so he or she knows of the problem, but you can add any number of custom scripts to this directory as well, and they will be run in alphabetical order. When smartd finds a problem, it executes your script and passes the full path to the error file as an argument, so within your script you can access it via the $1 variable, for instance. Check the /etc/smartmontools/run.d/10mail script for a simple example on which you can base your scripts.

sysstat

Let's face it, you probably don't have terminals logged in to every system you manage with some tool like top running. Even if you did, you still won't know your system load or RAM statistics while you are asleep. Now some administrators solve this problem by running top via a cron job, but Ubuntu has a better system in place via sysstat. The sysstat package provides a number of useful system-monitoring tools, including `iostat`, which I cover in Chapter 11, Troubleshooting. These tools are useful for troubleshooting, but what makes them even more useful is that the `sysstat` package provides a simple mechanism to log system statistics like CPU load, RAM, and I/O stats. With these statistics, when someone complains that a system was slow around noon yesterday, you can play back these logs and see what could have caused the problem.

The first step is to install the `sysstat` package:

```
$ sudo apt-get install sysstat
```

Once the package is installed, you want to enable the data collection tool, so type

```
$ sudo dpkg-reconfigure sysstat
```

and answer Yes when prompted to activate `sysstat`'s cron job. Alternatively, you can also enable this in /etc/default/sysstat. Once enabled, `sysstat` gathers system stats every ten minutes and stores them under /var/log/sysstat. In addition, it will rotate out the statistics file every night before midnight. Both of these actions are run in the /etc/cron.d/sysstat script, so if you want to change how frequently `sysstat` gathers information, you can modify it from that file.

As `sysstat` gathers statistics, it stores them under /var/log/sysstat in files named sa and then the current day of the month. This means that you can go back up to a month from the current date and retrieve old statistics. Use the `sar` tool to view these statistics. By default `sar` outputs the CPU statistics for the current day:

```
$ sar
Linux 2.6.24-22-server (kickseed)       01/07/2009
. . .
07:44:20 PM     CPU     %user   %nice   %system %iowait %steal  %idle
07:45:01 PM     all     0.00    0.00    0.54    0.51    0.00    98.95
07:55:01 PM     all     0.54    0.00    1.66    1.26    0.00    96.54
08:05:01 PM     all     0.20    0.00    0.72    1.08    0.00    98.00
08:15:01 PM     all     0.49    0.00    1.12    0.62    0.00    97.77
08:25:01 PM     all     0.49    0.00    2.15    1.21    0.00    96.16
```

08:35:01 PM	all	0.22	0.00	0.98	0.58	0.00	98.23
08:45:01 PM	all	0.23	0.00	0.75	0.54	0.00	98.47
08:55:01 PM	all	0.20	0.00	0.78	0.50	0.00	98.52
09:01:18 PM	all	0.19	0.00	0.72	0.37	0.00	98.71
09:05:01 PM	all	0.24	0.00	1.10	0.54	0.00	98.12
Average:	all	0.32	0.00	1.12	0.78	0.00	97.78

From the output you can see many of the same CPU statistics you would view in top output. At the bottom sar provides an overall average as well. The sysstat cron job collects much more information than CPU load, though. For instance, to gather RAM statistics instead, use the -r option:

```
$ sar -r
Linux 2.6.24-22-server (kickseed)      01/07/2009
```

07:44:20 PM	kbmemfree	kbmemused	%memused	kbbuffers	kbcached	kbswpfree
kbswpused	%swpused	kbswpcad				
07:45:01 PM	322064	193384	37.52	16056	142900	88316
0	0.00	0				
07:55:01 PM	318484	196964	38.21	17152	144672	88316
0	0.00	0				
08:05:01 PM	318228	197220	38.26	17648	144700	88316
0	0.00	0				
08:15:01 PM	297669	217780	42.25	18384	154408	88316
0	0.00	0				
08:25:01 PM	284152	231296	44.87	20072	173724	88316
0	0.00	0				
08:35:01 PM	283096	232352	45.08	20612	173756	88316
0	0.00	0				
08:45:01 PM	283284	232164	45.04	21116	173780	88316
0	0.00	0				
08:55:01 PM	282556	232892	45.18	21624	173804	88316
0	0.00	0				
09:01:18 PM	276632	238816	46.33	21964	173896	88316
0	0.00	0				
09:05:01 PM	281876	233572	45.31	22188	173900	88316
0	0.00	0				
Average:	294804	220644	42.81	19682	162954	88316
0	0.00	0				

Here I can see how much free and used memory I have as well as view statistics about swap and the file cache similar to what you would see in either top or free output. If you aren't sure how to read or use these statistics, check out the Localhost Troubleshooting section of Chapter 11.

Another useful metric to pull from sar is disk statistics. The -b option gives you a basic list of disk I/O information:

```
$ sar -b
Linux 2.6.24-22-server (kickseed)   01/07/2009

07:44:20 PM       tps      rtps      wtps    bread/s    bwrtn/s
07:45:01 PM      8.03      0.00      8.03       0.00     106.61
07:55:01 PM      8.78      0.14      8.64       3.35     127.59
08:05:01 PM      7.16      0.00      7.16       0.00      61.14
08:15:01 PM      8.17      0.14      8.03       5.82     139.02
08:25:01 PM      9.50      0.06      9.44       4.09     212.62
08:35:01 PM      8.27      0.00      8.27       0.01      74.66
08:45:01 PM      8.04      0.00      8.04       0.00      71.51
08:55:01 PM      7.64      0.00      7.64       0.00      66.46
09:01:18 PM      7.11      0.00      7.11       0.36      63.73
09:05:01 PM      7.61      0.00      7.61       0.00      72.11
Average:         8.11      0.04      8.06       1.67     102.52
```

Here you can see the number of total transactions per second (tps) plus how many of those transactions were reads and writes (rtps and wtps respectively). The bread/s column doesn't measure bread I/O but instead tells you the average number of bytes read per second. The bwrtn/s similarly tells you average bytes written per second.

There are tons of individual arguments you can pass sar to pull out specific sets of data, but sometimes you just want to see everything all at once. For that just use the -A option. That will output all of the statistics from load average, CPU load, RAM, disk I/O, network I/O, and all sorts of other interesting statistics. This can give you a good idea of what sorts of statistics sar can output, so you can then read the sar manual (type man sar) to see what flags to pass sar to see particular statistics.

Of course, so far I've just listed how to pull all of the statistics for the current day. Often you want data from only a portion of the day. To pull out data for a certain time range, use the -s and -e arguments to specify the starting time and ending time you are interested in, respectively. For instance, if I wanted to pull CPU data just from 8:00 p.m. to 8:30 p.m., I would type

```
$ sar -s 20:00:00 -e 20:30:00
```

Below is the output from the sar command:

```
Linux 2.6.24-22-server (kickseed)        01/07/2009

08:05:01 PM    CPU    %user    %nice    %system    %iowait    %steal    %idle
08:15:01 PM    all     0.49     0.00      1.12       0.62      0.00     97.77
08:25:01 PM    all     0.49     0.00      2.15       1.21      0.00     96.16
Average:       all     0.49     0.00      1.63       0.91      0.00     96.96
```

If you want to pull data from a day other than today, just use the -f option followed by the full path to the particular statistics file stored under /var/log/sysstat. For instance, to pull data from the statistics on the sixth of the month I would type

```
$ sar -f /var/log/sysstat/sa06
```

You can use any of the other sar options as normal to pull out specific types of statistics.

Ganglia

Local monitoring is quite useful when you want a picture of the system from hours or days before, but the downside is that you have to log in to each host and pull those statistics. Also, sometimes it's easier to gauge a system's health when you have graphs or other visualization. There are a number of tools that can aggregate statistics for a network full of servers, but one of the simplest and most lightweight tools for this is called Ganglia.

Ganglia (http://ganglia.info) was designed to monitor clusters and provides a nice lightweight daemon called gmond that runs on each host and broadcasts its statistics to other hosts in the same cluster using a multicast IP address. I say "cluster" here, but you aren't required to have clustered servers to use Ganglia. For the rest of the chapter you can think of clusters simply as logical ways to group servers that provide the same kind of service. Since all of the hosts in a particular cluster listen and communicate with the same multicast address, all of them can be aware of each other's health.

In addition to the monitoring daemon gmond, Ganglia provides a server called gmetad that can be pointed at different clusters and can aggregate their data into local RRD files. RRD is a common format for small statistics databases, and a number of tools can use those files to generate graphs. Ganglia itself provides a nice PHP-based Web front end you can install on your gmetad host that will provide you with access to graphs of all sorts of statistics aggregated for an entire cluster or drilled down to individual hosts.

Install ganglia-monitor on All Hosts

The first step is to install the ganglia-monitor package, which provides gmond, on all machines you want Ganglia to monitor:

```
$ sudo apt-get install ganglia-monitor
```

The gmond program expects different clusters to communicate either on different multicast IPs or at least on different ports. All gmond configuration is done via the /etc/ganglia/gmond.conf file. By default /etc/ganglia/gmond.conf is already set up to communicate on multicast IP 239.2.11.71 and port 8649. If you just want to have one large cluster for all of your hosts, the only configuration changes you need to make are to add name = "*clustername*" in the cluster section of the /etc/ganglia/gmond.conf file. For my example I will name the cluster Ubuntu Cluster, so my section looks like:

```
cluster {
  name = "Ubuntu Cluster"
  owner = "unspecified"
  latlong = "unspecified"
  url = "unspecified"
}
```

to the bottom of gmond.conf and restart the ganglia-monitor service (sudo /etc/init.d/ganglia-monitor restart). The default gmond.conf is full of comments and example options you can set. Most of the options allow you to label a particular cluster with its location, latitude and longitude, and other such optional information. If you do decide to run multiple clusters, however, you need to change either the multicast channel or the multicast port on which gmond will communicate. You can change either or both for each cluster, depending on what is simpler for your network. Some administrators might want to keep the port the same and change the IP so that their local firewall configuration is simpler. Others might want to keep the IP the same and just change the port so they can keep all Ganglia traffic on one multicast IP. In either case, the options to change are mcast_join and port in the udp_send_channel section. Here is an example of both options set to their defaults:

```
udp_send_channel {
  mcast_join = 239.2.11.71
  port  = 8649
  ttl = 1
}
```

Once you have a gmond.conf configured for a cluster the way that you want it, deploy to all of the remaining servers in that cluster and restart the ganglia-monitor init script on all of them. If you do have any firewalls enabled, be sure that they allow traffic from the multicast IP and also that they allow traffic on TCP and UDP port 8649 (or the specific port you set up). Once gmond is set up properly, you can log in to a particular host and telnet to port 8649 on localhost and you should get a bunch of XML output:

```
$ telnet localhost 8649
Trying 127.0.0.1...
Connected to localhost.
Escape character is '^]'.
<?xml version="1.0" encoding="ISO-8859-1" standalone="yes"?>
<!DOCTYPE GANGLIA_XML [
   <!ELEMENT GANGLIA_XML (GRID)*>
      <!ATTLIST GANGLIA_XML VERSION CDATA #REQUIRED>
. . .
<METRIC NAME="swap_free" VAL="88316" TYPE="uint32" UNITS="KB"
   TN="77" TMAX="180" DMAX="0" SLOPE="both" SOURCE="gmond"/>
<METRIC NAME="os_name" VAL="Linux" TYPE="string" UNITS=""
   TN="612" TMAX="1200" DMAX="0" SLOPE="zero" SOURCE="gmond"/>
<METRIC NAME="pkts_out" VAL="0.19" TYPE="float" UNITS="packets/
   sec" TN="93" TMAX="300" DMAX="0" SLOPE="both" SOURCE="gmond"/>
</HOST>
</CLUSTER>
</GANGLIA_XML>
```

You can also use the `tcpdump` tool to confirm that a host can see traffic on the multicast IP:

```
$ sudo tcpdump dst host 239.2.11.71
21:54:49.963993 IP 172.16.245.221.60305 > 239.2.11.71.8649: UDP,
   length 8
21:54:50.893289 IP 172.16.245.220.37462 > 239.2.11.71.8649: UDP,
   length 8
21:54:53.923391 IP 172.16.245.220.37462 > 239.2.11.71.8649: UDP,
   length 8
21:54:54.933453 IP 172.16.245.220.37462 > 239.2.11.71.8649: UDP,
   length 8
21:54:55.943464 IP 172.16.245.220.37462 > 239.2.11.71.8649: UDP,
   length 8
```

If you changed the multicast IP that you use for `gmond`, be sure to replace the default I used here with that. Here you can see that my host sees multicast packets from two hosts I have configured on 172.16.245.221 and 172.16.245.220.

Configure Ganglia Server

Once your Ganglia hosts are configured and communicating, the next step is to set up a Ganglia server that runs `gmetad` and the Web interface so you can store and view all of your statistics. In my example the Ganglia server will be called ganglia.example.org. First, install the `gmetad` package:

```
$ sudo apt-get install gmetad
```

All `gmetad` configuration is located at /etc/ganglia/gmetad.conf, and the `gmetad` package will provide a nice commented sample gmetad.conf file you can work from. Open /etc/ganglia/gmetad.conf in a text editor and locate the line in the file labeled

```
data_source "my cluster" localhost
```

The `data_source` line is used to define different clusters that `gmetad` will monitor. The syntax is to list the cluster name to monitor followed by a sample host or group of hosts that `gmetad` can query for statistics. Since I installed `ganglia-monitor` on this host and set it up to be on Ubuntu Cluster, I can just probe localhost, so I replace the line above with

```
data_source "Ubuntu Cluster" localhost
```

I listed `localhost` here because the machine that runs `gmetad` is also part of Ubuntu Cluster, but if you have multiple clusters configured, you will want to add `data_source` lines with IP addresses and `gmond` ports for a representative host or hosts from each cluster. So if I had set up a separate `gmond` cluster for my Web servers called Web Cluster and two of the hosts ran `gmond` on 192.168.10.5:8650 and 192.168.10.6:8650, I would add an additional line for that cluster, so the final configuration would look like this:

```
data_source "Ubuntu Cluster" localhost
data_source "Web Cluster" 192.168.10.5:8650 192.168.10.6:8650
```

Note that I didn't have to specify the port for localhost because it was configured to use the default port 8849. You will want to add multiple IP addresses for each cluster for redundancy so in case one host goes off-line you can still get statistics.

The preceding step is the only real setting that you must set in gmetad.conf for it to work. As you can see in the file, there are many other optional settings you can make either to add labels to your cluster or otherwise organize it. I will list a few of these options below.

Ganglia organizes systems into clusters and grids. A cluster is a group of machines and a grid is a group of clusters. The grid is the overarching name you want to apply to all of the different clusters this `gmetad` service monitors. If, for instance, you have one `gmetad` process for each data center, you might name the grid after the data center. Locate the section in the file that mentions the grid name:

```
# gridname "MyGrid"
```

and add a new line below it that names your grid:

```
gridname "London Datacenter"
```

The next optional setting allows you to configure gmetad so it points to your Ganglia Web service. Locate the section that references authority:

```
# authority "http://mycluster.org/newprefix/"
```

and add a line below it that points to your server. In my case I called my server ganglia.example.org:

```
authority "http://ganglia.example.org/ganglia/"
```

Now save your changes and restart the gmetad service:

```
$ sudo /etc/init.d/gmetad restart
```

If your gmetad host can access the hosts you set up under data_source, directories will be created for each cluster under /var/lib/ganglia/rrds. Under each cluster directory are directories for each host that contain RRD files for their various statistics.

Install the Ganglia Web Front End

Ganglia includes a Web front end written in PHP that lets you view all of the Ganglia graphs from an easy-to-use Web interface. This is an optional step, but the Web front end definitely makes it easier to view all the statistics. First install the ganglia-webfrontend package on your gmetad server:

```
$ sudo apt-get install ganglia-webfrontend
```

This will pull down all necessary programs and libraries you will need for the Ganglia Web front end to function. If you have a firewall enabled on the host, be sure to open up access to port 80. Finally, symlink Ganglia's Apache configuration into the standard Apache site directory and enable the site:

```
$ sudo ln -s /etc/ganglia-webfrontend/apache.conf
/etc/apache2/sites-available/ganglia
$ sudo a2ensite ganglia
```

Now go to any client on the network with a Web browser and browse to the Ganglia directory on the gmetad host. In my case I would go to http://

ganglia.example.org/ganglia/. You should see the main screen for your grid as shown in Figure 8-1. The nice thing about Ganglia is that it not only shows you statistics for individual hosts, it will combine statistics for the entire grid as well as each cluster you define. This can be useful if, for instance, you want to tell how much CPU load, RAM, or network traffic an entire Web cluster consumes or even how much load the entire data center (or grid) consumes.

You can use the drop-down menus on the main page to change the length of time you want to monitor as well as drill down into individual clusters or hosts within a cluster. Scroll down each page to see the full list of statistics Ganglia captures. All of the graphs are hyperlinked as well, so you can click on any of them to see a larger version of the graph.

Now your Ganglia monitoring system is complete. To add new hosts to a cluster, just be sure they have the ganglia-monitor package installed and that their /etc/ganglia/gmond.conf file is the same as you have on other members of the cluster. Once the ganglia-monitor init script restarts with the proper configuration, gmetad will automatically start logging that host's statistics and provide them via the Web interface.

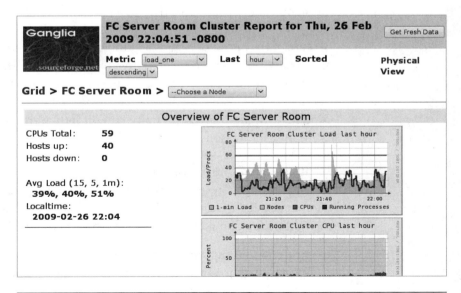

Figure 8-1 Default Ganglia grid page

Nagios

Trending is an important part of any system monitoring, but collecting statistics is only one side of monitoring. The other side is getting alerts when a host or service goes down. There is a large number of great commercial and open source monitoring tools, but Nagios is the tool that seems to come up over and over. Nagios is an open source monitoring tool that has become popular among other reasons for its plug-in architecture. Not only is it relatively easy to write your own plug-ins to monitor specific things, but many of the common items you would want to monitor already have plug-ins written.

Nagios is a great tool, but if you talk to enough sysadmins who use it, you will find a common theme: It's great but it can be a pain to configure. Nagios uses a series of different configuration files to configure hosts to monitor, services to check on those hosts, groups of hosts, and the rest of its settings. The syntax for any particular file isn't too daunting in and of itself, but it does provide quite a learning curve for the uninitiated. If you have to monitor a large number of systems with Nagios, you end up doing one of two things: writing your own scripts to dump out Nagios configuration files, or using a Nagios front end for configuration. I tend to be on the side of not reinventing the wheel, so while I've written plenty of Nagios configuration files and scripts in my day, now I prefer the Web-based front ends.

Because of the power of Nagios a number of different individuals and companies have created monitoring software based on it. There are many excellent Nagios front ends to choose from, and choosing one to feature in this chapter is a tricky (and potentially controversial) task. In the end I settled on GroundWork Monitor Community Edition (http://groundworkopensource.com) for a few reasons:

▪ **It's an open source project.**
Even though GroundWork is created and supported by a company that also has a commercial version of the product, the Community Edition is a completely open source project that is also free of charge.

▪ **Professional support is available.**
Even though many Linux sysadmins are fine with not having commercial support for their software, often the people they work for aren't. The GroundWork company doesn't just offer support for its commer-

cial product but also has paid per-incident support for the Community Edition. This allows you to strike a nice middle ground between using software with an open license and having support if you need it.

- **There's a good balance between Nagios features and simplicity.** Nagios can be complicated to set up, especially at the outset, but GroundWork has a decent balance between offering you the full set of Nagios options and providing the beginner with a basic interface to get started.

- **There's an option for a fully commercial product.** Even though the Community Edition is great, it's nice to have the option to buy a different edition with more features if your enterprise needs it.

Install GroundWork

Nagios is a complicated piece of software, and while GroundWork simplifies administration of it, it still allows you access to all of that complexity if you want to tweak it. It also adds a large number of options on its own. You could really write an entire book about ways to configure host groups, tweak the available service checks and write your own, and configure escalation schedules for notifications, along with all of the other advanced options in this software. For the purposes of this example I will walk you through a basic configuration to monitor a few hosts with ping, show you how to add a service check, and describe how to configure GroundWork to e-mail you if a host goes down.

Unfortunately, GroundWork is not available for Ubuntu via the package manager, but it still is relatively simple to install. Unfortunately at the time of this writing, the Community Edition download link was rather difficult to find on the http://groundworkopensource.com page, but you should be able to find the latest version on http://sourceforge.net/projects/gwmos/files/. My example is based on version 6.0.1. GroundWork includes its own Apache, Nagios, MySQL, and the rest of its software as one big package, and the download comes in the form of a large .bin file that you then run to extract and install:

```
$ sudo chmod a+x groundwork-6.0.1-br124-linux-32-installer.bin
$ sudo ./groundwork-6.0.1-br124-linux-32-installer.bin
```

The binary includes both a graphical and a text-based installer, so if you do have an X server installed on your machine, you could potentially use the graphical installer. I will assume that you don't on this particular server, so when you run the program, the installer prompts you to continue in text mode. The installer starts by checking the specs of your system to make sure you have enough RAM and storage. If you don't meet the minimum requirements, the installer will exit out, but if you are above the minimum but below the recommended specs, it will just give you a warning and allow you to continue.

The installer is basically noninteractive at this point other than an initial prompt for a MySQL root password and an option to get software update notifications for GroundWork. After those options you will just see a progress bar as the software unpacks.

GroundWork File Conventions

It's good to know how GroundWork organizes all of its files, as it's a bit different from most other native Ubuntu software. Below I discuss the core file and directory locations in which the average administrator will be interested.

- **/usr/local/groundwork**
  This is the core GroundWork directory. Here you will find all of the included scripts and integrated programs like Nagios, Apache, and MySQL.

- **/usr/local/groundwork/apache2**
  Here you will find the complete GroundWork Apache installation, including all of the binaries and the Apache configuration.

- **/usr/local/groundwork/nagios**
  All of the Nagios configuration and supporting files are located in this directory. When you commit a new GroundWork configuration, it will convert the settings in its database to raw Nagios files within this directory. In this directory you will also find the Nagios log file under the var directory as well as all of the included Nagios checks within the libexec directory.

- /etc/init.d/groundwork

  This is the init script that starts GroundWork at boot time and is the script you can use to start, stop, and restart the service manually. This script will then go on to start or stop individual daemons like the Web interface, MySQL, and Nagios behind the scenes.

Initial Configuration

Once the GroundWork install completes, go to a Web browser and enter your GroundWork host's hostname. In my example that is groundwork .example.org. At the login screen, log in as admin with the password of *admin* and you will see the default GroundWork page. GroundWork divides different configuration and monitoring pages into tabs along the top of the screen. In Figure 8-2 you can see the default dashboard page. First, select the Administration tab. This screen allows you to configure the users, groups, and roles on this machine. With roles you can select which of the menu options a particular user can see, so if you don't want a user to be able to configure GroundWork, you can limit that user to the display options in the menu. Right now all we want to do, though, is change the admin password. Click the My Preferences link at the top right of the screen, select Edit Profile, and finally click Change Password.

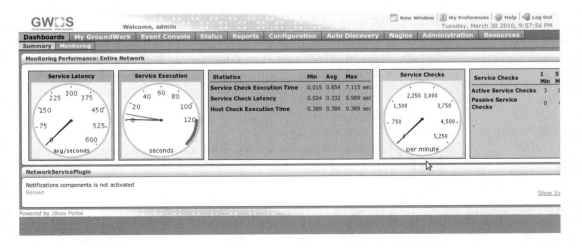

Figure 8-2 Groundwork default dashboard

NOTE   If you are in the Administration window, you could add your own user if you wanted. Click the User Management tab, then the Create new user account link in the right pane. Fill out your user information, and be sure to select the Administrators role when you get to the Assign Roles screen. Now when you log in as your user, you will have the same level of access as the administrator.

Initial Host Scan   One of the more annoying parts about a monitoring system is the initial configuration of every host. If you have a lot of hosts to monitor, it can be a pain to add them one by one to the system. Ground-Work provides a wizard that makes the initial configuration substantially simpler. Select Auto Discovery from the main row of tabs. There are a few different scanning modes to choose from: Interactive, Auto, and Auto Commit. The Interactive mode will prompt you at each phase of the process. The Auto mode will automatically add each host it detects to the GroundWork configuration but it won't commit the changes. The Auto Commit option is like Auto, but it will automatically commit the changes to Nagios as well. Start with the Interactive mode until you get a good grasp of how it works, then try out the other modes if you notice you always tend to add hosts GroundWork detects.

At the bottom of the screen you will see the option to define IP ranges to scan. You can define not only IPs to include here but also IPs you don't want to scan. Generally speaking, you at least want to scan the same subnet your monitoring server is on, so add that here. Once you add your subnets, uncheck the localhost subnet (127.0.1.*) so it won't add a lot of entries for your localhost interface, and then click the Go button at the top of the screen to proceed. After you confirm that you want to continue in the next screen, GroundWork will scan every IP in the subnets you defined. When it finds a particular host, it then scans it for open ports and attempts to detect services on the machine. For each service it detects that has an available Nagios check, GroundWork will automatically add that service check to that host.

Once the scan is complete, if you chose Interactive mode, click Next at the bottom of the screen and you will see a full list of hosts that GroundWork detected, as shown in Figure 8-3. If you chose Auto or Auto Commit mode,

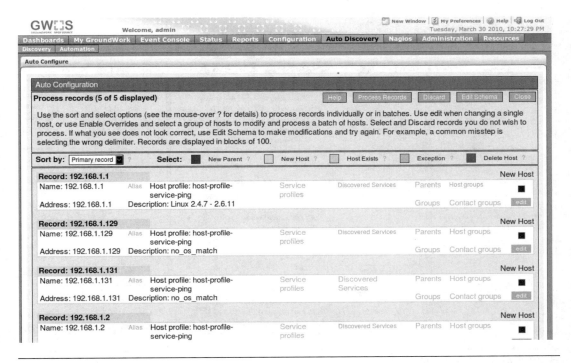

Figure 8-3 Auto scan results

it will bypass this screen. At a bare minimum each host will have ping monitoring enabled, but if other services are detected, appropriate Nagios checks will be added as well. Click the check box on the right-hand side of each host if you want to add it to your configuration. When you are finished selecting hosts, click Process Records to add the selected hosts to your configuration.

Check Host Status   Once you add the initial set of hosts and commit the changes, select the Status tab from the top of the screen. The status screen provides you with an overall view of the health of your network. Here you can see how many hosts and services are up or down at a glance. Each host group is listed in the left pane, and you can click any host groups you configure to gather statistics just for that group. Figure 8-4 shows a sample status page. The data updates in real time so as hosts recover, the status will change.

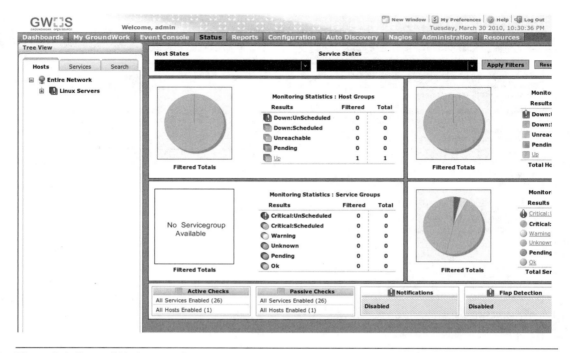

Figure 8-4 GroundWork status page

Configure Nagios

All Nagios configuration is done via the Configuration tab. GroundWork actually maintains its own configuration in a MySQL database. When you make changes here, it actually changes them in the database first. It isn't until you commit changes that GroundWork converts the configuration into the individual Nagios configuration files and reloads Nagios.

The configuration page is divided into a number of different categories via a smaller row of tabs at the top of the page:

▪ **Services**
This category lets you configure all of the service checks available for Nagios. Here you can change the options used by service checks, such as their warning and critical thresholds, and you can add new service checks.

- **Profiles**

  Profiles allow you to define different templates you can use for different types of hosts. You can set up service profiles that group certain service checks together, so, for instance, a default service profile might include checks for the services you know all of your servers have, such as SSH. A service profile for your Web servers might include a number of different Apache checks.

  The host profiles let you create templates for host settings such as how often to check if the host is up and whether to monitor the host 24x7. You can also add service profiles to a host profile. This way you could set up a host profile for your production Web servers that makes sure they are monitored 24x7, includes a default service profile for SSH and other default services, and adds your Web service profile.

- **Hosts**

  The hosts configuration contains all of the hosts you have added to GroundWork. Here you can select individual hosts and tweak their settings; add, remove, or change settings for their services; and configure what group they are in. This page also contains host group configurations so you can group different sets of servers together to make it easier to monitor their status.

- **Contacts**

  The contacts page lets you add contact information for people who will receive notifications when services go down. You can also set up contact groups that contain multiple individual contacts, then assign those contact groups to hosts so that the entire group will get notified. Within these contacts you can also configure what sorts of notifications a particular contact should receive, how to contact the person, and even at what times of day.

- **Escalations**

  Escalations are very useful if you rotate on-call duties or have on-call staff in different parts of the globe. You can set up escalations so that the first three alerts, for instance, go to your on-call person, and if that person doesn't respond by the third alert, the rest will go to the secondary contact. You can also define time periods to go with the escalations so that if you have nighttime on-call staff and daytime on-call staff, you can contact one or the other based on the time of day.

▪ **Commands**

It's easy to confuse commands and services. Commands are the Nagios check scripts that typically live in /usr/local/groundwork/nagios/libexec. These are usually generic commands that accept a whole host of options. Services will then point to one of these commands and run them with a particular set of options. For instance, there is a generic command called check_tcp that will test a TCP connection on a particular port. If you wanted to test port 80, for instance, you could set up a service you call check_port80 that calls the check_tcp command to test port 80 only. Use this page if you wrote your own custom Nagios plug-in and want to make it available to GroundWork.

▪ **Time periods**

As the name indicates, this page lets you configure different time periods to which Nagios can refer. By default some standard time periods are already defined, such as 24x7, work hours, and non-work hours. These can be handy if you want to monitor certain services only during certain hours.

▪ **Groups**

On this page you can configure particular groups within the Ground-Work interface. These groups would contain groups of hosts, contact groups, and other settings. With these groups defined you can easily change a particular setting (such as add a new service check) and deploy it to all of the hosts within a particular group. This is really handy when you manage large numbers of hosts and want to be able to change entire groups at a time.

▪ **Control**

The control page is where you go whenever you want to commit your changes. Here you can also view the Nagios configuration and test your current changes before you commit them.

- **Tools**

   The tools page provides a few extra GroundWork tools. Here you can export your settings to a file and also delete groups of hosts or services based on a pattern.

- **Performance**

   On the performance page you can configure options for graphs and other metrics.

Commit Changes to Nagios

Since GroundWork maintains its settings in a separate database, changes you make in the Web interface don't directly load into Nagios. Whenever you make a change in the Web interface, you must commit it. The commit process translates GroundWork's configuration into valid Nagios files. To commit your changes, select Configuration from the main tab, then select the Control tab at the top of the page. From there select the Commit link in the left pane. You will have the option to back up your old configuration if you want; otherwise click the Commit button to update the Nagios config and restart Nagios.

Configure Contact List

After you set up your initial set of hosts, you will want to configure a contact to get the alerts. Select the Configuration tab, and then select the Contacts tab. Click the Contacts link in the left pane to expand it and reveal the New, Copy, and Modify options. Since we want to add a new contact, click New. Figure 8-5 gives an example of a contact entry. Fill out your contact's information and either set the notification period and other options manually or select a contact template from the drop-down menu that suits you. If none of the available options does suit you, you can also add a new contact template from the left pane with the settings you want to use. I chose generic-contact-2 because it has a good set of defaults for 24x7 monitoring.

GroundWork will set up a default contact group called nagiosadmin. The default templates that are already set up with GroundWork will use this contact group for notifications, so if you don't want to do much tweaking,

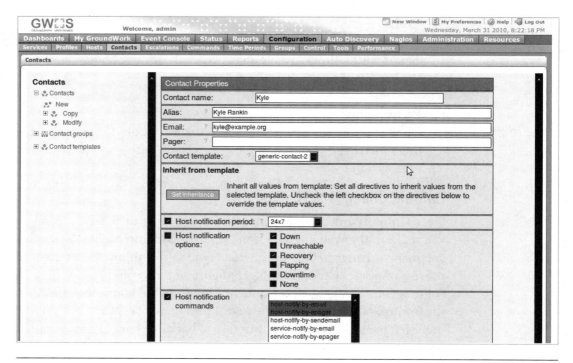

Figure 8-5 Sample contact properties page

click the "Contact groups" link in the left pane to expand it, click Modify, select nagiosadmin and change the settings so that you are added to the group and any default contacts are removed, then click Save. Alternatively, you could create your own contact group; just be sure to add that group to the hosts you monitor so you will get alerts. Once you change all of your contact settings, remember to commit the changes.

Enable Notifications for Nagios

Even if you set up a contact and it is part of the correct contact group, by default GroundWork will not send out notifications until you explicitly tell it to start. This is a good default because you can set up all of your hosts first and tweak service checks so that everything is online before you trigger notifications. That way you won't get unnecessary e-mails or pages until you are ready. When you *are* ready to enable notifications, click the Control tab at the top of any Configuration page, then select "Nagios main configuration" in the left pane of the page that loads. Around the middle of the right pane you will see an option called "Enable notifications." Check that option and then scroll to the bottom and click Save and Next. You will have to click Save and Next through a few more screens until you see and click Save and Done. Now click Commit in the left pane and commit your changes to Nagios. Now you will start to get alerts to any configured contacts.

NOTE   If you set up notifications via e-mail, be sure that your host has a functioning local mail server configured; otherwise notifications will never get to you. For more information on how to configure a mail server on Ubuntu, check out the Mail Server section of Chapter 5.

Add a Service Check to a Host

For most hosts you should at least do some sort of ping probe to see if the server is up. Most people, though, want to monitor more than that. Ground-Work supplies a number of different service checks out of the box along with a number of commands you can reference to create your own custom service checks. For starters, I will walk you through adding a new service check to a host to check whether SSH is alive.

First select the Configuration tab, and then select the Hosts tab. Expand the Hosts tree in the left pane until you can find the host you want to change. Once you expand that host, you will see a Detail link that you can click to configure all of the settings for that host. Each set of options is organized into different tabs in the right pane, so click the Services tab to configure the services monitored on this host. The ssh_alive service is what you can use to test that SSH is available, so I select that service along with any others I might want to add on this page and then click the Add Services button to add it to the list. Then click the Host Detail tab, scroll down to the bottom of that tab, and click Save to save your changes. Now commit your changes to Nagios so they will take effect.

Add a New Host

To add a new host to GroundWork outside of automatic scanning, select the Configuration tab and then click the Hosts tab at the top of the page. In the left pane, locate the link named "Host wizard" and click it. Fill out the fields in the right pane with the hostname, an alias, the IP address, and a host profile to use for the host. If you haven't configured any custom host profiles, the `host-profile-service-ping` option is a safe default. Once you are finished, click Next.

The next page lets you choose any host templates you might have configured along with any parents the host has. Choose the `generic-host` template unless you have set up a custom one. The `parents` field lets you choose previously configured hosts as the parent of this host. When a host is another host's parent, if it goes down Nagios will consider the child host down as well. This helps you build a dependency tree from your network equipment to your hosts. If you aren't sure what parents to configure, it's fine to leave this blank.

On the next page you can assign your new host to any host groups you have defined. If you want to use Nagios's mapping feature, you can also enter map coordinates here. This page also is where you would select any escalation trees if you have defined them. If you are just starting out, you will probably leave most of these options blank.

The next page is where you configure what services to monitor on this host. If you have any service profiles configured, you can add them here; otherwise you can manually select services. Once you click Next, you will be at the final page of the wizard. You have the option to save all of your settings as a profile. This can be handy if you know you are going to repeat this wizard for a group of hosts and they will all have the same sets of options. You can just save this as a profile and then choose it when you add the next host. Click Continue to finish adding the host to GroundWork. Don't forget to commit your changes once you are finished adding hosts.

Advanced Configuration

While there are far too many options in Nagios to be described here, I discuss a few principles that will help you as you navigate through the long list of settings. I start with host settings and then describe how to add a new custom service check to GroundWork.

When you look at the custom options for a host, you will notice that each option has a check box on the left; a check box, drop-down menu, or text entry box on the right; and a small question mark. Figure 8-6 shows a sample host configuration page. The right check box, text entry, or menu will show the current state of a particular setting.

The left check box tells you whether this particular setting is currently getting its value from a template. If the box is checked, you won't be able to change that setting manually. When you change it and save your changes, you will notice it will revert back to whatever was set in the template. So uncheck the left check box if you want to override a setting; just realize that if you do update that option in the template, it will no longer get passed to this host. Generally speaking, unless you are making an exception, it's simpler to make changes with templates than to go host by host.

The question mark accompanies most configuration options in Ground-Work, and if you roll your mouse over it you will get a more in-depth explanation of a particular option. With so many options, tips like this definitely come in handy.

You can also override the default settings for a particular service check on a host. Just click that service check in the left pane under the host and

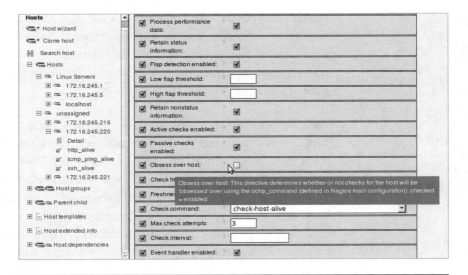

Figure 8-6 GroundWork host configuration options

make your changes. The Service Check tab here lets you change the default arguments you will pass to a service check. This comes in handy when you want to modify the warning and critical thresholds for a particular server. For instance, if you get alerts for high load, but you know that a particular server sometimes exceeds your default threshold but for it that higher load is normal, you can tweak its threshold and leave the rest of the hosts alone.

Create a New Service Check   Even though there are a fair number of service checks in GroundWork by default, the amount you can create once you understand how some of the core Nagios commands work is staggering. For this example I show how to add a custom service check I call `tcp_smtp` that checks whether port 25 (the SMTP port) is open on a host.

First select the Configuration tab. Then click the smaller Services tab on the top of the page. Click "New service" in the left pane to create a new service check. On the first page I am prompted for the name of my service and what service template to use. I name it `tcp_smtp` , select the `generic-service` template, and then click Add.

Once the service is added, I can see all sorts of default options that the `generic-service` template sets, such as whether to check the service 24x7, how often to check it, and how many retries to make before an alert. I'm going to leave these at the defaults, but depending on how sensitive your service is, you might want to tweak these options to monitor the service more or less often.

What I am most interested in is the Service Check tab. It is there I can define what command to use for this service. I click that tab and then locate the "Check command" drop-down menu. Now at this point if you are new to Nagios you might not know what to select. You can get some hints by the service name, but realistically what you will need to do is check out what the standard Nagios commands do, either with research online or by going to /usr/local/groundwork/nagios/libexec and running the commands manually. Many of the commands are just shell scripts, so you can even open them and see how they work. From my own experience I know that I want the command named `check_smtp` so I select it here.

Once you select a command, the "Command line" text entry box will get loaded with the command and each of its default arguments separated by exclamation points. In my case I have ARG1 and ARG2. When I look at the command definition, I can see that it passes ARG1 to check_smtp's -w argument and ARG2 to -c. Most standard Nagios commands use -w and -c to set warning and critical thresholds, respectively, but again you will need to do some research here. In this case they are looking for the number of seconds it takes SMTP to respond to my test. Different SMTP servers have different response times, but I set this to warn me if it takes five seconds to respond, and to send an alert if it takes ten seconds. So in the "Command line" text entry box in place of

```
check_smtp!ARG1!ARG2
```

I put

```
check_smtp!5!10
```

You can see an example of my Service Check tab in Figure 8-7. Now I click Save to save my changes. From this point I can go to the host configuration section and add this check to any hosts I want to monitor. Again, remember to commit your changes to Nagios for them to take effect.

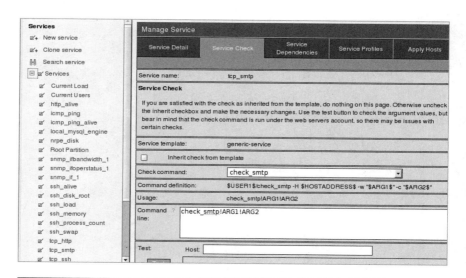

Figure 8-7 Service Check settings for a new service

More GroundWork Information

I've really only scratched the surface of Nagios and GroundWork configuration. GroundWork includes its own documentation via the Bookshelf link at the top of the Web interface. Click that and a new window will pop up with a searchable index and a predefined list of documentation topics you can browse through. In addition, http://groundworkopensource.com has a number of different configuration guides as well as a forum you can join to ask questions and get tips from other GroundWork users.

## CHAPTER 9

Virtualization

ONE OF THE HOTTEST TRENDS in system administration today is virtualization. With virtualization you can create multiple instances of Ubuntu that all run on the same hardware. You can allocate parts of your server's resources to each virtual machine. There are incredible amounts of processing power in a modern server, and with virtualization you can get much more out of the hardware you have. I even used virtual machines as a test lab for this book; it is much faster to set up a new Ubuntu server and try out a particular package when you can do so within a virtual machine rather than setting aside multiple hardware machines.

There are a number of different virtualization technologies available under Ubuntu Server, and in this chapter I cover two of the most popular, VMware Server and KVM. VMware Server is a free product produced by VMware, and KVM (Kernel-based Virtual Machine) is free software with support built into the Linux kernel. Finally I discuss some of the new Cloud features available to Ubuntu Server.

KVM

KVM is the default virtualization technology supported by Ubuntu. This software takes advantage of virtualization support built into Intel and AMD processors and allows you to run a number of different distributions and operating systems as VMs (virtual machines) on a single host.

Install KVM

The one "gotcha" about KVM is that it doesn't just take advantage of virtualization support in processors, it requires it. So before you do anything else, you should confirm that your processor has virtualization extensions. Run the following command on your host:

```
$ egrep '(vmx|svm)' /proc/cpuinfo
```

If you get some output, then your server has the necessary extensions and you can move on. If not, then you won't be able to use KVM on this machine. You aren't out of luck, though; just move on to the VMware

Server section later in the chapter as that product doesn't require those extensions.

Enable Support in BIOS

Once you have confirmed that your server will support KVM, you still will probably need to enable those extensions in your BIOS. Each BIOS is different, but reboot the machine and look for a section of the BIOS settings that includes processor settings or perhaps advanced settings and make sure that virtualization extensions are enabled.

Install KVM Packages

Once the BIOS is all set, boot back into your server and install all of the packages you will need for KVM:

```
$ sudo apt-get install gemu-kvm libvirt-bin ubuntu-vm-builder
```

In addition to the KVM software and necessary libraries, this group of packages will also provide you with the virsh command-line tool you will need to manage your VMs. This will also install the ubuntu-vm-builder script, which makes spinning up new Ubuntu VMs incredibly easy.

Along with the root user you will probably want to set up at least one other user on the system who can directly manage VMs. To do this you simply need to add that user to the libvirtd group:

```
$ sudo adduser username libvirtd
```

Replace username with the name of your user. Note that you will have to log out and log back in for the group changes to take effect. Once you log back in, run the groups command and make sure that libvirtd is among your user's list of groups. At this point you are ready to test whether KVM is functioning and your user can manage it, so run the following virsh command:

```
$ virsh -c qemu:///system list
Connecting to uri: qemu:///system
 Id Name                 State
----------------------------------
```

You will use this `virsh` command a lot. In this case it outputs the list of all VMs currently running on this machine. We haven't set up any yet, but the fact that we got valid output and not an error means that we are ready to proceed. If you got some sort of permissions error, it is likely because your user is not part of the libvirtd group.

Configure KVM Networking

There are two main ways you can set up networking for your VMs. The default networking setup provides a private network under 192.168.122.0/24. A DHCP server will hand out the rest of the IPs; alternatively, you can set up static IPs for your VM. The KVM host has the IP 192.168.122.1, and VMs then communicate with the outside world via that gateway using NAT (Network Address Translation). This works fine, especially for VMs on a desktop, but since we are talking about servers here, my assumption is that you want machines outside of the KVM host to be able to communicate with your VMs. While you could certainly set up some sort of `iptables` DNAT rules and forward traffic back in, that solution doesn't scale very well. The real solution is to set up bridged networking so that your VMs appear to be on the same network as your host.

It is relatively simple to set up the br0 bridge interface on Ubuntu. Essentially you identify the interface over which you want to bridge traffic (probably eth0 or possibly bond0 if you set up bonding), transfer all if its configuration to br0 along with a few extra bridge options, and then change the original interface to manual mode. It makes more sense when you see the examples. For instance, if I had DHCP set up for eth0 and my old configuration in /etc/network/ interfaces looked like this:

```
auto eth0
iface eth0 inet dhcp
```

then my new configuration would look like this:

```
auto eth0
iface eth0 inet manual

auto br0
```

```
iface br0 inet dhcp
        bridge_ports eth0
        bridge_fd 9
        bridge_hello 2
        bridge_maxage 12
        bridge_stp off
```

Note that I changed the inet mode for eth0 from dhcp to manual. If eth0 had a static IP configured, I would just transfer all that configuration to br0 instead, so it would go from this:

```
auto eth0
iface eth0 inet static
        address 192.168.0.5
        network 192.168.0.0
        netmask 255.255.255.0
        broadcast 192.168.0.255
        gateway 192.168.0.1
```

to this:

```
auto eth0
iface eth0 inet manual

auto br0
iface br0 inet static
        address 192.168.0.5
        network 192.168.0.0
        netmask 255.255.255.0
        broadcast 192.168.0.255
        gateway 192.168.0.1
        bridge_ports eth0
        bridge_fd 9
        bridge_hello 2
        bridge_maxage 12
        bridge_stp off
```

Once I have set up /etc/network/interfaces to have the bridge, I then restart networking:

```
$ sudo /etc/init.d/networking restart
```

Now my `ifconfig` output should list my new bridged interface:

```
$ ifconfig
br0    Link encap:Ethernet  HWaddr 00:17:42:1f:18:be
       inet addr:192.168.0.5  Bcast:192.168.0.255  Mask:255.255.255.0
       inet6 addr: fe80::217:42ff:fe1f:18be/64 Scope:Link
       UP BROADCAST RUNNING MULTICAST  MTU:1500  Metric:1
       RX packets:17226 errors:0 dropped:0 overruns:0 frame:0
       TX packets:13277 errors:0 dropped:0 overruns:0 carrier:0
       collisions:0 txqueuelen:0
       RX bytes:16519186 (16.5 MB)  TX bytes:1455348 (1.4 MB)
```

NOTE Even though we are talking about servers with physical network connections here, I should bring up the fact that most wireless adapters don't support bridging, so if you try to set this up on your laptop and bridge over your wireless interface, bridged mode won't work.

Once the bridge interface is set up, the current KVM installation should be able to take advantage of it by default. Now you are ready to create your first VM.

Create a New VM

Once KVM and your bridged network are set up, you are ready to create your first VM. Ubuntu has set up a tool called `ubuntu-vm-builder` (in newer releases renamed `vmbuilder`) that you can use to automate the process of creating a VM. With `vmbuilder` you can define the settings for a VM, including what Ubuntu release you want, and the tool will create the local virtual disk and perform the base install for you. It will even register the VM with the system so that it's ready to go once it completes.

To streamline the process even further, Ubuntu has created a special Ubuntu installation known as JeOS (pronounced "juice") for virtual machines. All of the nonessential kernel modules have been removed, and the OS in general is tuned for better performance as a VM. In the examples that follow I create VMs based on JeOS.

The `vmbuilder` script can create VMs for a number of different platforms, including KVM, so when you run the command, the first two options you pass it are the virtualization technology (hypervisor) to use and what type of OS (suite) it will install. Here's the first segment of the command that we will build off of (but don't hit Enter just yet):

```
$ sudo vmbuilder kvm ubuntu
```

There are different options you can choose from based on which hypervisor and suite you choose, and you can pass the --help argument after each one to get a list of specific options:

```
$ sudo vmbuilder kvm ubuntu --help
```

The vmbuilder script will create a directory in your current directory and dump the VM's disk there, so if you have set aside a special place on the disk to store VM files, be sure to change to that directory first. Here's a sample relatively basic vmbuilder command that will create an Ubuntu Lucid VM called test1:

```
$ sudo vmbuilder kvm ubuntu --suite lucid --flavour virtual
  --arch i386 --hostname test1 --libvirt qemu:///system --
  rootsize=2048 --swapsize=256 --user ubuntu --pass insecure
  -d test1-kvm
2010-04-17 12:17:04,193 INFO : Calling hook: preflight_check
2010-04-17 12:17:04,196 INFO : Calling hook: set_defaults
2010-04-17 12:17:04,197 INFO : Calling hook: bootstrap
. . .
2009-02-27 16:52:31,480 INFO     Cleaning up
```

After I run the command, the script will go out and retrieve all of the packages and files it needs and automatically build the VM for me. Below I describe each of the options I chose:

- **--suite *lucid***
  The --suite option chooses which Ubuntu version to install. I chose lucid here but you could also choose dapper, feisty, gutsy, hardy, intrepid, jaunty, or karmic

- **--flavour *virtual***
  There are different kernel flavors available for Ubuntu. The virtual flavor chooses the JeOS kernel that's optimized for VMs, but there are

a number of different kernels from which you can choose, depending on which Ubuntu suite and architecture you choose.

▪ **--arch *i386***

This is the processor architecture to use for my VM. If I don't specify this, it will default to the host architecture. Valid options are i386, amd64, and lpia.

▪ **--hostname *test1***

If you don't specify a hostname, the VM will default to a hostname of ubuntu. This is fine until you decide you want to create more than one VM, at which point you will get an error that the domain ubuntu already exists. Use the --hostname option, so that not only can you specify the hostname within the OS, you can also specify the unique name that will be registered with KVM.

▪ **--libvirt *qemu:///system***

The --libvirt option will automatically add this VM to my local KVM instance.

▪ **--rootsize *2048* and --swapsize *256***

For basic VMs you probably just want a single disk with a root and swap partition. In that case you can use --rootsize and --swapsize to specify the root and swap partition sizes in megabytes. There is also an --optsize option that will set up a separate /opt partition.

▪ **--user *ubuntu* and --pass *insecure***

You will want some sort of default user on the system so once it is built you can log in to it, unless your network uses LDAP or some other network authentication. The --user and --pass arguments let me specify the default user and password to use; otherwise both will default to ubuntu. You can also use the --name option to set the full name of the user.

▪ **-d *test1-kvm***

By default, vmbuilder will install the VM's root disk under the ubuntu-kvm directory in the user's home directory. Of course, once you set up one VM, you won't be able to reuse the same directory, so the -d option lets you specify the location of the destination directory.

Once the install completes, I will see that a new test1-kvm directory was created in my current directory and inside is the disk file for that VM:

```
$ ls test1-kvm/
run.sh tmpHHSJGz.qcow2
```

In addition, my new VM will be registered with KVM, and its XML file, which defines its settings, will be installed under /etc/libvirt/qemu/test1.xml and look something like this:

```
<domain type='kvm'>
  <name>test1</name>
  <uuid>907a0091-e31f-e2b2-6181-dc2d1225ed65</uuid>
  <memory>131072</memory>
  <currentMemory>131072</currentMemory>
  <vcpu>1</vcpu>
  <os>
    <type arch='i686' machine='pc-0.12'>hvm</type>
    <boot dev='hd'/>
  </os>
  <features>
    <acpi/>
  </features>
  <clock offset='utc'/>
  <on_poweroff>destroy</on_poweroff>
  <on_reboot>restart</on_reboot>
  <on_crash>destroy</on_crash>
  <devices>
    <emulator>/usr/bin/kvm</emulator>
    <disk type='file' device='disk'>
      <source file='/home/ubuntu/vms/test1-kvm/tmpHHSJGz.qcow2'/>
      <target dev='hda' bus='ide'/>
    </disk>
    <interface type='network'>
      <mac address='52:54:00:c6:18:b7'/>
      <source network='default'/>
      <model type='virtio'/>
    </interface>
    <input type='mouse' bus='ps2'/>
    <graphics type='vnc' port='-1' autoport='yes' listen='127.0.0.1'/>
    <video>
      <model type='cirrus' vram='9216' heads='1'/>
    </video>
  </devices>
</domain>
```

Extra vmbuilder Options

The example `vmbuilder` command I gave will certainly work, but the script supports a large number of additional options that might be useful for your VMs. For instance, in my example I list the `--rootsize` and `--swapsize` options to set the root and swap partitions in my VM's disk. You might decide that you want a more complex partition layout than just a root and swap partition, in which case you can use the `--part` option. The `--part` option reads from a file you create that contains partition information and uses it when it sets up disks. The file has a very basic syntax. Each line contains a mount point followed by a partition size in megabytes. You can even set up multiple disks—just use `---` on its own line to separate one disk from another.

For instance, let's say I wanted to create two disks. The first disk would have a 100Mb /boot partition, a 2Gb / partition, and a 512Mb swap. The second disk would have a 5Gb /var partition. I could create a file called test1.partitions containing the following data:

```
/boot 100
root 2000
swap 512
---
/var 5000
```

Now when I run `vm-builder` I replace the `--root 2000 --swap 256` lines in my command with `--part /path/to/test1.partitions`. The final command would look like this:

```
$ sudo vmbuilder kvm ubuntu --suite lucid --flavour virtual
  --arch i386 --hostname test1 --libvirt qemu:///system
  --part /home/ubuntu/vminfo/test1.partitions --user ubuntu
  --pass insecure -d test1-kvm
```

Package Management   The `vmbuilder` script also has a number of handy preseed-like options for automating your install. Here are some options specifically aimed at package management:

■ **--addpkg** *packagename* and **--removepkg** *packagename*
The `--addpkg` and `--removepkg` commands will respectively add and remove a package you specify as an argument. You can add multiple

--addpkg or --removepkg commands on the command line if you want to add or remove more than one package. Keep in mind that any packages that are interactive when they install (i.e., they ask you questions) won't work here.

▪ **--mirror** *URL*
Use the --mirror command followed by the URL for a specific Ubuntu mirror if you want to use something other than the default Ubuntu servers. This is handy if you have set up a local Ubuntu mirror, as the install will go much faster.

▪ **--components** *main,universe*
If you want to add particular repositories to your Ubuntu VM such as universe or multiverse, for instance, use the --components argument followed by a comma-separated list of repositories.

▪ **--ppa** *PPA*
If there is a particular PPA (Personal Package Archive) from ppa.launchpad.net that you want to add, just specify its name here.

Network Settings   By default VMs will be created using DHCP for their network information. You can optionally specify a static network setting on the command line. Here is a description of each network option along with a sample setting:

▪ **--domain** *example.org*
This sets the default domain of the VM; otherwise it is set to the domain of the host.

▪ **--ip** *192.168.0.100*
Here you set the static IP address to assign the VM.

▪ **--mask** *255.255.255.0*
This value is set to the subnet mask.

▪ **--net** *192.168.0.0*
This value is set to the address for the network of the host.

▪ **--bcast** *192.168.0.255*
Here you can specify the broadcast address.

▪ **--gw** *192.168.0.1*
If you don't specify a gateway address with this option, the first address of your network will be chosen.

▪ **--dns** *192.168.0.5*
Like the gateway address, if you don't specify an address here, it will use the first address on your network.

Post-install Scripts There are a number of options you can set with vmbuilder that can set up post-install scripts and other actions to help automate your install further. Here is a description of some of the main options you might use:

▪ **--ssh-key** */root/.ssh/authorized_keys* **and** *--ssh-user-key /home/username/.ssh/authorized_keys*
These options take the full path to your SSH authorized keys file for either the root user (--ssh-key) or a regular user (--ssh-user-key) and copy it to the host. You might set this up so that you can automatically SSH into a VM after it is installed and start without a password.

▪ **--copy** *filename*
This option reads in a file you specify that contains a list of source and destination files, such as

```
/home/ubuntu/vmfiles/filename /etc/filename
```

It will copy the file from the source file on the host to the destination file on the VM.

▪ **--execscript** *script*
This argument will run a script you specify on the command line within the VM using chroot at the end of the install.

- **--firstboot** *script*

  This option is like `--execscript` except it copies the script you specify into the VM and executes it the first time the VM boots.

- **--firstlogin** *script*

  The downside to most of the automated installer options is that they require that scripts be noninteractive. The `--firstlogin` option doesn't have that limitation. It will take a script you specify and execute it the first time a user logs in to the VM. Since the first user who logs in will see the script, you have the option of making it interactive. You might also want to use this script to install any packages on your VM that have an interactive installer.

Once you have successfully created a VM with `vmbuilder`, you are ready to start your VM for the first time and manage it with `virsh`.

Manage VMs with virsh

The `virsh` command is one of the main tools you will use to manage your VMs. The basic syntax for KVM is `virsh -c qemu:///system` followed by some sort of command. For instance, to list all of the running VMs, type

```
$ virsh -c qemu:///system list
Connecting to uri: qemu:///system
 Id Name                 State
----------------------------------
```

Now that you have created a new VM, you can use the `start` command to start it:

```
$ virsh -c qemu:///system start test1
Connecting to uri: qemu:///system
Domain test1 started

$ virsh -c qemu:///system list
Connecting to uri: qemu:///system
 Id Name                 State
----------------------------------
 9 test1                 running
```

Note that the start command is followed by the VM that you want to start. Similar commands to start are shutdown and destroy, which will shut down and pull the power from the VM, respectively. If you want the VM to start at boot time, use the autostart command:

```
$ virsh -c qemu:///system autostart test1
Connecting to uri: qemu:///system
Domain test1 marked as autostarted
```

If you want to remove the autostart option, add --disable to the command:

```
$ virsh -c qemu:///system autostart --disable test1
Connecting to uri: qemu:///system
Domain test1 unmarked as autostarted
```

KVM also supports snapshotting so you can save the current state of your VM and roll back to it later. To take a snapshot, use the save command followed by the VM and the file in which to save the state:

```
$ virsh -c qemu:///system save test1 test1-snapshot.state
Connecting to uri: qemu:///system
Domain test1 saved to test1-snapshot.state
```

Later you can use the restore command followed by the state file you saved previously to restore the VM to that state:

```
$ virsh -c qemu:///system restore test1-snapshot.state
Connecting to uri: qemu:///system
Domain restored from test1-snapshot.state
```

You can also suspend and resume VMs with the suspend and resume commands. Keep in mind that suspended VMs still do consume memory resources. Suspended VMs will show up in a list with the paused state:

```
$ virsh -c qemu:///system suspend test1
Connecting to uri: qemu:///system
Domain test1 suspended

$ virsh -c qemu:///system list
Connecting to uri: qemu:///system
```

```
Id Name                   State
--------------------------------
11 test2                  running
12 test1                  paused

$ virsh -c qemu:///system resume test1
Connecting to uri: qemu:///system
Domain test1 resumed

$ virsh -c qemu:///system list
Connecting to uri: qemu:///system
 Id Name                   State
--------------------------------
11 test2                  running
12 test1                  running
```

One particularly nice feature of using VMs is that if a VM needs more
RAM and your host has it available, you can make the change rather easily.
First use the dominfo command to see the amount of RAM currently used
by the VM. Once the VM is shut down, use the setmaxmem command to
change the maximum RAM available to the VM and the setmem command
to change the RAM the VM can currently use (the two can be different values, provided the maximum memory is larger). Once you restart the VM,
it will come up with the new amount of RAM:

```
$ virsh -c qemu:///system dominfo test1
Connecting to uri: qemu:///system
Id:             -
Name:           test1
UUID:           e1c9cbd2-a160-bef6-771d-18c762efa098
OS Type:        hvm
State:          shut off
CPU(s):         1
Max memory:     131072 kB
Used memory:    131072 kB
Autostart:      disable
Security model: apparmor
Security DOI:   0

$ virsh -c qemu:///system setmaxmem test1 262144
Connecting to uri: qemu:///system

$ virsh -c qemu:///system dominfo test1
Connecting to uri: qemu:///system
```

```
Id:            -
Name:          test1
UUID:          e1c9cbd2-a160-bef6-771d-18c762efa098
OS Type:       hvm
State:         shut off
CPU(s):        1
Max memory:    262144 kB
Used memory:   131072 kB
Autostart:     disable
Security model: apparmor
Security DOI:  0

$ virsh -c qemu:///system setmem test1 262144
Connecting to uri: qemu:///system

$ virsh -c qemu:///system dominfo test1
Connecting to uri: qemu:///system
Id:            -
Name:          test1
UUID:          e1c9cbd2-a160-bef6-771d-18c762efa098
OS Type:       hvm
State:         shut off
CPU(s):        1
Max memory:    262144 kB
Used memory:   262144 kB
Autostart:     disable
Security model: apparmor
Security DOI:  0
```

KVM Graphical Console and Management Tools

There are a number of ways that you can get a console into a KVM VM. Some people simply set up SSH ahead of time and SSH into the machine, while others set up some sort of remote desktop with VNC. When you first get started, however, you might not have all of that infrastructure in place, so it's nice to have some sort of tool to get a graphical console on your VM. The virt-manager utility makes this process simple.

First, install the virt-manager packages with sudo apt-get install virt-manager. If your server has some sort of graphical desktop, you can run it from there. You will see a display of the potential local KVM instances to which you can connect. Double-click the localhost (System) entry and it will connect and expand to show you all of your available VMs, as shown in Figure 9-1. If any VMs are currently running, you will be able to see their current CPU and memory statistics.

If you select a particular VM from the main screen and click the Open button, it will open up a graphical console into the machine as shown in Figure 9-2. From that window you can log in to your VM and run commands just as if you had a keyboard, mouse, and monitor connected to it. You can also power off, suspend, and take snapshots from within this interface.

Back at the main menu you can also get more detailed information about a VM. Select the VM and then click Edit_Machine Details. From here not only can you see more detailed graphs of its current load, but if you click the Hardware tab (Figure 9-3), you can view, add, and remove hardware, although the host will need to be powered off, depending on what you want to change.

Remote KVM Management   This tool isn't limited to local KVM management as there's a good chance that you don't have a graphical environment

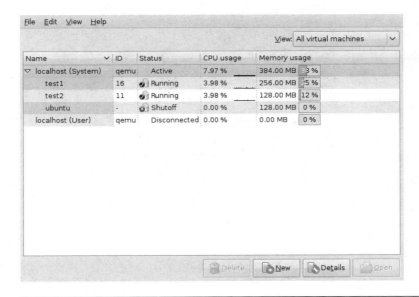

Figure 9-1 Virtual Machine Manager default screen

Virtual Machine   View   Send key   Help

▷   ⏸   ⏻
Run   Pause   Shutdown

```
* Setting preliminary keymap...
* Setting the system clock
* Starting basic networking...                            [ OK ]
* Starting kernel event manager...                        [ OK ]
* Loading hardware drivers...                             [ OK ]
* Setting the system clock
* Loading kernel modules...
* Loading manual drivers...                               [ OK ]
* Setting kernel variables...                             [ OK ]
* Activating swap...                                       [ OK ]
* Checking file systems...
fsck 1.40.8 (13-Mar-2008)
                                                          [ OK ]
* Mounting local filesystems...                           [ OK ]
* Activating swapfile swap...                             [ OK ]
* Checking minimum space in /tmp...                       [ OK ]
* Configuring network interfaces...                       [ OK ]
* Setting up console font and keymap...                   [ OK ]
* Starting system log daemon...                           [ OK ]
* Starting kernel log daemon...                           [ OK ]
* Running local boot scripts (/etc/rc.local)              [ OK ]

Ubuntu 8.04.2 test1 tty1

test1 login: _
```

Figure 9-2 Graphical VM console

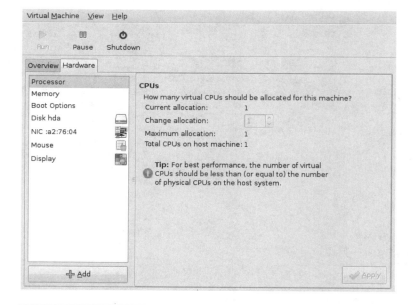

Figure 9-3 VM hardware details

on your server. You can also install the package to a desktop on your network and then connect to your KVM server via an SSH tunnel. Just make sure that you have SSH set up and then click File->Open Connection from the main Virtual Machine Manager window. Then select "Remote tunnel over SSH" in the Connection drop-down menu, make sure the hypervisor is set to QEMU, and then type in the hostname for your KVM server and click Connect.

VMware Server

VMware Server is one of many virtualization products created by VMware. This particular product is not open source software but it is free to download from http://vmware.com after you register with the site. VMware Server offers nice graphical management of VMs via a Web interface and provides full virtualization of the x86 hardware so you can run both Linux and even Windows VMs from the same Ubuntu server.

Install VMware Server

To install VMware Server you need to go to the Products section of http://vmware.com and select VMware Server. You need to create an account on the site so you can download the software and get a free license. At the download page you will see a number of different download options, including Windows .exe and Linux .rpm and .tar.gz images. Choose the Linux .tar.gz image.

While the package downloads, install the `build-essential` package on your Ubuntu server so that the installer can build its special kernel modules. You also need to install the Linux kernel `headers` package for your particular kernel:

```
$ sudo apt-get install build-essential linux-headers-'uname -r'
```

Once the tarball downloads, copy it to your Ubuntu server, extract it, and go inside the vmware-server-distrib directory.

```
$ tar xzvf VMware-server-2.0.2-203138.i386.tar.gz
$ cd vmware-server-distrib
```

Unfortunately the current version of Vmware Server won't build properly on the 2.6.32 kernel included with Lucid, so you will have to extract and patch some files before you run the installer.

```
$ cd lib/modules/source/
$ sudo tar xf vmci.tar
$ sudo tar xf vmmon.tar
$ sudo tar xf vmnet.tar
$ sudo tar xf vsock.tar
```

The community has provided different patches you can use to make the edits. Download and use the patch file in the same directory where you extracted the tarballs:

```
$ cd ../../../
$ wget -N http://risesecurity.org/~rcvalle/VMware-server-2.0.2-
  203138-update.patch
$ sudo patch -p1 < Vmware-server-2.0.2-203138-update.patch
```

Next, update the tar files you extracted so they have your changes, go back to the root vmware-server-distrib directory, and run the vmware-install.pl script as root:

```
$ cd lib/modules/source/
$ sudo tar cf vmci.tar vmci-only
$ sudo tar cf vmmon.tar vmmon-only
$ sudo tar cf vmnet.tar vmnet-only
$ sudo tar cf vsock.tar vsock-only
$ cd ../../../
$ sudo ./vmware-install.pl
```

If you have an old version of VMware Server installed on the machine, the installer will first remove it. Once the install script begins, you will be asked a few questions about your system. The defaults work fine; however, I prefer to install the binary files in /usr/local/bin instead of /usr/bin so they are separated. It's fine to answer the rest of the questions in the installer with the defaults unless you know what some of the settings do and want to change them. The installer will take care of creating any directories it needs.

Configure VMware Server

At the end of the installation program you will be prompted to run the vmware-config.pl script, included wherever you installed the VMware binaries. This script will configure VMware Server to run on your system and will also set up networking devices, so answer Yes when prompted to run it. You can also run the script manually any time you want to change your default answers. VMware Server doesn't contain Ubuntu Server kernel modules, so the configuration script will prompt you to compile the vmmod module. It's possible you will get a warning at this stage because the kernel was compiled with a different version of gcc than you currently have on your system. Tell the program to continue anyway. At this point the program should be able to locate your kernel headers, so you can accept the defaults as it asks you to compile extra modules.

Once all of the modules compile, vmware-config.pl will prompt you to set up networking for the virtual machines, so answer Yes here. VMware has a concept of three different network types:

- **Bridged**
  If a VM is connected to the bridged network, all traffic from it will go out from the server's Ethernet interface as though it were a separate machine. In this mode, if you have DHCP set up on your network, VMs can potentially grab a regular lease.

- **NAT**
  On the NAT network VMware will create an internal subnet on which VMs will communicate and set its virtual network interface on that subnet as a gateway. All VMs on the NAT network can communicate with each other, and if they want to talk outside of their subnet, VMware will use NAT so that all of their traffic appears to come from the host's IP address instead of the VM's.

- **Host-only**
  A host-only network is a private network. VMware will probe for an unused private subnet to use, and all hosts on the host-only network will be able to communicate with each other but won't be able to access the outside network.

As the configuration script proceeds, unless you know what you are doing it's safe to go with VMware's default settings as they will create a new VMware network interface for each of the three network types. If you have multiple Ethernet interfaces on your host, you will be prompted to choose one for the bridged network. Unless you want to set your own internal private IPs to use, VMware will probe for unused private subnets for NAT and host-only networks.

Next the configuration tool will compile the vmnet kernel module and prompt you for which ports to use for remote connections, HTTP connections, and HTTPS connections. Accept all of the defaults here. When you are prompted to specify a VMware Server administrator, choose a user on your system whom you want to log in to manage VMware over the Web interface. Accept the default location to store VMs (/var/lib/vmware/Virtual Machines) unless you have a separate directory set up for them. Finally, enter the serial number you should have received over e-mail when you downloaded the .tar.gz image. The very last step will install the VIX software on the system (a set of APIs so that you can control VMware from outside programs), and then VMware Server will start up.

All of VMware Server's configuration files are stored within /etc/vmware as regular text files, so if you know what you are doing, you could go inside that directory and edit the configuration by hand. In general, I recommend sticking with the vmware-config.pl script whenever you want to make a configuration change.

VMware Server Init Scripts

The installation tool will set up init scripts for VMware so it automatically starts at boot. The /etc/init.d/vmware script is the main one you will use if you ever want to manually start or stop VMware. Just keep in mind that when you do stop the service, all of the VMs that it manages will also stop or suspend (depending on how you configure them).

Once VMware starts, if you look at the output of ifconfig you should notice that at least two vmnet interfaces have been created for your NAT and host-only networks:

```
$ /sbin/ifconfig
. . .
vmnet1    Link encap:Ethernet  HWaddr 00:50:56:c0:00:01
          inet addr:192.168.170.1  Bcast:192.168.170.255
          Mask:255.255.255.0
          inet6 addr: fe80::250:56ff:fec0:1/64 Scope:Link
          UP BROADCAST RUNNING MULTICAST  MTU:1500  Metric:1
          RX packets:0 errors:0 dropped:0 overruns:0 frame:0
          TX packets:6 errors:0 dropped:0 overruns:0 carrier:0
          collisions:0 txqueuelen:1000
          RX bytes:0 (0.0 B)  TX bytes:0 (0.0 B)

vmnet8    Link encap:Ethernet  HWaddr 00:50:56:c0:00:08
          inet addr:172.16.45.1  Bcast:172.16.45.255
          Mask:255.255.255.0
          inet6 addr: fe80::250:56ff:fec0:8/64 Scope:Link
          UP BROADCAST RUNNING MULTICAST  MTU:1500  Metric:1
          RX packets:0 errors:0 dropped:0 overruns:0 frame:0
          TX packets:6 errors:0 dropped:0 overruns:0 carrier:0
          collisions:0 txqueuelen:1000
          RX bytes:0 (0.0 B)  TX bytes:0 (0.0 B)
```

With these interfaces in place, you can connect to any VMs you have created on the same networks via SSH or other network tools on this host.

VMware Web Administration

In the past VMware has offered local applications you could use to manage VMware, but starting with VMware Server 2.0, all VM management is done via a Web interface. This interface by default listens on port 8222 for HTTP and port 8333 for HTTPS, so open a Web browser and browse to your VMware Server. If the server's hostname was vmhost.example.org, you would browse to http://vmhost.example.org:8222 or https://vmhost .example.org:8333, but in either case you would be redirected to the HTTPS session. Once you accept the self-signed cert and load the page, you will be prompted for a username and password, so use the credentials for the user you told the VMware configuration tool you would use for administration. Once you log in, you will see the default VMware management page as shown in Figure 9-4.

On the default management page you can see the CPU and memory usage for the machine along with all data stores VMware Server is using. The

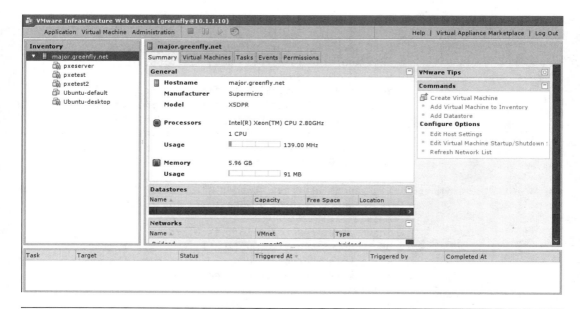

Figure 9-4 Default VMware management page

interface is pretty intuitive; use the tabs in the main pane to move between different displays.

NOTE   If you need additional help navigating the Web administration tool, click the Help link along the top of the page. This will open a new window with complete documentation of VMware Server, the Web interface, and documentation for running and tuning virtual machines.

Create a New Virtual Machine

To create a new VM, click the Virtual Machine button at the top of the page and choose Create Virtual Machine. This will start a wizard that will ask you a number of different questions about your host, such as its name, what type of operating system you will install on it, and how much RAM and storage to give it. All of these options will of course vary depending on what kind of VM you want to create, but it is relatively simple to navigate through the menu and make your selections.

NOTE   **Storage Settings**
When you create a new disk, be aware of some of the options you have. If you are concerned about space, you can tell VMware to grow the disk file as needed, so even though you have set up a 20Gb disk, if the disk is only 20% full, it will take up only that much storage. This saves on space but it can hurt disk performance. When you create the disk, you will have to decide between performance and storage. You also have the option to save VMware disks as 2Gb max files. Unless you plan to move your VM to a file system that has a 2Gb maximum file size limit, leave this option unchecked.

When you get to the Network Adapter section, you will be able to choose between the bridged, NAT, and host-only networks you have set up previously. Again, what you choose here will depend largely on whether you want to isolate this VM from the rest of the network or not. If you want the VM to appear as though it's any other machine on the network, choose Bridged. If you want to give it access to the rest of the network but want it on its own private network, choose NAT. If you want it completely isolated, choose Host-only.

When you get to the CD/DVD drive section, you will be able to choose between giving this VM access to a physical CD-ROM drive on your server or an ISO on your system. The ISO option is handy since you can store ISOs for multiple install and rescue CDs on the server and boot from them with a few clicks. I create a directory called isos under /var/lib/vmware/ Virtual Machines that I use to store all of the ISOs I want to use. You can also add virtual floppy drives and USB controllers if you want.

Once you finish with the wizard, your host will show up in the left pane along with any other VMs you have created. Click on it to see a screen like Figure 9-5 that shows the VM's Summary screen. From this screen you can monitor the CPU and RAM usage of the VM, check out what hardware it currently has configured, and add personal notes.

Along the top of the screen you will see shortcut icons shaped like the standard stop, pause, and play icons along with one for resetting power. The stop button will remove power from your VM just as though you held down the power button on a server or unplugged it from the wall. The play button will power on the machine, and the pause button will suspend its

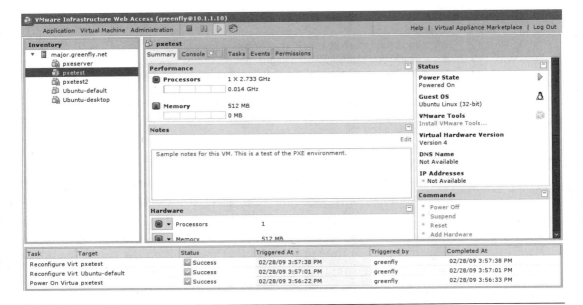

Figure 9-5 VM Summary screen

current state to disk. Finally, the reset button will act as though you hit the reset button on the front of a server. On the main pane along the right side you will see a Commands section that has links to perform the same set of actions along with snapshot options, which I cover next, and options to add hardware and configure the VM.

VM Console Access

When you power on a VM, it will start the boot process and run in the background. Of course, if this is the first time you have powered on the machine, it won't have an operating system on it, so you will likely want some sort of console access so you can install the OS. One of the tabs available for each VM is labeled Console. When you click on this tab the first time, you will be prompted to install a browser plug-in. After the plug-in is installed, each time you enter this tab you can click within to launch a separate window on your screen that gives you console access to your machine as though you had a remote desktop or KVM session into it. Figure 9-6 shows an example remote console screen where my VM is at the Ubuntu Server install CD boot screen.

Figure 9-6 VMware console with Ubuntu CD boot screen

Click within the screen or hit Ctrl-G for it to intercept your keyboard and mouse input. If you want the keyboard and mouse to return to your regular desktop, just hit Ctrl and Alt together. The tricky part about the console screen is that usually by the time it launches, the BIOS screen is gone. If you want to reset the VM at that point to see the BIOS screen, hit Ctrl-Alt-Insert from within the console screen to send a Ctrl-Alt-Del and reset it. At the BIOS screen you can hit Esc to choose the device from which to boot, F12 to boot from the network, and F2 to enter a basic BIOS configuration screen where you can hard-set the boot device order. You can close the console window at any time to leave the VM running in the background.

Snapshots

A particularly handy feature of VMware Server is the ability to create a snapshot for a VM. A snapshot freezes a VM's disk and RAM state in time so you can revert to it. To take a snapshot, select the VM, and then click Take a Snapshot from the Commands section in the right pane. At this point you can change settings, install or remove software, and even add and remove hardware, and all of the changes will be tracked on separate storage. If you want to go back to the snapshot state, just select the VM and click Revert to Snapshot from the Commands section.

Snapshots come in handy when you are about to perform a major upgrade on the server. Take a snapshot, perform the upgrade, and if there is a problem you know you can easily roll back and try again. I used snapshots extensively in writing this book. I would spin up one or two VMs and install the bare-bones default Ubuntu Server install on them. Then I took a snapshot. Whenever I wanted to demo a particular piece of software, I could then install and set it up on the VM. When I was done and ready to test entirely different software, I could revert to the snapshot and be back to a clean state. It took much less time than it would to reinstall Ubuntu each time.

NOTE   Keep an eye on your available storage when you use snapshots. Every change you make to your system has to be kept along with the original state. This means that depending on how much data has changed on the system since the last snapshot, you might have much more storage allocated than you expect.

Suspend

The suspend feature exists outside of any OS-level suspend support. With VMware suspend, the entire state of the VM is suspended to disk, much like a snapshot. Once a machine is suspended, you can move its files around, even to other VMware servers, and then unsuspend it and it will pick up where it left off.

The suspend feature is particularly useful for forensics after your machine has been hacked. Once you confirm a VM has been hacked, suspend it to disk and make a copy of the VM's entire directory. That way you have a pristine RAM and disk image that might even have the attacker's processes still running in memory. You can then take that VM to other VMware servers and replay the attacked state over and over again.

Local VM Storage

VMware Server uses /var/lib/vmware/Virtual Machines as the default location to store all of the VM files. You typically want as much storage as possible at this location and want the storage to be as fast as possible, since potentially multiple VMs will be stored here and will access the storage at the same time. Each VM keeps all of its files within its own directory named after the VM. Here are the sample files that were created for my test VM:

```
$ ls /var/lib/vmware/Virtual\ Machines/Test/
Test.nvram  Test.vmdk  Test.vmsd  Test.vmx  Test.vmxf  vmware-0.log
  vmware.log
```

The .nvram file stores the VM's BIOS and all of the BIOS settings. If you see a .vmsn or .vmsd file, those are what VMware uses to store snapshot data and snapshot metadata, respectively. If you see a .vmem file, VMware has made a copy of the VM's paging file. Generally, this happens when the VM is running or if it has crashed. Any .vmdk files are virtual disk files. These files are likely what will take up the bulk of your storage apart from potential snapshot files.

All of a VM's settings, such as how much RAM it has, what hard drives or CD-ROM drives are attached, and its network settings, are stored in the .vmx file. While you should generally not modify this file by hand unless you really know what you are doing, it is just a text file. The contents of a .vmx file are just key and value pairs and look something like this:

```
#!/usr/local/bin/vmware
.encoding = "UTF-8"
config.version = "8"
virtualHW.version = "7"
floppy0.present = "FALSE"
mks.enable3d = "TRUE"
. . .
vmci0.present = "TRUE"
nvram = "Test.nvram"

scsi0.present = "TRUE"
scsi0.sharedBus = "none"
scsi0.virtualDev = "lsilogic"
memsize = "512"
scsi0:0.present = "TRUE"
scsi0:0.fileName = "Test.vmdk"
scsi0:0.writeThrough = "TRUE"
ide1:0.present = "TRUE"
ide1:0.fileName = "/var/lib/vmware/Virtual Machines/isos/
  ubuntu-8.04.1-server-i386.iso"
ide1:0.deviceType = "cdrom-image"
ide1:0.allowGuestConnectionControl = "FALSE"
```

The .log files inside each VM's directory maintain a log of all of the events that happen to a VM. You can access a subset of these logs from within the Web interface, but the log files themselves contain much more detailed information. Look here if a VM crashed for some unexpected reason or if you just want a lower-level understanding of what VMware does when you start or stop a VM.

Since everything that makes up a VM is really just a file on the system, provided that a VM is suspended or powered off, you can move the files around with regular Linux commands like mv, cp, and rsync. If you want to migrate or copy a VM from one machine to another, you could just make sure it is powered off or suspended and then use rsync or scp to transfer it. Keep in mind that when you do move or copy a VM and start it back up on a new host, VMware will detect it and prompt you to generate a new UUID (a universal string that should be unique for each VM).

Virtual Appliances

Another useful aspect of all VM settings and disks residing in one directory is that a number of people have created what are known as "virtual appliances." Essentially a virtual appliance is a VM created for a particular purpose such as a spam filtering or a firewall. A number of companies have even set up virtual appliances that have their software pre-installed so you can easily demo it. Virtual appliances are generally compressed into a single .zip file, so once you download them, all you have to do to install them is extract the .zip file into /var/lib/vmware/Virtual Machines, go to the Web interface, click Virtual Machine_Add Virtual Machine to Inventory, and then browse to the new VM's .vmx file. VMware itself hosts a number of virtual appliances on its site and even has a link on the Web interface called Virtual Appliance Marketplace that will take you right there.

Ubuntu Enterprise Cloud

If you have been following the virtualization world at all, you no doubt have heard the term *cloud*, probably used in reference to Amazon's Elastic Computing Cloud (EC2) service. Amazon has built a large infrastructure of servers that can run VMs. Amazon then sells time and resources on these machines so that you can deploy your own virtual servers on Amazon's infrastructure and no longer have to worry about storage, RAM, or CPU resources or even what physical server your VM runs on. Instead the server runs somewhere on Amazon's cloud.

While it is straightforward and simple to deploy your own Ubuntu servers on EC2, some administrators prefer having full control over their infrastructure, both physical and virtual. Ubuntu has provided a solution called Ubuntu Enterprise Cloud (UEC) that allows you to set up your own "private cloud"—a set of your own servers that can run VMs and behaves much like EC2. With UEC you can add multiple nodes to your own cloud and manage it and all of your VMs from an easy-to-use interface.

While you might expect it to be rather difficult to deploy your own private cloud, Ubuntu has greatly automated the process, and as you'll find, it only takes a couple of steps. First though, let's go over what you will need.

UEC System Requirements

At a minimum you will need two physical servers to run UEC, a front-end server and one node. The front-end server will manage your private cloud and provide the following services:

- The Cloud Controller (known as cic)
- The Cluster Controller (known as cc)
- Walrus (the storage service like Amazon's S3)
- The Storage Controller (known as sc)

Since the front-end server itself will not run any VMs, you can use an older server that doesn't support virtualization extensions. The front-end server will also store all of the different server image types and deploy them to each node over the network so the more (and faster) storage and network speed you have for this machine, the better.

The node server is one of potentially many servers that are managed by the front end and will actually run the VMs themselves with the node controller (nc) service. Your node servers *will* need support for virtualization extensions just like if you set up a regular KVM server. The higher the resources (RAM, CPU, and disk) the node has, the more VMs it will be able to host.

Install UEC Front-End Server

The front-end server is as easy to install as any other Ubuntu Server instance. Just boot the machine off the Ubuntu Server CD, and at the boot menu you will see that the second option is Install Ubuntu Enterprise Cloud. Select that option and go through the standard Ubuntu install menus.

In the middle of the install, you will be asked a few questions so you can configure UEC. The installer automatically probes the network to see if a front-end server exists, and since presumably it won't (since we are setting it up right now), the installer defaults to setting up this instance as a front-end server. You are then asked to name your cluster, and finally you must provide a range of IP addresses that your front-end server can hand out to instances you create. Be sure to pick a range of IP addresses that aren't being used by any other machines and that your front-end server and nodes will be a member of. Finally, complete the install and reboot into your new server.

Install UEC Node Server

It is even easier to set up a node server than it is to install the front-end server. Just boot your node server off the Ubuntu Server install CD and select Install Ubuntu Enterprise Cloud from the boot menu. The installer automatically detects your front-end server and defaults to setting this machine up as a node. Just confirm the defaults and complete the install. The installer should automatically manage the node's registration with the cluster, so once the node has booted, you should be ready to get your credentials and manage your UEC cluster.

Manage Your Cloud

Once your servers are installed and running, the next step is to retrieve credentials from the cloud so that you can register and manage it. Everyone who will user the cloud must follow the same process.

Open a Web browser on your own computer or, optionally, on the front-end server itself, and browse to https://frontendserver:8443. Replace front-endserver with the hostname or IP address for your front-end server. Sign the certificate and log in with the username and password set to admin. The first time you login, you will go through a first-time configuration screen that will have you change the admin password and set a contact e-mail address to use. Once you complete this process, you will see the default UEC management screen (Figure 9-7).

On this screen, you can add other users who will have permission to view and manage cloud instances, but the first thing you should do is select the Credentials tab and click on Download Credentials. Then, on your local machine, create a directory named ~/.euca and unzip the credentials there:

```
$ mkdir ~/.euca
$ cd ~.euca/
$ unzip ~/Desktop/euca2-admin-x509.zip
Archive:  ~/euca2-admin-x509.zip
To setup the environment run: source /path/to/eucarc
  inflating: eucarc
  inflating: cloud-cert.pem
  inflating: jssecacerts
  inflating: euca2-admin-9f543bf5-pk.pem
  inflating: euca2-admin-9f543bf5-cert.pem
```

Figure 9-7 Ubuntu Enterprise Cloud management with the User tab selected

Finally, before you can manage your cloud, you need to install the euca2ools package on the machine where you have downloaded and extracted the credentials and test that your credentials work:

```
$ sudo apt-get install euca2ools
$ . ~/.euca/eucarc
$ euca-describe-availability-zones verbose
AVAILABILITYZONE    cluster1        192.168.0.74
AVAILABILITYZONE    |- vm types     free / max   cpu   ram   disk
AVAILABILITYZONE    |- m1.small     0002 / 0002    1   192    2
AVAILABILITYZONE    |- c1.medium    0002 / 0002    1   256    5
AVAILABILITYZONE    |- m1.large     0001 / 0001    2   512   10
AVAILABILITYZONE    |- m1.xlarge    0001 / 0001    2   1024   20
AVAILABILITYZONE    |- c1.xlarge    0000 / 0000    4   2048   20
```

Install a New Server Image

At long last, you are ready to set up your first server on your cluster. Go back to the Web interface on https://frontendserver:8443 and select the Store tab. The Store tab lists a number of server images that have already been built for you. All you have to do is select Install, and the image will download to your local cluster. Once the image has downloaded, click the "How to run?" link that appears under the Install button for instructions on how to run that image (Figure 9-8).

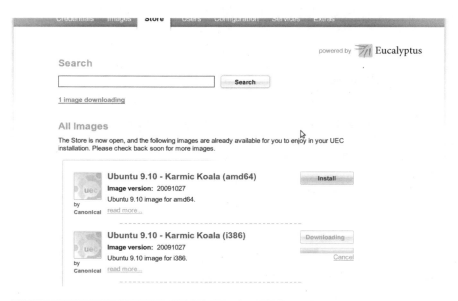

Figure 9-8 UEC Store downloading a Karmic i386 image

Start a New Instance

Now that you have at least one image downloaded and ready to install, you'll find there are a few different ways to start a new server based on this image, such as the command line via euca-run-instances or from other UEC management tools like Landscape or even with your Web browser using the ElasticFox Firefox extension. Since the graphical tools will likely be somewhat self-explanatory, I discuss how to use the command-line tool you should already have installed on your local system.

Create and Enable SSH Keypairs   You will need some SSH keypairs set up before you create a new instance on UEC. Without keypairs, you will have no way to remotely log into the server after it is created. The following script will create your keypairs:

```
if [ ! -e ~/.euca/mykey.priv ]; then
    mkdir -p -m 700 ~/.euca
    touch ~/.euca/mykey.priv
    chmod 0600 ~/.euca/mykey.priv
    euca-add-keypair mykey > ~/.euca/mykey.priv
fi
```

Now run this command to allow port 22 traffic on your instances:

```
$ euca-authorize default -P tcp -p 22 -s 0.0.0.0/0
GROUP       default
PERMISSION default ALLOWS tcp 22 22 FROM CIDR 0.0.0.0/0
```

View VM Types   UEC sets up a number of default VM types with different resources assigned to them. This way, when you create a new instance, you don't have to type in the amount of RAM, number of CPUs, and disk size for your instance and instead can refer to one of these shortcuts. If you click on the configuration tab on the UEC Web interface and scroll to the bottom, you will see the list of predefined VM types (Figure 9-9) and will have the ability to change them.

By default there are five configured VM types:

- **m1.small:** 1 CPU, 192MB RAM, 2GB disk

- **c1.medium:** 1CPU, 256MB RAM, 5GB disk

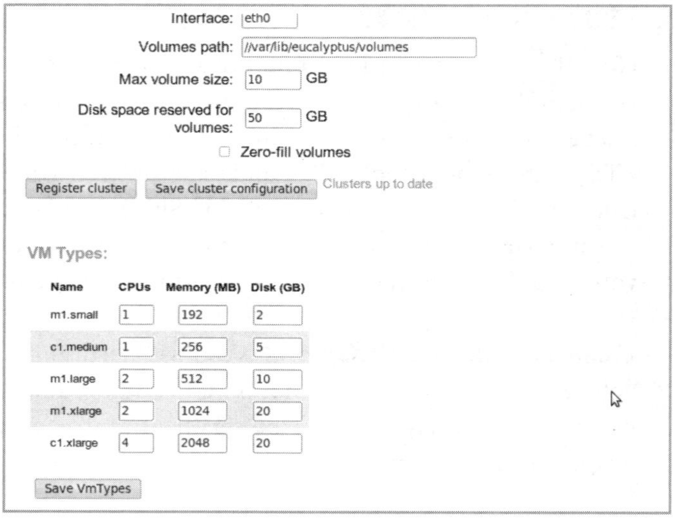

Figure 9-9 UEC VM types

- **m1.large:** 2CPUs, 512MB RAM, 10GB disk

- **m1.xlarge:** 2CPUs, 1024MB RAM, 20GB disk

- **c1.xlarge:** 4CPUs, 2048MB RAM, 20GB disk

Select Your Image   Now that you know what VM type you want to create, go back to the UEC Web front end and click on the Images tab. You should see at least one image ID that begins with emi-. Copy this ID and then, in a terminal, use the euca-run-instances tool to start your instance:

```
$ euca-run-instances -k mykey -t c1.medium emi-DE4C106E
RESERVATION  r-33F6071A      admin   admin-default
INSTANCE     i-3EFA0858      emi-DE4C106E    0.0.0.0 0.0.0.0 pending
    mykey  2010-04-17T22:04:54.647Z       eki-F43A10D7
    eri-08B41143
```

Once you run the instance, you will likely want to monitor the output of euca-describe-instances so you can tell when the instance's state has changed from pending to running:

```
$ euca-describe-instances
RESERVATION  r-41DB083A       admin   default
```

```
INSTANCE    i-48D40805    emi-DE4C106E    192.168.0.235
172.19.1.2  pending       mykey  0        c1.medium
    2010-04-17T22:50:37.016Z    cluster1    eki-F43A10D7
    eri-08B41143
```

If there is some problem creating your instance, you will find that the instance changes from pending to terminated. If this happens, check the output of /var/log/eucalyptus/nc.log on your node to get clues for why the instance will not start.

NOTE   When I started my first instance, I tested it out with the m1.small VM type. Unfortunately, the 2GB disk that VM type assigns was not large enough for the image, so the instance would never start—it went from pending to a terminated state. Finally I saw the error in /var/log/eucalyptus/nc.log, and when I tried again with a VM type that had more storage, the VM was created successfully. If your instances go straight to terminated, another thing to check is that virtualization extensions are enabled in your node's BIOS.

After the instance has changed to a running state, you can SSH to it and manage it like any other server. Just pull its IP address from euca-describe-instances and then SSH to that IP using the SSH key you created earlier. In this example, the IP address is 192.168.0.235:

```
$ euca-describe-instances
RESERVATION  r-41DB083A    admin    default
INSTANCE    i-48D40805    emi-DE4C106E    192.168.0.235
    172.19.1.2    running        mykey  0        c1.medium
    2010-04-17T22:50:37.016Z    cluster1    eki-F43A10D7
    eri-08B41143
$ ssh -i ~/.euca/mykey.priv ubuntu@192.168.0.235
```

When you are ready to terminate your instance, just make note of the instance ID that begins with the letter i. In my example, the instance ID is i-48D40805. To terminate the instance, you use euca-terminate-instances:

```
$ euca-terminate-instances i-48D40805
INSTANCE    i-48D40805
```

NOTE   If all of this command-line work is not for you, I recommend checking out ElasticFox or another graphical front end instead. It is relatively simple to set up and makes managing and monitoring your instances very easy.

## CHAPTER 10

Fault Tolerance

HARDWARE FAILS. Over the years I have had basically every major hardware component on a server fail, from CPUs to RAM to SCSI controllers and, of course, hard drives. In addition to hardware failure, system downtime is often the result of some other problem such as a bad configuration on a switch, a power outage, or even a sysadmin accidentally rebooting the wrong server. If you lose money whenever a service is down, you quickly come up with methods to keep that service up no matter what component fails.

In this chapter I discuss some of the methods you can use with Ubuntu servers to make them more fault-tolerant. I start with some general fault tolerance principles. Then I talk about ways to add fault tolerance to your storage and network with RAID and Ethernet bonding, respectively. I also cover Logical Volume Manager (LVM), even though it isn't technically used for fault tolerance. Of course, even with those procedures in place your server could crash or reboot, or you could lose a CPU, so finally I talk about how to set up a basic two-server cluster.

Fault Tolerance Principles

- **Build redundant systems.**
  The basic idea behind fault tolerance is to set up your systems so that you can lose any one component without an outage. These days servers with redundant power supplies and redundant disks are common. There are even servers that have redundant BIOSs and remote management ports. The downside with redundancy is that it is often wasteful. For instance, with RAID you typically lose at least one disk's worth of storage for redundancy. When compared to the cost of downtime, though, for most sysadmins it is worth the extra cost.

- **Favor hot-swappable components.**
  RAID is great because it protects you from losing data and your host going down because of a disk failure, but if you have to power down the host to replace the drive, you get little benefit. Where possible, favor components that are hot-swappable. These days servers are likely to offer at least hot-swappable drives and power supplies, and many have hot-swappable fans as well. In some higher-end blade servers you can even hot-swap integrated network and SAN switches and remote management cards.

- **Test your redundancy.**
  As with backups, if you haven't tested your fault tolerance, then you don't have fault tolerance. If possible, before you deploy a new redundant system such as Ethernet bonding or server clustering, be sure to simulate failures and understand both how the system responds to a failure as well as how it responds once the fault has been repaired. Systems can behave very differently in both how they handle a fault and how they resume after the fault is repaired, all based on how you configure them. This testing phase is also a good time to test any monitoring you have put in place to detect these failures.

- **Eliminate any single points of failure.**
  While having some redundancy is better than having none, try to go through the entire server stack and identify and eliminate any single points of failure. For instance, if you have set up redundant power sources for your data center and each server has a power supply hooked into one of the power sources, it is less useful if the servers are connected to one switch with a single power supply. For larger operations, even a data center itself is seen as a single point of failure, so in those cases servers are distributed across multiple data centers in entirely different geographical locations.

- **Respond to failures quickly.**
  When a component fails, try to identify and repair the problem as soon as you can. In RAID, for instance, many sysadmins set up a disk as a hot spare so that the moment a disk fails, a replacement can take its place. Provided the hot spare syncs before another drive fails, the data will still be intact. While you can't do this with every component, when you do have a fault, try to repair it before you lose the fail-over side as well.

RAID

The piece of server hardware most likely to fail is your hard drive, so if you want a fault-tolerant system, hard drive redundancy should be your first priority. This is generally accomplished using RAID. RAID stands for Redundant Array of Inexpensive Disks, although some people say it stands for Redundant Array of Independent Disks (those people must have priced out fiber channel drives).

RAID is generally referred to as either hardware or software RAID. With hardware RAID, your server has a component either built into the motherboard or available as an add-on card to which your hard drives connect. This hardware supports various RAID levels and typically has its own processor and memory to perform any calculations (such as parity calculations on RAID 5). The card then presents the storage as a single device (sometimes as a generic SCSI drive and other times as a different block device, depending on the vendor) that you can partition, format, and use. Any configuration, recovery, or monitoring typically requires special software on the host or work within the BIOS.

With software RAID, the operating system implements the RAID algorithms using the regular CPU with a driver or module. On Linux you can see both the original drives and partitions as well as a special device that represents the RAID storage. The advantage of Linux software RAID is that it doesn't require any special vendor support under Linux, and it actually performs surprisingly well, is surprisingly stable, and is free. Also, unless you invest in high-end RAID cards, Linux software RAID provides more flexibility in how you can expand a RAID. For the rest of the chapter I focus on Linux software RAID, and I will discuss how you can migrate a system from a single drive to RAID and from RAID 1 to RAID 5, as well as how to add a drive to a RAID 5 array.

NOTE   There's a third type of RAID that falls somewhere between hardware and software RAID. It can be found in cheap RAID cards that these days are even built into many desktop motherboards. Although there is hardware involved, the RAID itself is implemented via a driver that runs on the host, so it uses the host CPU. In addition, this hybrid RAID requires a vendor-specific driver so the OS can see the RAID drive.

RAID Levels

There are a number of different ways to implement RAID. Each has advantages and disadvantages, depending on what you want to accomplish. Next I cover the Linux software RAID types you are most likely to use.

RAID 0   You could consider RAID 0, also known as striping, to be a bit misleading. It is actually not a redundant array at all. With a RAID 0 array you need at least two disks. Each write to this array is striped across both disks so that in effect the two drives become one large disk. So if you have two 100GB hard drives in a RAID 0 array, you will have 200GB of storage. While RAID 0 offers great speed, the downside is that there is no redundancy. If you lose a drive in a RAID 0 array, all of your data is lost. For the examples in this chapter I use RAID 1 and 5; I just mention RAID 0 to illustrate the difference in RAID levels.

RAID 1   RAID 1 is also known as mirroring. In a RAID 1 array every bit that is written to one disk is copied to the other. As with RAID 0, RAID 1 requires at least two drives; however, in this case a RAID 1 array is only as big as one of its drives. So if you had two 100GB drives in a RAID 1 array, you would have 100GB of storage. The upside is that you could lose one of the drives in the array and still have all of your data.

RAID 5   RAID 5 is also known as striping plus parity. A RAID 5 array requires at least three drives. Every time the array is written to, the data is split across the three drives. In addition to the data, parity information is split among the drives so that any drive in the array can fail and not only will the remaining drives have all of the data, once the failed drive is replaced, the other drives can rebuild it. In a RAID 5 array you basically lose one drive's worth of storage, so in a RAID 5 array of three 100GB disks you would have 200GB of storage. A RAID 5 array of four 100GB disks would have 300GB of storage.

NOTE   **RAID 5 as a Root Partition**
It's important to note that while GRUB can read a software RAID 1 array, it can't read software RAID 5 arrays. This means that if you choose to have a RAID 5 array for your root partition, you must make a separate partition for the /boot directory that isn't RAID 5 for GRUB to use. A common scenario for a three-disk RAID is a three-partition RAID 1 array for /boot and a three-partition RAID 5 array for the root directory.

Configure RAID during Installation

You can set up a RAID array under Ubuntu either during the initial installation or afterward. The installer provides a nice graphical interface to create arrays that are ready to use after the install completes, so if you are installing a new machine, it makes sense to set up the RAID from the installer.

RAID configuration is done during the partitioning section of the install process. Once you see the main partition screen, select "Manual partitioning." In my example I set up RAID on a three-disk machine. I have a three-partition RAID 1 array for /boot, a three-partition RAID 5 array for /, and a three-partition RAID 5 array for swap.

The first step is to partition each of the disks so they have a /boot, /, and swap partition. When you size the partitions, keep in mind that RAID 1 arrays are only as big as one of the partitions, whereas RAID 5 arrays are as big as all of the partitions combined, minus the size of one partition. While it's not required that each partition be equal in size, the arrays base everything on the smallest partition, so if you can make each partition in an array the same size, you will have an easier time.

When you get to the partition settings for each new partition, the section where you can choose the file system and mount point, change the "Use as" option so that it says "physical volume for RAID," as shown in Figure 10-1.

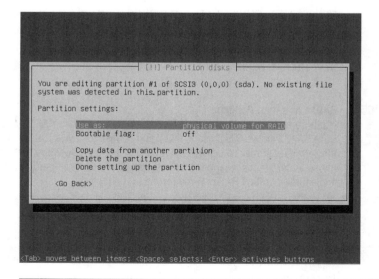

Figure 10-1 Partition settings for software RAID

Once you are finished partitioning, you will have a number of partitions on each drive of type K raid, as shown in Figure 10-2. At the top of the screen is the option "Configure software RAID." Select that option and at the next screen say Yes to write the changes to the partitioning tables of each of the disks, once you are sure each partition is the size you want.

The next step in the process is to create a multidisk (MD) device for each RAID array. In my case I want to create three MD devices, one for my RAID 1 /boot, one for my RAID 5 swap, and one for my RAID 5 /. For each of these MD devices, I select Create MD, then select the RAID level I want; then I choose the number of active and spare devices I want in the array. In my case I won't have any spare devices, so I set this option to three active devices for each array and zero spare devices. Finally, I select which partitions to use in a particular MD device. If you created each partition in the same order on your drives, this will be simple since /dev/sda1, /dev/sdb1, and /dev/sdc1 (in my case) are all part of the same MD device. Repeat this process until you have created all of the MD devices and then select Finish.

When you are finished, the partition screen will display your RAID devices as in Figure 10-3. What you will notice is that each of your SCSI drives

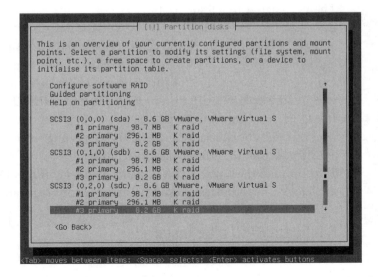

Figure 10-2 RAID partitioning completed

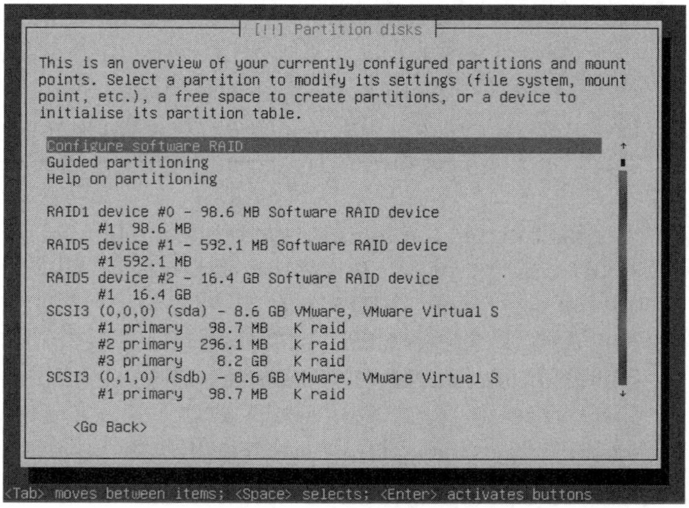

```
─┤ [!!] Partition disks ├─

This is an overview of your currently configured partitions and mount
points. Select a partition to modify its settings (file system, mount
point, etc.), a free space to create partitions, or a device to
initialise its partition table.

Configure software RAID
Guided partitioning
Help on partitioning

RAID1 device #0 - 98.6 MB Software RAID device
    #1  98.6 MB
RAID5 device #1 - 592.1 MB Software RAID device
    #1 592.1 MB
RAID5 device #2 - 16.4 GB Software RAID device
    #1  16.4 GB
SCSI3 (0,0,0) (sda) - 8.6 GB VMware, VMware Virtual S
    #1 primary    98.7 MB    K raid
    #2 primary   296.1 MB    K raid
    #3 primary     8.2 GB    K raid
SCSI3 (0,1,0) (sdb) - 8.6 GB VMware, VMware Virtual S
    #1 primary    98.7 MB    K raid

    <Go Back>

<Tab> moves between items; <Space> selects; <Enter> activates buttons
```

Figure 10-3 Partition menu with RAID devices created

appears as before, but above them are the RAID devices. These devices will be numbered and will display their RAID level as well as the overall size of the RAID device.

The next step is to tell the partitioner how to use each of these new RAID devices. Select the unlabeled partition on the line under each RAID device and hit Enter. From there you can configure the file system, mount point, and other options as if it were an ordinary partition. See Figure 10-4 for an example of how my final partition menu looked when I was done. Once you are finished, select "Finish partitioning" and write the changes to disk. If you get a prompt asking whether to boot when the array is degraded, read through the description of the risks of doing so and select Yes or No. The installation program will then continue the rest of the install process. Skip ahead to the Software RAID Management section to learn how to use the features of the mdadm package to manage your software RAID.

Configure RAID after Installation

You may choose to add RAID storage to a server after the initial installation. Later in the chapter I discuss how to migrate from a single disk to a RAID array and how to migrate from one RAID type to another, but for now I will

```
┌────────────────┤ [!!] Partition disks ├────────────────┐

 This is an overview of your currently configured partitions and mount
 points. Select a partition to modify its settings (file system, mount
 point, etc.), a free space to create partitions, or a device to
 initialise its partition table.

 Configure software RAID                                            ↑
 Guided partitioning
 Help on partitioning

 RAID1 device #0 - 98.6 MB Software RAID device
     #1   98.6 MB   f ext3       /boot
 RAID5 device #1 - 592.1 MB Software RAID device
     #1  592.1 MB   f swap       swap
 RAID5 device #2 - 16.4 GB Software RAID device
     #1   16.4 GB   f ext3       /
 SCSI3 (0,0,0) (sda) - 8.6 GB VMware, VMware Virtual S
     #1 primary    98.7 MB   K raid
     #2 primary   296.1 MB   K raid
     #3 primary     8.2 GB   K raid
 SCSI3 (0,1,0) (sdb) - 8.6 GB VMware, VMware Virtual S
     #1 primary    98.7 MB   K raid                                 ↓

     <Go Back>

<Tab> moves between items; <Space> selects; <Enter> activates buttons
```

Figure 10-4 Completed RAID partitioning

assume you simply want to add a RAID array to an existing server. For this example I will assume I have added three new drives, /dev/sdb, /dev/sdc, and /dev/sdd, and I want to partition the drives and create a RAID 5 array across all three partitions that I then mount at /mnt/storage.

Software RAID arrays are created and managed under Ubuntu with the mdadm tool. This tool might not be installed by default; if it isn't, run sudo apt-get install mdadm to install the package. The next step is to partition each of these drives. In my case I just create a single partition that spans the full drive. Use whichever partitioning tool you prefer (like fdisk or cfdisk) as though you were creating any other partition. The only difference here is to change the partition type from the default of 82 to fd. The fd partition type is set aside for Linux RAID autodetect. If a partition is set to that type, it tells Linux that it is part of a software RAID array.

Once your partitions are set up, you can use mdadm on the command line to create the MD device. In the case of a RAID 1 array you would type

```
$ sudo mdadm --create /dev/md0 --level=1 –raid-devices=2  /dev/sdb1
  /dev/sdc1
mdadm: array /dev/md0 started.
```

Most of the arguments here are pretty self-explanatory. The `--create` option tells `mdadm` that I want to create a new MD device at /dev/md0. If I already had a RAID array at /dev/md0, I would just pick the next number, such as /dev/md1. The `--level` option sets which RAID level to use for this array, `--raid-devices` sets the number of active devices, and finally you specify each partition you want to use for the array.

In my case I want to set up a RAID 5 array across /dev/sdb1, /dev/sdc1, and /dev/sdd1, so I would type

```
$ sudo mdadm --create /dev/md0 --level=5 --raid-devices=3 /dev/sdb1
  /dev/sdc1 /dev/sdd1
mdadm: array /dev/md0 started.
```

Once I have created the array, I can check out its current health in the /proc/mdstat file:

```
$ cat /proc/mdstat
Personalities : [raid6] [raid5] [raid4]
md0 : active raid5 sdd1[2] sdc1[1] sdb1[0]
    16771584 blocks level 5, 64k chunk, algorithm 2 [3/3] [UUU]

unused devices: <none>
```

Now I can treat /dev/md0 like any other partition and format it with a file system of my choice and then mount it:

```
$ sudo mkfs -t ext3 /dev/md0
$ sudo mkdir /mnt/storage
$ sudo mount /dev/md0 /mnt/storage
```

Now this array is up and functioning; however, it is not yet set up to automatically start and mount at boot time. If you don't set this up, you will have to run an `mdadm` command to assemble the array along with a `mount` command each time the system boots. To start the array at boot time, you need to configure /etc/mdadm/mdadm.conf with details about your array. Now you could certainly do this by hand, but `mdadm` provides a simpler way. The `mdadm --detail --scan` command will output an mdadm.conf-compatible string for each of your arrays, so all you have to do is redirect that output to the /etc/mdadm/mdadm.conf file:

```
$ sudo sh -c 'mdadm --detail --scan >> /etc/mdadm/mdadm.conf'
```

Now edit your /etc/fstab and add an entry for /dev/md0 as though it were any other mount point. In my case I would add

```
/dev/md0   /mnt/storage   ext3   defaults   0 0
```

Alternatively, I could specify the UUID for this device in fstab as with the rest of the partitions. To figure that out I would type

```
$ sudo blkid | grep /dev/md0
/dev/md0: UUID="99e190a7-dfe7-48ee-bf56-f426ef5343af" type="ext4"
```

Once /etc/mdadm/mdadm.conf and /etc/fstab are set up, I can reboot and then check /proc/mdstat to make sure the array comes up and then confirm it is mounted.

Software RAID Management

The bulk of the management of your software RAID arrays is done in two places: /proc/mdstat and mdadm. The /proc/mdstat file provides the current status of all of your running RAID arrays, including progress bars should any of them rebuild a disk. A standard /proc/mdstat file for a single RAID array might look like the following:

```
$ cat /proc/mdstat
Personalities : [raid6] [raid5] [raid4]
md0 : active raid5 sdd1[2] sdc1[1] sdb1[0]
      16771584 blocks level 5, 64k chunk, algorithm 2 [3/3] [UUU]

unused devices: <none>
```

In the output you can see which array is active (md0), what RAID level it uses (raid5), and which partitions it is using (sdd1, sdc1, and sdb1). In the final line you can see that the RAID is healthy in that it has three out of three disks all active ([3/3] [UUU]). That section will change if any disks become faulty, as we see below.

While you can get status from /proc/mdstat, the bulk of the actual RAID management is done with mdadm. For instance, this tool can report basic and more complete information about an array with the --query and --detail arguments respectively:

```
$ sudo mdadm --query /dev/md0
/dev/md0: 15.99GiB raid5 3 devices, 0 spares. Use mdadm --detail
  for more detail.
$ sudo mdadm --detail /dev/md0
/dev/md0:
          Version : 00.90.03
    Creation Time : Wed Feb 11 21:31:16 2009
       Raid Level : raid5
       Array Size : 16771584 (15.99 GiB 17.17 GB)
    Used Dev Size : 8385792 (8.00 GiB 8.59 GB)
     Raid Devices : 3
    Total Devices : 3
  Preferred Minor : 0
      Persistence : Superblock is persistent

      Update Time : Wed Feb 11 22:11:49 2009
            State : clean
   Active Devices : 3
  Working Devices : 3
   Failed Devices : 0
    Spare Devices : 0

           Layout : left-symmetric
       Chunk Size : 64K

             UUID : 37090db5:5fafad78:e368bf24:bd0fce41 (local to
                    host ubuntu)
           Events : 0.4

    Number   Major   Minor   RaidDevice State
       0       8       17        0      active sync   /dev/sdb1
       1       8       33        1      active sync   /dev/sdc1
       2       8       49        2      active sync   /dev/sdd1
```

Replace a Failed Disk While all of the information from mdadm can be useful, you will find you mostly use mdadm when a drive fails. When a drive fails, the mdadm daemon that runs on the system automatically sends an e-mail to the root user on the host. To change this, edit /etc/mdadm/ mdadm.conf and locate the MAILADDR option in the file. After you save your changes, run sudo /etc/init.d/mdadm reload to load the new options. Apart from the e-mail you can also see that a drive has failed from /proc/mdstat:

```
$ cat /proc/mdstat
Personalities : [linear] [multipath] [raid0] [raid1] [raid6]
  [raid5] [raid4] [raid10]
md0 : active raid5 sdb1[0] sdd1[3](F) sdc1[1]
    16771584 blocks level 5, 64k chunk, algorithm 2 [3/2] [UU_]

unused devices: <none>
```

Here you can see that sdd1 is marked with an (F) stating it has failed, and on the third line of output the array shows two out of three disks ([3/2] [UU_]). The next step is to remove the disk from /dev/md0 so that I can swap it out with a new drive. To do this I run mdadm with the --remove option:

```
$ sudo mdadm /dev/md0 --remove /dev/sdd1
```

The drive must be set as a failed drive for you to remove it, so if for some reason mdadm hasn't picked up the drive as faulty but you want to swap it out, you might need to set it as faulty before you remove it:

```
$ sudo mdadm /dev/md0 --fail /dev/sdd1
```

The mdadm command supports chaining commands, so you could fail and remove a drive in the same line:

```
$ sudo mdadm /dev/md0 --fail /dev/sdd1 --remove /dev/sdd1
```

Once you remove a drive from an array, it will be missing from /proc/mdstat:

```
$ cat /prod/mdstat
Personalities : [linear] [multipath] [raid0] [raid1] [raid6]
  [raid5] [raid4] [raid10]
md0 : active raid5 sdb1[0] sdc1[1]
    16771584 blocks level 5, 64k chunk, algorithm 2 [3/2] [UU_]

unused devices: <none>
```

Now you can swap out the drive with a fresh one and partition it. Be sure that when you replace drives you create new partitions to be equal or greater in size than the rest of the partitions in the RAID array. Once the new partition is ready, use the --add command to add it to the array:

```
$ sudo mdadm /dev/md0 --add /dev/sdd1
```

Now mdadm will start the process of resyncing data. This can take some time, depending on the speed and size of your disks. You can monitor the progress from /proc/mdstat:

```
$ cat /proc/mdstat

Personalities : [linear] [multipath] [raid0] [raid1] [raid6]
  [raid5] [raid4] [raid10]
md0 : active raid5 sdd1[3] sdb1[0] sdc1[1]
      16771584 blocks level 5, 64k chunk, algorithm 2 [3/2] [UU_]
      [>...................]  recovery =  2.0% (170112/8385792)
      finish=1.6min speed=85056K/sec

unused devices: <none>
```

Beyond this basic RAID management there are a number of different tweaks and customizations you can make to RAID arrays, particularly when you create them. For a full list of options and settings check out the mdadm manual (man mdadm).

Migrate Non-RAID to Software RAID

If you didn't build your system with RAID in mind, you might find yourself in a situation where you want to move a single-disk system to software RAID. I've even had situations where I had a RAID 1 array that I wanted to move to a RAID 5 to increase its storage. In this section I discuss how to perform both of these migrations, along with how to add a disk to a RAID 5 array.

In this example I will assume that I already have an installed system on /dev/sda. This is a basic Ubuntu install with a root partition at /dev/sda1 and a swap partition on /dev/sda5. I have added a second disk to the system at /dev/sdb1, and I'd like to make a RAID 1 array for both the root partition and the swap partition. Before I perform any additional steps, I want to make sure that the mdadm package is installed on my server, so I run

```
$ sudo apt-get install mdadm
```

Because I need to be able to copy all of the files from the old system to the new RAID array, I can't perform all of these steps from the running system. Instead, I need some sort of live CD or rescue disc so that no partitions are being written to. The Ubuntu Server install CD works OK for this; just boot from it and select the "Rescue a broken system" option. After you answer the basic keyboard and layout questions, you will get to a recovery menu with a few different recovery options. Here choose "Execute a shell in the installer environment."

Once you are in the installer environment, the first step is to use fdisk to partition /dev/sdb and at least create a /dev/sdb1 partition that is the same size as or larger than /dev/sda1. It's easier if the drives are the same size, because you can just re-create the partitions that are on /dev/sda, including the swap partition. As you create the partitions, remember to set their partition type to fd.

NOTE This example is for a RAID 1 array, but if you wanted to migrate from a single disk to a RAID 5 array, remember that GRUB can't read from RAID 5 arrays, so you must create a separate /boot partition and either leave it with no RAID or create a RAID 1 array for it.

Once the partitions are created, you are ready to create the arrays. Since we are currently using /dev/sda1 and /dev/sda5 on the system, we create the arrays in degraded mode, format them, copy all of the data to the new RAID arrays, boot off of the arrays in degraded mode, then finally hot-add the original partitions. This way we always have a safe copy of our data at every step. A degraded array is made much like a regular array, only in place of the missing drive you use the word missing:

```
# mdadm --create /dev/md0 --level=1 --raid-devices=2 /dev/sdb1 missing
mdadm: array /dev/md0 started
# mdadm --create /dev/md1 --level=1 --raid-devices=2 /dev/sdb5 missing
mdadm: array /dev/md1 started
```

Now I format /dev/md0 with an ext4 file system and /dev/md1 with a swap file system:

```
# mkfs.ext4 /dev/md0
# mkswap /dev/md1
```

Now you can create a temporary mount point for /dev/md0 and migrate all of the files from the root partition to this new partition. The Ubuntu recovery mode by default will mount the root partition under /target, but if you use another rescue disc, or if you need to mount and migrate multiple partitions to multiple arrays, you will have to mount those individually.

Unfortunately the Ubuntu Server recovery mode doesn't include the tools that I prefer to copy files to a new system, tools like cpio or rsync, and even the version of find is not full-featured, so instead I use the find and cpio commands from my server's root partition:

```
# mkdir /mnt/temp
# mount /dev/md0 /mnt/temp
# cd /target
# ./usr/bin/find . -xdev -print0 | ./bin/cpio -pa0V /mnt/temp
```

Of course, if you mounted your root partition (or the partition you wanted to migrate) somewhere other than /target, then cd to that directory instead. This command might take some time to run since it has to copy all of the files from the system.

Now that the system has been migrated to /dev/md0, you need to set up the array to automatically load at boot time. First we add the arrays we configured to /etc/mdadm/mdadm.conf inside where /dev/md0 is mounted. Then update its initramfs so it creates these devices at boot:

```
# mdadm --detail --scan >> /mnt/temp/etc/mdadm/mdadm.conf
# chroot /mnt/temp update-initramfs -u 2.6.32-19-generic-pae
update-initramfs: Generating /boot/initrd.img-2.6.32-19-generic-pae
```

Be sure to change the update-initramfs argument to point to your initrd file (check /mnt/temp/boot/ for the initramfs files from which you can choose).

Next I need to edit the /etc/fstab file on the RAID array so that it points to the RAID arrays instead of the partitions on /dev/sda. Since we have a limited set of tools on the rescue disc, this means using the nano text editor. First edit /mnt/temp/etc/fstab, comment out the current entry for /, and add a similar line that points to /dev/md0. Then do the same for the swap file line. You can add either the actual device name or the UUID for these devices here, but make a note of the UUIDs so you can refer to them later.

Now you are ready to reboot into the new system. Type exit in the shell you are in, and then select the "Reboot the system" option. When the system reboots and you see GRUB initially load, hit the Shift key to stop GRUB from booting so you can edit the boot options. Once you can see the list of boot choices, make sure the first option, which should be your main kernel, is highlighted, and then hit E to edit it. One of the lines will say `set root='(hd0,1)'`, or if not, it will point to your old root device, so change it to point to the new device. In my case I change it to `set root='(hd1,1)'`. Next there are two different lines that list the UUID for your original root partition. Change both of those UUIDs to the UUID of the new RAID device you jotted down. In my case the final GRUB options read

```
recordfail
insmod ext2
set root='(hd1,1)'
search --no-floppy --fs-uuid --set 65fc1772-3996-4012-af59-
    491d6b2e7e4e
linux /boot/vmlinuz-2.6.32-19-generic-pae
    root=UUID=65fc1772-3996-4012-af59-491d6b2e7e4e ro quiet splash
initrd /boot/initrd.img-2.6.32-19-generic-pae
```

Once you are finished changing these options, hit Ctrl-X boot into the system on the RAID array. If you set the boot arguments and the /etc/fstab correctly, when you boot and type df, you should see your root device is /dev/md0 (or what you assigned your RAID array):

```
$ df
Filesystem      1K-blocks      Used Available Use% Mounted on
/dev/md0         8231864     634492   7182500   9% /
. . .
```

When you check /proc/mdstat, you will see your active arrays running on a single disk:

```
$ cat /proc/mdstat
Personalities : [linear] [multipath] [raid0] [raid1] [raid6]
  [raid5] [raid4] [raid10]
md1 : active raid1 sdb5[0]
      88256 blocks [2/1] [U_]

md0 : active raid1 sdb1[0]
      8297472 blocks [2/1] [U_]

unused devices: <none>
```

Now you are ready to add the original partitions to each array:

```
$ sudo mdadm /dev/md0 --add /dev/sda1
$ sudo mdadm /dev/md1 --add /dev/sda5
$ cat /proc/mdstat
Personalities : [linear] [multipath] [raid0] [raid1] [raid6]
  [raid5] [raid4] [raid10]
md1 : active raid1 sda5[2] sdb5[0]
      88256 blocks [2/1] [U_]
              resync=DELAYED

md0 : active raid1 sda1[2] sdb1[0]
      8297472 blocks [2/1] [U_]
      [=>.................]  recovery =  5.6% (471936/8297472)
      finish=12.3min speed=10550K/sec

unused devices: <none>
```

The arrays will sync up in the background, but you can use your system in the meantime. Now you will want to update your GRUB configuration so that it points to the new UUIDs and devices (otherwise you would have to edit it by hand each time). In the past you would have to edit things by hand, but if you just type sudo update-grub, the update program will detect and change all of the relevant entries for you.

Now the problem you will find when you run a software RAID array is that GRUB will install only on the first disk. If you lose the first disk, the second disk won't automatically be able to boot the system. To fix this you have to manually install GRUB to the second disk. This is easy enough—just type sudo grub-install /dev/sdb. Change the device from /dev/sdb to your second RAID device if it's different. If you have a third RAID device, just run grub-install for that device as well.

The final step is to use a partitioning tool on /dev/sda and set both partitions to partition type fd so that they will automatically be detected as RAID devices. Reboot your system one final time to ensure it will boot to your RAID array. Now your system is fault-tolerant and ready to use.

Migrate from RAID 1 to RAID 5

At some point you might decide that a particular system needs to expand from RAID 1 to RAID 5. In most cases this is because your RAID array needs more storage. If you add an extra drive and migrate to RAID 5, you can double your available storage while keeping redundancy.

In this example I migrate the RAID 1 system I mentioned above into a RAID 5 system. Currently it has two RAID 1 arrays, /dev/md0 composed of /dev/sda1 and /dev/sdb1 for my / partition, and /dev/md1 composed of /dev/sda5 and /dev/sdb5, which I use for swap space. I add a third drive, /dev/sdc, and migrate the system to a RAID 5 array.

There are some special considerations when your root partition is on RAID 5 because GRUB can't directly boot from it. You need to set up a small /boot partition that is not RAID 5 for GRUB to boot from. You can still have fault tolerance here; you just have to make your /boot partition RAID 1.

Just as when I migrated from a single drive to a RAID 1 array, to migrate to a RAID 5 array, I need to use a rescue disc. I use the Ubuntu Server rescue mode in this case, so boot from your Ubuntu Server install CD and select "Rescue a broken system" at the boot menu. When you get to the section that lets you select your root file system, be sure to choose the correct MD device (in my case /dev/md0). At the main rescue operations menu choose "Execute a shell in the installer environment."

The general procedure for this migration is much like migrating from a single disk to RAID 1. We partition /dev/sdc the way we want the new array to look, remove /dev/sdb from both RAID 1 arrays, repartition it, then create our new degraded RAID arrays and set them up so the system can boot from them. Once we successfully boot from the new arrays, we destroy the old arrays, repartition the final drive, and hot-add it.

So first I partition /dev/sdc. I create a 100MB /boot partition at /dev/sdc1, then create my root and swap partitions with the remaining space. Since the RAID 5 arrays will be larger anyway, I don't have to worry that I'm robbing 100MB from the root partition. Remember to create each of the partitions as type fd. My final disk looks like this:

```
 Device  Boot Start    End   Blocks   Id  System
/dev/sdc1          1     13   104391   fd  Linux raid autodetect
/dev/sdc2         14   1033  8193150   fd  Linux raid autodetect
/dev/sdc3       1034   1044    88357+   5  Extended
/dev/sdc5       1034   1044    88326   fd  Linux raid autodetect
```

Now I use mdadm to remove /dev/sdb partitions from both RAID arrays:

```
# mdadm /dev/md0 --fail /dev/sdb1
mdadm: set /dev/sdb1 faulty in /dev/md0
# mdadm /dev/md0 --remove /dev/sdb1
mdadm: hot removed /dev/sdb1
# mdadm /dev/md1 --fail /dev/sdb5
mdadm: set /dev/sdb5 faulty in /dev/md1
# mdadm /dev/md1 --remove /dev/sdb5
mdadm: hot removed /dev/sdb5
```

Now use fdisk to change the partition table of /dev/sdb to match /dev/sdc. Once you change the partition table of /dev/sdb and write the changes, you might get an error that the kernel will use the old partition table until the system reboots. If that happens, you must reboot back into the rescue disc before you can continue. If you don't get that error, proceed to the next step.

At this point I'm ready to create my three new RAID arrays. My /boot partition will be a RAID 1 /dev/md2, my root partition a RAID 5 /dev/md3, and my new swap drives will be a RAID 5 /dev/md4. Use mdadm to create all of these in failed mode:

```
# mdadm --create /dev/md2 --level=1 --raid-devices=3 /dev/sdb1
  /dev/sdc1 missing
# mdadm --create /dev/md3 --level=5 --raid-devices=3 /dev/sdb2
  /dev/sdc2 missing
# mdadm --create /dev/md4 --level=5 --raid-devices=3 /dev/sdb5
  /dev/sdc5 missing
```

When you create these arrays, you will probably get a warning about the /dev/sdb partitions containing a file system, but that's expected, so type Y so it continues. Once I'm done, if I check /proc/mdstat, I will see all five of my RAID arrays in degraded mode:

```
# cat /proc/mdstat
Personalities : [linear] [multipath] [raid0] [raid1] [raid6]
  [raid5] [raid4] [raid10]
md4 : active raid5 sdc5[1] sdb5[0]
      176512 blocks level 5, 64k chunk, algorithm 2 [3/2] [UU_]

md3 : active raid5 sdc2[1] sdb1[0]
      16386048 blocks level 5, 64k chunk, algorithm 2 [3/2] [UU_]

md2 : active raid1 sdc1[1] sdb1[0]
      104320 blocks [3/2] [UU_]

md1 : active raid1 sda5[0]
      88256 blocks [2/1] [U_]

md0 : active raid1 sda1[0]
      8297472 blocks [2/1] [U_]

unused devices: <none>
```

Now you can format the new RAID arrays and create mount points for the new /boot and / partitions so you can transfer files to them:

```
# mkfs.ext4 /dev/md2
# mkfs.ext4 /dev/md3
# mkswap /dev/md4
# mkdir /mnt/boot
# mkdir /mnt/root
# mount /dev/md2 /mnt/boot
# mount /dev/md3 /mnt/root
```

Unfortunately, the Ubuntu Server recovery mode doesn't include the tools that I prefer to copy files to a new system, tools like cpio or rsync, and even the version of find is not full-featured, so instead I use the versions from my server. Finally I copy over the /boot directory to my new /boot RAID array and remount the drive under /mnt/root:

```
# cd /target
# ./usr/bin/find . -xdev -print0 | ./bin/cpio -pa0V /mnt/root
# mv /mnt/root/boot/* /mnt/boot/
# umount /mnt/boot
# mount /dev/md2 /mnt/root/boot
```

Now that the system has been migrated to /dev/md3 and /dev/md2, you need to set up the array to automatically load at boot time. First we add the arrays we configured to the /etc/mdadm/mdadm.conf file where we mounted /dev/md3 and update its initramfs so it creates these devices at boot:

```
# mdadm --detail --scan >> /mnt/root/etc/mdadm/mdadm.conf
# chroot /mnt/root update-initramfs -u 2.6.32-19-generic-pae
update-initramfs: Generating /boot/initrd.img-2.6.32-19-generic-pae
```

Be sure to change the update-initramfs argument to point to your initrd file (check /mnt/root/boot/ for the initramfs files from which you can choose).

Next I need to edit the /etc/fstab file on the RAID 5 array so that it points to the RAID 5 arrays instead of the /dev/md0. I also need to add a reference to my new /boot partition. First edit /mnt/root/etc/fstab, comment out the current entry for /, and add a similar line that points to /dev/md2. Then add a new line for /boot. Finally, do the same for the swap file line. You can add either the actual device name or the UUID for these devices here. Here's an example fstab file using the device names:

```
# /etc/fstab: static file system information.
#
# <file system> <mount point>  <type>  <options>      <dump>  <pass>
proc            /proc          proc    defaults       0       0
#/dev/md0       /       ext4    errors=remount-ro      0       1
/dev/md3        /       ext4    errors=remount-ro      0       1
```

```
/dev/md2        /boot   ext4    defaults        0       0
#/dev/md1       none    swap    sw      0       0
/dev/md4        none    swap    sw      0       0
/dev/scd0  /media/cdrom0  udf,iso9660  user,noauto,exec,utf8 0 0
/dev/fd0   /media/floppy0 auto    rw,user,noauto,exec,utf8 0 0
```

Even if you don't use UUIDs in the fstab file, be sure to jot down the new UUID for md3 and md2. Now you are ready to reboot into the new system. Type exit in the shell you are in, and then select the "Reboot the system" option. When the system reboots and you see GRUB initially load, hit the Shift key to stop GRUB from booting so you can edit the boot options. Once you can see the list of boot choices, make sure the first option, which should be your main kernel, is highlighted, and then hit E to edit it. One of the lines will say set root='(md0)', or if not, it will point to your old root device, so change it to point to the new device. In my case I change it to set root='(md3)'. Next there are two different lines that list the UUID for your original root partition. Change the UUID in the line that begins with search to the UUID of your new /boot partition (/dev/md2 in the example). That tells grub2 where to search for its files. Change the UUID in the line that beings with linux to the UUID of the new root device (/dev/md3). Also, since your boot partition is separate from the root partition, you will need to remove the /boot from any lines that reference it, because the initrd and kernel files will be within the main /boot directory. In my case the final GRUB options read

```
recordfail
insmod raid
insmod mdraid
insmod ext2
set root='(md2)'
search -no-floppy -fs-uuid -set 5452717c-727c-4ba9-8a75-
  4ac362f01ee6
linux /vmlinuz-2.6.32-19-generic-pae
  root=UUID=2bfc0697-f109-4986-83a5-117c162e37bf ro quiet splash
initrd /initrd.img-2.6.32-19-generic-pae
```

Once you are finished changing these options, hit Ctrl-X to boot into the system on the RAID array. If you set the boot arguments and the /etc/fstab correctly, when you boot and type df you should see that your root partition is /dev/md3 (or what you assigned your RAID array) along with your /boot partition:

```
$ df
Filesystem      1K-blocks        Used Available Use% Mounted on
/dev/md3        16254420       638276 14796844    5% /
. . .
/dev/md2          101018        23974    71828   26% /boot
```

When you check /proc/mdstat, you will see your active arrays running on a single disk:

```
$ cat /proc/mdstat
Personalities : [linear] [multipath] [raid0] [raid1] [raid6]
  [raid5] [raid4] [raid10]
md4 : active raid5 sdc5[1] sdb5[0]
      176512 blocks level 5, 64k chunk, algorithm 2 [3/2] [UU_]

md3 : active raid5 sdc2[1] sdb1[0]
    16386048 blocks level 5, 64k chunk, algorithm 2 [3/2] [UU_]

md2 : active raid1 sdc1[1] sdb1[0]
      104320 blocks [3/2] [UU_]

md1 : active raid1 sda5[0]
      88256 blocks [2/1] [U_]

md0 : active raid1 sda1[0]
      8297472 blocks [2/1] [U_]

unused devices: <none>
```

It's possible that md0 and md1 will not show up when you check /proc/mdstat. In that case, you won't need to destroy those arrays. Otherwise you must destroy the original RAID arrays /dev/md0 and /dev/md1 so we can repartition the drive and assign those new partitions the new arrays:

```
$ sudo mdadm --stop /dev/md0
mdadm: stopped /dev/md0
$ sudo mdadm --stop /dev/md1
mdadm: stopped /dev/md1
```

Once you are ready to repartition the original drive, you can check /proc/mdstat and see that those arrays are no longer available:

```
$ cat /proc/mdstat
Personalities : [linear] [multipath] [raid0] [raid1] [raid6]
   [raid5] [raid4] [raid10]
md4 : active raid5 sdc5[1] sdb5[0]
      176512 blocks level 5, 64k chunk, algorithm 2 [3/2] [UU_]

md3 : active raid5 sdc2[1] sdb1[0]
      16386048 blocks level 5, 64k chunk, algorithm 2 [3/2] [UU_]

md2 : active raid1 sdc1[1] sdb1[0]
      104320 blocks [3/2] [UU_]

unused devices: <none>
```

Now repartition /dev/sda as you did /dev/sdb so its partitions match the other two drives. Remember to set the partition types to fd. Once you save your changes, if fdisk complains that the kernel is going to use the old partition table, you have a small problem. You won't be able to safely add the new /dev/sda partitions to your RAID at this point. Instead, boot back into the rescue disc, select your RAID 5 root file system, then choose "Execute a shell in /dev/md3" (or the name of your root file system). Once you are at a prompt, type mount /boot so that the /boot partition is available. Otherwise, if fdisk doesn't give that complaint, proceed with the next steps.

Finally, you are ready to add the original partitions to each array:

```
$ sudo mdadm /dev/md2 --add /dev/sda1
$ sudo mdadm /dev/md3 --add /dev/sda2
$ sudo mdadm /dev/md4 --add /dev/sda5
$ cat /proc/mdstat
Personalities : [linear] [multipath] [raid0] [raid1] [raid6]
   [raid5] [raid4] [raid10]
md4 : active raid5 sda5[3] sdc5[1] sdb5[0]
      176512 blocks level 5, 64k chunk, algorithm 2 [3/2] [UU_]
         resync=DELAYED

md3 : active raid5 sda5[3] sdc2[1] sdb1[0]
      16386048 blocks level 5, 64k chunk, algorithm 2 [3/2] [UU_]
         [=>.................]  recovery =  5.6% (471936/8297472)
finish=12.3min speed=10550K/sec

md2 : active raid1 sda1[2] sdc1[1] sdb1[0]
      104320 blocks [3/3] [UUU]

unused devices: <none>
```

The arrays will sync up in the background, but you can use your system in the meantime. Now you will want to update your GRUB configuration so that it points to the new UUIDs and devices (otherwise you would have to edit it by hand each time). In the past you would have to edit things by hand, but if you just type sudo update-grub, the update program will detect and change all of the relevant entries for you. Now run sudo grub-install /dev/sda so that the GRUB instance on /dev/sda is updated.

Now the problem you will find when you run a software RAID array is that GRUB will install only on the first disk. If you lose the first disk, the second disk won't automatically be able to boot the system. To fix this you will have to manually install GRUB to the second disk. This is easy enough—just type sudo grub-install /dev/sdb. Change the device from /dev/sdb to your second RAID device if it's different. If you have a third or fourth RAID device, just run grub-install for that device as well.

The final step, if you haven't done so already, is to use a partitioning tool on /dev/sda and set both partitions to partition type fd so that they will automatically be detected as RAID devices. Reboot your system one final time to ensure it will boot to your RAID array. Now your system is fault tolerant and ready to use.

Add a Drive to a RAID 5 Array

It can be difficult to plan storage for a system. Even with the best plans in place, sometimes a machine's purpose changes. In any case, when you need more storage on a RAID 5 array, you have a few options. You could potentially back up all of the data, create a brand-new RAID 5 array with an extra drive, and then restore, or you could attempt to grow the RAID 5 array hot. Now growing a RAID 5 array hot isn't for the faint at heart. I would recommend you make a backup of your data if possible, just in case.

All warnings aside, let's assume I have a standard three-disk system using RAID 5 as in my previous RAID 1 to RAID 5 migration example. I have added a fourth disk, /dev/sdd, to the server, and I want to extend my RAID arrays across it. Since we want to grow the file system of our root partition, we need to do all of these steps from a rescue disc, so boot your Ubuntu Server install CD into recovery mode. When you are prompted to select a root file system, hit Alt-F2 to switch to a different console. We don't want to mount any file systems since we plan to grow them.

Once you are in the rescue mode shell, use fdisk to partition the new drive so that it matches the other drives. Once that has completed, use mdadm to add the new partitions to each of the RAID arrays:

```
# mdadm /dev/md2 --add /dev/sdd1
mdadm: added /dev/sdd1
# mdadm /dev/md3 --add /dev/sdd2
mdadm: added /dev/sdd2
# mdadm /dev/md4 --add /dev/sdd5
mdadm: added /dev/sdd5
# cat /proc/mdstat
Personalities : [linear] [multipath] [raid0] [raid1] [raid6]
  [raid5] [raid4] [raid10]
md4 : active raid5 sdd5[3](S) sda5[2] sdc5[1] sdb5[0]
      176512 blocks level 5, 64k chunk, algorithm 2 [3/3] [UUU]

md3 : active raid5 sdd2[3](S) sda2[2] sdc2[1] sdb1[0]
      16386048 blocks level 5, 64k chunk, algorithm 2 [3/3] [UUU]

md2 : active raid1 sdd1[3](S) sda1[2] sdc1[1] sdb1[0]
      104320 blocks [3/3] [UUU]

unused devices: <none>
```

Notice that the new partitions have been added to each array but they have an (S) after them to denote that they are currently hot spares. To extend the arrays to incorporate those drives as well, we need an additional mdadm command:

```
# mdadm --grow --raid-devices=4 /dev/md2
# mdadm --grow --raid-devices=4 /dev/md3
# mdadm --grow --raid-devices=4 /dev/md4
```

At this point all of your drives will get very busy as they shift data around evenly across all four drives. Since RAID 1 arrays just have to mirror and don't have to recalculate any parity, they should complete much faster, but it might take hours to grow the RAID 5 arrays. In the meantime you can watch /proc/mdstat to gauge the progress.

```
# while [ 1 ]; do cat /proc/mdstat; sleep 15; done;
```

Hit Ctrl-C to exit out of this script. After the RAID has finally resynced, you are ready to resize your file system. Different file systems have different tools they use to resize (if they support growing the file system), but with the standard case of an ext4 file system you run a file system check first (e2fsck) and then resize2fs:

```
# e2fsck -f /dev/md3
# resize2fs /dev/md3
```

Notice that I resized only the RAID 5 array and not /dev/md2. Since RAID 1 only mirrors, no matter how many drives you add to it, it will stay the same size. For the swap partition I just need to reformat it:

```
# mkswap /dev/md4
```

Now note that this will change the UUID for the swap partition, so if you reference the UUID in your /etc/fstab file, you must mount /dev/md3 to a temporary mount point and update your /etc/fstab. Once the file systems are resized, type Alt-F1 to go back to the rescue menu and select your root file system (in my case it is /dev/md3). Then select "Execute a shell in /dev/md3" (instead of /dev/md3 your rescue operations menu will reference the root partition you selected).

Once I'm in a shell within /dev/md3, I type mount /boot so the /boot partition is available. Then edit /etc/mdadm/mdadm.conf and update each ARRAY reference so that the num-devices value is equal to 4 instead of 3 (or if you updated your array from four disks to five, change this to 5). Save your changes, and then run update-initramfs so the initramfs file has the new mdadm.conf:

```
# update-initramfs -u 2.6.32-19-generic-pae
update-initramfs: Generating /boot/initrd.img-2.6.32-19-generic-pae
```

Replace 2.6.32-19-generic-pae with your kernel version if it's different. Now you can type exit to return to the rescue operations menu and select "Reboot the system" to reboot into your new expanded RAID array.

LVM
The Story of the Logical Volume Manager

Let's take a step back from our RAID adventure and look at the bigger picture in data storage. The entire situation is unpleasant. Hard drives are slow and fail often, and though abolished for working memory ages ago, fixed-size partitions are still the predominant mode of storage space allocation. As if worrying about speed and data loss weren't enough, you also have to worry about whether your partition size calculations were just right when you were installing a server or whether you'll wind up in the unenviable position of having a partition run out of space even though another partition is maybe mostly unused. And if you might have to move a partition across physical volume boundaries on a running system, well, woe is you.

RAID helps to some degree. It'll do wonders for your worries about performance and fault tolerance, but it operates at too low a level to help with the partition size or fluidity concerns. What we'd really want is a way to push the partition concept up one level of abstraction, so it doesn't operate directly on the underlying physical media. Then we could have partitions that are trivially resizable or that can span multiple drives, we could easily take some space from one partition and tack it on another, and we could juggle partitions around on physical drives on a live server. Sounds cool, right?

Very cool, and very doable via LVM, a system that shifts the fundamental unit of storage from physical drives to virtual or logical ones (although we harbor our suspicions that the term *logical* is a jab at the storage status quo, which is anything but). LVM has traditionally been a feature of expensive, enterprise UNIX operating systems or was available for purchase from third-party vendors. Through the magic of free software, a guy by the name of Heinz Mauelshagen wrote an implementation of a logical volume manager for Linux in 1998. LVM has undergone tremendous improvements since then and is widely used in production today, and just as you expect, the Ubuntu installer makes it easy for you to configure it on your server during installation.

LVM Theory and Jargon

Wrapping your head around LVM is a bit more difficult than with RAID because LVM rethinks the whole way of dealing with storage, which predictably introduces a bit of jargon that you need to learn. Under LVM, physical volumes, or PVs, are seen just as providers of disk space without any inherent organization (such as partitions mapping to a mount point in the OS). We group PVs into volume groups, or VGs, which are virtual storage pools that look like good old cookie-cutter hard drives. We carve those up into logical volumes, or LVs, that act like the normal partitions we're used to dealing with. We create filesystems on these LVs and mount them into our directory tree. And behind the scenes, LVM splits up PVs into small slabs of bytes (4MB by default), each of which is called a physical extent, or a PE.

Okay, so that was a mouthful of acronyms, but as long as you understand the progression, you're in good shape. You take a physical hard drive and set up one or more partitions on it that will be used for LVM. These partitions are now PVs, which are split into PEs and then grouped in VGs, on top of which you finally create LVs. It's the LVs, these virtual partitions, and not the ones on the physical hard drive, that carry a filesystem and are mapped and mounted into the OS. And if you're really confused about what possible benefit we get from adding all this complexity only to wind up with the same fixed-size partitions in the end, hang in there. It'll make sense in a second.

The reason LVM splits PVs into small, equally sized PEs is that the definition of a volume group (the space that'll be carved into logical volumes) then becomes "a collection of physical extents" rather than "a physical area on a physical drive," as with old-school partitions. Notice that "a collection of extents" says nothing about where the extents are coming from and certainly doesn't impose a fixed limit on the size of a VG. We can take PEs from a bunch of different drives and toss them into one VG, which addresses our desire to abstract partitions away from physical drives. We can take a VG and make it bigger simply by adding a few extents to it, maybe by taking them from another VG or maybe by tossing in a new PV and using extents from there. And we can take a VG and move it to different physical storage simply by telling it to relocate to a different collection of extents. Best of all, we can do all this on the fly, without any server downtime.

Do you smell that? That's the fresh smell of the storage revolution.

Setting Up LVM

By now, you must be convinced that LVM is the best thing since sliced bread. Which it is—and, surprisingly enough, setting it up during installation is no harder than setting up RAID. Create partitions on each physical drive you want to use for LVM, just as you did with RAID, but tell the installer to use them as physical space for LVM. Note that in this context, PVs are not actual physical hard drives; they are the partitions you're creating.

You don't have to devote your entire drive to partitions for LVM. If you'd like, you're free to create actual filesystem-containing partitions alongside the storage partitions used for LVM, but make sure you're satisfied with your partitioning choice before you proceed. Once you enter the LVM configurator in the installer, the partition layout on all drives that contain LVM partitions will be frozen.

Let's look back to our fictional server, but let's give it four drives, which are 10GB, 20GB, 80GB, and 120GB in size. Say we want to create an LVM partition, or PV, using all available space on each drive, and then combine the first two PVs into a 30GB VG and the latter two into a 200GB one. Each VG will act as a large virtual hard drive on top of which we can create LVs just as we would normal partitions.

As with RAID, arrowing over to the name of each drive and hitting Enter lets us erase the partition table. Then hitting Enter on the FREE SPACE entry lets us create a PV—a partition that we set to be used as a physical space for LVM. Once all three LVM partitions are in place, we select Configure the Logical Volume Manager on the partitioning menu.

After a warning about the partition layout, we get to a rather spartan LVM dialog that lets us modify VGs and LVs. According to our plan, we choose the former option and create the two VGs we want, choosing the appropriate PVs. We then select Modify Logical Volumes and create the LVs corresponding to the normal partitions we want to put on the system—say, one for each of /, /var, /home, and /tmp.

You can already see some of the partition fluidity that LVM brings you. If you decide you want a 25GB logical volume for /var, you can carve it out of the first VG you created, and /var will magically span the two smaller hard drives. If you later decide you've given /var too much space, you can shrink the filesystem and then simply move over some of the storage space from the first VG to the second. The possibilities are endless.

Last but not least, recent Ubuntu versions support encrypting your LVM volumes right from the installer, which is music to paranoid ears: It means you can now have full-disk encryption from the moment you install your machine. Encrypted LVM is offered as one of the "guided" options in the partitioning menu, but you can also accomplish the same result by hand.

TIP   **LVM Doesn't Provide Redundancy**
The point of LVM is storage fluidity, not fault tolerance. In our example, the logical volume containing the /var filesystem is sitting on a volume group that spans two hard drives. Unfortunately, this means that either drive failing will corrupt the entire filesystem, and LVM intentionally doesn't contain functionality to prevent this problem.

Instead, when you need fault tolerance, build your volume groups from physical volumes that are sitting on RAID! In our example, we could have made a partition spanning the entire size of the 10GB hard drive and allocated it to physical space for a RAID volume. Then, we could have made two 10GB partitions on the 20GB hard drive and made the first one also a physical space for RAID. Entering the RAID configurator, we would create a RAID 1 array from the 10GB RAID partitions on both drives, but instead of placing a regular filesystem on the RAID array as before, we'd actually designate the RAID array to be used as a physical space for LVM. When we get to LVM configuration, the RAID array would show up as any other physical volume, but we'd know that the physical volume is redundant. If a physical drive fails beneath it, LVM won't ever know, and no data loss will occur. Of course, standard RAID array caveats apply, so if enough drives fail and shut down the array, LVM will still come down kicking and screaming.

Ethernet Bonding

As you develop fault-tolerant systems, you quickly realize that after disk failures, network issues are probably the second area that requires redundancy. After all, switches need maintenance from time to time and they do fail, as do networking cards and even Ethernet cables. If you want to be able to survive switch failure or maintenance, you need a system with multiple Ethernet ports connected to redundant switches. Most servers these days come with at least two Ethernet ports if not more, so it makes sense to set up Ethernet bonding, especially when you see how easy it is.

Ethernet bonding is a feature built into the Linux kernel as a module. With Ethernet bonding you can have multiple Ethernet ports that answer to the same IP address. Depending on the bonding mode you choose, you could have an active/passive scenario where one port activates only if the other appears off-line, or you could have an active/active scenario where you accept traffic across all ports.

Full documentation of all of the Ethernet bonding modes is available in the Documentation/networking/bonding.txt file included with any Linux kernel source. Following is an excerpt from that documentation that describes each bond mode:

balance-rr or 0

Round-robin policy: Transmit packets in sequential order from the first available slave through the last. This mode provides load balancing and fault tolerance.

active-backup or 1

Active-backup policy: Only one slave in the bond is active. A different slave becomes active if, and only if, the active slave fails. The bond's MAC address is externally visible on only one port (network adapter) to avoid confusing the switch.

balance-xor or 2

XOR policy: Transmit based on the selected transmit hash policy. The default policy is a simple [(source MAC address XOR'd with destination MAC address) modulo slave count]. Alternate transmit policies may be selected via the xmit_hash_policy option, described below. This mode provides load balancing and fault tolerance.

broadcast or 3

Broadcast policy: transmits everything on all slave interfaces. This mode provides fault tolerance.

802.3ad or 4

IEEE 802.3ad Dynamic link aggregation. Creates aggregation groups that share the same speed and duplex settings. Utilizes all slaves in the active aggregator according to the 802.3ad specification.

balance-tlb or 5

Adaptive transmit load balancing: channel bonding that does not require any special switch support. The outgoing traffic is distributed according to the current load (computed relative to the speed) on each slave. Incoming traffic is received by the current slave. If the receiving slave fails, another slave takes over the MAC address of the failed receiving slave.

balance-alb or 6

Adaptive load balancing: includes balance-tlb plus receive load balancing (rlb) for IPV4 traffic, and does not require any special switch support. The receive load balancing is achieved by ARP negotiation. The bonding driver intercepts the ARP Replies sent by the local system on their way out and overwrites the source hardware address with the unique hardware address of one of the slaves in the bond such that different peers use different hardware addresses for the server.

So which bonding mode should you use? This can be a difficult question to answer as different networks support certain modes better than others. My recommendation is to try out some of the different bonding modes and test their fail-over by unplugging a cable while pinging the server. Different modes handle port failure differently, especially in the case where a cable is reconnected (or a switch is rebooted) and the port takes 30 seconds or so to come up. On some bonding modes pings will continue with no interruption, while on others you might have a 30-second outage while the port comes up. Note that because the bonding mode is set in the bonding module when it is loaded, if you change the bonding mode you will likely need to reboot (or at least take down the bond0 interface and unload and reload the module). For this example I choose bonding mode 1 because it has only one port active at a time, so it is relatively safe on any switch.

The first step to configure bonding is to install the ifenslave package:

```
$ sudo apt-get install ifenslave
```

This package includes the ifenslave utility, which the system will use to bond two interfaces together. The next step is to open /etc/modprobe.d/

aliases (or create it if it doesn't exist), scroll to the bottom of the file, and add

```
alias bond0 bonding
options bonding mode=1 miimon=100
```

The options line is what you can use to change your bonding mode. The miimon option tells the kernel how often to check the link state of the interface in milliseconds. In this case it is checked every 100 milliseconds.

The next step is to open your /etc/network/interfaces file and comment out any configuration lines for the network interfaces you will bond (you will probably have a configuration only for eth0). Also, if you have any references to auto eth0, comment those out as well. Then create a new configuration for the bond0 interface that mimics the settings you had for eth0. At the very end of the bond0 configuration you add an extra line called slaves that lists the different interfaces you want to bond together. Here's an example interfaces file for my server:

```
# This file describes the network interfaces available on your system
# and how to activate them. For more information, see interfaces(5).

# The loopback network interface
auto lo
iface lo inet loopback

# The primary network interface
#auto eth0
#iface eth0 inet static
#     address 192.168.0.5
#     netmask 255.255.255.0
#     gateway 192.168.0.1

auto bond0
iface bond0 inet static
      address 192.168.0.5
      netmask 255.255.255.0
      gateway 192.168.0.1
      slaves eth0 eth1
```

Save your changes and then run `sudo service networking restart` or `sudo /etc/init.d/networking restart`. Once you run `ifconfig`, you should see the new bond0 device:

```
$ sudo ifconfig
bond0     Link encap:Ethernet  HWaddr 00:0c:29:28:13:3b
          inet addr:192.168.0.5  Bcast:192.168.0.255
          Mask:255.255.255.0
          inet6 addr: fe80::20c:29ff:fe28:133b/64 Scope:Link
          UP BROADCAST RUNNING MASTER MULTICAST  MTU:1500  Metric:1
          RX packets:38 errors:0 dropped:0 overruns:0 frame:0
          TX packets:43 errors:0 dropped:0 overruns:0 carrier:0
          collisions:0 txqueuelen:0
          RX bytes:16644 (16.2 KB)  TX bytes:3282 (3.2 KB)

eth0      Link encap:Ethernet  HWaddr 00:0c:29:28:13:3b
          UP BROADCAST RUNNING SLAVE MULTICAST  MTU:1500  Metric:1
          RX packets:37 errors:0 dropped:0 overruns:0 frame:0
          TX packets:43 errors:0 dropped:0 overruns:0 carrier:0
          collisions:0 txqueuelen:1000
          RX bytes:16584 (16.1 KB)  TX bytes:3282 (3.2 KB)
          Interrupt:17 Base address:0x1400

eth1      Link encap:Ethernet  HWaddr 00:0c:29:28:13:3b
          UP BROADCAST RUNNING SLAVE MULTICAST  MTU:1500  Metric:1
          RX packets:1 errors:0 dropped:0 overruns:0 frame:0
          TX packets:0 errors:0 dropped:0 overruns:0 carrier:0
          collisions:0 txqueuelen:1000
          RX bytes:60 (60.0 B)  TX bytes:0 (0.0 B)
          Interrupt:18 Base address:0x1480

lo        Link encap:Local Loopback
          inet addr:127.0.0.1  Mask:255.0.0.0
          inet6 addr: ::1/128 Scope:Host
          UP LOOPBACK RUNNING  MTU:16436  Metric:1
          RX packets:0 errors:0 dropped:0 overruns:0 frame:0
          TX packets:0 errors:0 dropped:0 overruns:0 carrier:0
          collisions:0 txqueuelen:0
          RX bytes:0 (0.0 B)  TX bytes:0 (0.0 B)
```

Now you can test fail-over by unplugging eth0 while pinging the IP. Whenever a particular interface is down, the kernel will log both to dmesg and to /var/log/syslog. Here's an example log entry like one you would see if you unplugged eth0:

```
Feb 14 16:43:28 kickseed kernel: [ 2901.700054] eth0: link down
Feb 14 16:43:29 kickseed kernel: [ 2901.731190] bonding: bond0:
 link status definitely down for interface eth0, disabling it
Feb 14 16:43:29 kickseed kernel: [ 2901.731300] bonding: bond0:
 making interface eth1 the new active one.
```

Clusters

Even with RAID and Ethernet bonding on a host there are plenty of other components that can fail, from the CPU to the software on the host. If you need a service to stay up even when a host fails, then you need a cluster. There are a number of different ways to set up Linux clusters, and there are many different kinds of clusters as well. In this section I discuss one of the most common tools used in basic Linux clusters, Heartbeat, and how to use it to create a basic fault-tolerant service across two servers. Afterward I discuss how to use a tool called DRBD to replicate data between two servers over the network. These two tools provide a solid foundation you can use for any number of fault-tolerant services.

As you work with clusters, you will find that most clustering technologies use some of the same concepts for cluster management. Following are some of the basic rules and terminologies people use when they develop a cluster:

- **Floating IPs**
  In a standard active/passive Heartbeat cluster, each node (server) has its main IP and there is an additional floating IP that is shared between the nodes. Only the node that is considered active will use and answer to the floating IP address. Services are hosted off of the floating IP address so that when a particular host goes down and the fail-over node assumes the floating IP, it can take over the service.

- **Active/active versus active/passive**
  In an active/active cluster all nodes are running and accepting load at all times. In an active/passive cluster one node is considered the master and accepts all of the load while any other nodes take load only when the master goes down. My examples are based on an active/passive cluster.

▪ **Split-brain syndrome**

Split-brain syndrome occurs in an active/passive cluster when both nodes believe they are the master and try to assume the load. This can be disastrous for a cluster, especially in the case of shared storage and floating IPs, as both nodes will try to write to storage (that may not accept writes from multiple sources) as well as try to grab the floating IP for themselves. As you will see, one of the big challenges in clustering is identifying when a host is truly down and avoiding split-brain syndrome.

▪ **Quorum**

Clusters often use the concept of a quorum to determine when a host is down. The idea behind a quorum is to have a consensus among the members of your cluster about who can talk to whom. This typically works only when you have at least three hosts; in a two-node cluster if node A can't talk to node B, it can be difficult for node A to know whether its network is down or node B's network is down. With a third node you can set a quorum of two, so that at least two nodes must be unable to reach another node before that node is considered down.

▪ **Fencing**

Fencing is one of the methods used to avoid split-brain syndrome. The name is derived from the idea of building a fence around a downed node so that it can't become the active node again until its problems have been resolved. There are a number of ways to fence a machine, from turning off its network ports to rebooting it or triggering a kernel panic (aka shooting the other node in the head).

▪ **Shooting the other node in the head**

This term is used to describe a particularly direct response to fence a server. When a cluster determines a host is unavailable, it will often forcibly kill the server by either a reboot, a kernel panic, or even remotely power cycling the machine. The idea is that once the system reboots, it should be back to some sort of consistent state and should be able to rejoin the cluster safely.

▪ **Separate connection for node monitoring**

A common practice for clusters is to have a separate connection that the nodes use to monitor each other. The idea here is to prevent normal traffic from slowing down or interfering with communications between nodes. Some administrators solve this by monitoring over each node's serial port or connecting a crossover network cable between a second set of Ethernet ports.

Heartbeat

Heartbeat is one of the core Linux clustering tools. The idea behind Heartbeat is to provide a system to describe a cluster and then monitor each node to see if it is available. When a node is unavailable, Heartbeat can then take some sort of action in response. Responses might include moving a floating IP to a fail-over host, starting or stopping particular services, mounting particular file systems, and fencing the unavailable host.

There are two main methods of Heartbeat configuration these days. The classic Heartbeat configuration is based on a few basic text configuration files that are relatively easy to configure by hand. The traditional Heartbeat cluster works with only two nodes. The newer Heartbeat 2 configuration model relies on XML files and can support clusters of more than two nodes. These new features and file formats can introduce some complexity, especially when you are just getting started with clustering, so for the purposes of this chapter, since my example features only a two-node cluster, I am going to stick with the traditional Heartbeat configuration. The traditional Heartbeat configuration relies on three main configuration files: ha.cf, haresources, and authkeys.

■ **ha.cf**
This file defines all of the settings for a particular clustering, including the nodes in the cluster, what methods Heartbeat uses to communicate with each node, and also time-outs to use for any fail-over.

■ **haresources**
Here you will configure the responses a node will take as a result of a fail-over. This might be assuming a floating IP, mounting or unmounting file systems, or starting or stopping services.

■ **authkeys**
This file contains a secret key that all of the nodes have in common. This key is used as a method of authentication so that the nodes know they are speaking to valid members of the cluster.

Example Cluster   In my example I set up a two-node active/passive Apache cluster. I will assume that Apache hosts static files (i.e., I don't need replicated storage at this point). Here is the information about node1 and node2, the two different servers in my cluster:

```
node1
eth0: 172.16.245.220/255.255.255.0
eth1: 192.168.10.1/255.255.255.0

node2
eth0: 172.16.245.221/255.255.255.0
eth1: 192.168.10.2/255.255.255.0
```

I use eth0 to host the service. I use eth1 as a private network between each host. You could set this up either with a crossover cable between the ports on both servers or through a separate switch. In addition, I will set up a floating IP at 172.16.245.222 that any host that wants to access this Web site will use. I have already installed and configured Apache on each of these hosts.

Install and Configure Heartbeat   The Heartbeat software is packaged and available for Ubuntu Server as the package heartbeat, so you can use your preferred package manager to install it:

```
$ sudo apt-get install heartbeat
```

The package automatically creates the /etc/ha.d directory and the init scripts you need for the service, but it won't set up any of the main three configuration files, ha.cf, haresources, or authkeys, so I go into how to configure those here.

HA.CF   The Heartbeat package provides an annotated sample ha.cf file under /usr/share/doc/heartbeat, so be sure to use that as a resource if you want examples or further information. Here is the /etc/ha.d/ha.cf file I used in my cluster:

```
autojoin none
bcast eth1
warntime 5
deadtime 10
```

```
initdead 30
keepalive 2
logfacility local0
node node1.example.org
node node2.example.org
respawn hacluster /usr/lib/heartbeat/ipfail
ping 172.16.245.5 172.16.245.1
auto_failback off
```

A copy of this file will go on both node1 and node2. Each of these options is important, so I describe them here:

- **autojoin**

  You can choose to have nodes automatically join a cluster using the shared secret in the authkey file as authentication. For large clusters that constantly add or delete nodes this might be a useful option to enable so that you aren't constantly rolling out and updating your ha.cf file to list new nodes. In my case, since I have only two nodes, I have disabled this option.

- **bcast**

  There are a number of different ways each node can communicate to the others for Heartbeat and other communications. Each of these options is documented in /usr/share/doc/heartbeat/ha.cf.gz, but here is a summary. If you use the serial option, you can check Heartbeat over a null modem cable connected to each node's serial port. If you use mcast, you can define a multicast interface and IP address to use. In my case I used bcast, which broadcasts over my eth1 interface (the private network I set up). You can also specify ucast, which allows you to simply communicate via a unicast IP. That could be useful if you want to limit broadcast traffic or if you have only one interface (or a pair of bonded ports) and want to use your standard IP addresses to communicate. By default Heartbeat uses UDP port 694 for communication, so if you have a firewall enabled, be sure to add a rule to allow that access.

- **warntime**

  This is the time in seconds during which a communication can time out before Heartbeat will add a note in the logs that a node has a delayed heartbeat. No action will be taken yet.

▪ **deadtime**

This is the time in seconds during which a communication can time out before Heartbeat will consider it dead and start the fail-over process.

▪ **initdead**

On some machines it might take some time after Heartbeat starts for the rest of the services on the host to load. This option allows you to configure a special time-out setting that takes effect when the system boots before the node is considered dead.

▪ **keepalive**

This is the number of seconds between each heartbeat.

▪ **logfacility**

Here I can configure what syslog log facility to use. The `local0` value is a safe one to pick and causes Heartbeat to log in /var/log/syslog.

▪ **node**

The `node` lines are where you manually define each node that is in your cluster. The syntax is `node` *nodename*, where *nodename* is the hostname a particular node gives when you run `uname -n` on that host. Add `node` lines for each host in the cluster.

▪ **respawn**

Since I have a separate interface for Heartbeat communication and for the regular service, I want to enable the `ipfail` script. This script performs various network checks on each host so it can determine whether a host has been isolated from the network but can still communicate with other nodes. This `respawn` line tells Heartbeat to start the `ipfail` script as the hacluster user, and if it exits out, to respawn it.

▪ **ping**

This option goes along with the `ipfail` script. Here I can define extra hosts that a node can use to gauge its network connectivity. You want to choose stable hosts that aren't nodes in the cluster, so the network gateway or other network infrastructure hosts are good to add here.

- **auto_failback**

  This is an optional setting. Heartbeat defines what it considers a master node. This node is the default node from which the service runs. By default, when the master node goes down and then recovers, the cluster will fail back to that host. Just to avoid IPs and services flapping back and forth you may choose to disable the automatic failback.

Once the ha.cf file is saved and deployed to both node1 and node2, I can move on to haresources.

HARESOURCES   The /etc/ha.d/haresources file defines what resources the cluster is managing so it can determine what to do when it needs to failover. In this file you can define the floating IP to use and can also list services to start or stop, file systems to mount and unmount (which I discuss in the DRBD section), e-mails to send, and a number of other scripts that are located under /etc/ha.d/resource.d. In my case the haresources file is pretty simple:

```
node1 172.16.245.222 apache2
```

The first column defines which node is considered the default, in my case node1. Next I define the floating IP to use for this cluster, 172.16.245.222. Finally, I can define a list of services to start or stop when this node is active. Since Apache is started by /etc/init.d/apache2, I choose apache2 here. The example above used some configuration shorthand since I had some pretty basic needs. The longer form of the same line is

```
node1 IPaddr::172.16.245.222 apache2
```

The IPaddr section tells Heartbeat to use the /etc/ha.d/resource.d/IPaddr script and pass the 172.16.245.222 argument to it. With the default settings of the IPaddr script, the floating IP address will take on the same subnet and broadcast settings as the other IP address on the same interface. If I wanted the subnet mask to be /26, for instance, I could say

```
node1 IPaddr::172.16.245.222/26 apache2
```

The apache2 section at the end is also shorthand. By default Heartbeat will run the service with the start argument when a node becomes active and with the stop argument when a node is disabled. If you created a special script in /etc/ha.d/resource.d/ or /etc/init.d/ and wanted to pass special arguments, you would just list the service name, two colons, then the argument. For instance, if I created a special script called pageme that sent an SMS to a phone number, my haresources line might read

```
node1 172.16.245.222 apache2 pageme::650-555-1212
```

Once you have created your haresources file, copy it to /etc/ha.d/ on both nodes, and make sure that it stays identical.

AUTHKEYS   The final step in the process is the creation of the /etc/ha.d/ authkeys file. This file contains some method Heartbeat can use to authenticate a node with the rest of the cluster. The configuration file contains one line starting with auth, then a number that defines which line below it to use. The next line begins with a number and then a type of authentication method. If you use a secure private network like a crossover cable, your authkeys might just look like this:

```
auth 1
1 crc
```

This option doesn't require heavy CPU resources because the communications aren't signed with any particular key. If you are going to communicate over an open network, you will likely want to use either MD5 or SHA1 keys. In either case the syntax is similar:

```
auth 2
1 crc
2 sha1 thisisasecretsha1key
3 md5 thisisasecretmd5key
```

Here you can see I have defined all three potential options. The secret key you pass after sha1 or md5 is basically any secret you want to make up. Notice in the example above I set auth 2 at the top line so it will choose to authenticate with SHA1. If I had wanted to use MD5 in this example, I would set auth to 3 since the MD5 configuration is on the line that begins with 3. Once you create this file and deploy it on all nodes, be sure to set it so that only root can read it, since anyone who can read this file can potentially pretend to be a member of the cluster:

```
$ sudo chmod 600 /etc/ha.d/authkeys
```

Once these files are in place, you are ready to start the cluster. Start with the default node you chose in haresources (in my case node1) and type

```
$ sudo /etc/init.d/heartbeat start
```

Once it starts, move to the other node in the cluster and run the same command. You should be able to see Heartbeat start to ping nodes and confirm the health of the cluster in the /var/log/syslog file. At this point you are ready to test fail-over. Open a Web browser on a third host and try to access the Web server on the floating IP (in my case 172.16.245.222) and make sure it works. Then disconnect the main network interface on the active host. Depending on the time-outs you configured in /etc/ha.d/ha.cf, it will take a few seconds, but your fail-over host should start talking about the failure in the logs and will assume the floating IP and start any services it needs. Here's some sample output from a syslog file during a fail-over from node1 to node2:

```
Feb 16 17:37:56 node2 ipfail: [4340]: debug: Got asked for num_ping.
Feb 16 17:37:57 node2 ipfail: [4340]: debug: Found ping node
    172.16.245.1!
Feb 16 17:37:57 node2 ipfail: [4340]: debug: Found ping node
    172.16.245.5!
Feb 16 17:37:58 node2 ipfail: [4340]: info: Telling other node that we
    have more visible ping nodes.
Feb 16 17:37:58 node2 ipfail: [4340]: debug: Sending you_are_dead.
Feb 16 17:37:58 node2 ipfail: [4340]: debug: Message [you_are_dead]
    sent.
Feb 16 17:37:58 node2 ipfail: [4340]: debug: Got asked for num_ping.
Feb 16 17:37:58 node2 ipfail: [4340]: debug: Found ping node
    172.16.245.1!
Feb 16 17:37:59 node2 ipfail: [4340]: debug: Found ping node
    172.16.245.5!
Feb 16 17:37:59 node2 ipfail: [4340]: info: Telling other node that we
    have more visible ping nodes.
Feb 16 17:37:59 node2 ipfail: [4340]: debug: Sending you_are_dead.
```

```
Feb 16 17:37:59 node2 ipfail: [4340]: debug: Message [you_are_dead]
  sent.
Feb 16 17:38:05 node2 heartbeat: [4255]: info: node1 wants to go
  standby [all]
Feb 16 17:38:06 node2 ipfail: [4340]: debug: Other side is unstable.
Feb 16 17:38:06 node2 heartbeat: [4255]: info: standby: acquire [all]
  resources from node1
Feb 16 17:38:06 node2 heartbeat: [4443]: info: acquire all HA
  resources (standby).
Feb 16 17:38:06 node2 ResourceManager[4457]: info: Acquiring resource
  group: node1 172.16.245.222 apache2
Feb 16 17:38:06 node2 IPaddr[4483]: INFO:  Resource is stopped
Feb 16 17:38:06 node2 ResourceManager[4457]: info: Running
  /etc/ha.d/resource.d/IPaddr 172.16.245.222 start
Feb 16 17:38:06 node2 ResourceManager[4457]: debug: Starting
  /etc/ha.d/resource.d/IPaddr 172.16.245.222 start
Feb 16 17:38:07 node2 IPaddr[4554]: INFO: Using calculated nic for
  172.16.245.222: eth0
Feb 16 17:38:07 node2 IPaddr[4554]: INFO: Using calculated netmask
  for 172.16.245.222: 255.255.255.0
Feb 16 17:38:07 node2 IPaddr[4554]: DEBUG: Using calculated broadcast
  for 172.16.245.222: 172.16.245.255
Feb 16 17:38:07 node2 IPaddr[4554]: INFO: eval ifconfig eth0:0
  172.16.245.222 netmask 255.255.255.0 broadcast 172.16.245.255
Feb 16 17:38:07 node2 IPaddr[4554]: DEBUG: Sending Gratuitous Arp for
  172.16.245.222 on eth0:0 [eth0]
Feb 16 17:38:07 node2 kernel: [ 7391.316832] NET: Registered protocol
  family 17
Feb 16 17:38:07 node2 IPaddr[4539]: INFO:  Success
Feb 16 17:38:07 node2 ResourceManager[4457]: debug:
  /etc/ha.d/resource.d/IPaddr 172.16.245.222 start done. RC=0
Feb 16 17:38:07 node2 ResourceManager[4457]: info: Running
  /etc/init.d/apache2  start
Feb 16 17:38:07 node2 ResourceManager[4457]: debug: Starting
  /etc/init.d/apache2  start
Feb 16 17:38:07 node2 ResourceManager[4457]: debug:
  /etc/init.d/apache2  start done. RC=0
Feb 16 17:38:07 node2 heartbeat: [4443]: info: all HA resource
  acquisition completed (standby).
Feb 16 17:38:07 node2 heartbeat: [4255]: info: Standby resource
  acquisition done [all].
Feb 16 17:38:08 node2 heartbeat: [4255]: info: remote resource
  transition completed.
Feb 16 17:38:08 node2 ipfail: [4340]: debug: Other side is now stable.
Feb 16 17:38:08 node2 ipfail: [4340]: debug: Other side is now stable.
```

Now you can plug the interface back in. If you disabled automatic fail-over, the other node will still hold the floating IP. Otherwise the cluster will fail back. At this point your cluster should be ready for any remaining tests to tune the time-outs appropriately and then, finally, active use.

The previous example is a good starting place for your own clustered service but certainly doesn't cover everything that Heartbeat can do. For more information about Heartbeat along with more details on configuration options and additional guides, check out www.linux-ha.org.

DRBD

A common need in a cluster is replicated storage. When a host goes down, the fail-over host needs access to the same data. On a static Web server, or a Web server with a separate database server, this requirement is easily met since the data can be deployed to both members of the cluster. In many cases, though, such as more complex Web sites that allow file uploads, or with clustered NFS or Samba servers, you need a more sophisticated method to keep files synchronized across the cluster.

When faced with the need for synchronized storage, many administrators start with some basic replication method like an rsync command that runs periodically via cron. When you have a cluster, however, you want something more sophisticated. With DRBD you can set up a file system so that every write is replicated over the network to another host. Here I describe how to add DRBD to our Heartbeat cluster example from above. I have added a second drive to each node at /dev/sdb and created a partition that fills up the drive at /dev/sdb1. The goal is to have a replicated disk available at /mnt/shared on the active node.

The first step is to install the DRBD utilities. These are available in the drbd8-utils package, so install it with your preferred package manager:

```
$ sudo apt-get install drbd8-utils
```

The next step is to create a configuration file for DRBD to use. The package will automatically install a sample /etc/drbd.conf file that documents all of the major options. Definitely use this sample as a reference, but I recommend you move it out of the way and create a clean /etc/drbd.conf file for your cluster since, as you will see, the drbd.conf is relatively simple. Here's the /etc/drbd.conf I use for my cluster:

```
global {
    usage-count no;
}

common {
    protocol C;
}

resource r0 {
    on node1 {
    device   /dev/drbd1;
    disk     /dev/sdb1;
    address  192.168.10.1:7789;
    meta-disk internal;
    }
    on node2 {
    device   /dev/drbd1;
    disk     /dev/sdb1;
    address  192.168.10.2:7789;
    meta-disk internal;
    }
    net {
    after-sb-0pri   discard-younger-primary;
    after-sb-1pri   consensus;
    after-sb-2pri   disconnect;
    }
}
```

To simplify things, I break up this configuration file into sections and describe the options:

```
global {
    usage-count no;
}

common {
    protocol C;
}
```

The global section allows you to define certain options that apply outside of any individual resource. The usage-count option defines whether your

cluster will participate in DRBD's usage counter. If you want to participate, set this to Yes. Set it to No if you want your DRBD usage to be more
private.

The common section allows you to define options that apply to every resource
definition. For instance, the protocol option lets you define which transfer
protocol to use. The different transfer protocols are defined in the sample
drbd.conf included with the package. For protocol, choose C unless you
have a specific reason not to. Since I have a number of options in my
resource section that are the same for each node (like device, disk, and
meta-disk), I could actually put all of these options in the common section.
You just need to be aware that anything you place in the common section will
apply to all resources you define.

Each replicated file system you set up is known as a resource and has its
own resource definition. The resource definition is where you define which
nodes will be in your cluster, what DRBD disk to create, what actual partition to use on each host, and what network IP and port to use for the replication. Here is the resource section of my config for a resource called r0:

```
resource r0 {
    on node1 {
      device   /dev/drbd1;
      disk     /dev/sdb1;
      address  192.168.10.1:7789;
      meta-disk internal;
    }
    on node2 {
      device   /dev/drbd1;
      disk     /dev/sdb1;
      address  192.168.10.2:7789;
      meta-disk internal;
    }
    net {
      after-sb-0pri   discard-younger-primary;
      after-sb-1pri   consensus;
      after-sb-2pri   disconnect;
    }
}
```

As you can see, I have defined two nodes here, node1 and node2, and within
the node definitions are specific options for that host. I have decided to use

/dev/drbd1 as the DRBD virtual device each host will actually mount and access and to use /dev/sdb1 as the physical partition DRBD will use on each host. DRBD standardizes on port 7788 on up for each resource, so I have chosen port 7789 here. If you have enabled a firewall on your hosts, you will need to make sure that this port is unblocked. Note also that I have specified the IP addresses for the private network I was using before for Heartbeat and not the public IP addresses. Since I know this network is pretty stable (it's over a crossover cable), I want to use it to replicate the data. Otherwise you do want to make sure that any network you use for DRBD is fault-tolerant.

The final option for each node is meta-disk set to internal. DRBD needs some area to store its metadata. The ideal, simplest way to set this up is to use an internal metadisk. With an internal metadisk, DRBD will set aside the last portion of the partition (in this case /dev/sdb1) for its metadata. If you are setting up DRBD with a new, empty partition, I recommend you use an internal metadisk as it is much easier to maintain and you are guaranteed that the metadisk and the rest of the data are consistent when a disk fails. If you want to replicate a partition that you are already using, you will have to use an external metadisk on a separate partition and define it here in drbd.conf, or you risk having DRBD overwrite some of your data at the end of the partition. If you do need an external metadisk, visit www.drbd .org/docs/about/ and check out their formulas and examples of how to properly set up external metadisks.

The final part of my r0 resource is the following:

```
net {
  after-sb-0pri    discard-younger-primary;
  after-sb-1pri    consensus;
  after-sb-2pri    disconnect;
}
```

These are actually the default settings for DRBD, so I didn't need to explicitly list them here. I did so just so I could show how you can change DRBD's default split-brain policy. Remember that when a split brain occurs, neither node can communicate with the other and can't necessarily determine which node should be active. With DRBD, by default only one node is listed as the primary and the other is the secondary. In this section you can define behavior after different split-brain scenarios. The after-sb-0pri section defines what to do when both nodes are listed as secondary after a split brain. The default is to use the data from the node that was the primary before the split brain occurred. The next option sets what to do if one of the nodes was the primary after the split brain. The default is consensus. With consensus, the secondary's data will be discarded if the after-sb-0pri setting would also destroy it. Otherwise the nodes will disconnect from each other so you can decide which node will overwrite the other. The final after-sb-2pri option defines what to do if both nodes think they are the primary after a split brain. Here DRBD will disconnect the two nodes from each other so you can decide how to proceed. Check out the sample drbd.conf file for a full list of other options you can use for this section.

NOTE I could have condensed the configuration file quite a bit since both nodes will use the same type of metadisk, disk, and drive settings. Here's an example of a condensed drbd.conf:

```
global {
    usage-count no;
}

common {
    protocol C;
}

resource r0 {
    device   /dev/drbd1;
    disk     /dev/sdb1;
    meta-disk internal;
    on node1 {
        address  192.168.10.1:7789;
    }
    on node2 {
        address  192.168.10.2:7789;
    }
    net {
        after-sb-0pri   discard-younger-primary;
        after-sb-1pri   consensus;
        after-sb-2pri   disconnect;
    }
}
```

Initialize the DRBD Resource   Now that the /etc/drbd.conf file is set up, I make sure it exists on both nodes and then run the same set of commands on both nodes to initialize it. First I load the kernel DRBD module, then I create the metadata on my resource (r0), and then I bring the device up for the first time:

```
$ sudo modprobe drbd
$ sudo drbdadm create-md r0
$ sudo drbdadm up r0
```

Notice that I reference the r0 resource I have defined in drbd.conf. If you set up more than one resource in the file, you would need to perform the drbdadm commands for each of the resources the first time you set them up. After you run these commands on each node, you can check the /proc/drbd file on each node for the current status of the disk:

```
$ cat /proc/drbd
version: 8.0.11 (api:86/proto:86)
GIT-hash: b3fe2bdfd3b9f7c2f923186883eb9e2a0d3a5b1b build by
  phil@mescal, 2008-02-12 11:56:43

 1: cs:WFConnection st:Secondary/Unknown ds:Inconsistent/DUnknown
   C r---
    ns:0 nr:0 dw:0 dr:0 al:0 bm:0 lo:0 pe:0 ua:0 ap:0
    resync: used:0/31 hits:0 misses:0 starving:0 dirty:0 changed:0
    act_log: used:0/127 hits:0 misses:0 starving:0 dirty:0
      changed:0
```

In this output you can see that its current status (cs) is WFConnection, which means it is Waiting for a Connection. Currently no node has been assigned as the primary, so each will think that its state (st) is Secondary/ Unknown. Finally, the disk state (ds) will be Inconsistent because both DRBD resources have not been synced yet. It will also show Inconsistent here if you suffer a split brain on your cluster and DRBD can't recover from it automatically.

Next you are ready to perform the initial synchronization from one node to the other. This means you have to choose one node to act as the primary, and both nodes need to be able to communicate with each other over the network. Now if your disk already had data on it, it is crucial that you choose it as the primary. Otherwise the blank disk on the second node will overwrite all of your data. If both disks are currently empty, it doesn't matter as much. In my case I choose node1 as the primary and run the following command on it:

```
$ sudo drbdadm -- --overwrite-data-of-peer primary r0
```

At this point data will start to synchronize from node1 to node2. If I check the output of /proc/drbd, I can see its progress, much as with /proc/mdstat and software RAID:

```
$ cat /proc/drbd
version: 8.0.11 (api:86/proto:86)
GIT-hash: b3fe2bdfd3b9f7c2f923186883eb9e2a0d3a5b1b build by
  phil@mescal, 2008-02-12 11:56:43

 1: cs:SyncSource st:Primary/Secondary ds:UpToDate/Inconsistent
    C r---
    ns:9568 nr:0 dw:0 dr:9568 al:0 bm:0 lo:0 pe:0 ua:0 ap:0
    [>...................] sync'ed:  0.2% (8171/8181)M
    finish: 7:15:50 speed: 316 (316) K/sec
    resync: used:0/31 hits:597 misses:1 starving:0 dirty:0
      changed:1
    act_log: used:0/127 hits:0 misses:0 starving:0 dirty:0
      changed:0
```

Now you can see that the current status, state, and disk state have all changed. Once the synchronization starts, you can go ahead and start using /dev/drbd1 like a regular partition and put a file system on it and mount it. In my case the disk was empty, so I needed to do both on node1:

```
$ sudo mkfs -t ext3 /dev/drbd1
$ sudo mkdir /mnt/shared
$ sudo mount /dev/drbd1 /mnt/shared
```

Now go to node2 and make sure that the /mnt/shared directory exists there as well, but don't mount /dev/drbd1! Since I am using ext3 and not a clustering file system, I can mount /dev/drbd1 on only one node at a time. Once the file finishes syncing, the status will change to Connected and the disk state will change to UpToDate. You are then ready to set up Heartbeat so that it can fail-over DRBD properly.

NOTE Notice that I didn't say anything about /etc/fstab here. You do not want to add any DRBD devices to /etc/fstab because they will not necessarily automatically mount at boot time. Instead, Heartbeat will take care of mounting any DRBD disks on the active member of the cluster.

Configure Heartbeat Heartbeat includes DRBD support specifically in the form of a script under /etc/ha.d/resource.d/ called drbddisk. You can use this script to tell Heartbeat which resources to start or stop. Unless you use a clustering file system, only one node can mount and write to a DRBD device at a time, so you need to set up Heartbeat so that it will mount or unmount the file system based on which node is active. Previously the line in my /etc/ha.d/haresources file was

```
node1 172.16.245.222 apache2
```

Now I will change it to

```
node1 172.16.245.222 drbddisk::r0
  Filesystem::/dev/drbd1::/mnt/shared::ext3 apache2
```

Make similar changes to the haresources file on node2 as well. Once you change the /etc/ha.d/haresources file on both hosts, run

```
$ sudo /etc/init.d/heartbeat reload
```

Now your cluster is ready to go. You can simulate a failure by, for instance, rebooting the primary host. If you go to the second node, you should notice Heartbeat kick in almost immediately and mount /dev/drbd1, start Apache, and take over the floating IP. The /proc/drbd file will list the status as WFConnection since it is waiting for the other host to come back up and should show that the node is now the primary. Because we set up the

Heartbeat cluster previously to not fail back, even when node1 comes back, node2 will be the active member of the cluster. To test failback just reboot node2 and watch the disk shift over to node1.

NOTE To create a replicated-disk, fault-tolerant Samba or NFS cluster instead of an Apache cluster, just install and configure Samba or NFS on both nodes as normal and share out the /mnt/shared directory. Then replace apache2 in /etc/ha.d/haresources with either samba or nfs-user-server depending on which service you use so it will start or stop those init scripts instead of apache2. You could even set up both Samba and NFS on the same machine and list both samba and nfs-user-server in haresources.

---

drbdadm Disk Management Once you have a functioning DRBD disk, drbdadm is the primary tool you will use to manage your disk resources. The DRBD init script should take care of initializing your resources, but you can use

```
$ sudo drbdadm up r0
```

To bring up a resource, replace r0 with the name of the resource you want to start. Likewise, you can take down an inactive resource with

```
$ sudo drbdadm down r0
```

You can also manually change whether a node is in primary or secondary mode, although in a Heartbeat cluster I recommend you let Heartbeat take care of this. If you do decide to change over from primary to secondary mode, be sure to unmount the disk first. Also, if any node is currently primary, DRBD won't let you change it to secondary while the nodes are connected (the cs: value in /proc/drbd), so you will have to disconnect them from each other first. To set the primary or secondary mode manually for a particular resource, run

```
$ sudo drbdadm primary r0
$ sudo drbdadm secondary r0
```

CHANGE DRBD.CONF   At some point you might want to make changes in your /etc/drbd.conf file such as changing split-brain recovery modes. Whenever you make changes, make sure that the same change is added to /etc/drbd.conf on all of your nodes, and then run

```
$ sudo drbdadm adjust r0
```

on both nodes. Replace r0 with the name of the resource you want to change.

REPLACE A FAILED DISK   Ideally you will have any disks you use with DRBD set up in some sort of RAID so that a disk can fail without taking out the node. If you do have a DRBD disk set up on a single drive as I do in this example and the drive fails, you will need to run a few commands to add the fresh drive. In this example I will assume that /dev/sdb failed on my node1 server. First, by default DRBD should automatically detach and remove a disk when it has a failure, so unless you knowingly tweaked that default, DRBD should do that work for you. Once you add and partition the replacement drive (in my case it will be /dev/sdb1), then first you need to re-create the internal metadata on /dev/sdb1 and then attach the resource:

```
$ sudo drbdadm create-md r0
$ sudo drbdadm attach r0
```

MANUALLY SOLVE SPLIT BRAIN   DRBD will attempt to resolve split-brain problems automatically, but sometimes it is unable to determine which node should overwrite the other. In this case you might have two nodes that have both mounted their DRBD disk and are writing to it. If this happens you will have to make a decision as to which node has the version of data you want to preserve. Let's say in my case that node1 and node2 have a split brain and have disconnected from each other. I decide that node2 has the most up-to-date data and should become the primary and overwrite node1. In this case I have to tell node1 to discard its data, so I go to node1, make sure that any DRBD disk is unmounted, and type

```
$ sudo drbdadm secondary r0
$ sudo drbdadm -- --discard-my-data connect r0
```

If node2 is already in WFConnection state, it will automatically reconnect to node1 at this point. Otherwise I need to go to node2, the node that has the good data, and type

```
$ sudo drbdadm connect r0
```

Now node2 will synchronize its data over to node1.

These steps should get you up and running with a solid replicated disk for your cluster. For more detailed information about DRBD, including more advanced clustering options than I list here, visit the official site at www .drbd.org.

## CHAPTER 11

Troubleshooting

TROUBLESHOOTING IS A TOPIC that is near and dear to me. While there are many other areas of system administration that I enjoy, I don't think anything compares to the excitement of tracking down the root cause of an obscure problem. Good troubleshooting is a combination of Sherlock Holmes–style detective work, intuition, and a little luck. You might even argue that some people have a knack for troubleshooting while others struggle with it, but in my mind it's something that all sysadmins get better at the more problems they run into.

While this chapter discusses troubleshooting, there are a number of common problems that can cause your Ubuntu system to not boot or to run in an incomplete state. I have moved all of these topics into their own chapter on rescue and recovery and have provided specific steps to fix common problems with the Ubuntu rescue CD. So if you are trying to solve a problem at the moment, check Chapter 12, Rescue and Recovery, first to see if I have already outlined a solution. If not, come back here to get the more general steps to isolate the cause of your problem and work out its solution.

In this chapter I discuss some aspects of my general philosophy on troubleshooting that could be applied to a wide range of problems. Then I cover a few common problems that you might run into and introduce some tools and techniques to help solve them. By the end of the chapter you should have a head start the next time a problem turns up. After all, in many organizations downtime is measured in dollars, not minutes, so there is a lot to be said for someone who can find a root cause quickly.

General Troubleshooting Philosophy

While there are specific steps you can take to address certain computer problems, most troubleshooting techniques rely on the same set of rules. Here I discuss some of these rules that will help make you a better troubleshooter.

Divide the Problem Space

When I'm faced with an unknown issue, I apply the same techniques as when I have to pick a number between 1 and 100. If you have ever played this game, you know that most people fall into one of two categories: the random guessers and the narrowers. The random guessers might start by choosing 15, then hear that the number is higher and pick 23, then hear it is still higher. Eventually they might either luck into the right number or pick so many numbers that only the right number remains. In either case they use far more guesses than they need to. Many people approach troubleshooting the same way: They choose solutions randomly until one happens to work. Such a person might eventually find the problem, but it takes way longer than it should.

In contrast to the random guessers, the narrowers strategically choose numbers that narrow the problem in half each time. Let's say the number is 80, for instance; their guesses would go as follows: 50, 75, 88, 82, 78, 80. With each guess, the list of numbers that could contain the answer is reduced by half. When people like this troubleshoot a computer problem, their time is spent finding ways to divide the problem space in half as much as possible. As I go through specific problems in this chapter, you will see this methodology in practice.

Favor Quick, Simple Tests over Slow, Complex Tests

What I mean here is that as you narrow down the possible causes of a problem, you will often end up with a few hypotheses that are equally likely. One hypothesis can be tested quickly but the other takes some time. For instance, if a machine can't seem to communicate with the network, a quick test could be to see if the network cable is plugged in, while a longer test would involve more elaborate software tests on the host. If the quick test isolates the problem, you get the solution that much faster. If you still need to try the longer test, you aren't out that much extra time.

Favor Past Solutions

Unless you absolutely prevent a problem from ever happening again, it's likely that when a symptom that you've seen before pops up, it could have the same solution. Over the years you'll find that you develop a common list of things you try first when you see a particular problem to rule out all of the common causes before you move on to more exotic hypotheses. Of course, you will have problems you've never seen before, too—that's part of the fun of troubleshooting—but when you test some of your past solutions first, you will find you solve problems faster.

Good Communication Is Critical When Collaborating

If you are part of a team that is troubleshooting a problem, you absolutely *must* have good communication among team members. That could be as simple as yelling across cubicle walls, or it could mean setting up a chat room. A common problem when a team works an issue is multiple members testing the same hypothesis. With good communication each person can tackle a different hypothesis and report the results. These results can then lead to new hypotheses that can be divided among the team members. One final note: Favor communication methods that allow multiple people to communicate at the same time. This means that often chat rooms work much better than phones for problem solving, since over the phone everyone has to wait for a turn to speak; in a chat room multiple people can communicate at once.

Understand How Systems Work

The more deeply you understand how a system works, the faster you can rule out causes of problems. Over the years I've noticed that when a problem occurs, people first tend to blame the technology they understand the least. At one point in my career, every time a network problem occurred, everyone immediately blamed DNS, even when it appeared obvious (at least to me) that not only was DNS functioning correctly, it never had actually been the cause of any of the problems. One day we decided to hold a lecture to explain how DNS worked and traced an ordinary DNS request from the client to every DNS server and back. Afterward everyone who attended the class stopped jumping to DNS as the first cause of network problems. There are core technologies with which every sysadmin deals on a daily basis, such as TCP/IP networking, DNS, Linux processes, programming, and memory management; it is crucial that you learn about these in as much depth as possible if you want to find a solution to a problem quickly.

Document Your Problems and Solutions

Many organizations have as part of their standard practice a postmortem meeting after every production issue. A postmortem allows the team to document the troubleshooting steps they took to arrive at a root cause as well as what solution ultimately fixed the issue. Not only does this help make sure that there is no disagreement about what the root cause is, but when everyone is introduced to each troubleshooting step, it helps make all the team members better problem solvers going forward. When you document your problem-solving steps, you have a great guide you can go to the next time a similar problem crops up so it can be solved that much faster.

Use the Internet, but Carefully

The Internet is an incredibly valuable resource when you troubleshoot a problem, especially if you are able to articulate it in search terms. After all, you are rarely the only person to face a particular problem, and in many cases other people have already come up with the solution. Be careful with your Internet research, though. Often your results are only as good as your understanding of the problem. I've seen many people go off on completely wrong paths to solve a problem because of a potential solution they found on the Internet. After all, a search for "Ubuntu server not on network" will turn up all sorts of completely different problems irrelevant to your issue.

Resist Rebooting

OK, so those of us who have experience with Windows administration have learned over the years that when you have a weird problem, a reboot often fixes it. Resist this "technique" on your Ubuntu servers! I've had servers with uptimes measured in years because most problems found on a Linux machine can be solved without a reboot. The problem with rebooting a machine (besides ruining your uptime) is that if the problem does go away, you may never know what actually caused it. That means you can't solve it for good and will ultimately see the problem again. As attractive as rebooting might be, keep it as your last resort.

Localhost Troubleshooting

While I would say that a majority of problems you will find on a server have some basis in networking, there is still a class of issues that involves only the localhost. What makes this tricky is that some local and networking problems often create the same set of symptoms, and in fact local problems can create network problems and vice versa. In this section I will cover problems that occur specifically on a host and leave issues that impact the network to the next section.

Host Is Sluggish or Unresponsive

Probably one of the most common problems you will find on a host is that it is sluggish or completely unresponsive. Often this can be caused by network issues, but here I will discuss some local troubleshooting tools you can use to tell the difference between a loaded network and a loaded machine.

When a machine is sluggish, it is often because you have consumed all of a particular resource on the system. The main resources are CPU, RAM, disk I/O, and network (which I will leave to the next section). Overuse of any of these resources can cause a system to bog down to the point that often the only recourse is your last resort—a reboot. If you can log in to the system, however, there are a number of tools you can use to identify the cause.

System Load   System load average is probably the fundamental metric you start from when troubleshooting a sluggish system. One of the first commands I run when I'm troubleshooting a slow system is uptime:

```
$ uptime
13:35:03 up 103 days, 8 min, 5 users, load average: 2.03, 20.17, 15.09
```

The three numbers after the load average, 2.03, 20.17, and 15.09, represent the 1-, 5-, and 15-minute load averages on the machine, respectively. A system load average is equal to the average number of processes in a runnable or uninterruptible state. Runnable processes are either currently using the CPU or waiting to do so, and uninterruptible processes are waiting for I/O. A single-CPU system with a load average of 1 means the single CPU is under constant load. If that single-CPU system has a load average of 4, there is 4 times the load on the system that it can handle, so three out of four processes are waiting for resources. The load average reported on a system is not tweaked based on the number of CPUs you have, so if you have a two-CPU system with a load average of 1, one of your two CPUs is loaded at all times—i.e., you are 50% loaded. So a load of 1 on a single-

CPU system is the same as a load of 4 on a four-CPU system in terms of the amount of available resources used.

The 1-, 5-, and 15-minute load averages describe the average amount of load over that respective period of time and are valuable when you try to determine the current state of a system. The 1-minute load average will give you a good sense of what is currently happening on a system, so in my previous example you can see that I most recently had a load of 2 over the last minute, but the load had spiked over the last 5 minutes to an average of 20. Over the last 15 minutes the load was an average of 15. This tells me that the machine had been under high load for at least 15 minutes and the load appeared to increase around 5 minutes ago, but it appears to have subsided. Let's compare this with a completely different load average:

```
$ uptime
05:11:52 up 20 days, 55 min, 2 users, load average: 17.29, 0.12, 0.01
```

In this case both the 5- and 15-minute load averages are low, but the 1-minute load average is high, so I know that this spike in load is relatively recent. Often in this circumstance I will run uptime multiple times in a row (or use a tool like top, which I will discuss in a moment) to see whether the load is continuing to climb or is on its way back down.

WHAT IS A HIGH LOAD AVERAGE?   A fair question to ask is what load average you consider to be high. The short answer is "It depends on what is causing it." Since the load describes the average number of active processes that are using resources, a spike in load could mean a few things. What is important to determine is whether the load is CPU-bound (processes waiting on CPU resources), RAM-bound (specifically, high RAM usage that has moved into swap), or I/O-bound (processes fighting for disk or network I/O).

For instance, if you run an application that generates a high number of simultaneous threads at different points, and all of those threads are launched at once, you might see your load spike to 20, 40, or higher as they all compete for system resources. As they complete, the load might come right back down. In my experience systems seem to be more responsive when under CPU-bound load than when under I/O-bound load. I've seen systems with loads in the hundreds that were CPU-bound, and I could run diagnostic tools on those systems with pretty good response times. On the other hand, I've seen systems with relatively low I/O-bound loads on which just logging in took a minute, since the disk I/O was completely saturated. A system that runs out of RAM resources often appears to have I/O-bound load, since once the system starts using swap storage on the disk, it can consume disk resources and cause a downward spiral as processes slow to a halt.

top   One of the first tools I turn to when I need to diagnose high load is top. I have discussed the basics of how to use the top command in Chapter 2, so here I will focus more on how to use its output to diagnose load. The basic steps are to examine the top output to identify what resources you are running out of (CPU, RAM, disk I/O). Once you have figured that out, you can try to identify what processes are consuming those resources the most. First let's examine some standard top output from a system:

```
top - 14:08:25 up 38 days,  8:02,  1 user,  load average: 1.70, 1.77, 1.68
Tasks: 107 total,   3 running, 104 sleeping,   0 stopped,   0 zombie
Cpu(s): 11.4%us, 29.6%sy, 0.0%ni, 58.3%id, .7%wa, 0.0%hi, 0.0%si, 0.0%st
Mem:   1024176k total,   997408k used,    26768k free,    85520k buffers
Swap:  1004052k total,     4360k used,   999692k free,   286040k cached

  PID USER      PR  NI  VIRT  RES  SHR S %CPU %MEM    TIME+  COMMAND
 9463 mysql     16   0  686m 111m 3328 S   53  5.5 569:17.64 mysqld
18749 nagios    16   0  140m 134m 1868 S   12  6.6 1345:01 nagios2db_status
24636 nagios    17   0 34660  10m  712 S    8  0.5 1195:15 nagios
22442 nagios    24   0  6048 2024 1452 S    8  0.1  0:00.04 check_time.pl
```

The first line of output is the same as you would see from the uptime command. As you can see in this case, the machine isn't too heavily loaded for a four-CPU machine:

```
top - 14:08:25 up 38 days,  8:02,  1 user,  load average: 1.70, 1.77, 1.68
```

top provides you with extra metrics beyond standard system load, though. For instance, the Cpu(s) line gives you information about what the CPUs are currently doing:

```
Cpu(s): 11.4%us, 29.6%sy,  0.0%ni, 58.3%id,  0.7%wa,  0.0%hi,  0.0%si, 0.0%st
```

These abbreviations may not mean much if you don't know what they stand for, so I will break down each of them below.

- **us: user CPU time**
  This is the percentage of CPU time spent running users' processes that aren't niced (nicing a process allows you to change its priority in relation to other processes).

- **sy: system CPU time**
  This is the percentage of CPU time spent running the kernel and kernel processes.

- **ni: nice CPU time**
  If you have user processes that have been niced, this metric will tell you the percentage of CPU time spent running them.

- **id: CPU idle time**
  This is one of the metrics that you want to be high. It represents the percentage of CPU time that is spent idle. If you have a sluggish system but this number is high, you know the cause isn't high CPU load.

- **wa: I/O wait**
  This number represents the percentage of CPU time that is spent waiting for I/O. It is a particularly valuable metric when you are tracking down the cause of a sluggish system, because if this value is low, you can pretty safely rule out disk or network I/O as the cause.

- **hi: hardware interrupts**
  This is the percentage of CPU time spent servicing hardware interrupts.

- **si: software interrupts**
  This is the percentage of CPU time spent servicing software interrupts.

- **st: steal time**
  If you are running virtual machines, this metric will tell you the percentage of CPU time that was stolen from you for other tasks.

In my previous example, you can see that the system is over 50% idle, which matches a load of 1.70 on a four-CPU system. When I diagnose a slow system, one of the first values I look at is I/O wait so I can rule out disk I/O. If I/O wait is low, then I can look at the idle percentage. If I/O wait is high, then the next step is to diagnose what is causing high disk I/O, which I cover below. If I/O wait and idle times are low, then you will likely see a high user time percentage, so you must diagnose what is causing high user time. If the I/O wait is low and the idle percentage is high, you then know any sluggishness is not because of CPU resources and will have to start troubleshooting elsewhere. This might mean looking for network problems, or in the case of a Web server looking at slow queries to MySQL, for instance.

Diagnose High User Time A common and relatively simple problem to diagnose is high load due to a high percentage of user CPU time. This is common since the services on your server are likely to take the bulk of the system load and they are user processes. If you see high user CPU time but low I/O wait times, you simply need to identify which processes on the system are consuming the most CPU. By default, top will sort all of the processes by their CPU usage:

```
  PID USER      PR  NI  VIRT  RES  SHR S %CPU %MEM    TIME+  COMMAND
 9463 mysql     16   0  686m 111m 3328 S   53  5.5 569:17.64 mysqld
18749 nagios     1   0  140m 134m 1868 S   12  6.6  1345:01 nagios2db_status
24636 nagios    17   0 34660  10m  712 S    8  0.5  1195:15 nagios
22442 nagios    24   0  6048 2024 1452 S    8  0.1  0:00.04 check_time.pl
```

In this example the mysqld process is consuming 53% of the CPU and the nagios2db_status process is consuming 12%. Note that this is the percentage of a single CPU, so if you have a four-CPU machine you could possibly see more than one process consuming 99% CPU.

The most common high-CPU-load situations you will see are all of the CPUs being consumed either by one or two processes or by a large number of processes. Either case is easy to identify since in the first case the top process or two will have a very high percentage of CPU and the rest will be relatively low. In that case, to solve the issue you could simply kill the process that is using the CPU (hit K and then type in the PID number for the process).

In the case of multiple processes, you might simply have a case of one system doing too many things. You might, for instance, have a large number of Apache processes running on a Web server along with some log parsing scripts that run from cron. All of these processes might be consuming more or less the same amount of CPU. The solution to problems like this can be trickier for the long term, as in the Web server example you do need all of those Apache processes to run, yet you might need the log parsing programs as well. In the short term you can kill (or possibly postpone) some processes until the load comes down, but in the long term you might need to consider increasing the resources on the machine or splitting some of the functions across more than one server.

Diagnose Out-of-Memory Issues   The next two lines in the top output provide valuable information about RAM usage. Before diagnosing specific system problems, it's important to be able to rule out memory issues.

```
Mem:   1024176k total,   997408k used,   26768k free,    85520k buffers
Swap:  1004052k total,     4360k used,  999692k free,   286040k cached
```

The first line tells me how much physical RAM is available, used, free, and buffered. The second line gives me similar information about swap usage, along with how much RAM is used by the Linux file cache. At first glance it might look as if the system is almost out of RAM since the system reports that only 26,768k is free. A number of beginner sysadmins are misled by the used and free lines in the output because of the Linux file cache. Once Linux loads a file into RAM, it doesn't necessarily remove it from RAM when a program is done with it. If there is RAM available, Linux will cache the file in RAM so that if a program accesses the file again, it can do so much more quickly. If the system does need RAM for active processes, it won't cache as many files.

To find out how much RAM is really being used by processes, you must subtract the file cache from the used RAM. In the example above, out of the 997,408k RAM that is used, 286,040k is being used by the Linux file cache, so that means that only 711,368k is actually being used.

In my example the system still has plenty of available memory and is barely using any swap at all. Even if you do see some swap being used, it is not necessarily an indicator of a problem. If a process becomes idle, Linux will often page its memory to swap to free up RAM for other processes. A good way to tell whether you are running out of RAM is to look at the file cache. If your actual used memory minus the file cache is high, and the swap usage is also high, you probably do have a memory problem.

If you do find you have a memory problem, the next step is to identify which processes are consuming RAM. top sorts processes by their CPU usage by default, so you will want to change this to sort by RAM usage instead. To do this, keep top open and hit the M key on your keyboard. This will cause top to sort all of the processes on the page by their RAM usage:

```
 PID USER     PR NI  VIRT  RES  SHR S %CPU %MEM   TIME+  COMMAND
18749 nagios  16  0  140m 134m 1868 S   12  6.6 1345:01 nagios2db_status
 9463 mysql   16  0  686m 111m 3328 S   53  5.5  569:17 mysqld
24636 nagios  17  0 34660  10m  712 S    8  0.5 1195:15 nagios
22442 nagios  24  0  6048 2024 1452 S    8  0.1  0:00.04 check_time.pl
```

Look at the %MEM column and see if the top processes are consuming a majority of the RAM. If you do find the processes that are causing high RAM usage, you can decide to kill them, or, depending on the program, you might need to perform specific troubleshooting to find out what is making that process use so much RAM.

NOTE   top can actually sort its output by any of the columns. To change which column top sorts by, hit the F key to change to a screen where you can choose the sort column. After you hit a key that corresponds to a particular column (for instance, K for the CPU column), you can hit Enter to return to the main top screen.

OOM KILLER   The Linux kernel also has an out-of-memory (OOM) killer that can kick in if the system runs dangerously low on RAM. When a system is almost out of RAM, the OOM killer will start killing processes. In some cases this might be the process that is consuming all of the RAM, but this isn't guaranteed. I've seen the OOM killer end up killing programs like sshd or other processes instead of the real culprit. In many cases the system is unstable enough after one of these events that you find you have to reboot it to ensure that all of the system processes are running. If the

OOM killer does kick in, you will see lines like the following in your /var/log/syslog:

```
1228419127.32453_1704.hostname:2,S:Out of Memory: Killed process
    21389 (java).
1228419127.32453_1710.hostname:2,S:Out of Memory: Killed process
    21389 (java).
```

Diagnose High I/O Wait   When I see high I/O wait, one of the first things I check is whether the machine is using a lot of swap. Since a hard drive is much slower than RAM, when a system runs out of RAM and starts using swap, the performance of almost any machine suffers. Anything that wants to access the disk has to compete with swap for disk I/O. So first diagnose whether you are out of memory and, if so, manage the problem there. If you do have plenty of RAM, you will need to figure out which program is consuming the most I/O.

It can sometimes be difficult to figure out exactly which process is using the I/O, but if you have multiple partitions on your system, you can narrow it down by figuring out which partition most of the I/O is on. To do this you will need the iostat program, which is provided by the sysstat Ubuntu package, so type

```
$ sudo apt-get install sysstat
```

Preferably you will have this program installed before you need to diagnose an issue. Once the program is installed, you can run iostat without any arguments to see an overall glimpse of your system:

```
$ sudo iostat
Linux 2.6.24-19-server (hostname)    01/31/2009

avg-cpu:  %user   %nice %system %iowait  %steal   %idle
           5.73    0.07    2.03    0.53    0.00   91.64

Device:            tps   Blk_read/s   Blk_wrtn/s   Blk_read   Blk_wrtn
sda               9.82       417.96        27.53   30227262    1990625
sda1              6.55       219.10         7.12   15845129     515216
sda2              0.04         0.74         3.31      53506     239328
sda3              3.24       198.12        17.09   14328323    1236081
```

The first bit of output gives CPU information similar to what you would see in top. Below it are I/O stats on all of the disk devices on the system as well as their individual partitions. Here is what each of the columns represents:

▪ **tps**
This lists the transfers per second to the device. "Transfers" is another way to say I/O requests sent to the device.

▪ **Blk_read/s**
This is the number of blocks read from the device per second.

▪ **Blk_wrtn/s**
This is the number of blocks written to the device per second.

▪ **Blk_read**
In this column is the total number of blocks read from the device.

▪ **Blk_wrtn**
In this column is the total number of blocks written to the device.

When you have a system under heavy I/O load, the first step is to look at each of the partitions and identify which partition is getting the heaviest I/O load. Say, for instance, that I have a database server and the database itself is stored on /dev/sda3. If I see that the bulk of the I/O is coming from there, I have a good clue that the database is likely consuming the I/O. Once you figure that out, the next step is to identify whether the I/O is mostly from reads or writes. Let's say that I suspect that a backup job is causing the increase in I/O. Since the backup job is mostly concerned with reading files from the file system and writing them over the network to the backup server, I could possibly rule that out if I see that the bulk of the I/O is due to writes, not reads.

NOTE   You will probably have to run iostat more than one time to get an accurate sense of the current I/O on your system. If you specify a number on the command line as an argument, iostat will continue to run and give you new output after that many seconds. For instance, if I wanted to see iostat output every two seconds, I could type sudo iostat 2. Another useful argument to iostat if you have any NFS shares is -n. When you specify -n, iostat will give you I/O statistics about all of your NFS shares.

In addition to `iostat`, these days we have a much simpler tool available in Ubuntu called `iotop`. In effect it is a blend of `top` and `iostat` in that it shows you all of the running processes on the system sorted by their I/O statistics. The program isn't installed by default but is provided by the `iotop` Ubuntu package, so type

```
$ sudo apt-get install iotop
```

Once the package is installed, you can run `iotop` as root and see output like the following:

```
$ sudo iotop
Total DISK READ: 189.52 K/s | Total DISK WRITE: 0.00 B/s

  TID PRIO  USER     DISK READ  DISK WRITE  SWAPIN      IO>
     COMMAND

 8169 be/4 root      189.52 K/s   0.00 B/s  0.00 %  0.00 %
     rsync --server --se

 4243 be/4 kyle        0.00 B/s   3.79 K/s  0.00 %  0.00 %
     cli /usr/lib/gnome-

 4244 be/4 kyle        0.00 B/s   3.79 K/s  0.00 %  0.00 %
     cli /usr/lib/gnome-

    1 be/4 root        0.00 B/s   0.00 B/s  0.00 %  0.00 %
     init
```

In this case, I can see that there is an `rsync` process tying up my read I/O.

Out of Disk Space

Another common problem system administrators run into is a system that has run out of free disk space. If your monitoring is set up to catch such a thing, you might already know which file system is out of space, but if not, then you can use the `df` tool to check:

```
$ sudo df -h

Filesystem         Size  Used Avail Use% Mounted on
/dev/sda1          7.9G  541M  7.0G   8% /
varrun             189M   40K  189M   1% /var/run
varlock            189M     0  189M   0% /var/run
```

```
udev                    189M   44K  189M   1% /dev
devshm                  189M     0  189M   0% /dev/shm
/dev/sda3                20G   15G  5.9G  71% /home
```

The df command lets you know how much space is used by each file system, but after you know that, you still need to figure out what is consuming all of that disk space. The similarly named du command is invaluable for this purpose. This command with the right arguments can scan through a file system and report how much disk space is consumed by each directory. If you pipe it to a sort command, you can then easily see which directories consume the most disk space. What I like to do is save the results in /tmp (if there's enough free space, that is) so I can refer to the output multiple times and not have to rerun du. I affectionately call this the "duck command":

```
$ cd /
$ sudo du -ckx | sort -n > /tmp/duck-root
```

This command won't output anything to the screen but instead creates a sorted list of what directories consume the most space and outputs the list to /tmp/duck-root. If I then use tail on that file, I can see the top ten directories that use space:

```
$ sudo tail /tmp/duck-root
67872   /lib/modules/2.6.24-19-server
67876   /lib/modules
69092   /var/cache/apt
69448   /var/cache
76924   /usr/share
82832   /lib
124164  /usr
404168  /
404168  total
```

In this case I can see that /usr takes up the most space, followed by /lib, /usr/share, and then /var/cache. Note that the output separates out /var/cache/apt and /var/cache so I can tell that /var/cache/apt is the subdirectory that consumes the most space under /var/cache. Of course, I might have to open the duck-root file with a tool like less or a text editor so I can see more than the last ten directories.

So what can you do with this output? In some cases the directory that takes up the most space can't be touched (as with /usr), but often when the free space disappears quickly it is because of log files growing out of control. If you do see /var/log consuming a large percentage of your disk, you could then go to the directory and type `sudo ls -lS` to list all of the files sorted by their size. At that point you could truncate (basically erase the contents of) a particular file:

```
$ sudo sh -c "> /var/log/messages"
```

Alternatively, if one of the large files has already been rotated (it ends in something like .1 or .2), you could either gzip it if it isn't already gzipped, or you could simply delete it if you don't need the log anymore.

NOTE **Full / due to /tmp**
I can't count how many times I've been alerted about a full / file system (a dangerous situation that can often cause the system to freeze up) only to find out that it was caused by large files in /tmp. Specifically, these were large .swp files. When `vim` opens a file, it copies the entire contents into a .swp file. Certain versions of `vim` store this .swp file in /tmp, others in /var/tmp, and still others in ~/tmp. In any case, what had happened was that a particular user on the system decided to view an Apache log file that was gigabytes in size. When the user opened the file, it created a multigigabyte .swp file in /tmp and filled up the root file system. To solve the issue I had to locate and kill the offending `vim` process.

Out of Inodes   Another less common but tricky situation in which you might find yourself is the case of a file system that claims it is full, yet when you run `df` you see that there is more than enough space. If this ever happens to you, the first thing you should check is whether you have run out of inodes. When you format a file system, the `mkfs` tool decides at that point the maximum number of inodes to use as a function of the size of the partition. Each new file that is created on that file system gets its own unique inode, and once you run out of inodes, no new files can be created. Generally speaking, you never get close to that maximum; however, certain servers store millions of files on a particular file system, and in those cases you might hit the upper limit. The `df -i` command will give you information on your inode usage:

```
$ df -i
Filesystem       Inodes   IUsed   IFree IUse% Mounted on
/dev/sda         520192   17539  502653   4% /
```

In this example my root partition has 520,192 total inodes but only 17,539 are used. That means I can create another 502,653 files on that file system. In the case where 100% of your inodes are used, there are only a few options at your disposal. Either you can try to identify a large number of files you can delete or move to another file system, possibly archive a group of files into a tar archive, or back up the files on your current file system, reformat it with more inodes, and copy the files back.

Network Troubleshooting

Most servers these days are attached to some sort of network and generally use the network to provide some sort of service. Many different problems can creep up on a network, so network troubleshooting skills become crucial for any system administrator. Linux provides a large set of network troubleshooting tools, and next I discuss a few common network problems along with how to use some of the tools available for Ubuntu to track down the root cause.

Server A Can't Talk to Server B

Probably the most common network troubleshooting scenario involves one server being unable to communicate with another server on the network. I use an example in which a server named ubuntu1 can't access the Web service (port 80) on a second server named web1. There are any number of different problems that could cause this, so I run step by step through tests you can perform to isolate the cause of the problem. Normally when troubleshooting a problem like this, I might skip a few of these initial steps (such as checking link), since tests further down the line will also rule them out. For instance, if I test and confirm that DNS works, I've proven that my host can communicate on the local network. For this guide, though, I walk through each intermediary step to illustrate how you might test each level.

Client or Server Problem   One quick test you can perform to narrow down the cause of your problem is to go to another host on the same network and try to access the server. In my example, I would find another server on the same network as ubuntu1, such as ubuntu2, and try to access web1. If ubuntu2 also can't access web1, then I know the problem is more likely on web1, or on the network between ubuntu1 and ubuntu2, and web1. If ubuntu2 *can* access web1, then I know the problem is more likely on ubuntu1. To start, let's assume that ubuntu2 can access web1, so we will focus our troubleshooting on ubuntu1.

Is It Plugged In? The first troubleshooting steps to perform are on the client. You first want to verify that your client's connection to the network is healthy. To do this you can use the ethtool program (installed via the ethtool package) to verify that your link is up (the Ethernet device is physically connected to the network), so if your Ethernet device was at eth0:

```
$ sudo ethtool eth0
Settings for eth0:
     Supported ports: [ TP ]
     Supported link modes:   10baseT/Half 10baseT/Full
                             100baseT/Half 100baseT/Full
                             1000baseT/Half 1000baseT/Full
     Supports auto-negotiation: Yes
     Advertised link modes:  10baseT/Half 10baseT/Full
                             100baseT/Half 100baseT/Full
                             1000baseT/Half 1000baseT/Full
     Advertised auto-negotiation: Yes
     Speed: 100Mb/s
     Duplex: Full
     Port: Twisted Pair
     PHYAD: 0
     Transceiver: internal
     Auto-negotiation: on
     Supports Wake-on: pg
     Wake-on: d
     Current message level: 0x000000ff (255)
     Link detected: yes
```

Here on the final line you can see that Link detected is set to yes so ubuntu1 is physically connected to the network. If this were set to no you would need to physically inspect ubuntu1's network connection and make sure it is connected. Since it is physically connected, I can move on.

NOTE   **Slow Network Speeds**

ethtool has uses beyond simply checking for link. It can also be used to diagnose and correct duplex issues. When a Linux server connects to a network, typically it autonegotiates with the network to see what speeds it can use and whether the network supports full duplex. The Speed and Duplex lines in the example ethtool output illustrate what a 100Mb/s, full duplex network should report. If you notice slow network speeds on a host, its speed and duplex settings are a good place to look. Run `ethtool` as in the example above, and if you notice `Duplex` set to `Half`, then run:

```
$ sudo ethtool -s eth0 autoneg off duplex full
```

Replace `eth0` with your Ethernet device.

Is My Interface Up? Once you have established that you are physically connected to the network, the next step is to confirm that the network interface is configured correctly on your host. The best way to check this is to run the `ifconfig` command with your interface as an argument, so to test eth0's settings I would run

```
$ sudo ifconfig eth0
eth0      Link encap:Ethernet  HWaddr 00:17:42:1f:18:be
          inet addr:10.1.1.7  Bcast:10.1.1.255  Mask:255.255.255.0
          inet6 addr: fe80::217:42ff:fe1f:18be/64 Scope:Link
          UP BROADCAST MULTICAST  MTU:1500  Metric:1
          RX packets:1 errors:0 dropped:0 overruns:0 frame:0
          TX packets:11 errors:0 dropped:0 overruns:0 carrier:0
          collisions:0 txqueuelen:1000
          RX bytes:229 (229.0 B)  TX bytes:2178 (2.1 KB)
          Interrupt:10
```

Probably the most important line in this output is the second line, which tells us our host has an IP address (10.1.1.7) and subnet mask (255.255.255.0) configured. Now whether these are the right settings for this host is something you will need to confirm. If the interface is not configured, try running `sudo ifup eth0` and then run `ifconfig` again to see if the interface comes up. If the settings are wrong or the interface won't come up, inspect /etc/network/interfaces. There you can correct any errors in the network settings. Now if the host gets its IP through DHCP, you will need to move your troubleshooting to the DHCP host to find out why you aren't getting a lease.

Is It on the Local Network? Once you see that the interface is up, the next step is to see if a default gateway has been set and whether you can access it. The `route` command will display your current routing table, including your default gateway:

```
$ sudo route -n
Kernel IP routing table
Destination     Gateway        Genmask          Flags Metric Ref    Use Iface
10.1.1.0        *              255.255.255.0    U     0      0        0 eth0
default         10.1.1.1       0.0.0.0          UG    100    0        0 eth0
```

The line you are interested in is the last line that starts with `default`. Here you can see that my host has a gateway of 10.1.1.1. Note that I used the `-n` option with `route` so it wouldn't try to resolve any of these IP addresses into hostnames. For one thing, the command runs more quickly, but more important, I don't want to cloud my troubleshooting with any potential DNS errors. Now if you don't see a default gateway configured here, and the host you want to reach is on a different subnet (say, web1, which is on 10.1.2.5), that is the likely cause of your problem. Either be sure to set the gateway in /etc/network/interfaces, or if you get your IP via DHCP, be sure it is set correctly on the DHCP server and then reset your interface with `sudo service networking restart`.

Once you have identified the gateway, use the `ping` command to confirm that you can communicate with the gateway:

```
$ ping -c 5 10.1.1.1
PING 10.1.1.1 (10.1.1.1) 56(84) bytes of data.
64 bytes from 10.1.1.1: icmp_seq=1 ttl=64 time=3.13 ms
64 bytes from 10.1.1.1: icmp_seq=2 ttl=64 time=1.43 ms
64 bytes from 10.1.1.1: icmp_seq=3 ttl=64 time=1.79 ms
64 bytes from 10.1.1.1: icmp_seq=5 ttl=64 time=1.50 ms

--- 10.1.1.1 ping statistics ---
5 packets transmitted, 4 received, 20% packet loss, time 4020ms
rtt min/avg/max/mdev = 1.436/1.966/3.132/0.686 ms
```

As you can see, I was able to successfully ping the gateway, which means that I can at least communicate with the 10.1.1.0 network. If you couldn't ping the gateway, it could mean a few things. It could mean that your gateway is blocking ICMP packets. If so, tell your network administrator that blocking ICMP is an annoying practice with negligible security benefits and then try to ping another Linux host on the same subnet. If ICMP isn't being blocked, then it's possible that the switch port on your host is set to the wrong VLAN, so you will need to further inspect the switch to which it is connected.

Is DNS Working?   Once you have confirmed that you can speak to the gateway, the next thing to test is whether DNS functions. The `nslookup` and `dig` tools both can be used to troubleshoot DNS issues, but since I need to perform only basic testing at this point, I just use `nslookup` to see if I can resolve web1 into an IP:

```
$ nslookup web1
Server:     10.1.1.3
Address:    10.1.1.3#53

Name:   web1.example.net
Address: 10.1.2.5
```

In this example DNS is working. The web1 host expands into web1 .example.net and resolves to the address 10.1.2.5. Of course, make sure that this IP matches the IP that web1 is supposed to have! In this case DNS works, so we can move on to the next section; however, there are also a number of ways DNS could fail.

NO NAME SERVER CONFIGURED OR INACCESSIBLE NAME SERVER

```
$ nslookup web1
;; connection timed out; no servers could be reached
```

If you see this error, it could mean either you have no name servers configured for your host, or they are inaccessible. In either case you will need to inspect /etc/resolv.conf and see if any name servers are configured there. If you don't see any IP addresses configured there, you will need to add a name server to the file. Otherwise, if you see something like

```
search example.net
nameserver 10.1.1.3
```

you now need to start troubleshooting your connection with your name server, starting off with `ping`. If you can't ping the name server and its IP address is in the *same* subnet (in this case 10.1.1.3 is within my subnet), the name server itself could be completely down. If you can't ping the name server and its IP address is in a *different* subnet, then skip ahead to the Can I Route to the Remote Host? section, only apply those troubleshooting steps to the name server's IP. If you can ping the name server but it isn't responding, skip ahead to the Is the Remote Port Open? section.

MISSING SEARCH PATH OR NAME SERVER PROBLEM   It is also possible that you will get the following error for your nslookup command:

```
$ nslookup web1
Server:      10.1.1.3
Address:     10.1.1.3#53

** server can't find web1: NXDOMAIN
```

Here you see that the server did respond, since it gave a response server can't find web1. This could mean two different things. One, it could mean that web1's domain name is not in your DNS search path. This is set in /etc/resolv.conf in the line that begins with search. A good way to test this is to perform the same nslookup command, only use the fully qualified domain name (in this case web1.example.net). If it does resolve, then either always use the fully qualified domain name, or if you want to be able to use just the hostname, add the domain name to the search path in /etc/resolv.conf.

If even the fully qualified domain name doesn't resolve, then the problem is on the name server. The complete method to troubleshoot all DNS issues is a bit beyond the scope of this chapter, but here are some basic pointers. If the name server is supposed to have that record, then that zone's configuration needs to be examined. If it is a recursive name server, then you will have to test whether recursion is not working on the name server by looking up some other domain. If you can look up other domains, then you must check whether the problem is on the remote name server that does contain the zones.

Can I Route to the Remote Host?

After you have ruled out DNS issues and see that web1 is resolved into its IP 10.1.2.5, you must test whether you can route to the remote host. Assuming ICMP is enabled on your network, one quick test might be to ping web1. If you can ping the host, you know your packets are being routed there and you can move to the next section, Is the Remote Port Open? If you can't ping web1, try to identify another host on that network and see if you can ping it. If you can, then it's possible web1 is down or blocking your requests, so move to the next section.

If you can't ping any hosts on the network, packets aren't being routed correctly. One of the best tools to test routing issues is traceroute. Once you provide traceroute a host, it will test each hop between you and the host. For example, a successful traceroute between ubuntu1 and web1 would look like the following:

```
$ traceroute 10.1.2.5
traceroute to 10.1.2.5 (10.1.2.5), 30 hops max, 40 byte packets
 1  10.1.1.1 (10.1.1.1)  5.432 ms  5.206 ms  5.472 ms
 2  web1 (10.1.2.5)  8.039 ms  8.348 ms  8.643 ms
```

Here you can see that packets go from ubuntu1 to its gateway (10.1.1.1), and then the next hop is web1. This means it's likely that 10.1.1.1 is the gateway for both subnets. On your network you might see a slightly different output if there are more routers between you and your host. If you can't ping web1, your output would look more like the following:

```
$ traceroute 10.1.2.5
traceroute to 10.1.2.5 (10.1.2.5), 30 hops max, 40 byte packets
 1  10.1.1.1 (10.1.1.1)  5.432 ms  5.206 ms  5.472 ms
 2  * * *
 3  * * *
```

Once you start seeing asterisks in your output, you know that the problem is on your gateway. You will need to go to that router and investigate why it can't route packets between the two networks. If instead you see something more like

```
$ traceroute 10.1.2.5
traceroute to 10.1.2.5 (10.1.2.5), 30 hops max, 40 byte packets
 1  10.1.1.1 (10.1.1.1)  5.432 ms  5.206 ms  5.472 ms
 1  10.1.1.1 (10.1.1.1)  3006.477 ms !H  3006.779 ms !H  3007.072 ms
```

then you know that the ping timed out at the gateway, so the host is likely down or inaccessible even from the same subnet. At this point if I hadn't tried to access web1 from a machine on the same subnet as web1, I would try pings and other tests now.

NOTE   If you have one of those annoying networks that block ICMP, don't worry, you can still troubleshoot routing issues. You will just need to install the `tcptraceroute` package (`sudo apt-get install tcptraceroute`), then run the same commands as for `traceroute`, only substitute `tcptraceroute` for `traceroute`.

Is the Remote Port Open?   So you can route to the machine but you still can't access the Web server on port 80. The next test is to see whether the port is even open. There are a number of different ways to do this. For one, you could try `telnet`:

```
$ telnet 10.1.2.5 80
Trying 10.1.2.5...
telnet: Unable to connect to remote host: Connection refused
```

If you see `Connection refused`, then either the port is down (likely Apache isn't running on the remote host or isn't listening on that port) or the firewall is blocking your access. If `telnet` can connect, then, well, you don't have a networking problem at all. If the Web service isn't working the way you suspected, you need to investigate your Apache configuration on web1. Instead of `telnet`, I prefer to use `nmap` to test ports because it can often detect firewalls for me. If `nmap` isn't installed, run `sudo apt-get install nmap` to install it. To test web1 I would type the following:

```
$ nmap -p 80 10.1.2.5

Starting Nmap 4.62 ( http://nmap.org ) at 2009-02-05 18:49 PST
Interesting ports on web1 (10.1.2.5):
PORT   STATE  SERVICE
80/tcp filtered http
```

Aha! `nmap` is smart enough that it can often tell the difference between a closed port that is truly closed and a closed port behind a firewall. Now normally when a port is actually down, `nmap` will report it as `closed`. Here it reported it as `filtered`. What this tells me is that there is some firewall in the way that is dropping my packets to the floor. This means I need to investigate any firewall rules on my gateway (10.1.1.1) and on web1 itself to see if port 80 is being blocked.

Test the Remote Host Locally

At this point we have either been able to narrow the problem down to a network issue or we believe the problem is on the host itself. If we think the problem is on the host itself, there are a few things we can do to test whether port 80 is available.

Test for Listening Ports   One of the first things I would do on web1 is test whether port 80 is listening. The `netstat -lnp` command will list all ports that are listening along with the process that has the port open. I could just run that and parse through the output for anything that is listening on port 80, or I could use `grep` to show me only things listening on port 80:

```
$ sudo netstat -lnp | grep :80
tcp     0     0 0.0.0.0:80     0.0.0.0:*     LISTEN     919/apache
```

The first column tells you what protocol the port is using. The second and third columns are the receive and send queues (both set to 0 here). The column you want to pay attention to is the fourth column, as it lists the local address on which the host is listening. Here the `0.0.0.0:80` tells us that the host is listening on all of its IPs for port 80 traffic. If Apache were listening only on web1's Ethernet address, I would see `10.1.2.5:80` here. The final column will tell you which process has the port open. Here I can see that Apache is running and listening. If you do not see this in your `netstat` output, you need to start your Apache server.

Firewall Rules   If the process is running and listening on port 80, it's possible that web1 has some sort of firewall in place. Use the `ufw` command to list all of your firewall rules. If your firewall is disabled, your output would look like this:

```
$ sudo ufw status
Status: inactive
```

If your firewall is enabled but has no rules, it might look like this:

```
$ sudo ufw status
Status: inactive
```

It's possible, though, that your firewall is set to deny all packets by default even if it doesn't list any rules. A good way to test whether a firewall is in the way is to simply disable ufw temporarily if it is enabled and see if you can connect:

```
$ sudo ufw disable
```

On the other hand, if you had a firewall rule that blocked port 80, it might look like this:

```
$ sudo ufw status
Status: inactive

To          Action  From
--          ------  ----
80:tcp      DENY    Anywhere
```

Clearly in the latter case I would need to modify my firewall rules to allow port 80 traffic from my host. To find out more about firewall rules, review the Firewalls section of Chapter 6, Security.

Hardware Troubleshooting

For the most part you will probably spend your time troubleshooting host or network issues. After all, hardware is usually pretty obvious when it fails. A hard drive will completely crash; a CPU will likely take the entire system down. There are, however, a few circumstances when hardware doesn't completely fail and as a result causes random strange behavior. Here I describe how to test a few hardware components for errors.

Network Card Errors

When a network card starts to fail, it can be rather unnerving as you will try all sorts of network troubleshooting steps to no real avail. Often when a network card or some other network component to which your host is connected starts to fail, you can see it in packet errors on your system. The ifconfig command we used for network troubleshooting before can also tell you about TX (transmit) or RX (receive) errors for a card. Here's an example from a healthy card:

```
$ sudo ifconfig eth0
eth0      Link encap:Ethernet  HWaddr 00:17:42:1f:18:be
          inet addr:10.1.1.7  Bcast:10.1.1.255  Mask:255.255.255.0
          inet6 addr: fe80::217:42ff:fe1f:18be/64 Scope:Link
          UP BROADCAST MULTICAST  MTU:1500  Metric:1
          RX packets:1 errors:0 dropped:0 overruns:0 frame:0
          TX packets:11 errors:0 dropped:0 overruns:0 carrier:0
          collisions:0 txqueuelen:1000
          RX bytes:229 (229.0 B)  TX bytes:2178 (2.1 KB)
          Interrupt:10
```

The lines you are most interested in are

```
RX packets:1 errors:0 dropped:0 overruns:0 frame:0
TX packets:11 errors:0 dropped:0 overruns:0 carrier:0
collisions:0 txqueuelen:1000
```

These lines will tell you about any errors on the device. If you start to see lots of errors here, then it's worth troubleshooting your physical network components. It's possible a network card, cable, or switch port is going bad.

Test Hard Drives

Of all of the hardware on your system, your hard drives are the components most likely to fail. Most hard drives these days support SMART, a system that can predict when a hard drive failure is imminent. To test your drives, first install the smartmontools package (sudo apt-get install smartmontools). Next, to test a particular drive's health, pass the smartctl tool the -H option along with the device to scan. Here's an example from a healthy drive:

```
$ sudo smartctl -H /dev/sda
smartctl version 5.37 [i686-pc-linux-gnu] Copyright (C) 2002-6 Bruce Allen
Home page is http://smartmontools.sourceforge.net/

SMART Health Status: OK
```

This can be useful when a particular drive is suspect, but generally speaking, it would be nice to constantly monitor your drives' health and report to you. The smartmontools package is already set up for this purpose. All you need to do is open the /etc/default/smartmontools file in a text editor and uncomment the line that says

```
#start_smartd=yes
```

so that it looks like

```
start_smartd=yes
```

Then the next time the system reboots, smartd will launch automatically. Any errors will be e-mailed to the root user on the system. If you want to manually start the service, you can type sudo service smartmontools start or sudo /etc/init.d/smartmontools start.

Test RAM

Some of the most irritating types of errors to troubleshoot are those caused by bad RAM. Often errors in RAM cause random mayhem on your machine with programs crashing for no good reason, or even random kernel panics. Ubuntu ships with an easy-to-use RAM testing tool called Memtest86+ that is not only installed by default, it's ready as a boot option. At boot time, hit the Esc key to see the full boot menu. One of the options in the GRUB menu is Memtest86+. Select that option and Memtest86+ will immediately launch and start scanning your RAM, as shown in Figure 11-1.

Memtest86+ runs through a number of exhaustive tests that can identify different types of RAM errors. On the top right-hand side you can see which test is currently being run along with its progress, and in the Pass field you can see how far along you are with the complete test. A thorough memory test can take hours to run, and I know some administrators with questionable RAM who let the test run overnight or over multiple days if necessary to get more than one complete test through. If Memtest86+ does find any errors, they will be reported in the results output at the bottom of the screen.

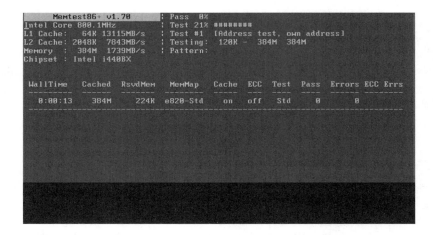

Figure 11-1 Memtest86+ RAM scan

## CHAPTER 12

Rescue and Recovery

YEARS OF LINUX ADMINISTRATION have convinced me that you learn the most about a system by repairing it when it is broken. Nothing pushes you to the limits of find arguments, dd commands, or general shell know-how like a critical system that no longer boots. I have had my share of broken systems over the years—some my fault and some not—and in this chapter I describe some of the recovery techniques I find I use over and over again.

There are three main recovery tools I describe in this chapter. The first is the recovery boot mode that is included with a default Ubuntu Server install. This mode provides the most limited set of recovery tools, as it requires a system that can at least partially boot. The second is the recovery CD mode that comes with your Ubuntu Server install CD. This option gives you all of the functionality of the recovery mode but adds extra recovery tools that you can run directly from the CD. Unfortunately, both of these tools are somewhat limited in the types of disasters from which they can recover, so the final section of the chapter will describe some recovery techniques that require a separate rescue disc. In this case I describe how to use the Ubuntu Desktop live CD for rescue, but you could use any live CD that allows you to install packages to the live CD such as Knoppix.

Ubuntu Recovery Mode

The Ubuntu recovery mode is a boot option that is included with your default server install. As you boot your system, GRUB will provide a basic prompt before it starts the boot process. After you press Shift, you will see that each kernel on your server has a recovery mode option beneath it. When you select the recovery mode, Ubuntu will start the normal boot process, but instead of launching all of the services on your system, once it completes you will be greeted with a recovery menu as shown in Figure 12-1. This menu provides you with six options:

- **resume**
  Choose this option to continue the boot process back to your regular system. You would pick this option if you accidentally chose the rescue mode or if you had successfully completed any fixes in the rescue mode and were ready to go back to the normal system.

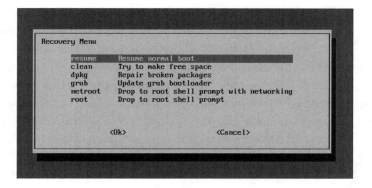

Figure 12-1 Ubuntu recovery mode menu

- **clean**
  The clean option attempts to clear up some free space on your system in case you have filled up / and can't access the system.

- **dpkg**
  This option will perform an `apt-get` update and upgrade and will attempt to repair any problems you might have with half-installed packages. You might choose this option if a package did not fully install or upgrade correctly and its init script is stalling out so the system can't boot fully. This choice could potentially fix the package problems.

- **grub**
  If you select this option, the rescue mode will update GRUB—handy if you have accidentally trashed your GRUB configuration.

- **netroot**
  This mode is the most useful of the options in this menu as it just drops you to a root shell on your booted server. I will spend the rest of this section focused on what you can recover with this option.

- **root**
  This mode is like the netroot option only without networking enabled.

In the rest of this section I discuss some potential rescue steps you can take once you choose the netroot option from the recovery menu. This drops you to a root-owned shell on the system, brings up your network, and is a bit further along the boot process. This recovery mode requires that you can at least partially boot and mount the root file system; depending on what is broken on your system, this may not be possible. If you can't boot into this mode and need to recover a system, move on to the Ubuntu Server Recovery CD section later in this chapter.

The rescue root shell is both limited and unlimited. It is limited in that there are no apparent automated tools to recover common problems on the system; however, it is unlimited in that you have full access to any tools already on your server. Usually you go into a rescue mode like this because your system won't fully boot, so I cover some of the common problems you might want to fix in this mode.

File Systems Won't Mount

The file systems in /etc/fstab generally are mounted as the system boots. If a file system won't mount at boot, you often need to drop to a rescue shell so you can either repair the file system or correct problems in /etc/fstab so it can mount. Of course, if the problem file system is the root file system, you probably won't even be able to get to this rescue mode, so skip ahead to the Ubuntu Server Rescue CD section.

File System Corruption   There are a number of scenarios when a file system might get corrupted through either a hard reboot or some other error. In these cases the default fsck that runs at boot might not be sufficient to repair the file system. Be sure before you run fsck on a file system that it is unmounted. You can run the mount command in the shell to see all mounted file systems and type umount *<devicename>* to unmount any that are mounted (except the root file system). We are assuming that since this file system is preventing you from completing the boot process, it isn't mounted. In this example let's assume that your /home directory is mounted on a separate partition at /dev/sda5. To scan and repair any file system errors on this file system, type

```
# fsck -y -C /dev/sda5
```

The -y option will automatically answer Yes to repair file system errors. Otherwise, if you do have any errors, you will find yourself hitting Y over and over again. The -C option gives you a nice progress bar so you can see how far along fsck is. A complete fsck can take some time on a large file system, so the progress bar can be handy.

Sometimes file systems are so corrupted that the primary superblock cannot be found. Luckily, file systems create backup superblocks in case this happens, so you can tell fsck to use this superblock instead. Now I don't expect you to automatically know the location of your backup superblock. You can use the mke2fs tool with the -n option to list all of the superblocks on a file system.

NOTE   **Warning**
Be sure to use the -n option here! Otherwise mke2fs will simply format your file system and erase all of your old data.

```
# mke2fs -n /dev/sda5
```

Once you see the list of superblocks in the output, choose one and pass it as an argument to the -b option for fsck:

```
# fsck -b 8193 -y -C /dev/sda5
```

When you specify an alternate superblock, fsck will automatically update your primary superblock after it completes the file system check.

Fstab Mistakes or UUID Changed   Another common problem you might face is that a file system won't mount because of a mistake in your /etc/fstab file. It might be that you migrated a file system from one partition to another and forgot to update its UUID in /etc/fstab. If this happens for the root partition, the same steps apply, but you will likely have to either run the commands from a rescue CD or edit the GRUB prompt at boot time so that the root= option points to the partition's device name instead of the UIID.

In any case, to discover the UUID for any file system, type

```
# ls -l /dev/disk/by-uuid
```

This directory provides symlinks between UUIDs and their partitions, so it's easy to see what is assigned where. Just make a note of the correct UUID, open /etc/fstab in a text editor, and update the UUID reference.

Problem Init Scripts

Sometimes an init script on a server stalls out. It could be that it requires a network connection that isn't available, or it could be any sort of other problem. No matter what the problem is, if an init script isn't written to automatically time out, when it stalls it can completely tie up the rest of the boot process. In these cases you might want to temporarily disable the init script from starting at boot time so you can fully boot the system and solve the problem.

The problem init script is likely in one of two locations. If it is a system init script, it will be located under /etc/rcS.d. Otherwise, since the default runlevel on an Ubuntu server is runlevel 2, it will likely be found under /etc/rc2.d. In either case, to disable an init script, locate it under one of these directories and then rename it so that the S at the beginning is now a D. For instance, if I was having some sort of problem with custom programs I put in my rc.local script that tied up the boot process, I would type the following to disable it:

```
# mv /etc/rc2.d/S99rc.local /etc/rc2.d/D99rc.local
```

Now I could resume the boot process normally and look into the problem init script. Once I finish, I just rename the file again and replace the D with an S.

Reset Passwords

A final system problem that might put you in a rescue mode is the situation where you have forgotten your user's password or you are taking over a system from a previous administrator and don't know the user password. In either case it is trivial to reset the password in the recovery shell. Just type passwd along with the name of the user to reset:

```
# passwd ubuntu

Enter new UNIX password:

Retype new UNIX password:
passwd: password updated successfully
```

If you get an error that the authentication token lock is busy, you likely forgot to remount the file system read/write, so first type

```
# mount -o remount,rw /
```

Then run your password command.

Once you are finished with any recovery from the root shell, you can type exit to return to the rescue menu, where you can choose to resume the boot process.

Ubuntu Server Recovery CD

While the Ubuntu recovery mode can help you fix certain problems, it requires that GRUB functions and that you can get through at least the beginning phase of the boot process. If your root file system is corrupted or GRUB stops working, you will need some other method to access and repair your server. The good news is that if you still have an Ubuntu Server install CD around, it has a built-in recovery mode. This recovery mode allows you to access the root file system as with the GRUB recovery mode, but since it boots from its own kernel and provides its own set of Linux tools, you can also use it to recover from problems with a root file system.

Unfortunately, the Ubuntu Server recovery CD has its own set of limitations. Essentially you will have access to a BusyBox shell prompt with a limited set of recovery tools. While you can certainly repair file systems and restore GRUB, if you want to do more sophisticated recovery such as deleted file recovery or partition table restoration, you will need a more advanced rescue disc that either includes tools like sleuthkit, gpart, and ddrescue or allows you to install these packages from the live CD. In this section I will discuss some of the situations beyond the GRUB recovery mode where you can use the Ubuntu Server recovery CD to repair your system.

Boot into the Recovery CD

To boot into the recovery CD, set your server to boot from the CD-ROM drive and insert the Ubuntu Server install CD. After you choose a language, you will see the standard installer screen. Instead of choosing the install option, use the arrow keys to select "Rescue a broken system" and then hit Enter. This will enter into a special recovery system on the installer.

After the recovery CD boots, you will be prompted with a lot of the same questions you might have seen in a standard server install such as language, keyboard, and time zone questions. Don't worry; this won't install over the top of the system (note the Rescue mode title in the top left of the display). Just answer the questions up until you see the prompt to select the root partition. Ideally you will already know which partition is the root partition, but if not I suppose at this point you will need to perform some trial and error until you locate it.

After you choose a root file system, you will see the main recovery operations menu as shown in Figure 12-2. The options are pretty self-explanatory:

▪ **Execute a shell in /dev/ubuntu/root**
This first option will open a shell in your root file system. Here I put /dev/ubuntu/root, but this menu will point to the partition you choose. This choice gives you essentially the same recovery options as in the GRUB recovery mode, as you can run any number of commands from inside the root file system such as package managers or other system tools.

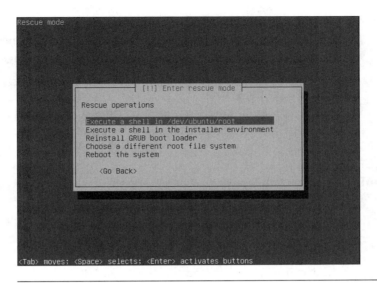

Figure 12-2 Recovery operations menu

▪ **Execute a shell in the installer environment**

The bulk of your recovery work will likely occur from this option.
Choose this and you will drop to a BusyBox shell on the install CD
itself. The root file system will be mounted under /target so you
could potentially edit configuration files from this mode. The
advantage to this mode is that it exists outside of the actual root
file system, so you can do things such as run fsck on the root partition—something that wouldn't be allowed if you had booted into
the system itself.

▪ **Reinstall GRUB boot loader**

One of the most common reasons why you might boot into a rescue
CD is that GRUB is broken. Without GRUB you can't boot into the
system without some serious Linux kung fu. Choose this option and
an automated script will reinstall GRUB onto the disk or partition of
your choice. Most people tend to install GRUB on the master boot
record, so when you are prompted for a location to install GRUB you
will probably choose (hd0). Note that if the rescue CD can't locate the
grub configuration files under /boot/grub, this won't appear.

- **Choose a different root file system**
  This option is pretty self-explanatory. If you happened to choose the wrong root file system, this option will let you change it.

- **Reboot the system**
  Here is another self-explanatory option. Once you are finished with your system recovery, choose this option to reboot.

NOTE When you are within either of the shell environments you can type exit to return to the rescue operations menu.

Recover GRUB

I have already mentioned the "Reinstall GRUB boot loader" option from the rescue operations menu. This will reinstall GRUB to the disk or partition of your choice, but sometimes GRUB itself is installed but its configuration file is missing or corrupted. When this happens, instead of a GRUB menu at boot time, you may not see anything at all. To fix this problem, choose the menu option to execute a shell within your root partition. Once there, run

```
# update-grub
```

This option will create a new /boot/grub/grub.cfg file based on your available kernels. Once it completes, you can type exit to return to the main menu and reboot the system.

Repair the Root File System

Typically the recovery CD will attempt to mount the root file system if possible. If it can mount the root file system, then you will not be able to unmount it and run any tools such as fsck on it. Of course, if the rescue CD were able to mount the file system, you wouldn't need to fsck it now, would you? If the root file system is corrupted and the rescue CD can't mount it, then drop to the installer shell and run

```
# fsck -y /dev/sda1
```

Replace /dev/sda1 with the path to your root partition. If fsck complains about a bad superblock, follow the steps in the File System Corruption section above under Ubuntu Recovery Mode. Otherwise, depending on how damaged your file system is, you might see fsck output the errors that it finds as it attempts to repair them.

In addition to the specific rescue steps I listed above, you should be able to perform all of the recovery steps from the GRUB recovery mode. Just choose the "Execute a shell in /dev/ubuntu/root" (it will replace /dev/ubuntu/root with the root partition you selected) from the recovery operations menu and follow the same steps.

Ubuntu Desktop Live CD

There are certain system rescues you need to perform that require you to boot outside of the server itself. Any system imaging, root partition fsck commands, or any other time that / needs to be unmounted you will need some sort of rescue disc. While I have already mentioned how you can use the Ubuntu Server install CD as a rescue disc, unfortunately you are limited by the tools present on that CD. There are a number of different live CDs available that provide the same set of tools, such as Knoppix and DSL, but since I assume it's more likely you will have an Ubuntu Desktop install CD around and it doubles as a live CD, I discuss some more advanced recovery techniques you can perform from the CD.

Boot the Live CD

The first step is to boot the live CD into the standard GNOME desktop. Don't worry if your server doesn't have a sophisticated video card since basically everything I describe can be done from the command line.

Add the Universe Repository

Once the live CD boots into the desktop, you need to add the universe repository to its list of package repositories. All of the tools I use here come from packages in the universe repository, so either click System_ Administration_Software Sources and make sure that the Community-maintained Open Source software (universe) option is checked, or open a terminal

(Applications_Accessories_Terminal) and then as root edit /etc/apt/ sources.list in your favorite text editor and change

```
deb http://us.archive.ubuntu.com/ubuntu lucid main restricted
```

to

```
deb http://us.archive.ubuntu.com/ubuntu lucid main restricted universe
```

Of course, if you are running a newer live CD than Lucid, you might see some other name here, so change the example to suit your Ubuntu live CD. Then from the same terminal run

```
$ sudo apt-get update
```

to update the list of available packages. Now you can install the tools for any of the following rescue tips.

Recover Deleted Files

It has happened to the best of us. I think every sysadmin has accidentally deleted the wrong file at one point in his or her career. For a long time I thought that once a file was deleted under Linux there was no way it could be recovered, but it turns out that's not entirely true. When you delete a file on Linux, the file system returns those blocks to the available space. Until another file uses those blocks, the data from the old file is still there and potentially recoverable. The key is to stop writing to that file system as soon as you can once you delete a file. That way you reduce the probability that the data will be overwritten.

In this example I assume you have halted the machine with the deleted file and have booted the Ubuntu live CD. Once the CD boots and you have added the universe repository, use the package manager to install the sleuthkit package or open a terminal and type

```
$ sudo apt-get install sleuthkit
```

Sleuth Kit is a set of forensics tools to aid investigation of a break-in on a system. Recovery of deleted files is a valuable thing for a forensics investigation, and Sleuth Kit has provided a pair of tools, fls (forensics ls) and icat (inode cat), that have deleted file recovery features.

For this example we assume that you have accidentally deleted the /etc/shadow file on your root file system /dev/sda1. Because these tools copy recovered files to another file system, you need to make sure that you have enough space to store them. Since /etc/shadow is a small file, the RAM disk used by the live CD is enough to store it, but if you need to restore a large number of files, or files that take up a lot of space, you will want to attach some sort of external storage or NFS share. I store everything under /home/ubuntu/, but if you mounted a USB drive at /media/disk, for instance, just replace occurrences of /home/ubuntu with /media/disk.

The first step is to create a directory to store the fls output and any files you recover. In this example I will call the directory recovery and put it under /home/ubuntu. Once the directory is created, use the fls tool to scan /dev/sda1 for any deleted files and output the results in a text file:

```
$ mkdir /home/ubuntu/recovery
$ sudo fls -f ext -d -r -p /dev/sda1 > /home/ubuntu/recovery/
  deleted_files.txt
```

Since the fls command has to scan through the entire /dev/sda1 partition, it might take some time to complete, depending on the size of the drive. To get more information about each of the fls arguments, you can type man fls in a terminal to see the full manual.

Once the command completes, I can open the deleted_files.txt file in a text editor and I will see a list of files and directories like the following:

```
d/d * 458:   etc/skel
r/r * 2094:  etc/shadow
r/r * 5423:  etc/wgetrc
```

The first column tells whether the file in question is a directory (d/d) or a file (r/r). The numerical column tells which inode this particular file uses, and finally you can see the full path to the file in the final column. Since we want to restore the etc/shadow file, we need to locate and copy inode 2094.

Sleuth Kit provides the `icat` tool for this purpose—it is like the `cat` command only it accepts inodes as arguments. To restore this file, I type

```
$ sudo icat -f ext -r -s /dev/sda1 2094 > /home/ubuntu/recovery/
  shadow
```

If the file is indeed recoverable, once this command completes I will see a copy of my shadow file under /home/ubuntu/recovery/shadow. Then I could mount the /dev/sda1 file system from the rescue disk and restore /etc/shadow from here. Now if you wanted to recover more than one file, either you could run this command multiple times and restore files one at a time or you could write a script to do it for you. There are a number of such scripts online, and the following is based off of a script originally found at http://forums.gentoo.org/viewtopic-t-365703.html that I then tidied up and improved:

```
#!/bin/bash

DISK=/dev/sda1 # disk to scan
RESTOREDIR=/home/ubuntu/recovery # directory to restore to

mkdir -p "$RESTOREDIR"
cat $1 |
while read line; do
    filetype=`echo "$line" | awk {'print $1'}`
    filenode=`echo "$line" | awk {'print $3'}`
    filenode=${filenode%:}
    filenode=${filenode%(*}
    filename=`echo "$line" | cut -f 2`

    echo "$filename"

    if [ $filetype == "d/d" ]; then
      mkdir -p "$RESTOREDIR/$filename"
    else
      mkdir -p "$RESTOREDIR/`dirname $filename`"
      icat -f ext -r -s "$DISK" "$filenode" > "$RESTOREDIR/$filename"
    fi
done
```

Save this file to /home/ubuntu/restore and change the DISK and RESTOREDIR variables to match the partition you want to scan and the directory you

want to restore into, respectively. Then to use the script, give it execute permissions and run it with the path to your complete list of deleted files as an
argument:

```
$ sudo chmod a+x /home/ubuntu/restore
$ sudo /home/ubuntu/restore /home/ubuntu/recovery/deleted_files.txt
```

The script will then systematically go through all of the files in the deleted_
files.txt file and attempt to restore them to RESTOREDIR. It will create directories as necessary as well, so once it is finished you should see a directory
structure matching that of your deleted files within RESTOREDIR.

Restore the Partition Table

The partition table is a 64-byte section of the 512 bytes at the beginning of a
hard drive known as the master boot record. These 64 bytes contain the settings for any primary or extended partitions you have created on the disk.
It's easy to take the partition table for granted. After all, it does take some
effort to erase or corrupt it. Then again, all it would take is an fdisk command on the wrong drive to make a hard drive unreadable by your server.

The good news is that even if a partition table is erased, the data for each
partition is still on the disk. All you need to do is figure out where each
partition begins and ends and you can reconstruct the partition table and
restore your data. Of course, this can be rather difficult to do manually, but
Linux has a tool called gpart (short for Guess Partition) that can do the
hard work for you.

The way that gpart works is to scan through the entire disk looking for
sections that match the beginning or end of a certain type of partition.
When it finds these sections, it makes a note of them and moves on. By the
time gpart is finished, it has what it believes is a complete partition table
for your disk.

Before I go into how to restore a partition table with gpart, it's worth dis-
cussing some of gpart's limitations. The primary limitation it has is with
extended partitions. While gpart is good at finding primary partitions,
extended partitions are more difficult to identify, so if your disk has extended

partitions you might get incomplete results. Also, gpart sometimes can be slightly off on where a partition begins (or more often) ends. I've seen gpart miss the end of a partition by a megabyte or two, but since most of us build partitions back to back, typically these sorts of small errors are easy to correct manually.

To install gpart on the live CD, either use the graphical package manager to install the gpart package or open a terminal and type

```
$ sudo apt-get install gpart
```

Once gpart is installed, run it in a terminal as root and pass it the drive to scan as an argument:

```
$ sudo gpart /dev/sda
```

Of course, replace /dev/sda with the path to your device. Once gpart is done, it outputs its results to the screen but does not write anything to disk. This way you can examine its output and see if it matches what you expect. Once you approve of the output, run gpart again, only this time with the -W option so it writes its changes to disk:

```
$ sudo gpart -W /dev/sda /dev/sda
```

The -W option takes a disk to write to as an argument, which is why you see /dev/sda here twice. Once gpart is finished scanning, you will be prompted to edit its results. In my opinion the gpart editor is a bit more difficult to use than fdisk or cfdisk, so I typically write the changes to disk and then do any minor corrections with fdisk or cfdisk. Remember, you can shift around the partition table and write it to disk without directly impacting your data, so it's OK to have gpart write an incorrect table that you then follow up and correct.

Rescue Dying Drives

If you have read Chapter 11, Troubleshooting, you will be acquainted with Smartmontools. This package can scan your hard drives and report when any of them appears unhealthy. Of course, what do you do when a hard drive is unhealthy or, worse, is so unhealthy that it will no longer mount? Usually the longer an unhealthy drive runs, the more data is lost, so you want to react quickly. Ubuntu has an excellent tool called ddrescue that you can use to create an image of a drive even if it has numerous errors.

The way that ddrescue works is to scan through a drive bit by bit. When it encounters errors on the drive, it makes a note of them and skips ahead. Since bad blocks are often in clusters, this means that ddrescue potentially skips ahead to good data. Once ddrescue finishes scanning the entire drive, it will divide and conquer the remaining bad block clusters until it has attempted to recover the entire drive. With this algorithm you have the best chance of recovering good data instead of spending all of your time trying to recover a cluster of bad blocks at the beginning of the disk, only to have the drive ultimately fail.

NOTE   **Why Not dd?**
The traditional tool that one might use to image a drive under Linux is dd. Unfortunately, dd is not ideally suited for hard drives with errors. By default when dd encounters an error, it will simply exit out of the program. While you can tell dd to ignore errors, doing so means it will simply skip that particular block and not write anything, so that you could end up with an image that is smaller than the original. These reasons, combined with the block cluster skipping algorithm and progress output, make ddrescue the better choice for this task.

To install ddrescue on your Ubuntu live CD, either install the ddrescue package using the graphical package manager, or open a terminal and type

```
$ sudo apt-get install ddrescue
```

Before you image a dying drive, make sure that you can store it somewhere. The ddrescue tool can image a hard drive or partition to either another hard drive or a file, but you need to make sure that the other device is equal to or greater in size than the drive you are imaging. The great thing about this is that you don't even necessarily need to connect extra storage to your server. If you have an NFS server with enough capacity, you can mount the NFS share on your live CD and have ddrescue image to that. For this example I assume that you want to image one partition, /dev/sda1, on your server, you have attached an external USB drive to the server, and the desktop has found it and mounted it under /media/disk. To image the drive you simply run ddrescue and list the drive to image and the location to image to as arguments:

```
$ sudo ddrescue /dev/sda1 /media/disk/sda1_image.img /media/disk/
  sda1_image_logfile
```

Replace /dev/sda1 with the partition or complete drive you want to image, and /media/disk/sda1_image.img with the mount point and file you want to image to. If you wanted to image from /dev/sda1 to /dev/sdb1, you would just replace /media/disk/sda1_image.img with /dev/sdb1. Notice that I added a third argument, /media/disk/sda1_image_logfile. The third argument tells ddrescue where to store an optional log file of its progress. With this log file in place you can actually stop ddrescue at any time, and when you start it again it can resume where it left off.

The great thing about ddrescue is that it provides you with a nice progress bar so you can keep track of how much longer it has to go. That, combined with its resume feature, means if you do need to interrupt it for some reason, you know you can go back and complete the job later.

NOTE   **Image Drives or Partitions?**
You may have noticed that in my example I chose to image a single partition instead of the entire drive. I did this because partition images are much easier to fsck and mount loop-back when you image to a file. Generally speaking, it's much simpler if you image each partition on a disk one at a time, especially if you image to a file. If you plan to image directly to another drive, then image the entire drive since you can then easily access each partition individually.

Once ddrescue completes, check the image you have created for any file system errors by running fsck on it:

```
$ sudo fsck -y -C /media/disk/sda1_image.img
```

Once fsck has completed, you can mount the image loopback and recover any files you need from the disk or, alternatively, you can use a tool like dd to copy this image to yet another drive. To mount the drive loopback, I create a temporary mount point at /mnt/temp and mount the drive there:

```
$ sudo mkdir /mnt/temp
$ sudo mount -o loop /media/disk/sda1_image.img /mnt/temp
```

From here I can copy particular files from /mnt/temp to some other storage or otherwise just confirm that the data on the drive is intact. Later I can use a regular imaging tool like dd or even rsync to copy the data from this file back to a partition.

## CHAPTER 13

Help and Resources

YOU HAVE UBUNTU SERVER installed, or you are beginning the process of doing so. The system is new to you, and you have questions or need help. Where do you turn? What are your options?

That is the whole point of this chapter: You aren't on your own. Whether you work for a major corporation in a large industrial setting or you are a hobbyist setting up your first server in your basement, there are help options available that are suitable to your needs.

Paid Support from Canonical

Most system administrators prefer to do their own support, at least to the extent possible. We are a unique breed who usually feel as if we can solve any problem, and if we can't, then we can learn how. But occasionally we are wrong, and we need help.

Corporate managers want to minimize risk. The idea that something could go wrong, even when the chances are small, is not something they want to consider without a contingency plan in place. Network and system downtime equals lost opportunities and possibly lost income. These guys and gals want to have some assurance of a safety net.

Canonical, the company that stands behind Ubuntu, offers a paid professional support option that is perfect for these instances. They promise to give quick and quality assistance with installation and deployment, security and performance optimization, protection against IP infringement claims, and more.

There are paid support options for servers, desktop systems (for when you convince the powers that be to allow you to migrate the entire corporate infrastructure after your successful and amazing server migration), and thin clients/clusters. You can pay for support during business hours, or full 24x7. (There is no per-incident support option available at this time.) The options are extensive and easily adapted to the needs of anyone from small businesses to large corporations. You can find out more at *www.ubuntu.com/support/paid/* or *www.canonical.com/services/support*. Support assistance can be requested using the telephone, the Web, or e-mail.

One of the things that makes this support attractive for some is that there is guaranteed help available for software upgrades. Even with paid support from Canonical, the software used is the standard Ubuntu releases, either the most current Long-Term Support (LTS) release or the most current regular release. There is no difference between what you get with the paid support option and what would otherwise be used, except that you have the company that funds and organizes much of the Ubuntu development process standing behind you in case you encounter problems. As is the case for everyone using Ubuntu, security updates are guaranteed for a regular release for 18 months. An LTS release receives security updates for a longer period of time, three years on the desktop and five years on the server.

Paid support customers will receive a wonderful tool called Landscape free of charge. This is a system management and monitoring service that allows you to manage multiple Ubuntu machines at the same time. Landscape allows the administrator to perform software updates, manage users and processes, monitor resource usage on multiple machines, and do far more just as easily as it would be done on one machine, perhaps more easily since it uses a simple Web interface. Landscape is also available by subscription for customers who do not need paid support. Find out more at www.canonical.com/projects/landscape.

Forums

The Ubuntu community offers free, volunteer support via Web forums. Anyone may sign up for a free account and ask questions that are read and answered by other Ubuntu users. The main support forum is found at http://ubuntuforums.org and at the time of this writing has nearly 1 million registered members.

It is likely that you will find the answer to any common problem you have by just searching the forum. In most cases, someone has already asked the same question and received a great answer that will be applicable to your situation. If not, the community there is friendly and welcoming to newcomers, as well as filled with knowledgeable and helpful people, so feel free to register for an account and ask away.

Internet Relay Chat

In the event that you have an urgent need for help, or just prefer real-time discussion, you can use Internet Relay Chat (IRC). Set your IRC client to point to the Freenode network at irc.freenode.net, and pick a channel that is best suited for your question.

The best place to start for general help with Ubuntu is #ubuntu, but there is also an excellent channel available dedicated to running an Ubuntu server at #ubuntu-server. There are helpful and knowledgeable users in each of these channels and others. You can find a full list of current channels and help getting started at ***http://help.ubuntu.com/community/InternetRelayChat***.

To get started using IRC on an Ubuntu desktop machine, you can install a program called XChat, which is available for installation from the software repositories. Once you have it installed, you can launch it in Ubuntu from the menu at Applications Internet XChat IRC.

The first time you start XChat, you will be asked to select the network(s) to connect to. For our purposes, select Ubuntu Servers from the list and click Connect, as in Figure 13-1.

Next, if you are running on an Ubuntu desktop computer, you will automatically be logged in to the main Ubuntu support channel, #ubuntu. You can begin asking questions here by typing something in the box next to your username at the bottom of the XChat screen and pressing Enter, as seen in Figure 13-2.

To leave a channel, right-click on the channel name in the list of channels and select Close (Figure 13-3). Text commands in IRC have been standardized for years and may be issued from the text entry line, the same place where you would otherwise type your questions. Commands are prefaced by /. For example, you can type /part in the bottom box to issue a command to leave the channel.

You may join a channel using a text command as well, if you know the channel name, as shown in Figure 13-4.

Figure 13-1 XChat Network List, the first screen you will see

Figure 13-2 The main XChat screen

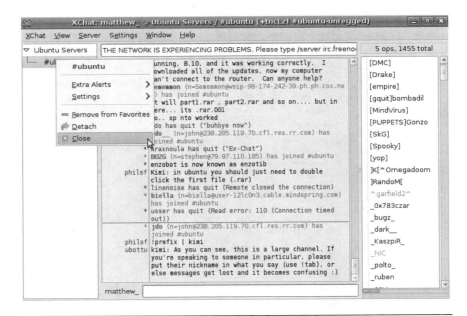

Figure 13-3 Leaving a channel in Xchat

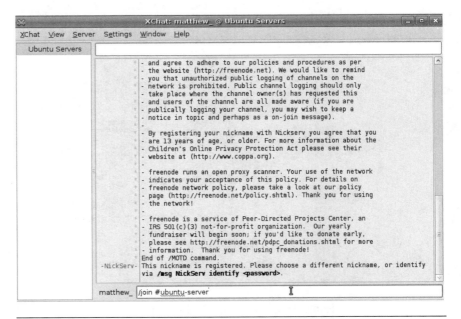

Figure 13-4 Joining a channel in XChat using a text command

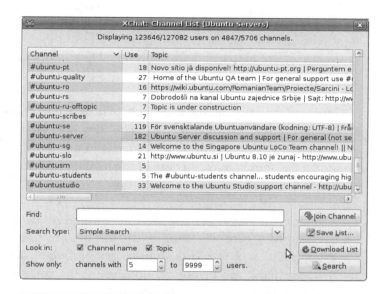

Figure 13-5 Joining a channel in XChat using the graphical channel list

You may also join a channel and find a list of available channels via the XChat menu at Server List of Channels... This brings up a new window, which starts out mostly empty. To get a list of channels on your current server, click Download List at the lower right and after a few moments your window will look like Figure 13-5. You may then scroll up and down to find a channel that interests you, such as #ubuntu-server. Select it with a left click, and click the Join Channel button near the lower right.

When you are done, you may quit XChat from the menu at XChat Quit or by typing /quit and closing the program.

Mailing Lists

Most of the development and other work that goes into creating the Ubuntu distribution and making it a technical success happens on mailing lists. These are good places to ask questions in a place that will be seen by the developer community, and a great place to read continuing technical discussions or receive notices and announcements, but they are not a great place for general assistance.

The developers welcome useful feedback and interesting contributions to discussions but are focused on making Ubuntu the best it can be. Other resources are better and are more highly recommended for immediate help needs.

More information about mailing lists is available at *www.ubuntu.com/support/community/mailinglists*. The first link on that page discusses mailing list etiquette. Reading, understanding, and conforming to those guidelines should make any use of the mailing lists a pleasant and beneficial experience.

A full list of available mailing lists can be found at *http://lists.ubuntu.com*. User support generally happens in the ubuntu-users support-focused mailing list at *https://lists.ubuntu.com/mailman/listinfo/ubuntu-users*. Be aware that if you sign up for this mailing list, you can expect to receive at least 200 e-mails a day just from this list.

Online Documentation

There are two sets of documentation available for Ubuntu: official and community.

The official set comes directly from and is maintained by the Ubuntu Documentation Project. This is pulled together by members of the Ubuntu Documentation Team and includes information that is vetted for accuracy and usefulness. It is shipped with each of the desktop versions of Ubuntu, made available both in the main desktop menu as well as online for all users at *https://help.ubuntu.com/*.

The community documentation is not intended so much for user support as to provide a way for interested users to discuss ideas and store information for various teams (such as the LoCos, discussed next, or the Documentation Team that was just mentioned). Even so, it often contains very interesting and useful tidbits that make it worth mentioning. You can investigate further at *https://wiki.ubuntu.com*.

Localhost Documentation

There are already several pieces of wonderful documentation available on your server. When a package is installed from the Ubuntu repositories, it usually includes at least one, and often several, forms of documentation that you can use. I discuss two of the most common and most important: man pages and doc files.

Man pages are included with nearly every command and with many programs when they are installed. They are not intended to be how-to guides or hold-your-hand-style introductions but are generally concise yet full guides to the syntax of any command or program usage from the command line. They are generally the easiest way to find out all of the options available for anything you might want to try to do and are also a fabulous way to quickly refresh your memory when you can't quite remember the options you wanted to use while doing an `rsync` backup, as in `man rsync`. If you know the command or program you want to use, starting with the man page is always a good bet.

Man pages use a standard organization that is clear, making it easy to find the details you need quickly. Not all man pages use every section, but these are the most common sections you will find. A man page always begins with the NAME of the command and a quick one-sentence description of what it does. This is followed by a longer SYNOPSIS of the command that gives standardized examples of how to use it. Following this is a DESCRIPTION section that chronicles in greater detail what the command or program is designed to do and outlines its features. You may find a GENERAL section after this, which gives other details that are interesting and useful but which may not be vital for understanding what you need (that doesn't mean it isn't worth reading, though). Often this is followed by a SETUP section, which may either describe installation and configuration or tell you where to get this information. The most important section for most needs is USAGE, where the man page will discuss specifically how to use the program to do a task and may include several good examples. Some commands and packages include a DOCUMENTATION section that explicitly states where to find more information on your localhost. You may also find sections like ADVANCED USAGE, EXAMPLES, OPTIONS, and a SUMMARY, each of which is extremely useful when present.

Doc files are a great resource, especially when you have installed a new package and aren't sure what to do next. One of the first things that many system administrators do when installing a new program on an Ubuntu server is read the README.Debian.gz file at /usr/share/doc/*<packagename>*. For example, you could use `sudo zless /usr/share/doc/apache2.2-common/README.Debian.gz` to read the Apache 2.2 common documentation, and hit *Q* to quit when done. For some programs and packages, there may be only one or two docs available, but others have many great ones, sometimes in subdirectories, like the example of an apache2.conf file found at /usr/share/doc/apache2.2-common/examples/apache2/apache2.conf.gz.

Spend some time digging around any time you have a question and you may discover the answer without having to ask anyone or even looking for documentation outside of your server.

Local Community Teams

Some of us prefer face-to-face interaction. This option is one of the more enjoyable and useful for nonprofessional uses, like the hobby-level enthusiast who has a server at home or the university student looking to find others with whom to learn. The Local Community, or LoCo Teams, operate all over the world. Much of their planning and coordination is done online in their own mailing lists, IRC channels, and forums (often as subforums in the main Ubuntu forums discussed earlier). In many places, LoCo Teams operate in other languages, which may be better for users whose native language is other than English.

LoCo Teams often arrange gatherings to discuss new developments, to help one another with technical issues, or just to have fun spending time with people who share similar interests. Many hold special gatherings around the time of new Ubuntu version releases called "release parties" or "installfests" to celebrate the accomplishment of a completed release cycle, install or upgrade their operating systems at the same time, and help users install Ubuntu on their equipment (if needed). More information about LoCo Teams can be found at ***https://wiki.ubuntu.com/LoCoTeamList***.

Other Languages

Several of the resources already mentioned have options in other languages for people who do not speak English as their native tongue. One of the initial and continuing focuses of Ubuntu as a distribution is to make Ubuntu available to as many people as possible worldwide, and this means translating the interfaces for the software into other languages as well as providing means for non-English speakers to find quality support in their native language.

The job is not yet complete, but Ubuntu has support and installation options available in a very large number of languages. Most of the resources just listed include other language options on their Web pages. These include forums, IRC channels, LoCo Teams, and more. For more information look at *www.ubuntu.com/support/community/locallanguage*.

Tech Answers System (Launchpad)

Canonical is involved in projects outside of Ubuntu as well, including their wonderful collaboration and code hosting platform service, Launchpad (*https://launchpad.net*), which is used by a large number of software projects, including Ubuntu. Launchpad provides a central location for code development, bug reporting, and even questions and answers. It isn't as complete or as user-friendly as a Web forum, for example, but it is an excellent resource for more advanced users.

Here is the URL for Ubuntu-related questions: *https://answers.launchpad.net/ubuntu*.

Bug Reporting

Sometimes you encounter problems that are not covered in any documentation anywhere and for which you cannot seem to find help. It may be that you have discovered a flaw, or bug, in a program. Congratulations! To assist the developers in their task and desire to make Ubuntu work as well as possible, you can file a bug report. This will directly inform the people who maintain the specific package about a problem. They will then examine the report, try to reproduce the behavior, and, if it is confirmed as a problem, get to work on trying to fix it.

To file a bug report for Ubuntu, you first need a Launchpad account. Launchpad is the system that is used to track bugs and help with other areas of development. You can sign up for an account by clicking the Register link at ***https://launchpad.net*** and following the instructions you are given. It is a useful and versatile system. I focus here on one small aspect of how it may be used.

Once you have your Launchpad account, open ***https://bugs/launchpad .net/ubuntu*** to go to the main page for the Ubuntu project. From there, you can search current bugs to see if there is one that is similar or identical to what you are experiencing. If so, feel free to add your comments to currently existing bug reports to help confirm the problem or add information that may help the developers understand and fix it.

If you don't find anything that fits your issue, you can file a new bug report by clicking the red Report a Bug button in the middle of the page. You will be given a text box in which to write a short summary of the problem, preferably something short, clear, and descriptive, but less than a sentence: for example, would be "LDTP server crashes when running the update-manager testcase." Click Continue.

You will be given a list of bugs found by Launchpad that may be similar. Take a look. If one is the same as what you are experiencing, you can subscribe to receive notifications as the bug report is updated with new information, work-arounds, or a solution. If not, check "No, I'd like to report a new bug" to move to the next step.

You will be asked in which package you found the bug. If you know, you can enter it to assist the developers. If you don't, you can click "I don't know" and let them try to figure it out from the summary you will write under "Further Information."

In the section titled "Further information:" enter a clear description of the problem, using as much specific information as you can without rambling. You should include things like the steps to take to reproduce the unexpected behavior, and an outline of what you were doing and trying to accomplish at the time. You may be asked for further information later. There is also a nice list of guidelines at the bottom of this page to help you know what information to include to make your bug report as useful, and as likely to receive assistance, as possible. You can also include an attachment, like a text file copy of a configuration file or error log. When you are done, click the Submit Bug Report button at the bottom of the page to finish the process.

Summary

Switching to a new system can be overwhelming. Using an established system is not a guarantee that you will never have questions. In each instance, there are times when support is needed. This chapter described several wonderful options. For further information, check the official Ubuntu Web site for the most up-to-date list of support options at *www.ubuntu .com/support*.

## CHAPTER 14

Basic Linux Administration

IN CHAPTER 2, Essential System Administration, I discussed some core tools any administrator should know. In this chapter I expand on that foundation and describe more basic shell concepts and tools. Then I will talk about some different Linux file types: hard and symbolic links and device files. Finally I describe how to use cron and at to schedule programs to run at different times.

Shell Globs

When you work on the command line, you often need to run a command against more than one file at a time. For instance, you might want to copy all of the files from one directory to another, or you might want to move only the files that match a particular pattern. While you could certainly type each of these filenames one at a time, the bash shell provides a few different shortcuts to the process with shell globs and other pattern matching.

A shell glob is a special character that you can think of like a wildcard. For instance, you can use the ? symbol in place of any single character. Let's say that I have a directory with five files, a.txt, b.txt, c.txt, d.doc, and e.tar:

```
$ ls
a.txt  b.txt  c.txt  d.doc  e.tar
```

If I wanted to see only the .txt files, I could type all of filenames by hand:

```
$ ls a.txt b.txt c.txt
a.txt  b.txt  c.txt
```

or I could use ? as a wildcard:

```
$ ls ?.txt
a.txt  b.txt  c.txt
```

You can use multiple shell globs as well, so if I also wanted to match e.tar, I could type:

```
$ ls ?.t??
a.txt  b.txt  c.txt  e.tar
```

Probably one of the most useful shell globs is the * symbol. This wildcard matches any number of characters, including zero. In this example, let's say I had the following files in my directory:

```
$ ls
aa.txt  ac.txt  a.txt  b.txt  c.txt  d.doc  e.tar
```

If I wanted to list only the files that begin with a, I could type

```
$ ls a*
aa.txt  ac.txt  a.txt
```

Note that the * symbol acts as a wildcard for a number of different characters in the filename. If I wanted to move these files to the /tmp directory, for instance, I could type

```
$ mv a* /tmp/
```

If, instead, I wanted to move all of the .txt files to the /tmp directory, I would type

```
$ mv *.txt /tmp/
```

Unlike with the ? wildcard, when I use * I also match aa.txt and ac.txt.

Regular Expressions

Regular expressions is probably too dense a topic for a chapter like this, but essentially it is a special language used to describe patterns. The bash command line supports a basic set of regular expressions you can use to describe patterns in filenames beyond what you could achieve just with shell globs. For instance, say I wanted to list all of the files in the example directory above that began with a *or* b. One way would be to type

```
$ ls a* b*
aa.txt  ac.txt  a.txt  b.txt
```

Or I could use this regular expression:

```
$ ls [ab]*
aa.txt  ac.txt  a.txt  b.txt
```

When I put a set of characters inside brackets, this sets up a *character class*. A character class defines a set of characters that will match. It's important to note that this character class matches only *one* character. So why use this when a shell glob can accomplish the same thing? I find I use it often when I'm trying to manage a directory full of logs. When logs in /var/log/ rotate, they end up appending a number to the file and then compressing it. For instance:

```
$ ls /var/log/messages*
/var/log/messages        /var/log/messages.2.gz
/var/log/messages.5.gz
/var/log/messages.0      /var/log/messages.3.gz
/var/log/messages.6.gz
/var/log/messages.1.gz  /var/log/messages.4.gz
```

Often you will find when you need to free up space on a disk that /var/log is a good place to start. Let's say that I wanted to remove only the last three messages logs. While I could certainly type them all in manually, I could also type

```
$ rm /var/log/messages.[456].gz
```

NOTE   As you learn about shell globs and regular expressions, you will find out that often the pattern you match is different from the pattern you thought you'd match. To be safe, always run ls or echo with your pattern first and see what files match before you do something like mv or rm, which are difficult or almost impossible to undo.

Pipes and Redirection
Pipes

If there is one tool that I think best illustrates the power of the command line, it's the pipe. If you look at a lot of command examples, one of the first things you will see is the | symbol. This is known as a pipe and is used to take the output from one program and feed it to another program as input. You can use pipes to chain multiple commands together so that one command generates output, and the next command filters through that output and changes it and then outputs it to some other program.

grep   One of the best examples of the use of pipes is also one of the most useful command-line tools: grep. At its core, the grep command filters its input for a keyword or pattern that you specify and then outputs anything that matches that pattern. For instance:

```
$ ls
anotherfile.txt somedir somefile1.txt somefile2.txt
$ ls | grep some
somedir
somefile1.txt
somefile2.txt
```

In the second command you can see that I piped the output of the ls command to grep, and then told grep to filter only text that contained the keyword some. If I had wanted to see only text that had the word file in it, I could type

```
$ ls | grep file
anotherfile.txt
somefile1.txt
somefile2.txt
```

You can also chain multiple grep commands together using pipes. For instance, say after I ran the command above I decided that I wanted to filter the output again, only this time to show only files that contained 1 in their name:

```
$ ls | grep file | grep 1
somefile1.txt
```

You will often see grep used in this way to filter output from one command and pipe it to another command to act on the new filtered input. grep can also be used to filter text that is inside a file. Just continue to list your keyword as the first argument to grep and then follow it with the file to filter through. For instance, let's say our somefile1.txt file contained the following lines:

```
1. Line 1
2. Another line
3. Final line
4. Some other text
```

If I wanted to see any lines that contained the word `line`, I would type

```
$ grep line somefile1.txt
2. Another line
3. Final line
```

Now notice that it didn't display 1. `Line 1`. That's because in that case the L in `Line` was capitalized and by default `grep` is case-sensitive. If you want to do a case-insensitive match, then use `grep` with the -i argument:

```
$ grep -i line somefile1.txt
1. Line 1
2. Another line
3. Final line
```

You will find you use `grep` a lot to search through log files for particular keywords. Sometimes, though, as you filter through certain keywords you will notice you get extra output that you aren't interested in. If you pass the -v argument to `grep`, it will invert what it does; that is to say, it will show you only lines that *don't* match your keyword. For instance, in the same somefile1.txt that I listed above, let's say that I wanted to show all of the lines that *didn't* contain the word `Another`:

```
$ grep -v Another somefile1.txt
1. Line 1
3. Final line
4. Some other text
```

sort   Another useful command-line tool is `sort`. As its name indicates, the sort command takes input and sorts it. For instance, let's take two files, somefile2.txt:

```
5. Another example
5. Another example
6. Linux
```

and our same somefile1.txt:

```
1. Line 1
2. Another line
3. Final line
4. Some other text
```

If we run the cat command with both of these files as arguments, it will output the contents of both files one after the other. Let's say that I list somefile2.txt first and then somefile1.txt:

```
$ cat somefile2.txt somefile1.txt
5. Another example
5. Another example
6. Linux
1. Line 1
2. Another line
3. Final line
4. Some other text
```

If I pipe this to the sort command, it will sort all of the input for me:

```
$ cat somefile2.txt somefile1.txt | sort
1. Line 1
2. Another line
3. Final line
4. Some other text
5. Another example
5. Another example
6. Linux
```

NOTE   By default the sort command actually sorts alphabetically. Sometimes, though, you want to sort output numerically. In that case pass sort the -n option.

---

uniq   If you look at the output from the sort command, you will notice that there are two identical lines. That might be fine, but often when you sort through files you want to remove any lines that are duplicated. This might be especially true if you are merging the contents of two text files as I am here. In that case you can use the uniq command. The uniq command will remove any duplicates it gets from input, but that input *must* already be sorted. The beauty of pipes is that you can pipe output to the sort command first to sort it, then to the uniq command to strip out any duplicates. For instance, if we wanted to strip out the duplicate 5. Another example line from the previous output, we would just pipe the sort output to uniq:

```
$ cat somefile2.txt somefile1.txt | sort | uniq
1. Line 1
2. Another line
3. Final line
4. Some other text
5. Another example
6. Linux
```

Redirection

As you parse through and filter text files and other output on the command line, often you will find it useful to put that output in another file. For instance, you might run grep on a log file to pull out specific log entries that you then want to save to a file. This is where redirection comes in.

Redirection uses the >, >>, and < symbols on the command line. For instance, the > character will redirect output to a file and overwrite anything that was previously in the file. If I had the same somefile1.txt and somefile2.txt files from the previous examples and I wanted to cat somefile1.txt and then save the output to somefile3.txt, I would type

```
$ cat somefile1.txt > somefile3.txt
$ cat somefile3.txt
1. Line 1
2. Another line
3. Final line
4. Some other text
```

Now notice what happens if I run the same command only with somefile2.txt. It will overwrite what used to be in somefile3.txt with new data:

```
$ cat somefile2.txt > somefile3.txt
$ cat somefile3.txt
5. Another example
5. Another example
6. Linux
```

Because > will overwrite the destination file, you should be particularly careful when you use it so that you don't accidentally blow away valuable data. Now what if you had actually wanted the contents of both some-file2.txt and somefile1.txt in the new file? In that case you can use the >> operator, which like > will redirect output to a file but will append the new data to the end of the file:

```
$ cat somefile1.txt >> somefile3.txt
$ cat somefile3.txt
5. Another example
5. Another example
6. Linux
1. Line 1
2. Another line
3. Final line
4. Some other text
```

One example of where you might append instead of overwrite redirected output is when you grep multiple log files for data to store in some other text file. After you run the grep command on one file, when you run it a second time on a different log file you don't want to blow away the first set of output, so you will use the >> operator.

The < operator is a bit different from the other two in that it redirects input, not output. For instance, if I wanted to sort the somefile3.txt that I just created, I could type

```
$ sort < somefile3.txt
1. Line 1
2. Another line
3. Final line
4. Some other text
5. Another example
5. Another example
6. Linux
```

You can even chain together input and output redirection, so if I wanted to sort somefile3.txt and redirect the output to somefile4.txt, I could type

```
$ sort < somefile3.txt > somefile4.txt
```

File Permissions and Ownership

Ubuntu (and Linux as a whole) has a file permission model that is based on UNIX. In this permission model each file or directory essentially has three different permissions: read (whether you can look at the contents of a file), write (whether you can modify the contents of a file), and execute (whether you can run the script or program). In addition to these permissions, the UNIX permission model sets up three categories of people on the system: users, groups, and other. The user category represents each login on a system. When you install your Ubuntu server, for instance, you are prompted to choose a username that you will use to log in to the system. That username is your particular user. UNIX (and Linux) was designed with the expectation that more than one person might use the same system at the same time. Some users on the system might even need to share files or directories with each other. With groups, you can add multiple users to a particular group. Then you can set group permissions on a particular file so that anyone who is a member of that group can then access the file with those permissions. Finally, there is the other category. This category represents the rest of the users on the system. You will see how all of these categories and permissions come into play below.

In Chapter 2 I briefly mentioned how to read ls output to see the permissions on a file. Use the -l argument with ls to see file ownership and permissions on files in a directory:

```
$ ls -l
total 12
-rw-r--r-- 1 kyle admin 17 2009-04-04 15:13 a.txt
-rw-r--r-- 1 kyle admin  8 2009-04-04 15:13 b.txt
-rwxr-xr-- 1 kyle admin 52 2009-04-04 15:13 c.sh
```

The first column in the ls -l output shows the permissions on each file. These permissions are split into three categories: user permissions, group permissions, and other permissions. Each of these sections has three different permissions you can enable. Read permissions (represented by r) give a particular category the right to read the file. Write permissions (represented by w) allow a category to write to the file. Finally, execute permissions (represented by x) allow a category to execute a file (such as a shell script or other program). If a particular permission is replaced by a - symbol, it means that permission is disabled. Let's start with the permissions of a.txt in the output above. That file's permissions are rw-r--r--. This means that the user category has read and write permissions (execute is disabled), the group category has read permissions (write and execute are disabled), and the other category also has read permissions (write and execute are disabled).

After the permissions for a.txt you will notice two columns containing the words kyle and admin. The first column shows what user on the system owns the file (in this case the kyle user). The second column shows what group owns the file (in this case the admin group). You can combine a file's permissions with these ownership columns to find out who can do what to the file. In the case of a.txt, the kyle user can read and write to the file, the admin group can read the file, and the rest of the users on the system (other category) can read the file. Contrast this with the c.sh file:

```
-rwxr-xr-- 1 kyle admin 52 2009-04-04 15:13 c.sh
```

In this case the kyle user can read, write, and execute the file. The admin group can read and execute the file, and everyone else can only read the file.

NOTE As you work with group permissions, you will find it handy to check what groups your user is a member of. While you could potentially read /etc/group to find this out, you can also just run the groups command on the command line:

```
$ groups
kyle adm dialout cdrom floppy audio dip video plugdev scanner
  lpadmin admin netdev powerdev polkituser sambashare libvirtd
```

Because your default user can also become root, you will notice it will probably be a member of extra groups compared to any other users on the system.

---

chmod

The chmod command allows you to change permissions on a file. There are a number of different ways to describe permissions for a file (type man chmod to see a full list), but one common way is to list u, g, or o for user, group, or other categories followed by a + or - sign, and then the permission to add or remove. So if I wanted to remove write access for the user who owns a file, I would type chmod u-w *filename*. If I wanted to add read permissions for a file's group I would type chmod g+r *filename*. To add read permissions on a file for other users on the system, I would type chmod o+w *filename*. Let's take our c.sh file as an example:

```
-rwxr-xr-- 1 kyle admin 52 2009-04-04 15:13 c.sh
```

If I wanted to allow other users on the system to execute this file, I would type

```
$ chmod o+x c.sh
$ ls -l c.sh
-rwxr-xr-x 1 kyle admin 52 2009-04-04 15:13 c.sh
```

In addition to u (user), g (group), and o (other), the chmod command also accepts a for all categories. If, for instance, you wanted to remove execute permissions for user, group, and other, you could type

```
$ chmod a-x c.sh
$ ls -l c.sh
-rw-r--r-- 1 kyle admin 52 2009-04-04 15:13 c.sh
```

To undo what I just did, I would just change it to a+x:

```
$ chmod a+x c.sh
$ ls -l c.sh
-rwxr-xr-x 1 kyle admin 52 2009-04-04 15:13 c.sh
```

Linux File Types

Most people who have used a computer for some time are familiar with the two most common types of files, regular files and directories. On a Linux system, though, everything from hard drives to other physical devices is represented by a file. While the beginning administrator probably won't deal with named pipes or socket files much, there are three file types that you will run into and use: symbolic links, hard links, and device files.

Symbolic Links

Symbolic links, or symlinks, are a special kind of small file that points to another file. If you come from a Windows background, symlinks might remind you of Windows shortcut files. When you perform an operation on a symlink, such as opening it with another program or writing to it, the data actually goes to the original file instead.

So why would you want to use a symlink? Often administrators use symlinks when they need the same set of files in more than one location. This can be handy if you want to share a system directory or other file with a new Linux user—you can just create a symlink to the directory in that user's home directory. You will also see administrators use a symlink when the name of a configuration file has changed but they still want the old filename to appear.

To create a symlink, use the `ln` command along with the `-s` argument followed by the file you want to link to and the path to the symlink you want to create. For instance, if I wanted to store my Web site under my home directory at /home/kyle/example.net/ (possibly because it has more space) but still show up under /var/www/, since that's the standard place an administrator would look, I could create a symlink:

```
$ sudo ln -s /home/kyle/example.net /var/www/example.net
```

When you use the `ls` command with the `-l` argument against the symlink, you can easily tell that it is a symlink by the fact that it has an arrow pointing to the source file or directory. Note that if you delete the file to which a symlink points, the symlink file will still exist on the system, but the data itself will be gone.

```
$ ls -l /var/www/example.net
lrwxrwxrwx 1 root root 26 2009-04-09 19:11 /var/www/example.net ->
  /home/kyle/example.net
```

Hard Links

Hard links are similar to symlinks, only where symlinks point to another file, a hard link actually *is* the file. If you want to understand hard links, it helps to understand what an inode is. Each file that you create on a partition stores its data in an inode. That inode has a unique number compared to any other inodes on the partition, and within the inode there is information such as the permissions on the file, who owns the file, and pointers to the actual data of the file, among other things. When you create a file in a directory, the directory actually just contains the file's name and its inode number. When you then access the file, you get directed to that inode and read its data. In the case of a hard link, a second file gets created somewhere on the partition that also points to that same inode.

Since a hard link shares the same exact inode information as the original file, for all intents and purposes it is that file; it's just potentially in a different directory. Unlike with symlinks, if you create a hard link to a file, you can delete the original file and the hard link will still work.

When would you use a hard link? Hard links are very useful when you want to reference the same file in two locations (say, a large DVD image or other file) on the file system. With a hard link both files have the same permissions and the correct file size, and they operate as normal files. You will find that some backup software will use hard links so that if two servers have some identical files, the backup server has to store the file only once. So why would you use one type of link rather than the other? Well, for one thing, you can't use a hard link for directories. Second, hard links work only on the same file system, so if you had a root partition and a separate /home partition, you couldn't create a hard link between the two.

To create a hard link, just use the ln command *without* the -s option. So if I wanted a copy of my Ubuntu server ISO file from /home/kyle/isos/ on my desktop without taking up a lot of space, I could type

```
$ ln /home/kyle/isos/ubuntu-8.04.1-server.i386.iso
/home/kyle/Desktop/ubuntu-8.04.1-server.i386.iso
```

This hard link looks no different from the original file:

```
$ ls -l /home/kyle/isos/ubuntu-8.04.1-server-i386.iso
-rw-r--r-- 2 kyle kyle 584722432 2008-10-08 20:26 /home/kyle/isos/
  ubuntu-8.04.1-server-i386.iso
$ ls -l /home/kyle/Desktop/ubuntu-8.04.1-server-i386.iso
-rw-r--r-- 2 kyle kyle 584722432 2008-10-08 20:26 /home/kyle/
  Desktop/ubuntu-8.04.1-server-i386.iso
```

Device Files

Eventually as you learn about Linux you will hear someone talk about how under Linux everything is a file. This can be strange if you are used to other operating systems, but under Linux everything, including the hardware on your computer, is a file. These device files are mostly stored under the /dev directory on a Linux system. You will commonly hear about these device files as you start to work with Linux partitions. For instance, the first SCSI drive on your system is represented by a file named /dev/sda, and all of the partitions on that drive are numbered starting with 1, so the first partition on the drive is /dev/sda1. Even though this is a special device file, many of the file-based tools on your Linux system will work with it just like any other file. For instance, a common way to image drives under Linux is to use a tool called dd that reads from a file one bit at a time to read from one device file, say, /dev/sda1, and write to another device file, say, /dev/sdb1.

So how can you tell a device file from a regular file? Well, typically all device files reside inside the /dev directory. In addition to that, if you run ls -l on a device file, you will see either a b or a c before the file's permissions. The b tells you that this is a block (unbuffered) device, and the c means it is a character (buffered) device:

```
$ ls -l /dev/sda
brw-rw---- 1 root disk 8, 0 2009-04-03 06:17 /dev/sda
$ ls -l /dev/zero
crw-rw-rw- 1 root root 1, 5 2009-04-03 06:17 /dev/zero
```

I already mentioned that /dev/sda is the device file for the first SCSI drive on my system, but /dev/zero is a special device. When you read input from /dev/zero, you will simply get an unending string of zeros. This can be useful when you want to write over a hard drive with zeros, by the way; just use dd to read from /dev/zero and write to the drive you want to erase. Here are some other interesting device files:

- **/dev/mem**
  This file is actually a complete copy of your system RAM.

- **/dev/random and /dev/urandom**
  These devices operate like /dev/zero only they output random numbers.

- **/dev/ttyS0**
  This is the first serial port on the system.

- **/dev/null**
  This is the "black hole" on your Ubuntu system. Any data that you write to this file will essentially disappear without the file growing in size. Administrators often redirect program output to this file so that it doesn't show up on the console.

At and Cron

As you get more comfortable with Linux and running programs from the command line, eventually you will find that you need a program to run when you aren't around. For instance, you might set up a script that backs up your system, but you would like it to run at 2 AM when no one is using the system. Linux includes two different services, at and cron, that allow you to run programs at predefined times. You use at when you want a program to be run at a particular time, and generally only once. When you want to run a program periodically (such as once per day or once every hour), you use cron.

At

To use at, first type the command at in a terminal followed by the time you want the command to be run. At can accept times and dates in many different formats, but be sure to not confuse AM and PM. You can even substitute words like "tomorrow" for hard dates. Once you press Enter, you will be in an interactive shell:

```
$ at 9pm

warning: commands will be executed using /bin/sh

at>
```

Inside this shell you can type all of the commands you would like at to run, just as though you were in a terminal. If you want to run multiple commands, just hit Enter after each command to go to a new at> prompt. When you have entered all the commands you want to run at that time, hit Ctrl-D on the empty at> prompt, and the job will be queued.

```
$ at 9pm

warning: commands will be executed using /bin/sh

at>

at> /usr/local/bin/my_backup_script

at> <EOT>

job 1 at Sat Apr 17 21:00:00 2010
```

Once a command has been queued, you can use the atq command to see all of your queued jobs. The output will list the job number, the time it will be executed, and the user it will be executed as (the same user who originally ran the at command):

```
$ atq

1    Sat Apr 17 21:00:00 2010 a kyle
```

If you want to remote a job from the queue, just use the atrm command followed by the job to remove:

```
$ atrm 1
$
```

Cron

Most of the time, you will find that instead of using at, you will want to run commands periodically. For that you will use cron. Cron is a daemon that runs in the background on your Linux system. Each user and the system itself has a cron table (called crontab) that lists what jobs they would like run as well as how frequently they should be run.

The systemwide crontab is located at /etc/crontab and is a good place to look to get an idea of cron's syntax:

```
$ cat /etc/crontab
# /etc/crontab: system-wide crontab
# Unlike any other crontab, you don't have to run the 'crontab'
# command to install the new version when you edit this file
# and files in /etc/cron.d. These files also have username fields,
# that none of the other crontabs do.

SHELL=/bin/sh

PATH=/usr/local/sbin:/usr/local/bin:/sbin:/bin:/usr/sbin:/usr/bin

# m h dom mon dow user        command

17 * * * *    root    cd / && run-parts -report /etc/cron.hourly

25 6 * * *    root    test -x /usr/sbin/anacron ||
   ( cd / && run-parts -report /etc/cron.daily )

47 6 * * 7    root    test -x /usr/sbin/anacron ||
   ( cd / && run-parts -report /etc/cron.weekly )

52 6 1 * *    root    test -x /usr/sbin/anacron ||
   ( cd / && run-parts -report /etc/cron.monthly )

#
```

Each crontab entry in this file starts with a few fields that tell cron when that entry should be run. Then the entry states which user will execute the command (root in these examples), and finally it lists the command to run. Let's look at a few of these lines to see how the syntax works:

```
25 6 * * *    root    test -x /usr/sbin/anacron ||
   ( cd / && run-parts -report /etc/cron.daily )
```

The first field in this line tells cron what minute on the hour to trigger the command, and the second field sets which hour. In this example the command will be triggered at 6:25 AM. The next three fields allow you to set the day of the month, the month, or the day of the week to run the command. In our case we have * in each of those fields, which acts like a wildcard so that cron will run the command at 6:25 AM every day.

The next line in the crontab shows you how to have a command run once a week:

```
47 6 * * 7   root   test -x /usr/sbin/anacron ||
   ( cd / && run-parts —report /etc/cron.weekly )
```

In this command the minute field is set to 47, the hour field is set to 6 (so 6:47 AM), the day of month and month fields are wildcards, and the day of week field is set to 7. The day of week field can accept a number between 0 and 7 with either 0 or 7 representing Sunday, 1 representing Monday, 2 Tuesday, and so on. In this case the command will be run every Sunday at 6:47 AM.

The final line in the file shows you how to have cron execute a command once per month:

```
52 6 1 * *   root   test -x /usr/sbin/anacron ||
   ( cd / && run-parts —report /etc/cron.monthly )
```

Here we see that the minute field is set to 52, the hour field is set to 6, and the day of month field is set to 1, while the rest of the fields are wildcards. This tells cron to run that command on the first day of the month at 6:52 AM. If I wanted the command to run on the 20th day of the month, I would change the 1 to a 20.

In addition to the standard numbers you can put in each field, cron accepts ranges and multiple numbers separated by commas. You can define a range by putting a dash between two numbers. For instance, if I wanted to run a command every 15 minutes, my fields would look like

```
0,15,30,45 * * * *     root   mycommand
```

This way cron will run the command at 0, 15, 30, and 45 minutes after the hour. If I wanted to run a command at 9 AM only on Monday through Friday I could say

```
0 9  *  * 1-5    root    mycommand
```

Finally, cron also accepts fractions, which saves you from having to type in all of the comma-separated numbers. For instance, a shorthand form of the above command that runs every 15 minutes could be

```
*/15 *  *  *  *    root    mycommand
```

While in the past many administrators would put their commands directly into the /etc/crontab file, over time that caused the file to get quite large and difficult to manage. Realistically, you usually want to run a command either every hour, every day, every week, or every month. Instead of putting those commands directly into /etc/crontab, all you have to do is create a file that has the shell script you want to run and then place it in either /etc/cron.hourly/, /etc/cron.daily/, /etc/cron.weekly/, or /etc/cron.monthly/, and cron will run it at that frequency. If you look in those directories, you'll find that a number of other services on your system already have scripts set up there that you can emulate.

Even if you do have a command you want to run that doesn't conveniently fit into one of the above directories, you still don't want to add it directly to /etc/crontab. Instead, Ubuntu has set up an /etc/cron.d/ directory. To use this directory, create your custom /etc/crontab-style file that follows the proper syntax, and then place it in this directory. For instance, if I wanted to run my special backup script located at /usr/local/sbin/mybackup at 7 AM every day, I could create a file named /etc/cron.d/mybackup that would contain the following:

```
# /etc/cron.d/mybackup: run my backup script outside of
# regular cron.daily

SHELL=/bin/sh

PATH=/usr/local/sbin:/usr/local/bin:/sbin:/bin:/usr/sbin:/usr/bin

0 7   *  *  *   root  /usr/local/sbin/mybackup
```

User crontabs While you will likely run programs in cron as the root user, sometimes you'd like to run programs as a regular user. You could create a system cron entry and specify that user, but what if you didn't have root permissions on the system? In that circumstance, you can use the `crontab -e` command on the command line as your regular user. The first time you run the command, it will let you select which text editor to use and then drop you into that text editor. From there you can define your own crontab entries.

NOTE Because these commands will be run as your user, the user field does not exist in this crontab. Just enter the time and date fields followed by your command.

After you add your entries to your user's crontab, save the file, and that crontab will go into effect. If you want to see the contents of your crontab, just type `crontab -l`.

Finally, if you want to see all of the user crontabs and at jobs, go to the /var/spool/cron directory on your system as the root user. You will see an atjobs and atspool directory that contains information for at along with a crontabs directory that lists every user's crontab.

Cool Tips and Tricks

ONE OF THE MOST AMAZING things about Linux is just how flexible the command line is. Over the years I've learned a lot of useful command-line tricks. Some are time-saving and others are life-saving. No matter how long you've used Linux, it seems as if you learn new tips like this all the time. In this section I have compiled some of my favorite short command-line tips and tricks.

Avoid That grep Command in grep Output

One of the main ways I use grep is when I am looking for a particular process on the system. The problem is that the grep command itself always seems to match and shows up in the output:

```
$ ps -ef | grep bash
kyle    982  2077  0 19:50 pts/2     00:00:00 grep bash
kyle   2077  6668  0 Apr06 pts/2     00:00:01 bash
kyle   6859  6668  0 Apr03 pts/1     00:00:00 bash
```

As you can see here, I have two valid bash processes running, but I get the grep command in my output as well. That can be annoying if you want to count the number of Apache processes on the system, for instance, as you always have to subtract one for the grep command—that is, unless you surround the first character of your keyword with brackets:

```
$ ps -ef | grep [b]ash
kyle   2077  6668  0 Apr06 pts/2     00:00:01 bash
kyle   6859  6668  0 Apr03 pts/1     00:00:00 bash
```

This works because of the power of regular expressions. When I surround the first character with brackets, I'm telling grep to search within a character class. Usually you use character classes so you can list a number of different characters to match, but in this case, since there is only one character in it, it acts just as if I were grepping for bash. Of course, since the grep command itself has brackets in it, it doesn't show up in the result.

Shortcut to a Command Path

There are times when you want to look at a shell script you have in your binary path but you can't quite remember whether it's in /bin, /sbin, /usr/bin, /usr/local/bin, or somewhere else. While you could just keep hitting the tab key until you find it, the which command will search through your path and output the full path to the command you list:

```
$ which vim
/usr/bin/vim
```

If I wanted to run ls -l against the vim binary but I wasn't sure what directory it was in, I could just type

```
$ ls -l `which vim`
lrwxrwxrwx 1 root root 21 2008-03-21 22:22 /usr/bin/vim ->
/etc/alternatives/vim
```

When you surround a command with backticks (`), it will run the command and the output will appear in its place. I especially like to do this when I want to edit a custom shell script I've written and don't know where I saved it.

Wipe a Drive in One Line

Be careful with this command! As a sysadmin you often have systems you need to get rid of and need to erase the hard drives so no private company data gets out. A simple way to do this is to use the dd command to read from the special /dev/zero device and output to the drive you want to erase. When the command is done, the entire drive will be all zeros. So if I wanted to completely erase /dev/sdb, I would type

```
$ sudo dd if=/dev/zero of=/dev/sdb
```

Run a Command Over and Over

Often I will be copying a file from one file system or server to another and I want to monitor the copy progress. While I could just type `ls -l` over and over, a better method is to use the `watch` command. The `watch` program takes a command as an argument and then runs that command every two seconds and shows its output on the screen. So, for instance, if I wanted to monitor the size of ubuntu.iso, I would type `watch "ls -l ubuntu.iso"`. The `watch` command accepts a few arguments such as the `-n` argument so that you can adjust how many seconds it will wait before it runs the program again.

Make a Noise When the Server Comes Back Up

When I work I usually have more than one thing going on at a time. When I'm working on a server and need to reboot it, usually I want to know right away when it comes back up so I can log in to it and finish whatever work I was doing. Of course, what usually happens is that I start to reboot a server, then get distracted by other work while I wait for it to come back up and completely forget about it until later. A nice solution to this problem is to use the `ping` program with the `-a` argument. The `-a` argument tells `ping` to play an audible bell (the beep you hear when you hit Tab on the keyboard sometimes) for every `ping` response. When a system is up, this just means one beep after another. What I like to do is run `ping -a` against a particular hostname as I reboot it. Then I can go do some other work and once the server comes back up on the network, my terminal will beep over and over until I stop the `ping` process.

Search and Replace Text in a File

There are many different ways to search and replace text in a file, from `sed` and `awk` scripts to opening the file in a text editor. One of my favorite ways is with what I like to call my "Perl pie" script. If I wanted to replace all instances of `kyle` with `Kyle` in a file.txt, I would type:

```
$ perl -pi -e 's/kyle/Kyle/' file.txt
```

Since this one-liner uses Perl, it also means that you can take advantage of Perl's advanced regular expression engine.

find and exec Commands

A very common command-line need is to locate all the files within a directory and all its subdirectories with a certain attribute and run some command on them. For instance, let's say I wanted to move all files that end in .txt within my current directory and all the directories below it into the ~/Documents directory. If you wanted to just list all of the files, you would run the following find command:

```
$ find ./ -name "*.txt"
```

In your output you would get a list of each file that ended with .txt along with its path. To then execute some program against these files you would use the -exec argument to find:

```
$ find ./ -name "*.txt" -exec mv {} ~/Documents/ \;
```

The -exec command will replace the {} in each file with the full path to that file. In this case it would run the mv command against the file and move it to the ~/Documents directory. Notice that strange \; text at the end of the command. That is required when you use the -exec argument so that it knows it is at the end of the command.

Be careful when you run this command. People make mistakes, and often you'll find either your find output is different from what you thought it would be or you have some mistake in your -exec command. I recommend before you run anything risky that you test your -exec command with echo. That way you see what -exec would run before it actually does anything. For instance, I would test the command above with

```
$ find ./ -name "*.txt" -exec echo mv {} ~/Documents/ \;
```

Bash Commands with Too Many Arguments

As you start to run more and more find -exec commands, you will eventually run across a situation when there are too many files in the output and will get some sort of error message like "too many arguments." There are a limited number of arguments you can have in your shell, but luckily if this happens to you, there is a good way around it using the xargs program. The xargs program will accept a set of arguments that are piped to it and will run a command against those arguments one by one. So, for instance, if I got that error in my find command, I could instead type

```
$ find ./ -name "*.txt" -print0 | xargs mv ~/Documents
```

Use Your Bash History

While it's always advisable to document all of your procedures, especially when you fix a problem, sometimes you don't get around to it and have to figure out what you did the last time to fix a system. It can be easy to forget that bash logs all of your previous commands to its history file. One of the first things I do when I can't remember exactly how I ran a command previously is type history and look through the output for more details.

Are These Files Identical?

As you troubleshoot problems on a system, you commonly wonder whether the problem stems from one server having a different configuration file from another working server. While you can definitely open both files and compare them line by line or run diff against them, both methods can be tedious. A quick way to test whether two files are identical is to use the md5sum tool to create a checksum of both. If the output matches, the files are identical:

```
$ md5sum bar
d41d8cd98f00b204e9800998ecf8427e  bar
$ md5sum foo
d41d8cd98f00b204e9800998ecf8427e  foo
```

Go Back to Your Previous Directory

This is a nice quick tip. When you move around directories on a system, sometimes it would be nice if you could quickly jump back to the directory you were previously in. Just type

```
$ cd -
```

Bash will replace the - symbol with the value of $OLDPWD—an environment variable bash uses to keep track of your previous directory.

Find Out Who Is Tying Up a File System You Want to Unmount

Linux won't let you unmount a file system if a file is opened on that file system. Often you will see this if you have a shell in a directory on that file system. In that case you can fix the problem just by changing to a different directory, and then you can unmount the file system; but sometimes you aren't sure what program is tying it up. In that case you can use the lsof command. The lsof command will list all of the open files on the system. All you need to do is grep for the file system you want to unmount and you will see what processes have open files on that file system. Let's say, for instance, that I want to unmount /media/cdrom. I would type

```
$ sudo lsof | grep /media/cdrom
```

In the lsof output I would see a list of all of the processes with open files on that file system, their process IDs, and even what files they had opened. Then I could close that program or kill the process and unmount the file system.

Send a Test E-mail Using telnet

A mail server listens on port 25 for SMTP connections, and when you connect to that port, if you know what SMTP commands to issue, you can pretend to be another mail server. A very handy trick is to be able to test a mail server just by connecting to port 25 on the machine with telnet and typing a raw e-mail message:

```
$ telnet localhost 25
Trying 127.0.0.1...
Connected to localhost.
Escape character is '^]'.
220 minimus ESMTP Postfix (Ubuntu)
HELO kyle
250 minimus
MAIL FROM: kyle@example.net
```

```
250 2.1.0 Ok
RCPT TO: kyle@localhost
250 2.1.5 Ok
DATA
354 End data with <CR><LF>.<CR><LF>
Subject: test
This is just a test
.
250 2.0.0 Ok: queued as 1ADD057CD0
quit
221 2.0.0 Bye
Connection closed by foreign host.
```

The first command you type is HELO followed by the name you want the system to know you as. Next type MAIL FROM: followed by the e-mail address you want the e-mail to appear to come from. After that type RCPT TO: followed by the e-mail address you want to send to. Then type DATA. At that point everything else you type will be considered the body of the e-mail. In my example I added a Subject: field but even that is optional. Just continue to type out your message and then when you are finished, type enter then type a period, then type enter again. Finally type quit to end the session.

Easy SSH Key Sharing

One of the annoying parts of setting up key authentication on SSH is having to move all the public keys around to each system's authorized_keys file. For years I would do some fancy shell scripting to copy keys around, but then I found out that the openssh packages included a tool called ssh-copy-id just for that purpose. To use the program just type ssh-copy-id followed by the remote server (and optionally the remote username) you want the key copied to. For instance, if I wanted to copy my current user's key to a server named web1, I could type:

```
$ ssh-copy-id web1
```

Or if I wanted to copy the key to the kyle user's account on a server named db4, I would type:

```
$ ssh-copy-id kyle@db4
```

Get the Most Out of Dig

A number of people (myself included) still use nslookup for a number of DNS queries even though it's been deprecated for years, just because it's what we are used to using. Dig, after all, has different syntax, and usually you get a lot of output you have to pore through to find the info you wanted. That is true unless you use dig's +short option. With that option dig will give you just the output you want:

```
$ dig www.ubuntu.com +short
91.189.90.40
```

Another great option for dig is the +trace option. Usually dig will give you the final result you are searching for, but what you may not realize is that there are a number of DNS servers between your query and the answer (if the answers aren't cached). If you add +trace to a dig query, it will act a lot like traceroute in that it will trace through the dig query and show you all the hops your DNS request took.

```
$ dig www.ubuntu.com +trace
; <<>> DiG 9.6.1-P2 <<>> www.ubuntu.com +trace
;; global options: +cmd
.                       163547  IN      NS      b.root-servers.net.
.                       163547  IN      NS      c.root-servers.net.
.                       163547  IN      NS      d.root-servers.net.
.                       163547  IN      NS      e.root-servers.net.
.                       163547  IN      NS      f.root-servers.net.
.                       163547  IN      NS      g.root-servers.net.
.                       163547  IN      NS      h.root-servers.net.
.                       163547  IN      NS      i.root-servers.net.
.                       163547  IN      NS      j.root-servers.net.
.                       163547  IN      NS      k.root-servers.net.
.                       163547  IN      NS      l.root-servers.net.
.                       163547  IN      NS      m.root-servers.net.
.                       163547  IN      NS      a.root-servers.net.
;; Received 244 bytes from 192.168.0.1#53(192.168.0.1) in 5 ms

com.                    172800  IN      NS      H.GTLD-SERVERS.NET.
com.                    172800  IN      NS      L.GTLD-SERVERS.NET.
com.                    172800  IN      NS      D.GTLD-SERVERS.NET.
com.                    172800  IN      NS      F.GTLD-SERVERS.NET.
com.                    172800  IN      NS      C.GTLD-SERVERS.NET.
com.                    172800  IN      NS      B.GTLD-SERVERS.NET.
com.                    172800  IN      NS      K.GTLD-SERVERS.NET.
```

```
com.                    172800  IN      NS      J.GTLD-SERVERS.NET.
com.                    172800  IN      NS      A.GTLD-SERVERS.NET.
com.                    172800  IN      NS      M.GTLD-SERVERS.NET.
com.                    172800  IN      NS      G.GTLD-SERVERS.NET.
com.                    172800  IN      NS      E.GTLD-SERVERS.NET.
com.                    172800  IN      NS      I.GTLD-SERVERS.NET.
;; Received 504 bytes from 192.58.128.30#53(j.root-servers.net)
   in 110 ms

ubuntu.com.             172800  IN      NS      ns1.canonical.com.
ubuntu.com.             172800  IN      NS      ns2.canonical.com.
ubuntu.com.             172800  IN      NS      ns3.canonical.com.
;; Received 144 bytes from 192.41.162.30#53(L.GTLD-SERVERS.NET)
   in 91 ms

www.ubuntu.com.                 600     IN      A       91.189.90.41
ubuntu.com.             172800  IN      NS      ns1.canonical.com.
ubuntu.com.             172800  IN      NS      ns2.canonical.com.
ubuntu.com.             172800  IN      NS      ns3.canonical.com.
;; Received 160 bytes from 91.189.94.173#53(ns1.canonical.com)
   in 151 ms
```

Index

Also Available:
The Official Ubuntu Book, Fifth Edition

Benjamin Mako Hill, Matthew Helmke, Corey Burger

ISBN-13: 978-0-13-708130-1

Written by leading Ubuntu community experts, *The Official Ubuntu Book, Fifth Edition*, covers everything you need to know to make the most of Ubuntu 10.04, whether you're a home user, small-business user, server administrator, or programmer.

The authors explain Ubuntu 10.04 from start to finish: installation, configuration, desktop productivity, games, management, support, and much more. Among the many topics covered in this edition: Kubuntu, Ubuntu Netbook Edition, and Ubuntu Server. The accompanying DVD includes the complete Ubuntu Linux operating system for installation on PC platforms, preconfigured with an outstanding desktop environment for both home and business computing.

Disc Warranty

Prentice Hall warrants the enclosed CD and DVD to be free of defects in materials and faulty workmanship under normal use for a period of ninety days after purchase (when purchased new). If a defect is discovered in the CD/DVD during this warranty period, a replacement CD/DVD can be obtained at no charge by sending the defective CD/DVD, postage prepaid, with proof of purchase to:

Disc Exchange
Prentice Hall
Pearson Technology Group
75 Arlington Street, Suite 300
Boston, MA 02116
Email: AWPro@aw.com

Prentice Hall makes no warranty or representation, either expressed or implied, with respect to this software, its quality, performance, merchantability, or fitness for a particular purpose. In no event will Prentice Hall, its distributors, or dealers be liable for direct, indirect, special, incidental, or consequential damages arising out of the use or inability to use the software. The exclusion of implied warranties is not permitted in some states. Therefore, the above exclusion may not apply to you. This warranty provides you with specific legal rights. There may be other rights that you may have that vary from state to state.

More information and updates are available at:
informit.com/ph

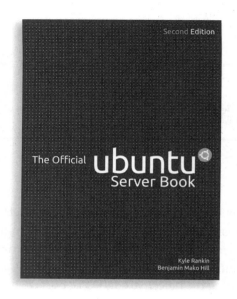

FREE Online Edition

Your purchase of *The Official Ubuntu Server Book, Second Edition* includes access to a free online edition for 45 days through the Safari Books Online subscription service. Nearly every Prentice Hall book is available online through Safari Books Online, along with more than 5,000 other technical books and videos from publishers such as Addison-Wesley Professional, Cisco Press, Exam Cram, IBM Press, O'Reilly, Que, and Sams.

SAFARI BOOKS ONLINE allows you to search for a specific answer, cut and paste code, download chapters, and stay current with emerging technologies.

Activate your FREE Online Edition at
www.informit.com/safarifree

> **STEP 1:** Enter the coupon code: HDDYAZG.

> **STEP 2:** New Safari users, complete the brief registration form.
> Safari subscribers, just log in.

If you have difficulty registering on Safari or accessing the online edition, please e-mail customer-service@safaribooksonline.com